The New York Times

BOOK OF

SPORTS LEGENDS

**Profiles of 50 of This
Century's Greatest Athletes—
By the Legendary Sportswriters
Who Covered Them**

EDITED BY JOSEPH J. VECCHIONE

INTRODUCTION BY IRA BERKOW

A FIRESIDE BOOK
Published by Simon & Schuster
New York London Toronto Sydney Tokyo Singapore

FIRESIDE
Simon & Schuster Building
Rockefeller Center
1230 Avenue of the Americas
New York, New York 10020

First Fireside Edition, 1992
Published by arrangement with Times Books, a division of
Random House, Inc.

FIRESIDE and colophon are registered trademarks of
Simon & Schuster Inc.

Designed by Robert Bull Design
Manufactured in the United States of America

1   3   5   7   9   10   8   6   4   2

Library of Congress Cataloging in Publication Data
is available

ISBN: 0-671-76039-4

To Elizabeth:
You did all the work.

ACKNOWLEDGMENTS

First and foremost, I would like to thank my wife, Elizabeth, who did most of the early research and kept my nose to the grindstone throughout the project. Then, Ira Berkow, for his highly readable introduction, his suggestions, and his encouragement. Steve Fine, who did a fine job of collecting the photographs. All those people who were so willing to help us find the material—Bob Medina, head of *The New York Times* news morgue, and his staffers, Ricardo Campbell, Bob Fowlow, and Joe Wroclawski. My former colleagues in *The Times* sports department who were always able to come up with the information I needed—in particular, Ray Corio, Rich Goldstein, Leslie Chambliss, and Judy Miceli. Last, but certainly not least, Paul Golob, the editor at Times Books who asked the right questions, caught the errors, and made a better book of it.

J. J. V.

CONTENTS

INTRODUCTION

By IRA BERKOW

A S THE STORY GOES, the Carlisle School track team of 1912 was
booked to meet the Lafayette team at Easton, Pennsylvania. A welcoming committee was dispatched and was understandably puzzled when only two
Carlisle lads stepped off the train.

"Where's your team?" they asked.

"This is the team," replied Jim Thorpe.

"Only two of you?"

"Only one," said Thorpe, with a smile. "This fellow's the manager."

The Carlisle contingent was more than enough, however, to handle the
Lafayette team. Shortly after, Thorpe was participating in the Olympics in
Stockholm, where he won both the decathlon and the pentathlon. When
he stood before the royal box to receive a gold medal, the king of Sweden, Gustaf V, said to the black-haired Sac and Fox Indian, "Sir, you are the greatest
athlete in the world."

Then followed a most bittersweet life: the medals were stripped from him
because he was ruled a professional, having played semipro baseball under an
assumed name. He went on to play major league baseball and professional
football and, after that, knocked around, becoming an alcoholic, and drifting
out of the public eye until it was discovered in the late 1940s that he was
destitute. Groups throughout the country then raised thousands of dollars for
him. Jim Thorpe died of a heart attack in 1953, but his memory, and his legend,
live on.

In this book, which recounts fifty of America's greatest sports heroes of
the twentieth century, Thorpe's story, like those of Babe Ruth and Babe Didrikson Zaharias, of Jack Dempsey and Jackie Robinson, of Joe Louis and Joe
Lapchick, of Knute Rockne and Bill Tilden and Maureen Connolly and Bobby
Jones and John McGraw and Hank Greenberg, and a sportswriter, Red Smith,
and even a racehorse, Secretariat, are told, for the most part, with and without
tears.

That is, the facts and details of their lives are presented in straightforward
fashion in *The New York Times* obituaries that ran immediately after their
deaths. But the emotions, the stuff embracing human life, are here, too: the
grimness of tragedy as well as the joy of achievement and the laughter during
unforgettable moments.

These stories not only describe the sports hero in his finest moments, as
those who have demonstrated the spectacular possibilities of the human body

and mind in tandem, but also depict the frailties and the sometimes all-too-humanness of these people.

There is also life beyond the obituary in this book, which includes *Times* feature stories on these legends. These pieces round out and give a fuller flavor to the lives of these remarkable men and women, who added such flavor to the lives of the rest of us. Sports goes beyond the playing field, of course. It touches most of us, sometimes whether we know it or not. It is in our sociology, in our psychology, in our blood. It entertains; it fascinates; it inspires.

Not only is Vince Lombardi's life described here, and his finally getting a professional head coach's job at the relatively advanced age of forty-six, but also included is a vivid account of the first Super Bowl, on January 15, 1967, in which his Green Bay Packers walloped the Kansas City Chiefs, which was probably the highlight of Lombardi's career.

Also here is the afternoon of July 4, 1939, Lou Gehrig Appreciation Day at Yankee Stadium, when the Iron Horse, now bowed with a deadly disease that would soon end his life, made his memorable speech about being "the luckiest man on the face of the earth." "In perhaps as colorful and dramatic a pageant as ever was enacted on a baseball field," wrote John Drebinger from the press box that day, "61,808 fans thundered a hail and farewell to Henry Louis Gehrig."

And a sports event on another Independence Day, in 1910, that stirred the nation was the heavyweight title fight between the black champion, Jack Johnson, and the original great white hope, the aging ex-champ, Jim Jeffries. The *Times* had asked John L. Sullivan, the celebrated ex-heavyweight champion, to write an account of the fight. His story is in the section on Jack Johnson and tells as much or more about race relations in America during that period—the fact that Sullivan wrote it and the fact that the *Times* published it—as we might get from any history book.

"The Negro had few friends," Sullivan wrote from ringside, "but there was no real demonstration against him. . . . I have never witnessed a fight where I was in such a peculiar position. I all along refused to announce my choice as to the winner. I refused on Jeff's account, because he was sensitive. . . . I refused on Johnson's account, because of my well-known antipathy to his race."

Among the pleasures of this book are sometimes remarkable insights, like Satchel Paige's dictum that "if your stomach disputes you, lie down and pacify it with cool thoughts." Or Lefty Gomez's observation that he succeeded as a pitcher with the Yankees because of "clean living and a fast outfield." And there was the moment, described by Red Smith in a column titled "A Sense of Dignity," when Joe Louis, then an unlettered twenty-one-year-old in 1935, was asked to pose for a photograph while eating watermelon. Louis understood that this would simply be perpetuating the black stereotype and refused, saying he didn't like watermelon.

" 'And the funny thing is,' said Harry Markson, telling the story, 'Joe loves watermelon.' "

It is not just the stories, to be sure, but the writers of those stories that give this book its special quality. And some of America's finest sportswriters are included, such as Red Smith and John Kieran and Arthur Daley and Robert

Lipsyte and Dave Anderson and George Vecsey and Leonard Koppett and Tony Kornheiser and Joe Durso and Gerry Eskenazi.

The editor of this undertaking, Joe Vecchione, who for ten years was the sports editor of the *Times,* has chosen the subjects wisely. But the nature of sports is argument, and so, one might ask, where are such heroes as Gene Tunney or Tris Speaker or Judge Kenesaw Mountain Landis or Johnny Weissmuller or Tommy Hitchcock or Earl Sande, or even such notables as Avery Brundage or Shoeless Joe Jackson?

At one point, as in a golf tournament, some simply don't make the cut. Unlike a golf tournament, it was not the number of strokes of a golf club here that eliminated, but the stroke of the editor's pen.

And though some may voice disapproval, few can dispute that the fifty selected are anything but worthy, and each a legitimate sports legend.

The New York Times
BOOK OF
SPORTS LEGENDS

GROVER CLEVELAND ALEXANDER

1887–1950

R ANKED AMONG baseball's immortals, Grover Cleveland Alexander was an outstanding right-handed pitcher for nearly twenty years. Nicknamed Old Pete and Alex the Great by his admirers, he proved a thorn to major league batsmen from 1911 to 1930, and during that period compiled several pitching records.

He was born in St. Paul, Nebraska, on February 26, 1887, learned to play the game on the prairies, and was a sensation in his first season as a major leaguer after a brief stay in the minors. Alexander was obtained by the Philadelphia Phillies in 1911 and won twenty-eight games that year, a remarkable achievement for a rookie.

His curveball and perfect control brought him thirty or more triumphs in successive seasons from 1915 through 1917. Alexander won thirty-one victories in 1915, thirty-three in 1916, and thirty in 1917.

Although he never pitched a no-hit, no-run game, he registered many amazing records. He pitched 696 contests for three teams, the Phillies, Chicago Cubs, and St. Louis Cardinals, during his National League career, and won 373 of them. For six years he led the circuit in complete games pitched, and in 1915 he established a National League earned-run mark of 1.22 for pitchers working in 250 innings or more.

Alexander enjoyed his most successful year in 1916, and in that campaign scored sixteen shutout triumphs. During his entire career in the majors, he blanked his rivals on ninety occasions, a feat still unequaled in National League history.

After seven years with the Phillies, Alexander was sent with his battery mate, Bill Killifer, to the Chicago Cubs for $55,000 and several players, an enormous price at the time. He twirled the opening game of the 1918 campaign for the Cubs and then became a member of the American Expeditionary Force. He saw service overseas during World War I and was made a sergeant.

In 1919 Alexander picked up the thread of his spectacular feats with the Cubs and was an idol of Wrigley Field fans in Chicago for eight years. When he appeared to be losing his mastery, the Cubs sent him on waivers to the St. Louis Cardinals in June 1926, but in a sensational comeback, he became the hero of the World Series that fall.

Alexander proceeded to win twelve of twenty-two games during the regular campaign and then hurled the Cardinals to two victories over the New York Yankees in the World Series. His pitching in the sixth game enabled St. Louis

to tie the count at three-all in the baseball classic, and excitement ran high at Yankee Stadium as the seventh and deciding contest moved into the seventh inning with the Cardinals holding a 3–2 lead over the American League pennant winners.

Although denied by Alexander, the story circulated through the Stadium that afternoon that he had celebrated his previous day's triumph too well and was catching up on his sleep in the bull pen when a teammate told him that Manager Rogers Hornsby wanted him to enter the game as relief pitcher.

When he was summoned, the bases were filled, there were two out, and Tony Lazzeri, slugging second baseman of the Yankees, was at bat. Alexander trudged slowly to the mound looking dejected, but fanned Lazzeri on three pitched balls to quell the Yankee threat. He continued to tame the New Yorkers during the remaining two frames and clinched the world championship for the Cards.

Exultant St. Louis fans gave the club a roaring welcome when Alexander and his mates returned to that city after their capture of the World Series. One of the most conspicuous banners carried in the St. Louis victory parade bore the inscription "Alexander for President."

During his last big season, in 1927, Alexander won twenty-one games and lost ten for the Cards. He scored sixteen victories the next year but lost his effectiveness thereafter and returned to the Phillies after the 1929 campaign. The Phils handed him his unconditional release on June 3, 1930, thus ending his major league career.

Later he pitched for a brief time for Dallas in the Texas League, and in 1938 he was still twirling an occasional game for the House of David and other independent clubs, when he was voted into baseball's Hall of Fame, at Cooperstown, New York. Alexander was the fourth pitcher to receive that honor—the others were Mathewson, Walter Johnson, and Cy Young.

Alexander, who saw action in the 1915 World Series with the Phillies as well as in the 1926 and 1928 classics with the Cards, was carefree and had an utter disregard for training rules. His inclination to break training frequently got him in difficulties with his managers, and in later years club owners hesitated to take a chance on him as a team leader.

Hard times resulted for Alexander and he turned to various odd jobs. One summer he sold tickets at a midwestern racetrack. In his later years he was an added attraction at a sideshow on New York's West Forty-second Street, where in a low, soft voice, he enthralled the customers with stories concerning baseball heroes of bygone days.

Alexander survived a skull fracture in 1941, and when it became generally known that he was in need of money, baseball fans rallied and contributed handsomely to a fund for the old-timer. During World War II he was employed at a Cincinnati airplane factory. At that time he wanted it known that his physical condition was such that he would welcome a job in baseball, as a pitching coach or in some other capacity.

Apparently, no one found a need for old Pete in the game that had made him famous.

On November 4, 1950, he was found dead in his room in St. Paul. An unfinished letter to his divorced wife, Aimee, was found in his typewriter.

Alexander the Great

By ARTHUR DALEY

"Don't let it go to your head, Alex," pleaded Manager Bill McKechnie of the Cardinals. "Please don't do anything foolish. I'm warning you. If you're not back here on time, you'll get a ticket to somewhere else."

Grover Cleveland Alexander had just scored his 373rd major league victory. According to the record books of that era he thereby had broken Christy Mathewson's National League record of 372 triumphs. Ol' Pete was obviously in the twilight of his remarkable career and great was his delight that he'd shattered the mark of the immortal Matty. And Ol' Pete knew only one way to celebrate.

"I'm just gonna see a friend, Bill," he told McKechnie. Alex's best friend—and his worst one—was John Barleycorn. They had a long visit. It marked the end of Pete as a member of the Cardinals. He was shipped to the Phillies, where he failed to win another game. Then it was the minors and oblivion.

Grover Cleveland Alexander led a tragic life. John Barleycorn, the invincible one, robbed him of health, wealth, happiness, and everything else. The National League tried valiantly in his declining years to help him—this never was publicized—but it was hopeless. He lost everything. Ironically, he also lost his record in a fashion that never has been explained.

In the 1940s, some statistician delved deeply into ancient files and discovered a game, hitherto uncredited to him, that had presumably been won by Matty in 1902. The Al Munro Elias Bureau, keeper of the archives, added it to Matty's record in the Little Red Book. The *Sporting News* added it in its *Baseball Register*. Both Matty and Alex now are bracketed as the twin record holders at 373 victories. Who authorized the changes? No one seems to know.

The greatest pitchers in history were Cy Young, Walter Johnson, Matty, and Alex. They were off in a class by themselves with nobody else even close. Yet Ol' Pete never could rank with the other idols as a model for American youth. Baseball men were truly horrified when he reached such a low point as to appear as a sideshow attraction for a flea circus off Times Square.

But Alexander's weaknesses were only off the field. On the mound he had nary a weakness. His pitching motion was poetry itself. His control was as close to perfection as control could be. And there never was any wasted effort to him. He'd win 'em in an hour or so, fast, sure, and confident.

The last game that Cy Young ever pitched was in 1911 when he was beaten, 1–0, by a strong-armed rookie.

"When the kids can beat you, it's time to quit," philosophized Cy and he never pitched again. Little did he realize that the kid who beat him was to become another of baseball's all-time greats—Grover Cleveland Alexander.

Alex won twenty-eight games in his freshman year. Then it was nineteen, twenty-two, twenty-seven, and—this almost takes your breath away—thirty-one, thirty-three, and thirty. What is more, his earned-run average was as low as 1.22, and it was under two runs a game for six straight years. He pitched shutout after shutout in the bandbox Baker Bowl, the burying ground for all other pitchers.

In spite of the handicap of neighborly fences, Ol' Pete always could throw the ball exactly where he wanted to throw it. Batters just couldn't hit him solidly. One modern gauge of judging the ability of a pitcher is to match the walks he gives against his strikeouts. If he fans more than he walks, he's deemed to have excellent control. Not many qualify in accordance with those standards.

Let's take Pete's three thirty-game years as a sample. In 1915 he fanned 241 but walked only 64. Then it was 167 and 50. Then it was 200 and 56. Where the moderns are happy if they do better than a fifty-fifty ratio, Alex was spinning away on a 4-to-1 or 3-to-1 basis. What is more important, he achieved his greatness in spite of the fact that John Barleycorn was hanging around his neck like an Old Man of the Sea.

In a left-handed sort of way this right-handed ace was responsible for the making of Joe McCarthy as a manager. When Marse Joe came to the Cubs from Louisville in 1925, the veterans on the club were a trifle scornful of his abilities. Their tendency was to regard him as an unproven bush leaguer—which he was.

So McCarthy traded Alexander, the idol of the fans, to the Cardinals. It was a daring gamble. But it demonstrated that Marse Joe's training rules had to be obeyed and that he was demanding the respect of his hired hands. It established his authority, and McCarthy was always the boss from that point on.

And now Alexander the Great is gone, a tragic figure off the field but one of the true titans of the game on it.

BEAR BRYANT

1913–1983

By JOSEPH DURSO

B EAR BRYANT died of a heart attack only thirty-seven days after he retired as head football coach at the University of Alabama with the most victories in major college football history to that time. Bryant ended his thirty-eight-year career with a record of 323 victories, 85 losses, and 17 ties compiled at four schools: Maryland, Kentucky, Texas A&M, and for his last twenty-five years, Alabama. Six of his teams at Alabama were rated No. 1 nationally by the wire service polls. And when Alabama defeated Auburn, 28–17, on November 28, 1981, for his 315th victory, he surpassed the record that had been set earlier in the century by Amos Alonzo Stagg.

Bryant's impact on football everywhere was assured through the scores of men who had played or coached under "the Bear." In his time, he developed star quarterbacks such as Joe Namath, George Blanda, Babe Parilli, Ken Stabler, Steve Sloan, and Richard Todd. More than forty of his former players became head college coaches, including Jerry Claiborne, Howard Schnellenberger, Jackie Sherrill, Steve Sloan, and Pat Dye.

He also became instrumental in recruiting black athletes for Alabama. His first black player was Wilbur Jackson, a running back, in 1971. In his final season, 54 of the 128 football players at Alabama were black. Later, he remembered that he had wanted to recruit black football players at Kentucky, and said, "They wouldn't let me. Then, at Alabama all those years, my hands were tied. To tell you the truth, Sam Cunningham did more for integration at Alabama than anybody else. He was a black running back for Southern Cal. Came down here in 1970 and ran all over my skinny little white boys. Scored three touchdowns."

Two weeks after he announced his retirement as coach, the Bryant era ended on December 29, 1982, when Alabama defeated Illinois in the Liberty Bowl, 21–15. It was the eighth victory of the season for Alabama after four defeats, the first time in thirteen years the team had lost as many as four games. It was also his twenty-ninth bowl game, a record for a coach that included twenty-four straight at Alabama, and the last appearance in a stadium for the craggy-faced figure roaming the sidelines in the houndstooth hat.

Paul William Bryant was born September 11, 1913, in Moro Bottom, Arkansas, which he described as "a little piece of bottomland on the Moro Creek, about seven miles north of Fordyce." He was one of eleven children in a poor family, and he remembered that he had an inferiority complex and "wasn't very smart in school, and lazy to boot."

But he was big, eventually growing to 6 feet 4 inches. And he recalled that he acquired his nickname as a teenager in high school when he accepted a dare to wrestle a bear.

"It was outside the Lyric Theater," he said. "There was a poster out front with a picture of a bear, and a guy was offering a dollar a minute to anyone who would wrestle the bear. The guy who was supposed to wrestle the bear didn't show up, so they egged me on. They let me and my friends into the picture show free, and I wrestled this scrawny bear to the floor. I went around later to get my money, but the guy with the bear had flown the coop. All I got out of the whole thing was a nickname."

As a strapping and aggressive tackle on the Fordyce High School football team, Bryant lived up to his nickname by winning all-state honors. Then he was recruited for the University of Alabama by Hank Crisp, an assistant to Frank Thomas, and played right end. His principal assignment, he remembered, was to do the blocking while Don Hutson, the left end, was the star pass receiver. Hutson was later elected to the College Football Hall of Fame. But the team thrived, winning twenty-three games and losing only three in Bryant's years as a player, and the Crimson Tide defeated Stanford in the 1935 Rose Bowl game, 29–13.

After his class had graduated, Bryant stayed at Alabama as an assistant coach. Four years later, he switched to Vanderbilt as an assistant. But two years after that, in 1941, he joined the navy and served in World War II, part of the time as a football coach at the preflight school in North Carolina. He was discharged in 1945, in time to become head coach at Maryland, where he opened his long and sometimes stormy career.

He was an instant success, partly because he had taken the precaution of bringing along several good players from the navy preflight team. In his first game, Maryland whipped Guilford College, 60–6. That first season, Maryland won six games, lost two, and tied one.

But he also was an instant center of controversy. He suspended a player for breaking training rules, was overruled by the school's president, and promptly quit and took over as coach at Kentucky.

He stayed eight seasons, and his teams won sixty games and lost twenty-three, appeared in four postseason games, and won the school's only Southeastern Conference championship. The highlight was a 13–7 victory over Oklahoma in the 1950 Sugar Bowl that broke a thirty-one-game winning streak for Oklahoma.

After he left, in 1954, he conceded that one problem had been a conflict of personalities with Adolph Rupp, the highly successful basketball coach.

"The trouble," he said, "was that we were too much alike. He wanted basketball to be No. 1, and I wanted football No. 1. In an environment like that, one or the other has to go."

The next stop was Texas A&M, where Bryant stayed four seasons with a record of twenty-five victories and fourteen defeats and a Southwestern Conference title in 1956. He also developed the talents of John David Crow, a running back who won the Heisman Trophy as the nation's best player. But more controversy arose when the school was placed on probation for violating the rules on recruiting players, and Bryant acknowledged later that some of his players had been paid, though not by him.

Finally, he went "home" in 1958 to his alma mater, Alabama. "It was like when you were out in the field, and you heard your mama calling you to dinner," he said, explaining his joy at returning. "Mama called."

Alabama had won only four football games in three years. But in his first season, the Crimson Tide won five games and lost four. And in 1961, he received his first No. 1 ranking nationally. For the rest of his career, his teams averaged 8.5 victories a year and did not suffer a losing season.

Controversy followed him home, however. An article in the *Saturday Evening Post* said that he and Wally Butts, the coach at Georgia, had arranged to fix the result of a game in 1962. Alabama won the game, 35–0. Butts won a libel suit against the publisher, and Bryant won a substantial out-of-court settlement.

Although he acknowledged an obsession for winning, he was a forbidding figure when it came to training rules. Not even Namath escaped his discipline. In 1964, he removed Namath as quarterback for breaking training and kept him on the sidelines during the Sugar Bowl game. At other times, he also disciplined Lee Roy Jordan, Scott Hunter, John Hannah, Ken Stabler, Steve Sloan, and even Ray Perkins, the man who would eventually succeed him as head coach.

Bryant was a tireless worker who customarily rose at five in the morning and did not stop until late in the evening. He often supervised practice sessions from a tower overlooking two fields, one covered with grass, the other with artificial turf. One of his quarterbacks, Steadman Shealy, once said, "There's something about him up in that tower that makes you want to run through a wall."

He was married to his college sweetheart, Mary Harmon Black, who had been a campus beauty queen when he played football at Alabama. They had two children, Paul William, Jr., and May Martin Tyson, and four grandchildren.

Mr. Bryant's stature at Alabama was so great that his salary became something of a protocol problem. Eventually, it reached $120,000. But, for years, the university made an effort to keep the football coach's salary below that of the school's president. The president made $100,000 a year; Mr. Bryant was paid $99,999.99.

He Breaks Stagg's Record

By MALCOLM MORAN

Paul Bryant of the University of Alabama, who once wrestled a bear to earn his nickname and long ago achieved immortality in these parts, coached his 315th victory on November 28, 1981, more than any other major college football coach up until that time.

Despite the absence of two players who were dismissed from the team two days earlier and the problem of two fumbled punts that led to scores and put his team behind in the fourth quarter, Alabama defeated Auburn that day,

28–17. The game was played before a national television audience and a frenzied crowd of 78,170 at Legion Field in Birmingham, Alabama, that included Joe Namath and other former Bryant players, assistants, and friends.

Bryant, who passed Glenn "Pop" Warner with a victory two weeks earlier at Penn State, moved ahead of Amos Alonzo Stagg, who won 314 games in fifty-seven seasons. Bryant, in thirty-eight years at Maryland, Kentucky, Texas A&M, and Alabama would end his career with a record of 323–85–17.

His players, following instructions, surrounded Bryant at the end of the game. Bryant's houndstooth hat, his trademark, disappeared from view and was taken to a safe place. He received the game ball from Bart Krout, a senior tight end from Birmingham who was born in October 1959, one year after Bryant came to Alabama.

It was nearly an hour after the game before someone wanted to know about the next game, the Cotton Bowl against Texas on January 1. "How can I have plans for the Cotton Bowl when I haven't quit shaking from the end of this game," Bryant replied.

Auburn took the lead for the first time with 12 minutes 58 seconds to play after the second Alabama fumble of a punt had led to a score. Alabama lost four fumbles and had one pass intercepted, but it was the two fumbles by Joey Jones, the punt returner, that gave Alabama its biggest problems.

The score was tied, 7–7, at halftime. Alan Gray, the first of three Alabama quarterbacks, gained 63 yards on an option run to set up his 1-yard touchdown midway through the first quarter. George Peoples, the Auburn fullback, tied the score with 3:58 to go in the half.

Alabama regained the lead on its first possession of the third period, when Ken Coley, its third quarterback, shoveled the ball ahead to the split end, Jesse Bendross, who turned the left corner and went 21 yards for the touchdown.

After Jones's first fumbled punt, and the high-speed chase for the bouncing ball, Chuck Clanton, an Auburn defensive back, recovered at the Alabama 2, and Lionel James scored from there.

And after Mike Hicks recovered Jones's second fumble at the Alabama 32, Al Del Greco kicked a 19-yard field goal ten plays later, and the Tigers led for the first time.

Auburn had not beaten Alabama since 1972, when the late Ralph "Shug" Jordan was the coach. Before Pat Dye, a former Alabama assistant, became the coach in 1980, Bryant told Dye not to take the job. "He said I would never beat him," Dye said. "I didn't tell him I would. We're going to let the players decide that."

Now, leading by 17–14, Auburn had its greatest chance, and Bryant was in danger of being embarrassed. It was several years earlier when rival schools had been telling recruits that Bryant would soon retire. To answer the opposition and reassure recruits, Bryant said he intended to break Stagg's record. "If someone has to be the winningest coach," he said then, "it might as well be me."

And his current players were eager to share in the historic occasion.

"I really wanted to go out saying I'm a part of it," said Warren Lyles, a senior middle guard.

"Every time we lined up in the third and fourth quarters," said Benny

Perrin, a senior defensive back, "we would say in the huddle, 'We can't give up, this is for 315 and the record.' "

At the start of the fourth quarter, all of that seemed to be slipping away. And then suddenly it all turned around.

But there was no need for another time. Walter Lewis, the second of the three Alabama quarterbacks, threw a 38-yard touchdown pass to Bendross to regain the lead. And after three Auburn plays and a punt, Linnie Patrick, a sophomore halfback who carried the ball just once in the first 51 minutes of play, gained 47 yards in two carries. His 15-yard touchdown, with 7:07 to go, gave the Tide an eleven-point lead and secured the record.

There was enough depth that Bob Cayavec, an all-conference offensive tackle, and Gary Bramblett, a guard, were hardly missed. They had been dismissed from the team the previous Thursday, after Cayavec was reportedly arrested for drunken driving with Bramblett a passenger.

Being Bear Bryant has been a difficult job this year. But after the record was set, the coach made certain to thank the players, coaches, and friends who could not be here: Carney Laslie and Frank Moseley, coaches who had died; Ermal Allen, who had recently suffered a heart attack; Frank McGough, Marlin Mooneyham, Ralph Genito, and Nick Odlivak, who were ill at the time.

He thanked President Reagan and former President Jimmy Carter, who called the locker room.

"Did the president call you?" Dye said, excited.

"Sure he called me," Bryant said, trying to sound matter of fact.

Bryant smiled. He hoped the day his team won No. 315 would end like so many others. "I want to go home and get the TV on and hold my grand-daughters," he said.

ROBERTO CLEMENTE

1934–1972

O N DECEMBER 31, 1972, Roberto Clemente, star outfielder for the Pittsburgh Pirates, died in the crash of a cargo plane carrying relief supplies to the victims of the earthquake that struck Nicaragua earlier that month.

Three days of national mourning for Clemente were proclaimed in his native Puerto Rico, where he was the most popular sports figure in the island's history. He was later enshrined in baseball's Hall of Fame. He was only the eleventh man in baseball history to get 3,000 hits, and at his death, his lifetime batting average of .317 was the highest among active players.

Clemente, who was thirty-eight years old, won the National League batting championship four times in his eighteen-season career, was named to the All-Star team twelve times, and in 1966 was named the league's Most Valuable Player. He was also one of the finest defensive outfielders, with a very strong throwing arm. He led the Pittsburgh Pirates to two world championships, in 1960 and 1971, the latter time being named the Most Valuable Player in the World Series.

Clemente was the leader of Puerto Rican efforts to aid the Nicaraguan victims and was aboard the plane because he suspected that relief supplies were falling into the hands of profiteers.

An Involved Player

By LEONARD KOPPETT

The way Roberto Clemente died had more to do with the way he had lived than all the spectacular baseball statistics for which, in due course, he was enshrined in the Hall of Fame.

Few men, if any, have played professional baseball better than Clemente did during his eighteen-year career with the Pittsburgh Pirates. And few players put as much passion into other aspects of life as he did.

Not halfway through his thirty-ninth year, he was personally involved in a mission of mercy, trying to relieve the suffering of strangers caused by an earthquake in a country he had previously visited only briefly. Most athletes, or anyone else earning nearly $200,000 a year, as Clemente did, lend their

names, financial support, or even their exhortations to some worthy cause and let it go at that. But Clemente had to go in person.

This capacity for involvement characterized him as a ball player and helped generate some of the misunderstandings that made him a controversial personality.

But in the end—the brutally abrupt end—his baseball skills remained the achievement of his life and the reason his personality mattered to so many people.

He made exactly 3,000 hits, and only fifteen players in more than a hundred years of major league baseball had made as many. He won four National League batting championships and a Most Valuable Player award. He helped his team to victory the only two times it reached the World Series. His career batting average was .317, highest of all active players with at least a few years of service.

In addition he was acknowledged as one of the greatest fielders of his day with an exceptionally strong and accurate throwing arm, and a first-rate base runner. As the "complete player," his only peers as contemporaries were Willie Mays and Hank Aaron, each of whom got greater recognition because they hit more home runs.

Clemente was Puerto Rican and black, and fiercely proud of his identity. His status as a national hero in Puerto Rico stemmed as much from his outspoken expression of such pride as from his baseball feats. Other Puerto Ricans had won baseball glory but few had made such explicit demands for respect and recognition.

His destiny was baseball from the start. He was born on August 18, 1934, in Carolina, the San Juan suburb that remained his home. He was the youngest child in a large, financially comfortable family. His father was a foreman on a sugar plantation, and his plans for Roberto pointed toward engineering.

But while still in high school at seventeen, he was playing baseball so spectacularly that he was given a $500 bonus to join the Santurce team in the Puerto Rican League, in which professionals from the States also played. In his third season, the winter of 1953–54, he hit .356, and the major league scouts had no doubts.

In 1954 there was still an unspoken quota system limiting the number of black players a team would use, although Jackie Robinson had already completed seven seasons with the Brooklyn Dodgers. There was also a distinct set of prejudices about "Spanish-speaking players." And there was a "bonus rule" that forced a major league team to keep on its active roster any player to whom it had paid more than $4,000 for signing—a deterrent to giving bonuses to a player not ready to play in the majors immediately.

But Clemente's talent was so evident that all three deterrents were disregarded. After some bidding, the Dodgers landed him for $10,000 outright and a $5,000 salary to play for their Montreal club. That meant he could be drafted by another team for $4,000 after the 1954 season.

There are conflicting versions of what happened next. The facts are that Clemente played part-time for Montreal, batted .257, and was drafted by Pittsburgh, which had first choice because it finished last in 1953.

The Dodgers had won the pennant in 1953 by a huge margin and couldn't have signed Clemente without a bonus. They knew, they said afterward, they would lose him in the draft, but it was worth the money to keep him from signing with the New York Giants, who already had Mays. The idea of a Mays and Clemente playing side by side was too frightening for the Dodgers to allow.

Another version is that the Dodgers hoped to sneak Clemente through the draft by not playing him much (to hide his ability) and by loading the Montreal roster with other attractive draft picks. But the Pirates, under the direction of Branch Rickey, who had left Brooklyn three years before, were not fooled.

Clemente started the 1955 season with a Pittsburgh club that had lost 317 games in three years, finishing last each time. He was not yet twenty-one and was among a half-dozen young players who were to make Pittsburgh a World Series winner by 1960—Dick Groat, Bill Mazeroski, Roy Face, Vern Law, Don Hoak, and Bill Virdon.

Clemente's bitterness about nonrecognition dates to the 1960 season. A key member of that team, he felt unjustly neglected when so much of the praise was heaped on others who had done no more. For the next decade, during which he won his four batting championships and the M.V.P. in 1966, a feeling of being unappreciated marred his satisfaction with increasing fame and wealth.

Recognition finally came in full measure in 1971. By then the acknowledged leader of the Pirates, he led them into the World Series and, as underdogs, to a dramatic seven-game victory over Baltimore. He hit .414 in that Series, but was even more dominating by his involvement in key plays and was finally hailed by the widest possible audience for what he had been all along: a player of all-round excellence second to none.

By that time he was deep into his dream of building a "Sports City" in Puerto Rico to encourage children and youngsters to play. It was a project that needed financing but could not provide profit—quite different from the usual "baseball school camp."

He had been to Nicaragua for an amateur baseball tournament. That was enough of a tie to impel him to head a relief committee after the earthquake, interrupting his activities with baseball for youngsters.

A Man of Two Worlds

By JOSEPH DURSO

On New Year's Day, 1973, Tom Seaver sat by the Christmas tree in his home in Greenwich, Connecticut, and reflected on the life and times of Roberto Walker Clemente. He agreed that the key word in everything Clemente did for thirty-eight years, nearby half of them in the big leagues, was *passion.*

"Also compassion," Seaver said. "Emotional, sincere, a compassionate type of person. I could not believe what I heard on the radio, that he was gone. It was just chills, period. It's a horrible loss, not only to his family and teammates but to all of us, especially to the young players. I mean, you look up to Henry Aaron and Sandy Koufax and Roberto Clemente."

Since 1955, when he became a rookie outfielder with the Pittsburgh Pirates, Roberto Clemente lived in two worlds and they had one thing in common: passion. On the baseball field, he played eighteen seasons with passion, often complaining of aches and pains as he attacked National League pitching. Off the field, he would retreat to his handsome house in Puerto Rico to spend the winter with his wife and three sons while resting those aches and pains, but then he would become involved with passion in civic projects until spring training.

"I had a rough winter," Clemente said the previous February as he sat exhausted in the Pirates' training camp in Bradenton, Florida, four months after he had hit .414 in the World Series at the age of thirty-seven. "I didn't do any exercise, I kept going from one place to another and never had enough time home. My father was very ill. I lost ten pounds and now I have stomach trouble.

"In addition to my house, I have a place in the mountains, and I said I would spend a lot of time there. I got there three times all winter.

"For a month and a half, my wife and I couldn't sleep. Our house was like a museum—people flocking down the street, ringing our bell day and night, walking through our rooms. People from the town, even tourists.

"Then I had so many things going on down there, and I just couldn't say no. Every day I was doing something different. The governor sent for me, the park administration, civic clubs. We tried to get away to South America for a vacation and were called back because my father took sick."

Even at his peak moments on the ball field, Clemente related his baseball world to his world back home. After the Pirates had dethroned the Baltimore Orioles in the 1971 Series, he was called to the microphones in the tumultuous locker room. He asked permission to include a few words in Spanish to his mother and father in Puerto Rico, then said, "On this, the proudest moment of my life, I ask your blessing."

"I thought he was great," Brooks Robinson was saying in the losers' locker room at the same time, "but now that I've seen him more than I ever had, he's greater than I thought."

"When a guy gets older, you usually see him slow up," Don Buford, of the Orioles, was saying. "But not Clemente."

"Very few players can win a game in as many different ways," observed Bill Mazeroski, his teammate for seventeen years.

"The very special thing about Roberto physically," Tom Seaver reflected, "was his hands. So very powerful. He stood there far away from the plate with that great big, long bat, and with those strong hands he controlled it like crazy, hitting pitches on the other side of the plate.

"There was that one area out there at the knees off the outside corner. If you hit that spot with a pitch, he'd look and walk away. If you missed it, he'd hit the ball very hard."

"His weakness was so close to his strength that you were always in danger," said Jim Russo, chief scout for the Orioles. "I mean, I told our pitchers they could throw low and away. But if they made a mistake, he'd hit it out of sight to right field."

They will remember Roberto Clemente as one of the rare ones in his world of baseball: twelve All-Star games, eleven times the Golden Glove winner in right field, five times the league leader in throwing out base runners from the outfield, the best career batting average (.317) on the scene, the eleventh player in history to total 3,000 hits. Now there are fifteen.

They even named a race horse after him—Roberto, winner of the 1972 English Derby and owned by John W. Galbreath, who also owned the Pittsburgh Pirates. And in a special election a few months later, he became the first Latin player elected to baseball's Hall of Fame.

But for all his honors on the field, it may well be that Robert Clemente will be remembered longer and more lovingly off the field, in that "other" world back home, the world where his strong bronze face and his passion made him a folk hero, where his house was like a museum and where he couldn't say no.

A Genuine Superstar

By ARTHUR DALEY

During his eighteen years with the Pittsburgh Pirates the gifted Roberto had gained recognition as a man of towering dignity, highly esteemed not only as a person but as a ball player. He was a genuine superstar, and few of his contemporaries could surpass him in skill. Roberto was the complete ball player. He did everything extraordinarily well. He could run, throw, field, hit, and hit with power. These are the five ingredients on which players are rated, and the Pirate outfielder ranked at or near the top in each.

He won four batting championships and one Most Valuable Player award. He had thirteen years of over .300 and he still hit .312 in his last season, when he supposedly was easing into the twilight of his career. Twilight? Roberto just didn't seem to acknowledge it. At the somewhat advanced age of thirty-seven in 1971 he batted .414 in the World Series with at least one hit in each of the seven games, thereby duplicating a feat he had performed eleven years earlier in another Series against the Yankees.

If there was a smoldering resentment within Roberto that he never got the acclaim he deserved, he was entitled to such an attitude. Willie Mays was given instant acclaim when he first arrived on the scene and was endowed with superstardom almost immediately. But Willie the Wonder had the advantage of starting with the New York Giants and that put him in a matchless showcase. Roberto never had one in Pittsburgh.

When Giant writers in those early days would rattle off a list of Willie's impossible catches, Pirate writers would dutifully recite impossible catches that Roberto made, all of equal value. But only Willie's stuck in memory.

Many of Mays's throws also became engraved enduringly in consciousness, but Roberto had a better and more accurate arm, one that never seemed to diminish in strength. He once made a throw home from the iron gate at right field in old Forbes Field. It reached the catcher on the fly. The distance was 460 feet. Such was his reputation that he scared runners, causing many to hold up rather than risk being shot down by his gunner's arm.

Once he threw out a runner on a bunt, a rather fancy play for any outfielder to make. Bill Mazeroski, a teammate, attests to it, and he is a man of great probity. It was a freak play, of course. It would have to be. The Pirate strategy with runners on first and second with none out was to have the third baseman race in for a bunt while the shortstop covered third. Outfielders instinctively played shallow. But this particular batter mangled his bunt, tapping the ball on the fly to the vacated shortstop spot. Base runners hesitated and held up. Roberto came tearing in from the outfield, made a quick pickup and forced a runner at third.

Originally signed by the Brooklyn Dodgers, he may have been victimized by a quota system that some said was in effect in those unenlightened days. The Pirates drafted him from the Dodger farm system and thus did his advance toward stardom begin. Perhaps it would have been swifter and more noticeable in Brooklyn. Who knows? Also unknown is whether this would have made him a different kind of ball player.

Ebbets Field was a neat little playpen with all fences within easy reach of the Dodger clout circus of that era. But Roberto landed instead in Forbes Field, the most spacious ball park in the majors. Smart man that he was, he shunned the home run, which might have tempted him in Brooklyn.

He became a line-drive hitter, spraying them in all directions, but his favorite target was the opposite field, right field. Awesome was his accummulation of hits over the years, and in 1972 he achieved a goal that only ten ball players in all recorded history had ever reached before him. A few days before the end of the season, Roberto lashed a double off the wall on one hop and the scoreboard became alive with the number 3,000. He had just made his 3,000th hit.

"Roberto is the greatest ball player I ever saw," often said his former manager, Danny Murtaugh. It is not too extravagant an estimate. Roberto was a great one in so many ways. He even went out with a flourish typical of the man, seeking to extend a helping hand to those in need.

TY COBB

1887–1961

T Y COBB was the No. 1 player elected to baseball's Hall of Fame and probably the greatest star in the game's history.

The famed Georgia Peach, a giant in baseball almost from the start of his major league career in 1905, was one of the most feared players in the game because of his daring and his short-fused temper.

After playing twenty-two years with the Detroit Tigers and two years with the Philadelphia Athletics, Cobb was the first player chosen in 1936 to the Hall of Fame. He beat out Babe Ruth by seven votes.

Tall (6 feet), tough, and fiery, Cobb was noted for the deadly use of his spikes on the base paths, his dramatic base stealing, and his skill at bat.

Among his numerous records were highest career batting average (.367), most batting championships (twelve), most stolen bases (892), and most base hits (4,191). The last two records were subsequently eclipsed by Lou Brock (938 steals), Rickey Henderson (936 steals, as of 1990), and Pete Rose (4,256 hits).

During fourteen of his years in the major leagues, he batted when the old "dead" ball was still in use and when there was virtually no limit on the tricks a pitcher could use.

Cobb started with Detroit on August 30, 1905, at the age of eighteen. The Tigers had paid between $700 and $750 to get him from Augusta in the South Atlantic League. Cobb hit a double off Jack Chesbro in his first time at bat.

His first-year batting average was .240 for forty-one games, but from then until he called it quits in 1928 he never fell below .322. Three times, he batted more than .400 in a season.

Batting left-handed and throwing right-handed, the center-field star played in 3,033 games, scored 2,244 runs, hit 297 triples, and nine times made more than 200 hits in a season. In 1915 he stole ninety-six bases, a mark that stood for forty-seven years.

The nickname Georgia Peach was given to Cobb by Grantland Rice, the sportswriter, who was impressed with the daring, talented youngster in action with Augusta. After watching Cobb, Rice went back to his typewriter and recounted one dramatic play made by the lad he called the Georgia Peach. The name stuck.

A master of the hook and fall-away slide, Cobb raised base stealing to new heights. Several times Cobb stole second, third, and home in one inning. One manager reportedly asked his catcher:

"What do you do when Cobb breaks for second?"

The catcher replied:

"I throw to third."

Cobb was once home run champion of his league. He hit nine in 1909, helping Detroit win its third straight American League pennant. He also led the league in batting average and runs batted in that year, becoming the first player to win the Triple Crown.

It was not only his ability that inspired fear and respect in his foes, but also the temper of his playing. He once said that the reason he was so tough on the diamond was that he had entered baseball in the days when a player had to be tough to survive.

Often called the "stormy petrel" of the game, as well as less printable epithets, he played every game as if it were the deciding contest in the World Series.

At the height of his career he was frequently embroiled in fights with other players and with fans. In 1912 the Tigers went on strike because he was suspended for attacking a heckler who happened to be handicapped. In another famous scrap, Cobb squared off with George Moriarty, an umpire, in a bout under the stands.

In his later years Cobb became a "mellow sort of fellow," in the words of a man who knew him and was impressed with the apparent turnabout in his personality.

Where as a player he had battled with his own teammates as well as with opposing team members, and had only a few intimates, he seemed in his later years to want to atone for his long period of aggressiveness.

In a soft-spoken way he liked to make jokes about his days as a "difficult player," and it was a habit of his to attend many of the old-time affairs and reminisce.

He continued to take long hikes and to go hunting for many years, activities that in his playing years he credited with developing his endurance and quick awareness.

As a manager, as well as a player, Cobb gave the fans repeated thrills and excitement. In the off-season of 1920, he signed to manage the team on which he had starred for so long. He brought the Tigers home second in 1923, but that was his best.

In his last years as player-manager, Cobb drove fans and opposition to distraction by jogging back and forth from center field to talk to his pitcher, shift his infield, or otherwise evolve strategy. But he was still batting .339 when he resigned as manager in 1926.

Soon afterward he figured in a potential scandal that threatened to become another "Black Sox" affair. With Tris Speaker, another of baseball's old-time heroes, he was accused by Dutch Leonard, a former Tiger pitcher, of figuring in an agreement to throw a game in 1919—the year of the crooked Series between Cincinnati and Chicago.

But on January 27, 1927, the two stars were exonerated by Judge Kenesaw Mountain Landis, and Cobb said at once he felt "honor bound" to put in at least one more "big year."

Connie Mack signed him for the Athletics for a reported $75,000, and

Cobb promptly predicted a pennant. But Mack's lineup of stars—he had signed Eddie Collins and Zach Wheat as well—lost to the Yankees that year. Cobb never had another chance to be on a pennant winner. He played in ninety-five games in 1928, batting .323, or forty-four points below his career average.

Waspish as he was on the field, Cobb was a quiet man away from the diamond. Known to have invested his money wisely, he became a millionaire, largely on the investments he had made in Coca-Cola stock.

After he left the game as a player he rarely went to a ball park. He insisted that the game that he had played in the era of the fast, multiple steal, the squeeze bunt, and the dead ball was not matched in contemporary baseball.

Cobb died in Atlanta on July 17, 1961. He was seventy-four years old.

Larcenous Intent

By ARTHUR DALEY

Ty Cobb was more than just a great player, probably the greatest of them all. He was a diamond intellectual, analyst, and psychologist rolled into one. Not only could he hit better and run faster than anyone else, but he also could outthink any other ball player. Cold calculation motivated every action this firebrand made on a ball field.

"Rarely should a base runner risk a steal when the game is in the balance," he once told this reporter. "It's to be used when you can afford to fail."

When a fellow is privileged to listen to Cobb long enough and often enough, he gets such a glimpse of Ty's underlying philosophy that it's readily apparent why he was such a breathtaking, matchless performer.

"I couldn't even begin to count the number of times I was thrown out stealing when I knew I didn't have a chance to make it," he said. "But I went down anyway despite the realization I was going into a deliberate out. However, I only did this in a game which was already won. I wouldn't call it a failure, because I was gaining knowledge for the future. Maybe I'd learn something which could win a game later on.

"I'd be testing out the pitcher's ability to hold a man on base. I'd also be probing to see if I rattled him so that he was paying more attention to me than to the batter. I was testing out the catcher and his reactions. I was testing out the infielder who took the throw, maybe even experimenting with the kind of slide which would best avoid his type of tag.

"Most of all, though, I was saddling that team with a psychological burden so that they'd be muttering, 'Cobb is crazy. He'll run any time and in any situation.' It would help give them the jitters and they'd concentrate so much on me they weren't paying attention to the business at hand. My failures rarely were complete failures. They were more like future investments."

The Yankees' incomparable Hal Chase had a pet play that he kept trying to work on the Georgia Peach. When Cobb was the base runner on first, he thought nothing of going from first to third on an infield out. The adroit Chase, great fielder that he was, fell into the pattern of whipping the ball across the diamond to Jimmy Austin at third, not in the hope of heading off the mercury-footed Ty but in the hope that he might get him coming back from an overrun of the bag. And Cobb's overruns were getting dangerously long.

With the score tied with one out in the ninth, Cobb was on first and Wahoo Sam Crawford was at bat. The big slugger dribbled to Chase at first. Prince Hal stepped gracefully on the bag and in the same swoop rifled a throw to Austin at third. Austin sensed that Cobb had misplayed his hand by taking too much of a lead. His glove stabbed down at the base to tag the sliding Ty on his way back. He felt nothing and looked up just in time to see Cobb flashing over the plate with the winning run, scoring from first on an infield out.

Cobb's psychological maneuvers weren't always as subtle as that carefully plotted coup. It was on Lou Criger, who caught for the Red Sox, Browns, and Yankees, that he used the direct approach. Base stealers admit that they don't steal on the catchers. They steal on the pitchers. But Ty couldn't steal with Criger behind the plate no matter who was pitching. Then one day Ty singled.

"Watch out, you big baboon," shouted Cobb to Criger. "I'm going down on the first pitch." The catcher hurried his throw and Ty had his steal.

"I'm taking third on the next pitch," sang out Cobb derisively. He made it.

"Out of my way, ice wagon," snarled the Georgia Peach. "I'm coming home." He slid under the rattled Criger, stealing three bases on three successive pitches. He never had much trouble with the rifle-armed Criger thereafter.

Billy Sullivan, when he was with the Chicago White Sox, was another gunner who made stealing difficult. One day Ty stepped into the batter's box and calmly revealed his plans.

"When I get on base," he said, "I'm stealing second on the first pitch and third on the next pitch."

True to his boast, he stole second on the first pitch. But he remained disinterestedly anchored there as Billy called for a pitchout and fired a bullet to third. It was on the third pitch that Ty stole the other base because—or so he explained it—"I didn't want anyone to trust me at any time."

Cobb was obviously the inventor of the "war of nerves." Discount his failures on the bases. He knew what he was doing all the time.

The Cobb We Knew

By JOHN DREBINGER

It was not by accident or whim of choice that when they held the first poll for baseball's Hall of Fame in 1936, the name of Tyrus Raymond Cobb led all the rest. To be on top had been the only creed by which the Georgia Peach had lived through all the years of his spectacular—and at times turbulent—career.

His one goal was to win by any means the rules allowed. That, of course, got him into no end of fights. On and off the field the Georgia firebrand conducted countless feuds.

Even mild-mannered Eddie Collins, a great second baseman in Ty's heyday as a daring base stealer, confessed once that he had harbored a burning hatred for Cobb. Eddie used to go on hunting trips, but just for the exercise. He hadn't the heart to shoot a sparrow.

"But when that Cobb came sliding into me with those gleaming spikes, I saw red," said Eddie. "Throwing to first for a double play, I must have tried to nail him between the eyes with the ball a hundred times. But so agile was that demon in twisting out of reach I never got him once."

But Cobb didn't do all the spiking. He was sitting in a hotel room a few years after he had hung up his spikes for good when the talk got around to some of his more reckless exploits on the base paths.

"Yes," he admitted, "I guess I may have been a trifle rough. But take a look at this."

With that he rolled up his trousers and revealed a pair of shins crisscrossed with myriads of scars from ankles to knees.

"I didn't get those playing tiddlywinks," said Ty. "They gave it to me as hard as I gave it to them. The only difference was I never gave them the satisfaction of hearing me squawk. I'd sooner let them cut out my tongue than let them know I was hurt."

It was when the opposition was at its roughest and hostile crowds rode him hardest that he rose to his greatest heights as a player. Such was one memorable day at the Polo Grounds in 1920.

A few days before, the Yankees, who then made their home in the Polo Grounds, were playing the Indians. Carl Mays, a pitcher with a deceptive underhand or "submarine ball" delivery, was on the mound for the Yankees. A stray pitch struck Ray Chapman, a Cleveland infielder, in the head. He died without regaining consciousness.

The next day, Cobb, whose Tigers were playing elsewhere, was quoted as saying Mays had done it deliberately and should be driven from baseball. The New York fans and press rallied to Mays's support.

Cobb and his Tigers followed the Indians into New York and for the first game a capacity crowd packed the Polo Grounds. For more than an hour before game time they waited for Cobb. But throughout the pregame practice there was no Cobb.

Then, just as the umpires were getting ready to start the game, the clubhouse door in center field opened. Down the steps trotted the Georgia Peach. Up the middle of the field he marched, jauntily slapping his thigh with his glove, while the crowd jeered and booed with deafening noise. Unmindful of it all, Cobb strode to the press box, then in the front of the lower stands directly behind home plate. He doffed his cap with a mock bow. Then he walked to his dugout, where he gave the outraged gathering a final salute of utter disdain.

This done, the game started and the great Ty all but tore it apart with bat and glove. On his final hit the crowd gave him a standing ovation. You simply had to admire the guy.

"Yes," he said years later, "I guess you could say that was one of my biggest thrills."

There was, however, another side of Cobb's play that, perhaps, was not so well known and certainly not as much publicized. It was a side to which modern players could well pay close heed.

He was perhaps one of baseball's keenest students and at all times his own severest critic and taskmaster. He studied every type of batting form and mastered them all.

If any pitcher bothered him with a certain pitch, Cobb would be out early the next day wearing out his own batting-practice pitcher as he worked on that pitch over and over again. It was the same with his fielding. He had, of course, a wealth of natural talent, but he insisted on attaining perfection in all phases of the game.

"If I have any criticism of the modern player," he once said, "and I guess that could apply to my day as well, it is that so few will practice what they can't do. If a fellow can hit a long ball, that's all he tries for. He won't have any part of learning how to bunt or stroke a ball to the opposite field. My advice to young players is, Work at what doesn't come easy to you."

It was a formula that kept him on top for close to a quarter of a century with an incredible lifetime batting average of .367.

Cobb Often Went to Bat for Cobb

When Ty Cobb was seventeen years old, he played for a baseball team in Anniston, Alabama. Grantland Rice was the sports columnist of the *Atlanta Journal.*

Rice began getting a flood of mail from many Southern towns, all with different handwriting and different names but all with the same theme:

"Watch this fellow Ty Cobb. He is going places with his hitting and fielding."

Finally, Rice ran a paragraph in his column about young Ty Cobb. Cobb confessed to Rice years later that he had written all the letters.

"I wanted to get my name in his column," Cobb told the North American Newspaper Alliance. "My father read it regularly, and he would think I was making good."

One spring with the Tigers, Cobb noticed a rookie who was entertaining the players with tremendous broad jumps. The youngster had been a college broad jump star. Cobb challenged the rookie and couldn't come within six inches of him. Two weeks later he challenged the youngster again and beat him.

"No punk is going to outjump me," United Press International reported Cobb as saying.

What Cobb didn't say was that he had practiced secretly for two weeks.

In an Old-timers Game at Yankee Stadium in 1947, Cobb expressed concern about swinging a bat. He hadn't touched one since 1928, he complained.

"I'm way out of practice and I sure don't want to hit you when I swing," he said solicitously to the rival catcher, Benny Bengough. "Better move back a bit so you don't get hurt."

Bengough unsuspectingly obliged. Cobb bunted the first pitch and beat it out for a single while the red-faced Bengough huffed and puffed trying to catch up with the ball.

In 1959, an old-time major league player was interviewed by a broadcaster.

"What do you think Ty Cobb would bat today under modern conditions?" the player was asked.

"Oh, about .305 or .310," was the laconic reply.

"Only .305 or .310," exclaimed the astonished announcer. "Do you really think that is all the great Cobb could bat today?"

"Well," replied the old-timer, "you have to remember that he's seventy-two years old."

MAUREEN CONNOLLY

1934–1969

L ITTLE MO, the stocky prodigy, whose intense and powerful game won her three United States and Wimbledon crowns, became, in 1953, the first woman to achieve the grand slam of tennis—the national championships of the United States, Britain, France, and Australia.

Maureen Connolly's meteoric record of court successes began in 1951, when she won the United States national title then played at the West Side Tennis Club in Forest Hills, Queens, shortly before her seventeenth birthday.

She defended her United States crown successfully two more times and won the women's singles championship at Wimbledon three times before a horseback riding accident cut short her career in July 1954, when she was nineteen years old.

Riding a thoroughbred colt named Colonel Merryboy, which had been given to her by her neighbors in San Diego after a triumphant 1952 tour of Europe, Connolly approached a concrete mixer truck.

Her mount reared and slammed against the truck, crushing her right leg. She suffered a broken leg and deeply gashed muscles and tendons.

Although she had hoped to resume her tennis career upon recovery— probably as a professional—the injury proved more serious than was originally thought, and she announced her retirement in February 1955.

Later that year she was married to Norman Brinker, a former member of the United States Olympic equestrian team.

Until her death, Connolly had devoted herself to teaching the game to youngsters.

Named the female athlete of the year three times by the Associated Press, she was active with the Maureen Connolly Brinker Foundation for the advancement of tennis achievement among junior players in Texas.

In explaining her inability to play tournament tennis, although she was able to instruct children, she said, "I can teach adequately enough. I can hit the ball to my pupils and, if it comes back to me, I can hit it. My strokes are as good as ever. But if the ball is out of reach, I have to let it go."

At the time that her tournament play earned her comparisons with the great woman players of the country, there were few balls she could not reach, and most of them that she stroked did not recross the net.

Her game was marked by swiftness, powerful strokes, and a great competitive spirit.

Allison Danzig, the former tennis writer of *The New York Times*, said of

her: "Maureen, with her perfect timing, fluency, balance, and confidence, has developed the most overpowering stroke of its kind the game has known."

Maureen Connolly, the daughter of Martin and Jessamine Connolly, was born September 17, 1934, in San Diego. She started playing tennis at the age of ten when her mother bought her a racket and sent her to Eleanor Tennant for lessons. She won her first major title, the national outdoor junior championship, at fourteen and proceeded to national and international fame.

Harry Hopman, the captain of the Australian Davis Cup team, became one of her advisers and stressed to her the importance of physical condition.

The regimen she followed as a teenage champion was difficult. She once said, "Tennis can be a grind and there is always the danger of going stale if you think about it too much. You can get embittered if you train too hard and have nothing else on your mind. You have to be able to relax between matches and between tournaments."

Off the court, Maureen was a bubbling young girl, full of gaiety and friendliness for everyone, fond of hamburgers, baseball games, dancing, and music of every kind.

The tennis world was saddened at her retirement, but she accepted her fate philosophically.

"Tennis is a wonderful game and I leave it with no regrets," she said. "I've had a full life with lots of travel and I've met lots of wonderful people. Now I'm going to be a little housewife. It's a new career and I'm awfully happy with it."

She died of cancer in June 1969.

Little Girl, Big Racquet

By ALLISON DANZIG

Maureen Connolly at eighteen was the top woman tennis player in the world and the first in history to hold all four of the world's major crowns—American, British, Australian, and French—at one and the same time, winning the grand slam in 1953.

"Helen Wills was my model in building my game," Connolly said. "I tried to develop a baseline game like hers. I played against her once, in mixed doubles, and it was an experience I will never forget. She always knew where the ball was coming and she was always there ready to meet it."

Like Helen Wills, Connolly practiced against men because there were so few players of her sex who could give her a match and extend her sufficiently for her to profit from the workout. Not since Wills was in her prime had any woman played with such force as the little girl from San Diego. Possibly Helen may have hit harder from the forehand, with her greater weight behind the racquet, but from the backhand Connolly, with her perfect timing, fluency, balance, and confidence, developed the most overpowering stroke of its kind the game had known up until that time.

Again like Wills, Connolly won largely from the back of the court. She did not need to go to the net often when she could hit winners from the baseline. Wills had no affinity for the volley. She could hold her ground up forward, and with her height and reach, it was not easy to pass her or to lob successfully against her, but she was happier in the back court. Her footwork was not too good and that was another reason why she preferred to remain at the baseline.

Connolly, much faster afoot and quicker in her reaction, had no inhibitions about attacking up forward, but only after she won her first national title did she work to any great degree on her net attack. Eleanor "Teach" Tennant, who was her coach, wisely had her develop her ground strokes before she let her do much volleying.

Connolly gave Harry Hopman much of the credit for her game. "Mr. Hopman helped me with my game when I was in Australia, and he worked with me in Europe. I have a lot more confidence in my volley and overhead now and I feel my service is better. It still needs improving, though. My swing is wrong. It's too jerky. I am trying to correct it and swing like a man."

Hopman, the astute and successful captain of the Australian Davis Cup team, also persuaded Connolly to run and skip rope to improve her physical condition. Of training in general, the women's tennis champion said, "Tennis can be a grind and there is always the danger of going stale if you think about it too much. You can get embittered if you train too hard and have nothing else on your mind. You have to be able to relax between matches and between tournaments. There are also certain sacrifices you have to make. You have to go to bed early and be careful about what you eat—cut down on pastries, but have plenty of sugar and steak. And you have to avoid dancing too much and going to the movies too often, and swimming is out completely."

These sentiments came from the heart since Connolly loved a good time as much as any teenage girl and tried to have as much fun as any player of the top flight. Her hobbies were dancing and music of any and every kind. She liked to eat hamburgers and drink Cokes, go to baseball games and parties. On the court she was all business and had no thoughts for anything but beating her opponent into submission as quickly as she could. But once she was finished, she became a different person, a bubbling eighteen-year-old full of gaiety and friendliness for everyone. Some accused Connolly of letting success go to her head and of developing an exaggerated sense of her importance. They found fault with her because she didn't play in every tournament to which she was invited. Possibly some of the top-ranking players had made a habit of competing abroad too much and not supporting the tournaments at home enough, but they could hardly be blamed if they found it more exciting to travel and see the world, particularly when they were in their teens.

No player can compete week after week for months without feeling the strain and grind. All of them have to take time off now and then for relaxation. From all one observer saw of Connolly, he found nothing on which to fault her. She was just as friendly and unaffected as she was when she came east seeking her first big victory.

DIZZY DEAN

1911–1974

By JOSEPH DURSO

H IS FATHER WAS an itinerant sharecropper who wandered around the South picking cotton. His mother died when he was only three years old. His own education ended in the second grade in a place called Chickalah, Arkansas, and—he confessed later—"I didn't do so good in the first grade, either."

But, despite all such handicaps and the Ozark country boy image he carried into high places, Jay Hanna "Dizzy" Dean rose serenely and unflappably into a career as one of the best pitchers in modern baseball and as a folk hero who brought great turns of the English language to radio and television.

He could be vague about details of his early life and times. He suggested, on different occasions, that he had been born in Arkansas, Oklahoma, and Mississippi. He estimated the date as 1911, or thereabouts. He even gave his formal name variously as Jay Hanna or Jerome Herman Dean. Then, when he reached the big leagues in 1930 at the age of nineteen, his career barely covered the decade and included only half a dozen seasons of front-rank pitching.

But wherever he came from, and however long he held the spotlight, few personalities commanded the public's attention as joyously as Dizzy Dean.

In his first full season with the St. Louis Cardinals, he won eighteen games and led the National League in strikeouts and shutouts. In the following four seasons, he won a hundred and two games, including thirty in 1934 and twenty-eight in 1935. He once struck out seventeen Chicago Cubs in nine innings. And in the 1934 World Series, he and his younger brother, Paul "Daffy" Dean, pitched two victories apiece while the Gashouse Gang of St. Louis defeated the Detroit Tigers, four games to three.

When an injury shortened his baseball career a few years later, Dizzy switched his showmanship to behind a microphone and broadcast games for the Cardinals and Browns in St. Louis and for the Yankees in New York. Then he attained new heights as an innovator of language, coining words the way Casey Stengel coined paragraphs.

"Come on, Tommy, hit that old patata," he once said with the partisanship of a full fan. "This boy looks mighty hitterish to me," he observed another time. "Boy, they was really scrummin' that ball over today, wasn't they?" he reported on another occasion. And when purists complained over his statement that a base runner "slud into third," he would reply in self-defense, "Paul and me didn't get much education."

His style proved so unusual that, in the summer of 1946, a group of

Missouri schoolteachers complained to the Federal Communications Commission that his broadcasts were "replete with errors in grammar and syntax" and were having "a bad effect on the pupils." But in the public debate that followed, powerful voices were raised to champion Dizzy Dean, including that of the *Saturday Review of Literature.*

Norman Cousins, the guiding spirit of the magazine, extended his own approval of the Dean linguistic style to the great man's pitching style in these words:

"He was supposed to be as fast as Walter Johnson, and though he couldn't curve them and mix them up like the great Matty [Christy Mathewson], his assortment was better than most. You were attracted by the graceful rhythm of his pitching motion; the long majestic sweep of his arm as he let the ball fly; the poised alertness after the pitch. That was what counted, and you knew it when batter after batter swung ineptly at pitches they couldn't even see."

The man behind the fractured syntax and the fractured batting averages was a 6-foot-2-inch giant whose playing weight of 182 pounds expanded well above 200 during the twenty years he spent as a broadcaster, public speaker, raconteur, rancher, and golfer. The consensus is that he was born January 16, 1911, in Lucas, Arkansas, and Red Smith portrayed him in *The New York Times* in these words:

"As a ball player, Dean was a natural phenomenon, like the Grand Canyon or the Great Barrier Reef. Nobody ever taught him baseball and he never had to learn. He was just doing what came naturally when a scout named Don Curtis discovered him on a Texas sandlot and gave him his first contract."

That was in the fall of 1929, and Dean later recalled that his "bonus" amounted to $300. He earned it the next season by winning seventeen games at St. Joseph, Missouri, plus eight more at Houston in the Texas League. The Cardinals promoted him to the majors around Labor Day and he pitched once—beating the Pittsburgh Pirates.

He was still a teenager at the time, not far removed from the sixteen-year-old who had enlisted in the army, where he supposedly wore his first pair of good shoes. But he was a teenager with absolute confidence in his baseball ability, and he demonstrated the confidence after his debut by boasting that he could "pitch St. Louis to the pennant." The Cardinals responded by relegating him back to the minors in 1931, but he promptly demonstrated his ability there by winning 26 games.

Branch Rickey, who was running the Cardinals then, brought Dean back to St. Louis to stay in 1932, and Dizzy won 18 times, with 16 complete games and 191 strikeouts. Two years later, he touted Rickey on his brother Paul, and in 1934, the Dean boys pitched 49 victories (30 by Dizzy) and pitched the Cardinals to the world championship.

Pitchers may have had better seasons than Dizzy did that year, but not many. He was suspended briefly for insubordination and held out briefly for more money in midseason, yet he finished the summer with a 30–7 record that included these highlights down the home stretch of the pennant race:

On September 21, he pitched a three-hitter against the Brooklyn Dodgers (Paul pitched a no-hitter in the second game of the doubleheader). Two days later, Dizzy relieved in both games of a doubleheader in Cincinnati. Two days after that, he went nine innings and beat Pittsburgh, 3–2. Three days later, he stopped Cincinnati, 4–0. And two days after that, he shut out the Reds again, 9–0, to clinch the flag. Three days later, he beat Detroit in the opening game of the World Series.

"I always just went out there and struck out all the fellas I could," he remembered. "I didn't worry about winnin' this number of games or that number—and I ain't a-woofin' when I say that, either."

As one of the ringleaders of the rowdy Gashouse Gang that summer, Dean had plenty of support from Frank Frisch, Rip Collins, Joe Medwick, and the other Cardinals. They invaded hotel ballrooms in painters' overalls, they formed a hillbilly band, they nearly provoked a riot in the World Series. But they won, even though Dizzy was struck on the head by a thrown ball while running the bases.

Things started to unwind in 1937, when Dean was struck on the left foot by a line drive while pitching in the All-Star Game in Washington. He suffered a broken toe, but suffered more permanently when he tried to pitch despite the handicap and subsequently ruined his right arm. So in 1938, the Cardinals traded him to the Chicago Cubs for $185,000 and three players.

He did pitch in the World Series for the Cubs against the Yankees, but he was never his old fireballing self on the mound. And in May of 1941, at the age of thirty, he retired as a player with a career record of 150 victories and 83 losses for a winning percentage of .644, and an earned-run average of 3.03.

He was elected to baseball's Hall of Fame in 1953 (in an election in which Joe DiMaggio placed eighth). But by then, Dizzy Dean was already a folk legend that even Hollywood had tried to capture on film. It was titled *The Pride of St. Louis*, starring Dan Dailey as Dizzy, and Bosley Crowther wrote in his review in *The New York Times*:

"The magnetic thing is the nature of a great, big lovable lug who plays baseball for a living and lives just to play—or talk—baseball. It is not Dizzy Dean, the Cardinal pitcher, the powerhouse of the old Gashouse Gang, the man who won so many games in so many seasons, that is the hero of this film. It is Dizzy Dean, the character, the whiz from the Ozark hills, the braggart, the woeful grammarian, the humbled human being."

Through it all, Dean was abetted by Patricia Nash, a department store sales clerk he met while pitching for Houston. They were married in 1931 and later made their home in Dallas, where he played golf and did some ranching and eventually worked his vernacular into the broadcast booth.

"The players returned to their respectable bases," he once advised the radio audience. Then, when he got into television, he declared, "I'm through talking about things folks ain't seeing." And later: "The trouble with them boys is they ain't got enough spart."

When he was pressed for an explanation of that bit of Ozark inflection, Dizzy replied: "Spart is pretty much the same as fight or pep or gumption. Like the *Spart of St. Louis*, that plane Lindbergh flowed to Europe in."

Dean died of a heart attack in Reno, Nevada on July 17, 1974.

The Brilliant Dean Brothers

By ROSCOE McGOWEN

Those highly publicized Dean brothers lived up to every advance notice as they hurled the Cardinals to a double victory over the Dodgers at Ebbets Field on September 21, 1934. The elder brother, Dizzy, allowed three safeties, the first coming in the eighth inning, as the Cards took the opener, 13–0.

But good as Dizzy was, he went into eclipse behind the extraordinary feat of his youthful brother, who gave 18,000 fans the thrill that comes once in a baseball lifetime by hurling a no-hit game. The Cards made seven safe blows off Ray Benge to win, 3–0.

Paul's work was just one point short of perfection. He issued one pass, drawn by Len Koenecke in the first inning after two were out, but thereafter the Dodgers just marched to the plate and right back again with monotonous regularity.

By taking two games while the Giants were winning one from the Braves, the Cardinals advanced to within three games of the league-leading New Yorkers.

The tension among the players on the Cardinal bench and among the fans could almost be felt as Paul went to the mound in the ninth. Thousands of fans rose to their feet and leaned forward to watch every move on the field, while two or three Cardinals in the dugout could be seen holding their fingers crossed.

Dodger manager Casey Stengel gave Paul no break as the youngster was knocking on the door of baseball's Hall of Fame. Casey sent Jimmy Bucher, a dangerous southpaw hitter, to bat for catcher Al Lopez, and that youth cut viciously at the first pitch. But Paul slipped both the second and third strikes across the outside corner of the plate, and cheers cascaded from the stands.

Then Johnny McCarthy, another portside swinger, was sent in to bat for Ray Benge. He connected hard with the ball and for a split second the fans held their breath. But the ball went high in the air and nestled into Frankie Frisch's glove for the second out.

Now only Ralph Boyle stood between Paul and his goal, and Buzz came closest to spoiling everything. He drove a slashing grounder toward short that sizzled into Durocher's glove on the short hop and Leo couldn't hold it. But he pounced on the ball like a cat and by a lightning throw just beat Boyle to first to end the game.

As Umpire Sears waved high to signify the putout, thousands of fans swarmed onto the field and engulfed the young pitcher. But his brother Dizzy and several park policemen were there first and managed to clear a way for him off the field through the Brooklyn dugout.

Aside from Boyle's last-inning smash, there were only two other occasions when the Dodgers came close to hitting Paul safely. In the first inning Lonnie Frey sliced a drive toward left-center and Joe Medwick ran over fast to snare the ball.

In the seventh it was Sam Leslie who hit the ball hard, driving it close to the barrier in left-center, but again Medwick saved the day by racing over and making a gloved-hand catch.

Paul fanned six men, three of them in the last two innings, and thirteen other Dodgers were retired on balls not hit out of the infield.

It was the greatest day the Dean brothers ever experienced, a day in which one all-time record was smashed and two amazing predictions by Dizzy were fulfilled.

In winning his twenty-seventh game, Dizzy broke a mark established by Cy Young in 1899 as a Cardinal hurler to win the most games in a season. Cy won twenty-six and lost fifteen that season. Dizzy lost only seven.

When Paul won the nightcap it marked his eighteenth victory, and thus made good Dizzy's boast in the spring that "Paul and I will win forty-five games for the Cardinals this year."

The dizziest prophecy of all which was made good was voiced in the Cardinals' hotel yesterday morning, when the elder Dean told a St. Louis writer that "Zachary and Benge will be pitching against one-hit Dean and no-hit Dean today." Dizzy fell down only on his own assignment by allowing three hits instead of one.

As for the run scoring, which was almost lost sight of in the drama of Paul's performance, the Cardinals had a field day at bat in the opener against Tom Zachary, Lefty Clark, Owen Carroll, and Walter Beck.

They amassed seventeen hits, six of them for extra bases, including Jim Collins's thirty-fourth homer of the year, made off Carroll in the fourth. They counted twice in the first and five times in the third, when Zachary was driven to cover. Three more in the fourth, two in the sixth, and one in the seventh were made off Carroll. One hit and no runs were counted off Beck in the ninth.

Collins, who drove in six runs in the first encounter, batted in two of the three scored in the nightcap. The other was sent home by Pepper Martin, and it was Paul Dean who carried it across.

Paul scored in the sixth for the first run of the contest, paving the way by driving a two-bagger to deep left-center for the second hit off Benge.

Medwick doubled in the seventh and scored on Collins's single, and in the ninth banged a three-bagger to the exit gate. He tallied the final run as Collins grounded sharply to Jordan.

Enters the Hall

By ARTHUR DALEY

Things should be a lot livelier in the Hall of Fame from now on. The brash, impudent, and ever-laughing Dizzy Dean arrived as a full-fledged member on January 24, 1953, and the joint never will be the same again.

Ol' Diz was inordinately modest when he first heard the news that he had been elected. Said he, "It's doggone nice for an old cotton-picker from Arkansas to be up there with them fellers."

Yet that formal statement was hardly in character. It would have been much more like him to have declared airily, "What wuz them writin' fellers takin' so long for! They shoulda knowed from the start that Ol' Diz was the greatest pitcher who ever lived." Nope. There never was anything modest about Mr. Dean.

The Great Man once wrote a discreet autobiography of sorts and merely stated the facts. With remarkable self-restraint he set down these words:

"Anybody who's ever had the privilege of seein' me play ball knows that I am the greatest pitcher in the world. And them that ain't been fortunate enough to have a gander at Ol' Diz in action can look at the records."

Unfortunately, though, the records do not quite present an accurate picture. For five blazing years the buoyant Mr. Dean was exactly what he said he was, the best. But then he was hit on the toe by a line drive in the 1937 All-Star Game and his days of true greatness were at an end. With his easy pitching motion, his overpowering fastball, his courage, his skill, and his utter disdain for all hitters, he probably would have lasted another decade "effen I hadn't of tried to pitch too soon while my toe was still broke."

Flaming competitor that he was, he just couldn't wait for his toe to heal. He began to pitch, favoring the toe, and the new, unnatural muscle strain permanently injured his arm. What an arm that was!

Branch Rickey, his discoverer, couldn't believe his eyes the first time he saw Diz in action at a tryout camp. Each tyro pitcher tossed to three batters. But Diz gave the Mahatma hardly a glimpse of him. The big fellow fanned the three on nine pitches. So he was summoned back for a longer look. Nine more pitches added up to nine more strikes. Rickey assigned Diz to St. Joseph in the Western League despite the Great Man's protestations.

"Don't waste time sendin' me to St. Joe, Branch," urged the gangling Dean. "I kin win you twenty games for the Cardinals."

"By Judas Priest!" ruefully roared Rickey afterward, "I now believe Diz could have done it." As it was, he won seventeen for a last-place team.

Dean was a rookie out of the pages of Ring Lardner when he first reported to the Cards. His boasting drove Manager Gabby Street to the verge of distraction. And in one exhibition game in the spring the Cards were being clobbered by a fearsome Athletics team.

"I jes' wisht Ol' Diz wuz a-pitchin'," muttered Ol' Diz on the bench.

"Get in and pitch," screamed Street. "And I hope they beat your brains out."

The bases were filled when the Great Man stepped in, almost without a warm-up. He was grinning jauntily in complete unconcern. He struck out Al Simmons. He struck out Jimmy Foxx. He struck out Mickey Cochrane.

Diz was a charter member of the famed Gashouse Gang and one of the ringleaders.

"Don't you worry none, Frankie," he told his astonished boss, Frank Frisch. "You string along with Ol' Diz and he'll make a great manager outa you."

That was in 1934, the year he announced to the Flash that "me 'n' Paul" would win forty-five games. It was the only time Dean underestimated himself. His younger brother, Paul, won nineteen. But Diz won thirty.

Late that season the brothers pitched a doubleheader against the Dodgers. Diz opened with a three-hitter and then Paul twirled a no-hitter. Diz was furious.

"Effen you'd only a-told me you wuz gonna pitch a no-hitter," he growled, "I'da pitched me one, too." He probably would have at that.

Against the Braves one day he strolled past the Boston dugout and made his announcement.

"I ain't pitchin' no curves today, fellers," he drawled, "Nuthin' but fastballs." He shut them out with three hits.

Diz was a fantastic performer. When Eldon Auker of Detroit was warming up before the seventh game of the 1934 World Series, Dean planted himself behind Cochrane, catcher and manager of the Tigers.

"He won't do, Mick," he said sadly. "He jes' won't do." He didn't. The Cards shelled him out early as Diz, laughing and clowning his way through, won 11–0. He got so playful that Frisch threatened to yank him.

"They ain't nobody yankin' Ol' Diz," announced Ol' Diz serenely, "when he's got hisself an eleven-run lead."

The self-confessed Great Man is a welcome addition to the Hall of Fame, though he lowers the humility quotient of the immortals down to virtually nothing.

And All Dizzy's Yesterdays

By RED SMITH

Jay Hanna Dean, who was also known as Jerome Herman Dean but answered more readily when addressed as Dizzy, was born in Lucas, Arkansas, or maybe Bond, Mississippi, or perhaps Holdenville, Oklahoma, sometime in 1911 or thereabouts, and approximately nineteen years later pitched his first game in the major leagues. He knocked off the Pittsburgh Pirates on three hits. The following winter he showed up unannounced in the Cardinals' offices in Sportsman's Park in St. Louis and went into executive session with Branch Rickey, the vice president and general manager. Two or three hours later, aware that newspapermen were on the premises, he departed by a rear door and Rickey trudged wearily into the outer office.

The Mahatma was coatless, his collar was unbuttoned and his necktie hung loose. His hair looked as though it had been slept in. He was sweating, and over the half-glasses on the end of his nose, his eyes were glassy. "By Judas Priest!" he said. "By Judas Priest! If there were one more like him in baseball, just one, as God is my judge I'd get out of the game!"

Young Mr. Dean, it seemed, had brought up the matter of his wage for the forthcoming baseball season and had expressed a preference for a figure higher than the $3,000 then considered fair for a rookie of promise. "He told me," Rickey said, "after one game this busher told me, 'Mr. Rickey, I'll put more people in the park than anybody since Babe Ruth!' "

Within three years, editorial changes were made in the handbills the

Cardinals posted on railroad station platforms and similar vantage points for a hundred miles around St. Louis. Formerly they had announced: "Double-header—Cardinals vs. New York Giants, Sunday, July 8," etc. Now the top line, set in type a mole could see at a hundred yards, read simply: "DIZZY DEAN," followed in smaller type by the promise: "Will pitch Sunday, July 8—." The busher was putting more people in the park than anybody else, including Ruth, who had never helped the Cardinals draw a dollar.

As a ball player, Dean was a natural phenomenon, like the Grand Canyon or the Great Barrier Reef. Nobody ever taught him baseball and he never had to learn. He was just doing what came naturally when a scout named Don Curtis discovered him on a Texas sandlot and gave him his first contract. It was the fall of 1929 and the contract committed him to pitch for St. Joseph, Missouri, the following season. Diz stayed in St. Joe long enough to win seventeen games, moved up to Houston, where he won eight, and joined the Cardinals around Labor Day. Gabby Street, the manager, waited until the Cardinals had won the pennant before using him, so he had only that one start against Pittsburgh and had to settle for twenty-six victories in his first professional season.

He knew how to pitch, he was by no means helpless with a bat in his hands, and he was a fine base runner. There was a game with the Giants in 1932, Dizzy's first full season in the big leagues (he had been sent back to Houston for 1931 on the amusing theory that it would teach him humility). With the score tied and a runner on third, he went to bat in a late inning and John McGraw pulled his infielders in to cut off the run.

With the aplomb of Willie Keeler, Dean lifted a swinging bunt over the infield. The run scored easily; caught off balance, the Giants threw the ball around in a panic; Dizzy kept running until he was home, laughing fit to split.

Nobody knew where or how or when he had learned to play like this and nobody ever found out from him, for Diz was cheerfully vague about matters like the date and place of his birth, length of army service, and other details of his background. This was partly because he had no background to speak of. He and his brothers, Paul and Elmer, and their father had been itinerant farmhands, picking cotton for fifty cents a day.

On one occasion they were on the move through the Southwest with other nomads. Dizzy, Paul, and Pop found seats in one car and Elmer hitched a ride in another. Reaching a grade crossing, the first car got over ahead of a train but the one carrying Elmer had to stop. It was four years before the family was reunited.

There were things in heaven and on earth not dreamed of then in Dizzy's philosophy, things like charge accounts and bank checks, whose existence he discovered after joining the Cardinals. He found that if he signed a check, a man would give him money and later Mr. Rickey would take care of the man. If he bought something and said, "Charge it," Mr. Rickey would take care of that. He took a simple, childish pleasure in these discoveries, until he was so far overdrawn that Sam Breadon, the Cardinals' owner, put him on a cash allowance of a dollar a day to be picked up each morning from Clarence Lloyd, the traveling secretary.

One morning in Boston Diz asked for ten dollars. Lloyd said he was sorry.

Diz pleaded. Lloyd inquired why he needed the extra money. Diz only begged harder. Lloyd said that he couldn't help him without a compelling reason. Diz was still a kid, a big, gangling gawk, appealing in his ungainliness. Painfully, he stammered the explanation: it was his bride's birthday and he wanted to buy Patricia a gift. He got the sawbuck.

In time, Pat taught him about money. Just living taught him other things, including an invincible philosophy.

"Hi, Diz, how's the old arm?" Grantland Rice hailed him when Dean was winding it up with the Chicago Cubs. "It ain't what it used to be, Granny," the philosopher said, "but what the hell is?"

JACK DEMPSEY

1895–1983

By RED SMITH

JACK DEMPSEY was one of the last of a dwindling company whose exploits distinguished the 1920s as "the golden age of sports." His contemporaries were Babe Ruth in baseball, Red Grange and the Four Horsemen of Notre Dame in football, Bobby Jones and Walter Hagen in golf, Bill Tilden, Helen Wills Moody, and Suzanne Lenglen in tennis, Johnny Weissmuller and Gertrude Ederle in swimming, Paavo Nurmi in track, Man o' War, the racehorse, and Earl Sande, the jockey. But none of the others enjoyed more lasting popularity than the man who ruled boxing between 1919 and 1926.

Strangely, though, Dempsey's popularity never approached its peak until he had lost the championship. He was reviled as a slacker during World War I, and although a jury exonerated him of a charge of draft dodging, the odium clung to him until the night Gene Tunney punched him almost blind and took his title.

"Lead me out there," Jack told his trainer after that bout. "I want to shake his hand."

Back in their hotel, Estelle Taylor Dempsey was appalled by her husband's battered face. "Ginsberg!" she cried, using her pet name for him. "What happened?"

"Honey," the former champion said, "I forgot to duck." From that day on, the gallant loser was a folk hero whose fame never diminished. Almost twenty-three years after he lost the championship, he was having breakfast with friends in Chicago, where Ezzard Charles and Jersey Joe Walcott were to box the following night for his old title, left vacant by the retirement of Joe Louis. A stranger passing their table recognized the old champion.

"Jack Dempsey!" he said, offering his hand. "Oh, boy, Jack, do I know you! Do I remember how you gave it to Jess Willard back there in Toledo!" Leaning forward, he put his face close to Jack's ear, and his voice dropped to a conspiratorial level. "I hope you beat hell out of that guy tomorrow night," he said and turned away.

Speechless for an instant, Dempsey stared after him. "Well, I'll be damned," he said. "He thinks I'm still champion!"

To many, Dempsey always remained the champion, and he always comported himself like one. He was warm and generous, a free spender when he had it and a soft touch for anybody down on his luck. After retirement from the ring, he made his headquarters in New York in Jack Dempsey's Restaurant, first at the corner of Fiftieth Street across Eighth Avenue from the old Madison Square

Garden and later at 1619 Broadway, where his partner was Jack Amiel, whose colt, Count Turf, won the 1957 Kentucky Derby.

At almost any hour, Dempsey was on hand to greet friends and strangers with a cordial, "Hiya, pal," in a voice close to a boyish treble. (He wasn't much better at remembering names than Babe Ruth, who called people "kid.") He posed for thousands of photographs with an arm around a customer's shoulders or—if the customer preferred, and many males did—squared off face-to-face. Autographing tens of thousands of menus, he never scribbled an impersonal "Jack Dempsey" but always took the trouble to write the recipient's name and add "good luck" or "keep punching." His ebullient good humor was even demonstrated against the occasional drunk who simply had to try out his Sunday punch on the old champion.

Grantland Rice said Dempsey was perhaps the finest gentleman, in the literal sense of gentle man, he had met in half a century of writing sports; Dempsey never knowingly hurt anyone except in the line of business.

In the ring, he was a tiger without mercy who shuffled forward in a bobbing crouch, humming a barely audible tune and punching to the rhythm of the song. He was 187 pounds of unbridled violence. That isn't big by heavyweight standards, yet in the judgment of some, this black-browed product of Western mining camps and hobo jungles was the best of all pugilists. In 1950, a poll by the Associated Press named Dempsey the greatest fighter of the half-century.

Certainly nobody surpassed him in color and crowd appeal. He drew boxing's first million-dollar gate in fighting Georges Carpentier, boxing's largest paid attendance in his first bout with Tunney, and the biggest "live" gate in their second meeting. As champion, Tunney received $990,445 for the latter fight, which grossed $2,658,660. He gave Tex Rickard, the promoter, his personal check for $9,555 and Rickard wrote a check for $1 million, the biggest purse ever collected for a single performance in sports before the days of closed-circuit television.

Dempsey was less than two weeks past his twenty-fourth birthday but had been through more than eighty professional fights, some unrecorded, when he burst upon the championship scene like a mortar shell. It was July 4, 1919, a blistering day on the shore of Maumee Bay outside Toledo, Ohio. Awaiting the opening bell as challenger for the heavyweight title, the 6-foot-1-inch contender was tanned and fit at 187 pounds. But he looked no more than half the size of Jess Willard, the champion, a pale tract of meat measuring 6 feet 6½ inches tall and weighing 245 pounds.

Three minutes later Willard looked like a case for the coroner. He had been down seven times, and one left hook had broken his cheekbone in thirteen places. Thinking the seventh knockdown had ended the fight, Dempsey and his manager, Jack "Doc" Kearns, left the ring but were called back.

After two more rounds the helpless Willard was spared further damage when one of his seconds signaled surrender by throwing a towel into the ring.

Now it was Dempsey, heavyweight champion of the world, and the bottom line of his record read: "KO 3." But the winner's jubilation was tempered by the discovery that Kearns had bet $10,000 of their guarantee on a first-round knockout, taking odds of 10 to 1, and the remaining $17,500 had gone for "training expenses," an omnibus term in the manager's lexicon.

In a ghost-written autobiography many years later, Kearns took partial credit for the destructive effect of his man's punches. He wrote that he had used plaster-of-Paris bandages on Dempsey's hand and that these had hardened into casts inside the gloves after being doused with water. Dempsey denied that his gloves had been loaded, and the tale never won general acceptance because Doc Kearns was known to be a creative artist who seldom let truth spoil a good story.

The destruction of Willard convinced boxing men of the new champion's greatness, but the public was slow to accept Dempsey because of his war record. Ostensibly doing essential work in a Philadelphia shipyard, he had posed for a news photograph holding a riveting gun and wearing overalls, with patent-leather shoes. The fancy footgear raised noisy doubts about his contribution to the war effort.

More than two years after the armistice, Rickard capitalized on this unfavorable publicity to build up the first million-dollar gate. Carpentier, the light-heavyweight champion, had been decorated in the French armed forces. When Rickard matched Dempsey with the Paris boulevardier in a wooden arena called Boyle's Thirty Acres in Jersey City, the "hero" became a sentimental favorite over the "slacker." A crowd of 80,183 paid $1,789,238 to see Dempsey win by a knockout in the fourth round.

Having broken all financial records, Dempsey and Kearns proceeded to break the city of Shelby, Montana. After an oil strike near their small community, Shelby boosters gave way to delusions of grandeur and promised the champion $250,000 to defend his title against the light-hitting Tommy Gibbons. The promotion laid an egg, but Kearns collected the entire guarantee and had a locomotive and caboose waiting to rush the money and the champion's party out of town as soon as Dempsey had won on points. Behind them, the banks that had put up the cash closed. Shelby had a hole in the seat of its civic breeches for a generation.

To those who saw it, the Dempsey-Firpo bout of 1923 was the most wildly exciting ever fought for the heavyweight title. Luis Angel Firpo of Argentina, unpolished and untamed, dazed the champion with a right to the jaw seconds after the opening bell. Only half-conscious, Dempsey dropped Firpo four times. Firpo knocked the champion into the press row, where reporters instinctively raised hands and shoved to protect themselves. Thus aided, Dempsey got back in the ring and put Firpo down once more before the bell. Two more knockdowns finished the Argentine in the second round.

The Firpo fight was Dempsey's fifth title defense (he had knocked out Billy Miske and Bill Brennan before meeting Carpentier). Three years later he made his sixth and last against Tunney, the Shakespeare-loving veteran of the Marine Corps who had moved into heavyweight ranks after winning the American light-heavyweight championship, losing it, and winning it back.

"I never seed anything like it," Rickard said, watching 120,757 customers crowd into the huge horseshoe in Philadelphia then called Sesquicentennial

Stadium. The promoter had been told the fight would draw big in Philadelphia, but he had not dreamed what a stir it would make.

Down in Maryland, for instance, was a racing official named Jim Milton. He was the starter when the Havre de Grace track opened in 1912, and when he retired half a century later he had started every race at that track except the last one on the program on September 23, 1926. He left that to an assistant starter and caught a train for Philadelphia and the fight.

Many years afterward Tunney was told about Milton's only dereliction. "He probably was betting on Dempsey," he said. If he was, he lost. Jabbing and circling through a drenching rainstorm, Tunney won going away.

One day less than a year later, the pair met again in Soldier Field in Chicago in a match that would make Dave Barry the world's most widely known referee. In the seventh round Tunney was knocked down for the first time in his life.

Gracious outside the ring, Dempsey in battle was no slave to the rules. In the early 1970s, when Joe Frazier was champion, he was scandalized by films of Dempsey crouching over a fallen Firpo ready to slug him as he rose. "That's bad for boxing," Frazier protested.

With Tunney on the floor, it did not occur to Dempsey to retire to a neutral corner until Barry stopped the count and led him across the ring. Returning, the referee started the count all over. Tunney got up at "nine"—it was established that he had had about fourteen seconds to recuperate—and won a clear decision, scoring a knockdown in the eighth round. To this day, the Dempsey cult believes Tunney was saved by the long count; Tunney always insisted he was in full control throughout.

That was the last time around for Dempsey as a fighter of importance. Thirty-two years had passed since his birth on June 24, 1895, in Manassa, Colorado, to Hyrum and Celia Dempsey, who had paused there with their brood on a meandering journey from Mudfork, West Virginia. Manassa was only one of many stops for a nomadic family, but years later the fact that Mrs. Dempsey had given birth there inspired Damon Runyon, the sportswriter, to dub the new champion the Manassa Mauler.

Hyrum Dempsey was a tough, restless descendant of Irish immigrants who had quit a job as schoolteacher to venture west. There was a strain of Indian blood in both parents, revealed in the baby's blue-black hair and high cheekbones. They named him William Harrison Dempsey and called him Harry, but at sixteen he went his own way and adopted his own names.

The first was Kid Blackie. For about three years he fought under that name in mountain mining camps. Between saloon bouts he worked in the mines, shined shoes, picked fruit, and hustled, riding the rods on trains and sleeping in hobo jungles. Meanwhile, his older brother, Bernie, was boxing as Jack Dempsey, having borrowed the name of an old-time middleweight known as the Nonpareil. One night in Denver, Harry substituted for Bernie and was introduced as Jack Dempsey. The name stuck.

He was managed for a while by one Jack Price and later by John "the Barber" Reisler before he and Kearns became partners. They started slowly but picked up speed as they moved. By the time they reached Maumee Bay and the rendezvous with Willard, Dempsey's record included twenty-one first-round knockouts. If any other puncher ever dealt such swift destruction to so many, the record books do not report it.

Willard had won the championship in 1915 and defended it once in a ten-round no-decision match with Frank Moran in 1916. On February 15, 1918, an item in *The New York Times* reported that Dempsey had knocked out Fireman Jim Flynn in one round, adding that Willard had agreed to meet the winner of a bout between Dempsey and Fred Fulton.

That bout took place on July 28, 1918. It lasted twenty-three seconds. One punch was thrown, a right by Dempsey. Fulton was counted out and his name entered in the long list of Dempsey's victims—Gunboat Smith, Carl Morris, Bill Brennan, Billy Miske, Battling Levinsky, Arthur Pelkey. There wasn't a heavyweight of repute Dempsey hadn't beaten, except Willard.

After taking care of that oversight, the new champion took his time about defending his title. In 1920 he took on two of his old victims, Miske and Brennan, and disposed of them. In 1921 he beat Carpentier, in 1922 he rested, and in 1923 he beat Tommy Gibbons and Firpo. Three years intervened before he fought again and lost to Tunney.

Like John L. Sullivan, Jim Corbett, and other champions before him, he gave the stage at least as much attention as he bestowed on the ring. He accepted a featured role on Broadway in a play called *The Big Fight*, directed by David Belasco. The feminine lead was Estelle Taylor, his wife.

In his early days in the mining camps, he had been married to Maxine Gates, a saloon piano player, but not for long. Taylor was a star of silent films whom he met in Hollywood. After their Broadway adventure, they went back to Hollywood and made a movie called *Manhattan Madness*, which was also a disaster.

By this time Dempsey and his manager had fallen out. A series of suits and countersuits kept them in litigation right up to the Philadelphia match with Tunney in 1926. The distraction was no help to Dempsey in his preparation for the bout, but when he lost, he did not mention this as an excuse.

He had learned that fighters suffer many distractions. "Some night," he told a young boxer, "you'll catch a punch between the eyes and all of a sudden you'll see three guys in the ring against you. Pick out the one in the middle and hit him, because he's the one who hit you."

Dempsey and Taylor were divorced, and he married the singer Hannah Williams. They had two daughters, Joan in 1934 and Barbara in 1936. He and Williams were divorced in 1943.

In 1958 he was married for the fourth time, to the former Deanna Piattelli. He later adopted her daughter from a previous marriage. She took the name Barbara Dempsey and helped him write his 1977 autobiography, *Dempsey*.

In 1938 Dempsey was the first winner of the Edward J. Neil Memorial Plaque, awarded by the New York Boxing Writers Association to the man who had done the most for boxing that year. He was elected to the Boxing Hall of Fame in 1954. Except during World War II, when he enlisted in the Coast Guard and was commissioned a lieutenant commander, he remained identified with the ring, as a referee of boxing and wrestling and a participant in various promotions.

In the early days of Joe Louis's reign as champion, Dempsey lent his name and restaurant facilities to a "white hope" tournament, a term that had survived in boxing long after its racial implications had evaporated. Dropping into Dempsey's, John Lardner, the writer, saw a horde of young males devouring steak and chops.

"Finest bunch of white hopes ever assembled," the proprietor said proudly. "What about him?" Lardner asked, indicating a husky young black in the middle of the pack. Dempsey fetched him a slap on the shoulder.

"You got a good eye for a fighter," he said. "He's the best prospect in the bunch."

A Close Call

In the shortest and fiercest battle ever fought between heavyweights, Jack Dempsey on September 15, 1923, knocked out Luis Angel Firpo, before a crowd of 90,000 people at the Polo Grounds fifty-seven seconds after the second round began.

But no champion ever had a closer call. In the first round, after Firpo had gone down seven times, one of his long smashing rights caught Dempsey fairly and knocked him clear through the ropes. The champion's head disappeared over the edge of the ring, his white-clad legs shot up in the air, and it seemed that a new world's champion was about to enter into his glory.

On the count of nine, Dempsey managed to stagger back into the ring, but the end of the round found him obviously badly shaken, and staggering as he had never staggered before.

To the spectators at the ringside it looked as if Dempsey was all gone, but his heart and his head were still there, and enough punching power to carry him through to victory in the second round. Firpo's right was too slow to reach the champion, who was striking in with all his power. He caught Firpo with a right and put him down. Two seconds later the challenger was up, but a moment more and Dempsey had him down again for the count of five.

Once more the "Wild Bull of the Pampas" staggered to his feet, but Dempsey was on him instantly, caught him with a left to the jaw, and then toppled him with a right as he sank. Bleeding slightly at the mouth, the huge brown man from the Argentine turned slowly over, striving vainly to rise as the referee's pumping arm marked the counts of eight and nine, and stiffened helplessly as the tenth count ended his championship hopes for the time.

In less than four minutes of fighting the champion had been knocked down twice and the challenger ten times. From the first instant the fight had been a fight, a fierce exchange of wallops unbroken by any strategic maneuvers. Dempsey won because he could hit faster and oftener, but above all because he could keep going and cash in on his advantages when he had them.

As for Firpo, he put up a terrific fight, and at the end of the first round had 90,000 more or less patriotic fans practically resigned to the loss of the championship. After the fight Firpo complained that he hadn't got an even break from Referee Jimmy Gallagher.

Firpo asserted that Gallagher had warned the fighters before the bout began that after a knockdown the man on his feet must move away to a neutral corner. Dempsey, he protested, stood over him and was on him instantly when he got off the canvas.

Whatever the justice in this complaint, there is no doubt that Dempsey won because he fought with his head as well as with hands, and Firpo had nothing but his hands and his courage. The question as to whether the Argentine fighter could "take it" was answered. He took a worse hammering even than Jess Willard took at Toledo, and if his brain had been as quick as his arm was powerful he would have survived it to win. He could also "give it."

But Dempsey, outweighed by twenty-four pounds, shorter, and with less reach, won because he had a super-fighting brain and a coolness that enabled him to hang on when everything seemed lost and to use all his powers in the desperate and successful effort to hold his time.

Firpo gained at least a certain consolation in his 12½ percent of the gate receipts. Promoter Tex Rickard reported that the ticket sale amounted to $1,250,000. Of this Dempsey got $468,750, and the challenger's share came to about $156,250, not to mention the incidental profits of moving pictures.

There were 85,800 paid admissions, and police, firemen, ushers, newspaper men, telegraph operators, refreshment vendors, and so on raised the total to 90,000. The receipts fell short of the $1,600,000 brought in by the Dempsey-Carpentier fight only because of the limit imposed in this state on the price of the ringside seats.

What might have happened had Dempsey utilized his superior boxing ability to stand off and take few chances until he had felt out Firpo no one can say. But he didn't do that. Realizing that most of his followers expected him to get in and fight, he rushed in furiously at the sound of the bell, and partly slipping, partly caught by one of Firpo's smashes, he dropped to one knee before the round was five seconds old. Yet he still stuck to his aggressive tactics and thereby showed the crowd that both he and Firpo were better men than anybody knew. It is a rare fight that enables both victor and vanquished to feel that they have surpassed themselves, all in the space of three minutes and fifty-seven seconds.

The Long Count

By JAMES P. DAWSON

His refusal to observe the boxing rules of the Illinois State Athletic Commission, or his ignorance of the rules, or both, cost Jack Dempsey the chance to regain the world's heavyweight championship in Chicago on September 22, 1927.

By the same token this disregard of rules of ring warfare, or this surprising ignorance, saved the title for Gene Tunney, the fighting ex-marine, who had been king of the ring for just a year.

The bout ended with Tunney getting the decision, and the vast majority in the staggering assemblage of 150,000 people at Soldier Field, who paid, it is estimated, $2,800,000 to see this great sport spectacle, approved the verdict.

The decision was given by Referee Dave Barry and Judges George Lytton, wealthy department store owner, and Commodore Sheldon Clark of the Sinclair Oil Company. It was announced as a unanimous decision, but this could not be verified in the excitement attending the finish of the battle. But it should have been unanimous according to all methods of reasoning and boxing scoring, for Tunney won seven of the ten rounds, losing only the third, sixth, and seventh, in the last of which, Dempsey made his great mistake. It is known that Judge Lytton voted for Tunney.

In that seventh round Dempsey was being peppered and buffeted about on the end of Tunney's left jabs and hooks and sharp though light right crosses, as he had been in every preceding round, with the exception of the third.

In a masterly exhibition of boxing Tunney was evading the attack of his heavier rival and was countering cleanly, superbly, skillfully, accurately for half of the round or so.

Then Dempsey, plunging in recklessly, charging bull-like, furiously and with utter contempt for the blows of the champion, since he had tasted of Tunney's best previously, suddenly lashed a long, wicked left to the jaw with the power of old. This he followed with a right to the jaw, the old "iron mike" as deadly as ever, and quickly drove another left hook to the jaw, under which Tunney toppled like a falling tree, hitting the canvas with a solid thud near Dempsey's corner, his hand reaching blindly for a helping rope which somehow or other refused to be within clutching distance.

Then Dempsey made his mistake, an error which, I believe, cost him the title he valued so highly.

The knockdown brought the knockdown timekeeper, Paul Beeler, to his feet automatically, watch in hand, eyes glued to the ticking seconds and he bawled "one" before he looked upon the scene in the ring.

There he saw Dempsey in his own corner, directly above the prostrate, brain-numbed Tunney, sitting there looking foolishly serious, his hand finally resting on the middle ring strand. Beeler's count stopped. Referee Barry never started one.

It is the referee's duty to see to it that a boxer scoring a knockdown goes to the corner farthest from his fallen foe, and it is the duty of the knockdown timekeeper to delay the count from the watch until this rule is obeyed. Beeler was simply observing the rule, which Dempsey either forgot to observe or refused to observe.

The challenging ex-champion stood there, arms akimbo on the top ropes of the ring in his own corner, watching his fallen rival, the characteristic Dempsey snarl o'erspreading his countenance, his expression saying more plainly than words, "Get up and I'll knock you down again, this time for keeps."

Dempsey had no eyes for Referee Barry, who was waving frantically for the former titleholder to run to a neutral corner, even as he kept an eye on the fallen Tunney. Instead, Dempsey merely looked down at Tunney squatting there, striving instinctively to regain his feet and waiting for his whirling brain to clear.

Finally, Dempsey took cognizance of the referee's frantic motions. He was galvanized into action and sped hurriedly across the ring to a neutral corner, away from Tunney.

If he had observed the rule to the letter, Dempsey should, in fact, have gone to Tunney's corner, which was farthest removed from the fallen champion.

But three or four, or possibly five precious seconds had elapsed before Dempsey realized at all what he should do. In that fleeting time of the watch Tunney got the advantage. No count was proceeding over him, and quickly his senses were returning. When Referee Barry started counting with Timekeeper Beeler, Tunney was in a state of mental revival where he could keep count with the tolling seconds and did, as his moving lips revealed.

Slowly the count proceeded. It seemed an eternity between each downward sweep of the arm of Referee Barry and the steady pounding of the fist of Timekeeper Beeler.

Seconds are like that in a crisis, and here was one if ever one existed.

Tunney's senses came back to him. He got to his feet with the assistance of the ring ropes and with visible effort at the count of "nine." He was groggy, stung, shaken, his head was whirling as so many other heads have whirled under the Dempsey punch.

But Dempsey was wild in this crisis, a floundering, plodding mankiller, as Tunney, backpedaling for dear life, took to full flight, beating an orderly, steady retreat with only light counter moves in the face of the plunging, desperate, vicious Dempsey, around now for the kill.

Dempsey plodded on so futilely and ineffectively that he tired from his own exertions. The former champion stopped dead in his tracks in midring and with a smile spreading over his scowling face, motioned disgustedly, daringly, for Tunney to come on and fight.

But Tunney was playing his own game, and it was a winning game. He did not want to expose himself to that deadly Dempsey punch again, and he would not.

Tunney backed steadily away from Dempsey, pecking and tantalizing with left jabs and grazing right hooks or crosses to the face or jaw. Which meant absolutely nothing to Dempsey. He brushed in against Tunney's blows but, in his eagerness, Dempsey was wild.

After motioning Tunney in, Dempsey backed the champion into the ropes near the challenger's corner and lunged forward savagely with a left and right to the jaw. But Tunney clinched under the blows and held Dempsey for dear life. And Dempsey never again got the chance that round to follow his advantage.

As the bell sounded the end of the round, Dempsey was warned for striking low with a left for the body. He was hurling his punches in a blind fury, not particularly concerned over where they landed, so long as they did land.

The crowd which witnessed this dramatic fight, and particularly the critical moments of the seventh round, experienced varying emotions at the crisis. Some yelled themselves hoarse. The shrieks of women mingled with the howls of staid, old businessmen and the thousands of the purely sporting fraternity clustered about the ringside and extending backward from the battle platform in serried rows of faces.

Society's blue bloods forgot decorum and yelled excitedly. Kings of finance and princes of industry were mingling their yells with those of governors, mayors, representatives in Congress, senators, lawyers, doctors, theater and movie folk, and just plain ordinary people.

It was a scene to grip the observer, a situation to send quickening throbs through the pulses of those at the ringside and in the other sections of Chicago's memorial to her dead heroes. Here was a war hero, a ring hero, a champion, on the floor, and everybody was affected.

Out over the ether wastes some 50 million people who listened to the fight broadcast by the National Broadcast Company, over the greatest hookup ever attempted for sport, had not the advantage of those actually watching the contest.

To those countless listeners it was plain that Dempsey was the victim of something, but just what only those who watched were aware. And there were some watching who did not realize the enormous consequences of this colossal mistake, because they are not versed in boxing rules. But it is safe to say that none among the 150,000 watching or among the 50 million listening will ever forget that particular elapse of time.

Leo P. Flynn, Dempsey's manager, made no effort after the fight to disguise or conceal his feelings or those of Dempsey. In plain words Flynn said that Dempsey had been robbed of victory because of that seventh-round situation.

"The watch in our corner showed fifteen seconds from the time Tunney hit the floor until he got up at the count of nine," Flynn said. "The legal count over a fallen boxer is ten seconds, not fifteen. Dempsey was jobbed. That's the way I look at it. But I'm going to appeal to the State Athletic Commission to reverse the decision, as is my privilege. Dempsey will fight him again and will knock him out if Tunney ever can be coaxed into meeting him again, just the way he knocked him out tonight."

In the final analysis, however, Dempsey was hoist on his own petard. The rule compelling a boxer to go to the corner farthest removed from a fallen foe is traceable to Dempsey himself. Its adoption followed the Manassa Mauler's battle in 1923 with the giant Firpo when Dempsey stood directly above the fallen Firpo striking the South American just as soon as his knees left the floor without waiting for Firpo to come erect after a knockdown.

Dempsey was permitted to do this then. His attempt to do it against Tunney was the most expensive mistake he would ever make in his life.

Some watches at the ringside showed twelve seconds on the knockdown, others fourteen, and Flynn holds that Dempsey's corner watch showed fifteen seconds.

But a rule is a rule in boxing as in other big business, adopted to be observed, and the Illinois boxing authorities are to be commended for enforcing their rules without regard to victims or cost. It was unfortunate that Dempsey should have been thus penalized.

It would have been none the less unfortunate, however, if Dempsey had been permitted to remain standing within punching distance of Tunney to strike down the champion before Tunney had actually come erect.

On the strength of that colossal mistake of Dempsey's, it is hard, indeed, to say that Tunney was the better man in the ring. Rather, the seventh round demonstrated what many have always contended despite assertions of Tunney and his associates to the contrary, that the real Dempsey would mow down the best Tunney like a cutting machine at work in a wheat field.

This is not said in an effort to detract from the victory of Tunney. He won and he won cleanly and clearly on points against the best Dempsey available. But he was knocked down, had the closest call of his career, and in the end, won only because of his superb boxing skill on defense and the little offense he attempted.

JIMMIE FOXX

1907–1967

J IMMIE FOXX, who helped the old Philadelphia Athletics achieve baseball dominance in the early 1930s, retired in 1945 with 534 major league home runs—second only to Babe Ruth at that time.

James Emory Foxx was born in Sudlersville, Maryland, on October 22, 1907. He was discovered by Franklin "Home Run" Baker, who urged Connie Mack, manager of the Philadelphia Athletics, to give him a trial. He was seventeen.

The big boy came to the A's as a catcher and batted .667 in ten games during the 1925 season. He was sent to the minors for more training and came back to the parent club in 1926 and 1927 for a few games each year.

Then in 1928 Foxx came up to stay.

He was one of the strongest right-handed batters who ever played baseball. Double X, as sportswriters called him, once hit a ball thrown by Vernon "Lefty" Gomez of the Yankees into the upper left-field stands of the Yankee Stadium. The ball broke a seat in the next to last row and might have gone out if it had been more to the right. No fair ball has ever been hit out of that stadium.

His greatest year of home run production was 1932. The 225-pound mild-mannered player hit 58, just two short of Ruth's record of 60, set in 1927. In 1938, after he had joined the Boston Red Sox, he hit 50.

While Foxx was a member of the A's, Mack moved him to first base and then to third. He played most of his major league games at those positions.

Near the end of his playing days, on August 20, 1945, Foxx got permission to pitch one game for the Philadelphia Phillies. He pitched 6⅔ innings to beat the Cincinnati Reds, 4–2.

In December 1935, he was sold by the Athletics to the Boston Red Sox in one of the biggest major league transactions up to that time. To get him, the Red Sox gave up a number of lesser players and $150,000. He was the last of Mack's great stars to be sold when the manager of the A's broke up his championship team of the early 1930s.

Foxx was one of the main reasons the A's won the pennants in 1929, 1930, and 1931, and he contributed to World Series victories in 1929 and 1930.

In the 1930 Series against the St. Louis Cardinals, he turned the tide in favor of the Athletics in the fifth game. With the series tied, he slammed a two-run homer off Burleigh Grimes in the top of the ninth for a 2–0 Philadelphia triumph. The A's easily won the next game, 7–1.

One of Foxx's claims to fame was as a strikeout victim. He was the middle

man when Carl Hubbell of the New York Giants fanned five successive sluggers in the 1934 All-Star Game. Ruth, Lou Gehrig, Foxx, Al Simmons, and Joe Cronin went down before the screwball hurler. Foxx had some consolation out of the incident. He was the only one of the five batters to hit a foul ball.

When Willie Mays hit his 535th home run in 1966, breaking Foxx's record as the most proficient right-handed power hitter in baseball, Foxx said, "I hope Mays hits 600. For twenty-five years, they thought only left-handers could hit the long ones. They even teach right-handed youngsters to hit left." By 1990 he had dropped to ninth on the all-time home run list.

Foxx turned to radio sports announcing after his major league career and briefly to managing the Bridgeport, Connecticut, Bees in the Colonial League.

In January 1951, he was elected to the Baseball Hall of Fame, along with Mel Ott, the former New York Giants star.

In 1958, Foxx, who had earned more than $250,000 as a player, was without a job and unable to pay his rent. After this was revealed by the Boston chapter of the Baseball Writers Association, he was offered jobs throughout the country.

Foxx always said that he had never gone after the homers.

"But if I had broken Ruth's record," he said, "it wouldn't have made any difference. Oh, it might have put a few more dollars in my pocket, but there was only one Ruth."

He died on July 21, 1967, in Miami, at the age of fifty-nine.

The Beast

By ARTHUR DALEY

There can be no disputing the election of James Emory Foxx into the Hall of Fame in 1951. He belongs. Only Babe Ruth had hit more home runs than Double X and not even the Babe could poleax a ball farther. The Maryland Strong Boy did it despite the disadvantage of being a right-handed hitter, which meant that he had more distant fences than the Babe everywhere except in Boston.

In view of the fact that Foxx was a quiet, amiable, and friendly sort of person it was almost surprising to discover that his teammates on the Athletics always referred to him as the Beast. His only beastly attributes were displayed when he was at bat, where he terrorized enemy pitchers.

It was Lefty Gomez who always brought Foxx into the discussion when he explained why he abandoned the use of glasses while on the mound.

"I was pitching this particular day," chuckled the Singular Señor, "when my glasses clouded up on me. I took them off to clean them, glanced toward the plate, and suddenly recognized the menacing figure of Jimmie Foxx at bat. This scared me so much that I never wore the glasses again."

Foxx is the lad who hit what was undoubtedly the longest home run ever struck in Yankee Stadium before Mickey Mantle's famous clout in 1963. Oddly enough, he hit it off Gomez. Lefty even had an explanation for that one.

"I actually got the ball halfway past him," he said. Then he ruefully added, "but it was the second half that was so tough."

The Maryland Strong Boy belted that one so hard that it broke the backrest of a seat. Hence there was no way of mistaking where the ball landed. It went into the upper deck of the left-field stands, a couple of rows from the very top. What is more, it was near the edge of the runway in the bull pen. It couldn't have been hit farther and still stay in the ball park.

When Ralph Kiner was with the Pirates and saw Comiskey Park for the first time at the 1950 All-Star Game, he gazed in respect at the distant left-field stands.

"That's a real wallop," he said, a note of awe in his voice. "Yet they tell me that Foxx hit four on the roof."

Maybe he did. But he also hammered a screamer clean over the roof, the ball bouncing in a playground across the street, a 520-footer at the very least.

If Foxx had not injured his wrist in August of 1932, he might very well have broken Ruth's one-season record of 60 homers. As it was, he wound up with 58.

"I doubt that I hit three homers during that entire month," he once told me, carelessly shrugging his shoulders.

If Foxx had come up with the Red Sox instead of the Athletics, he certainly would have surpassed the Bambino. Not until late in his career did he switch to Boston and that friendly left-field fence. He made 50 in the campaign of 1938.

There were two red-letter days in the life of the Maryland Strong Boy. One came in St. Louis in 1933. In the opening game of a doubleheader the muscular Jimmie slashed out two home runs. In the second encounter he cracked out two more homers, a double, and a triple. But each of these lesser blows bounced back onto the field of play from the top of the wall. In other words he was a total of only a few inches away from the startling feat of hitting six home runs in one afternoon.

It was in the 1930 World Series between the Cardinals and the Athletics that Burleigh Grimes, the master of the spitball, whipped across a curve for a third strike on Double X at one crucial moment.

"Gosh," said the wondering Jimmy to himself as he made the long trek back to the bench. "I didn't know he had a curve. I just hope he throws me another."

The two teams were in a scoreless tie in the ninth inning of the fifth game. Again Grimes was the pitcher and he walked Mickey Cochrane. Up to the plate strode the massive James Emory Foxx.

Grimes threw the curve. Foxx hit it for a homer. The Athletics won, 2–0.

Many months later Grimes encountered Foxx and they got to talking. "Remember those two curveballs I threw you in the World Series, Jimmy?" asked the Lord of Burleigh. "I fanned you on the first and you hit the second for a home run. I'll let you in on a secret. Those were the only two curves I threw in the entire World Series."

FRANKIE FRISCH

1898–1973

By JOSEPH DURSO

"THEN THERE WAS Mr. Frisch, which went to a university and could run fast besides," Casey Stengel once remembered. "He was the first second baseman that didn't pedal backwards when they hit the ball down the line. He'd put his head down and commence running like in a race, and he'd beat the ball there."

The old Fordham Flash—Frank Francis Frisch—commenced running fast from the time he stepped off the campus in 1919 and joined the New York Giants of John McGraw. For the next nineteen years, he was one of the most versatile and tempestuous performers in baseball, manager of the storied Gashouse Gang of St. Louis and an early member of the Hall of Fame.

He was also a remarkable study in contrasts, a hellcat in a baseball suit but a devotee of classical music and gardening at his home in New Rochelle, New York. To the public in the 1920s and 1930s, he was an accomplished infielder with a strong arm and strong features, speedy though slightly bow-legged, a strong batter who compiled a .316 career average as a switch-hitter.

Frisch's talents for trouble, mimicry, and umpire baiting were just as solid. As a player, he once disappeared after a tongue-lashing from McGraw and soon thereafter was traded to the Cardinals for Rogers Hornsby. As a manager, he once was ejected from a game for arguing and drew a five-day suspension the next afternoon for arguing again.

Even in his twilight, at the age of fifty-three, he led the National League in "thumbs" by being thrown out by umpires six times in one summer. The following year, he found Johnny Vander Meer sunning himself in Arizona instead of running laps around the ballpark. He unconditionally released the pitcher, whose achievements included consecutive no-hit games.

In one of his earlier capers, Frisch was put out of a game in the Polo Grounds and headed for the clubhouse in center field by a circuitous route, to annoy the umpires. He accidentally stepped through the wrong door, wandered beneath the stands and found himself standing on Eighth Avenue—locked out of the park in his uniform. He drew a crowd of autograph seekers until a policeman rescued him.

Another time, he was confronted by Bill Klem, the authoritarian dean of umpires, who often drew a line in the dirt with his spikes and said, "Don't you dare cross that line." Few would, but Frisch kept circling Klem while the umpire kept drawing lines until Frisch chortled, "Hey, Bill, you're all fenced in."

Red Smith, the columnist, once walked into Frisch's room in the Ben

Franklin Hotel in Philadelphia and asked teasingly if the manager had sent his check for a fine to the league president, Ford Frick. He was astonished when Frisch whipped out a check, signed it, and wrote in a note:

"Dear Ford: Here is my check for $25 to pay for the fine. Please use it for a good cause—like buying your umpires new caps. They now look like Civil War veterans."

"Rampaging, dictatorial managers have vanished with the bunny hug and the hip flask," Frisch lamented in 1954. "Gone are the feuds, fines, profanity, and fun. This is an era of love and kisses, of sciences and psychology."

"I love to get the Dutchman riled," once said Leo Durocher, the manager and a past master of riling competition. "He lets go with a full fireworks display. It's like the Fourth of July."

Yet for all his skyrockets on the field, Frankie Frisch somehow became a gentle, genial, and becalmed squire off the field, a man who liked to sit in his yard gazing at his flowers, magnolias, maples, and azalea bushes. He had a large collection of musical records and particularly favored Arthur Schnabel, the pianist.

He also liked to sit on a bench in his garden and watch a pair of cardinals, which he had named Musial and Slaughter.

He was, nevertheless, a complete athlete, one of the few in the early years of the century to graduate from college baseball to the big leagues.

He was born in New York on September 9, 1898, the son of Franz Frisch, and twenty-one years later he took the long stride to McGraw's Giants. They were then the toast of the town, and Frisch was the toast of the Fordham campus: the captain of the baseball, football, and basketball teams.

Inside two seasons, he was recognized as a pro, the sort of daredevil base runner and all-out player cast in McGraw's own image. Starting in 1921, the Giants won four straight National League pennants while Frisch batted .341, then .327, then .348, and .328. His headlong style carried over into the World Series, which the Giants won from the Yankees in 1921 and 1922 before losing to them in 1923 and to the Washington Senators in 1924.

Two years later, after his run-in with McGraw, he was abruptly traded to St. Louis. The move came as a shock to the Polo Grounds fans, who had assumed that Frisch would eventually succeed McGraw as manager. The two men's fiery dispositions collided, and they parted.

With the Cardinals, though, Frisch became just as popular. He played second base, third base, and shortstop, and helped the Redbirds win pennants in 1928, 1930, and 1931. In eleven seasons with two clubs, he had played on seven pennant winners, with more victories to come.

In 1933, he was still an active player when he was named manager of the Cardinals, who made sporting lore the next season as the rough-and-tumble Gashouse Gang. They were led by Paul and Dizzy Dean, Joe Medwick, Pepper Martin, Durocher, and Frisch, and they barreled to the pennant and then to a tumultuous World Series victory over the Detroit Tigers.

By 1937, Frisch was still the playing manager of the troupe—until he decided one day that his famous legs had lost their speed. He was on second base with Terry Moore on first when another Cardinal drove a hit between two outfielders. The forty-year-old Frisch huffed his way home, sliding safely across the plate with Moore sliding in just behind him.

"When they start to climb up the old Flash's back," he said clinically, "it's time to quit."

And he did, though he continued as manager through 1938. Then he led the Pittsburgh Pirates from 1940 through 1946 and finally, after a break, the Chicago Cubs for two and a half years, until July 1951. Meanwhile, he also worked as a coach with the Giants and emerged as a play-by-play radio announcer, whose oft-repeated "Oh, those bases on balls" became part of baseball lore.

He conducted a postgame show on early television, too, and in 1953 a critic wrote in *The New York Times*:

"The best postgame show on the air locally is that of Frankie Frisch, who appears over WPIX after each Giant game at the Polo Grounds. Most baseball players are not looked upon as performing talent except on the diamond, but as a former player and manager, Mr. Frisch knows how to talk in front of a camera.

"Oddly enough, and fortunately enough, he never even seems to know it's there. He's as calm as if he were at the plate with the count of 3 and 0."

Following a game between the Giants and the Philadelphia Phillies in 1956, Frisch, who was fifty-eight, completed his TV program and was stricken with a heart attack. He spent five weeks in New Rochelle Hospital. Later on he moved to Westerly, Rhode Island, where he lived more quietly, though he remained a spirited raconteur of baseball.

In his later years, he would occasionally show up in the Cardinals' spring-training camp in St. Petersburg, Florida, and reminisce with Stengel and other cronies.

He died on March 12, 1973, in an automobile accident. He was seventy-four.

The Flash Comes Home

By ARTHUR DALEY

The train was humming over the rails from Boston to St. Louis for the final lap of the 1946 World Series. Frank Frisch, an unemployed baseball manager, had just finished a complete, unexpurgated, and off-the-record recital of his troubles with the maddening Pittsburgh Pirates who had given him all those gray hairs. By the time he had ended his story, his listener couldn't help but wonder why anyone wanted to be a major league manager.

The Fordham Flash spoke eagerly of his chance to become a baseball broadcaster once again, a job that would permit him to leave his worries at the ball park instead of carrying them home with him. He talked with a growing enthusiasm of his radio job and then he suddenly paused and sighed.

"I dunno, though," he said slowly. "There's something about being a manager that gets in your blood until it's a part of your very life—the excitement of the games, the thrill of out-guessing the other fellow, the fascination of handling twenty-five players who differ so completely from one another, and even the smell of sweat and wintergreen in the dressing room. It gets you and you can't get away from it. Maybe it will catch me again, too."

It caught him again in 1948. The dulcet voice of ye olde Flash would no longer be heard over the air waves. He turned his back on a comparatively easy, well-paying job to get into a uniform once more. The chances are that only one team in baseball could have lured him away from the microphone, the Giants. Frisch always was a Giant at heart. He was McGraw's boy, the apple of the master's eye and marked by him to be his successor.

But the fates intervened before that ever could happen. Frisch was too much like McGraw, fiery, hot-headed, impetuous, and rebellious. They clashed. And the Flash jumped the team at St. Louis in 1926. His days were numbered then. The Little Napoleon, a heavy-fisted disciplinarian to the end, regretfully shipped him off to the Cardinals. When Frisch finally became a manager it was with the flamboyant Gashouse Gang of St. Louis rather than the Giants. But twenty-two years later, he finally came home as a coach of those same Giants.

The strangest part of this setup was that he would be working under Leo Durocher, who once used to work under him. The two had been buddies when they played side by side on the Cardinals, but a seemingly irreparable break came when Manager Frisch traded Shortstop Durocher to the Dodgers. Time heals all wounds, however, and the Lip and the Flash gradually regained their old palsy-walsy relationship.

Being a coach is not quite the same as being a manager, though. When Deacon Will McKechnie quit managing to become Lou Boudreau's coach with the Cleveland Indians, he said he never again would assume the managerial reins. "The responsibility is Lou's," he said, "and so are the decisions and the worries. I'm helping all I can, but the headaches are his, not mine." Former Phillies skipper Art Fletcher felt the same way when he was with the Yankees.

The Flash must have thought often about the headaches he had had. Perhaps he even wondered whether he had more riding herd on a good ball club in St. Louis or a bad one in Pittsburgh. The Gashouse Gang was easier to take, I suppose, even though they tormented him in merciless, high-spirited style. "I hope that Dutchman manages forever," once remarked Dizzy Dean, the arch-fiend of the waggish Gashousers, "because I jes' love to drive him nuts." He did, too.

There was, for instance, the time the Flash was conducting a clubhouse meeting, outlining the strength and weakness of each enemy hitter. "Keep the ball low and away from this guy," he warned. "Give him nothing but sweeping curves to the outside." Immediately Diz interrupted. "Hey, Frankie," he said, "not me. I don't give him nothin' but a high fast one. I mow him down with that." And Frisch would explode.

On another occasion the Cards were in a tight, tough, and crucial game during the vitally important September homestretch. Frisch called time and trotted to the mound to caution Dizzy about the next batter. Carefully he expounded all his theories on the proper procedure. Diz seemed to agree but then he impishly changed tactics. "Frankie," he drawled, "I cain't see how an

infielder like you kin know more about pitchin' than a great pitcher like me."
Yes, he sure liked to drive that Dutchman nuts.

The high point in the Frisch career undoubtedly came in the 1934 World
Series when he piloted the Cardinals to victory over the Tigers in seven games,
with some slight help from the Dean brothers, Dizzy and Paul, who won two
each. But he started sliding downhill after that and quit as a player three years
later. He was on second and Terry Moore on first when the batter slashed a
double to right. Frisch creaked around the paths. Moore just flew. He came so
fast that they practically slid home together in a dead heat.

"When they start climbing up the old Flash's back," sorrowfully commented the fastest man baseball ever produced, "it's time to quit. I'll never play
again." He never did, either.

What a man he was, though, in his prime! Arthur Devlin tipped off John
McGraw on him. "There's a kid at Fordham," he said excitedly, "who's ready
for the big leagues right now. You won't have to farm him out. I tell you he's
ready."

And so he was. You can count on the fingers of one hand the ball players
who went from the campus to the big leagues without seasoning in the minors.
One of them was Frisch. He went in for Larry Doyle in a crucial game in 1919
and they never got him out of the lineup again until he removed himself in 1937.
He was a clutch player, a money player of the type so dear to McGraw's heart.
When the stakes were highest, when a hit was needed most, or when an impossible fielding play was most required, the Flash would come through.

The picture of Frisch, the Giant, recklessly sliding headfirst into second
base at the Polo Grounds, his cap flying behind him, or playing third and
stopping grounders with his chest before pouncing on the ball for the putout will
always be part of baseball history.

LOU GEHRIG

1903–1941

WHEN LOU GEHRIG stepped into the batter's box as a pinch hitter for the New York Yankees on June 1, 1925, he started a record that many believe will never be equaled in baseball. From that day on he never missed a game through April 30, 1939—fifteen seasons of Yankee box scores with the name of Gehrig always in the lineup. He announced on May 2, 1939, that he would not play that day, and thus his streak came to an end.

But as brilliant as was his career, Lou will be remembered for more than his endurance record. He was a superb batter in his heyday and a prodigious clouter of home runs. The record book is liberally strewn with his feats at the plate.

Only in his first season, 1925, and in his last full campaign, 1938, did he fail to go over the .300 mark. Once he led the American League in hitting with .363, but on three occasions he went over that without winning the batting crown—.373, .374, and .379.

But baseball has had other great hitters before and other great all-around players. It was the durability of Gehrig combined with his other qualities that lifted him above the ordinary players and in a class all his own.

An odd little incident gave Gehrig his start, and an even stranger disease, one almost totally unknown for a robust athlete, brought it to an end. Columbia Lou's string of consecutive games began, innocently enough, when Yankee manager Miller Huggins sent him up to bat for Peewee Wanninger on June 1, 1925. The husky twenty-one-year-old promptly singled.

Huggins was impressed by the way Gehrig had delivered, but according to the tale, he had no notion of using him as a first baseman. The Yankees had a star at the initial sack in those days, Wally Pipp. But Pipp was troubled with frequent headaches.

On June 2 he was bothered by pains in his head.

"Has anyone an aspirin tablet?" asked Pipp.

Huggins overheard him and, on a sheer hunch, decided to use the "kid"— Gehrig—at first base. He never left the lineup again until his voluntary resignation fourteen years later. Perhaps that story is not cut from the whole cloth. Gehrig denied it, but Pipp insisted just as vehemently that it is true. At any rate, it is an interesting sidelight on how a spectacular career was begun.

The beginning of the Gehrig playing days was abrupt but the ending was a much slower process. In 1937 the Iron Horse batted .351, his twelfth succes-

sive season over the .300 mark. But in 1938 the Yankee captain slipped to .295, the same figure he had established in his 1925 campaign.

Not only his hitting but his fielding had lost much of its crispness. Batted balls that the Gehrig of old had gobbled up easily skidded past him for base hits. In fact, the situation had developed to such an extent that there was continual talk in spring training in 1939 that the endurance record was approaching its completion.

This became even more obvious in the early games of the campaign. Yankee followers were amazed to see how badly Gehrig had fallen from the peak. He was anchored firmly near first base and only the fielding wizardry of Joe Gordon to his right saved Gehrig from looking very bad. The second baseman overshifted to cover the hole between him and his captain. Lou couldn't go to his right any more.

At bat Gehrig was not even a pale shadow of his former self. Once he had the outfielders backing up to the fences when he stepped to the plate. But this time he could hardly raise the ball out of the infield. On one occasion when he caromed a looping single to left—a certain double for even a slow runner—Gehrig was thrown out at second, standing up.

That day he saw the handwriting on the wall. And on April 30, 1939, he played his last big league game against the Washington Senators. The Bombers lost and Gehrig realized that he was a detriment to his team. When the Yanks took to the field again in Detroit on May 2, Gehrig—his batting average down to .143—withdrew from the lineup, his first missed game after 2,130 straight.

He acted as nonplaying captain from that point on. On June 12, when the Yankees engaged in an exhibition game in Kansas City, Lou played the last three innings, did nothing, and promptly left for the Mayo Clinic. He was there a week, determined to discover just what was the matter with him. That something was wrong he was certain.

On June 21 the diagnosis was made—amyotrophic lateral sclerosis, a hardening of the spinal cord—and considered incurable. The illness has been called Lou Gehrig's disease ever since. His career thus was brought to an abrupt conclusion. And an amazing career it had been.

The public's reaction to Gehrig's swift retirement gave rise to one of the most inspiring and dramatic episodes in sport when on July 4, in ceremonies between the games of the afternoon's holiday doubleheader, a crowd of 61,808 joined in the Lou Gehrig Appreciation Day exercises at the Yankee Stadium and thundered a "hail and farewell" to baseball's stricken Iron Horse.

Players, officials, writers, and employees at the park showered Lou with gifts, the highlight of the spectacle coming when the Yankees themselves paraded on the field their world championship team of 1927. From far and wide these diamond stalwarts had returned to join in the tribute to their former teammate, who had managed to carry on long after their own retirement from the game.

The group included such Yankee immortals as Babe Ruth, Waite Hoyt, Bob Meusel, Herb Pennock, Joe Dugan, Tony Lazzeri, Mark Koenig, Benny Bengough, Wally Schang, Everett Scott, Wally Pipp, George Pipgras, and Bob Shawkey.

Overcome by this spontaneous reception, Gehrig finally mastered his emotions, and, in perhaps the most remarkable valedictory ever delivered in a sport arena, literally poured his heart out to his great throng of listeners, thanking them for their appreciation and assuring them, with characteristic pluck, that he still considered himself "the luckiest man on the face of the earth."

From then until the end of the season Gehrig stuck by his guns as retired field captain, and spent every day on the bench. He accompanied the club on all its road trips, and at the finish sat through all four of the 1939 World Series games in which his colleagues crushed the Cincinnati Reds.

With the close of the campaign, Lou retired himself within a small circle of close friends, spent much time fishing, a sport second only to baseball in its fascination for him. On October 11, in another surprise move, Mayor Fiorello La Guardia announced Gehrig's appointment to a ten-year term as a member of the three-man Municipal Parole Commission at a salary of $5,700 a year. He tackled with considerable enthusiasm this newest job, which was to launch him upon a new chapter in his astounding career.

Although anxious to go quietly about his new task and remain as much as possible in complete retirement, Gehrig was catapulted prominently into the spotlight again in mid-August of the 1940 pennant campaign when a New York newspaper, in a featured article, intimated that the extraordinary collapse of the four-time world champion Yankees might be attributable to the possibility that some of the players may have become infected with Gehrig's disease.

The story brought vehement protests from the Yankee players, who insisted they were suffering from no physical ailments, and then, as if in final rebuttal to the charge, the Yanks, within a few days after publication of the article, launched their spectacular drive, which was to lift them from fifth place into the thick of the flag race throughout the month of September.

Gehrig was born in New York on June 19, 1903.

His career began unobtrusively enough when, as a husky youngster, he reported for the High School of Commerce nine in New York. He was tried in the outfield, where he was no Joe DiMaggio at catching fly balls. He was tried as pitcher but was as wild. He was tried as a first baseman and clicked. In later years Lou explained that by saying, with his ever-ready grin, "We were mighty short on infielders in those days."

In his first season on the Commerce team he batted .170. Then he started hitting until he cracked the headlines with a crash in 1920. Commerce, the New York schoolboy champions, played Lane Tech of Chicago in a scholastic "world series." The single game was played at Wrigley Field, and Gehrig was awed by his surroundings. But he was not too awed. In the ninth inning with Commerce one run behind and the bases full he drove a home run over the right-field fence.

Buster Gehrig was beginning to take shape. He matriculated at Columbia, pitching, outfielding, and playing first base. He was a good enough college pitcher but did have the knack of hitting home runs. For one year there he also tried football, but that sport did not have the same appeal that baseball bore.

The diamond game carried such a zest for him that he quit before he had been long at Morningside Heights, joining the Yankees in 1923. He played thirteen games before Huggins decided that he was not yet ready for major league ball. Farmed out to Hartford in the Eastern League, he batted .304 for the rest of the season. Back with the Yanks the next campaign, he followed the identical procedure. He took part in ten games and then it was a return trip to Hartford, where he began to belabor the fences in the circuit, hitting .369. That figure was an eye-opener to Huggins, who recalled him the following season.

That was in 1925. Gehrig batted .295 in 126 games and then he began to rocket through the baseball firmament. His first full season showed him with .313, but after that his successive batting averages were .373, .374, .300, .379, .341, .349, .334, .363, .329, .354, .351, and finally he was back to .295 in his last full campaign. The .363 average gave him the batting championship in 1934, but signal honors had come to him before that. In 1927, his second full campaign with the Yankees, he was voted the Most Valuable Player in the American League.

Seven times he participated in World Series and oddly enough, was a star on the Yankees of 1926–27–28 and with the All-Star contingent of 1936–37–38. Each of these groups has its supporters as the greatest baseball team of all time. Ruth-Gehrig-Meusel, the famed Murderers' Row, or DiMaggio-Gehrig-Dickey? Those were the batting fulcrums around which the teams revolved. Columbia Lou was the lone tie between the two.

His Series deeds have been awe inspiring. His lifetime average in World Series games was .361—his full regular average .340—and twice he hit over the fantastic mark of .500, with .545 in 1928 and .529 in 1932. Babe Ruth, however, holds the Series record of .625 in 1928.

That is an oddity in itself, Gehrig with two terrific averages but still behind the Babe. Yet for the better part of his career the Iron Horse was to be in the shadow of Ruth. Lou entered baseball when the Babe was riding high, straddling the sport such as no man has straddled it before or since.

Gehrig never left that shadow. His all-time home run production was 493, a figure topped by only two men at the time of his death, Ruth and Jimmie Foxx. For many years Lou gave the Babe his closest pursuit in the home run derby, but he never caught him until the Babe's last year as a Yankee. Only when the king was on the decline did the crown prince win the home run championship of the league, forty-nine in 1934. Today, Gehrig is fifteenth on the all-time home run list, and Ruth is second.

For one thing, Gehrig did not have the flamboyant Ruth personality. They were teammates but far apart, one quiet, reserved, and efficient and the other boisterous, friendly, and efficient. Let it not be deduced that the Iron Horse was not of the friendly type. He was pleasant at all times, but unlike Ruth he never considered the world at large as his particular friend. Whereas the Babe would greet all and sundry with a booming "Hiya, kid!" Lou's was a more personalized welcome.

They were sharp contrasts, those two, both hulking men but as far apart as the two poles. Ruth was Gehrig's boyhood idol, and with the passing years Lou never lost that respect for the Home Run King. And in spite of his own tremendous record, Gehrig was always subordinated to Ruth.

What a pair they made at the plate, coming up to bat in order! Each was likely to drive the ball out of the park. Frequently either or both did just that.

In fact, one of the many records that Lou set was that of hitting the most home runs with the bases filled, a startling twenty-three. Another was of four homers in one game.

The Ruthian association affected Gehrig's salary in two respects. In one way the heavy blow that Ruth struck at the payroll kept Lou from getting a compensation as close to the Babe's as their relative batting averages would indicate. Yet, on the other hand, the Bambino lifted the scale so high that Gehrig probably received more than he would have had there been no Ruth to blaze the trail.

The general estimate is that the Iron Horse received a total of $361,500 in salary from the Yankees. Since he participated in seven World Series where the share always was heavy, his total income from baseball is estimated at $400,000.

Gehrig received $3,750 in his first season, $6,500 in his second year. This advanced $1,000 in 1927 and then the Iron Horse moved into the big-money class. He never dropped out of five figures for the rest of his career.

For the next five years he received $25,000 and then he dropped to $23,000 for 1933 and 1934, after which he received $31,000 in 1935 and 1936, $36,750 in 1937, $39,000 in 1938, and $35,000 for 1939, a campaign in which he played only eight games.

Baseball contracts were strictly one-way in those days. The club had the upper hand at all times and could sever any contract at will. Had they so desired, the Yanks could have dropped Gehrig the day the report from the Mayo Clinic arrived. But he was kept on full salary for the remainder of the year.

So firm was his place in the Yankee scheme of things that Manager Joe McCarthy refused to break the Gehrig string even when there was a clamor to the effect that the Iron Horse himself would benefit from it. Marse Joe shook his head to that. "Gehrig plays as long as he wants to play," he said. Not many ball players would be granted such a privilege.

But in this respect McCarthy knew his man and knew him well. He realized that once Lou discovered his form had departed and that he was hindering the progress of the team he would call it quits. And that is what happened.

Had it not been for the severity of the illness, Gehrig might have continued as a part-time performer. Ball players do not go as fast as he went. The disintegration always is gradual enough for managers and club owners to make preparations. But the Yankees were caught without an adequate substitute for him, only the light-hitting but sure-fielding Babe Dahlgren.

Previously, being Gehrig's replacement had been the height of frustration. There was just no hope that he ever would give way to anyone else. In their thorough fashion the Yankees had had several first basemen on their farm teams. All of them pleaded to be sold or traded elsewhere so that they would be able to play regularly.

One was Buddy Hassett, who later played first base for the Boston Braves. Another was George McQuinn, a hard-hitting initial sacker for the St. Louis Browns. Many others paraded into the Yankee orbit and out again, balked of their desire by the stalwart figure of Lou Gehrig.

The day before he entered the Mayo Clinic for the examination, baseball celebrated its centennial at Cooperstown and the Hall of Fame was dedicated. Ruth already had been elected to it and within a short time another bronze plaque joined the Babe's as Henry Louis Gehrig took his proper place among the all-time greats that this sport had produced.

For though baseball's Hall of Fame committee decided to hold no elections for new candidates in 1939, it chose, upon recommendation of the Baseball Writers Association of America, to make an exception and name Gehrig as the lone Hall of Fame award for the year.

For a year and a half, following his retirement from the game, Gehrig went to his office at the parole commission regularly. But, as his condition worsened, he was forced to spend the last month of his life at home.

He lost weight steadily during the final weeks and was said to be twenty-five pounds lighter shortly before he died. He was conscious until the end, on the evening of June 2, 1941.

The Streak Ends

By JAMES P. DAWSON

Lou Gehrig's matchless record of uninterrupted play that stretched over fifteen years and through 2,130 straight contests came to an end on May 2, 1939.

The mighty iron man, who at his peak had hit forty-nine home runs in a single season, took himself out of action before the Yanks marched on Briggs Stadium for their first game against the Detroit Tigers that season.

With the consent of Manager Joe McCarthy, Gehrig removed himself because he, better than anybody else, perhaps, recognized his competitive decline and was frankly aware of the fact he was doing the Yankees no good defensively or on the attack. He last played on April 30 in New York against the Washington Senators.

Gehrig never played another major league game.

Ellsworth "Babe" Dahlgren, baseball's greatest figure of frustration, started at first base. Manager McCarthy said he had no intention of transferring Tommy Henrich, the youthful outfielder whom he tried at first base at the Florida training camp. Dahlgren had been awaiting the summons for three years.

It was coincidental that Gehrig's string was broken almost in the presence of the man he succeeded as Yankee first baseman. At that time Wally Pipp, who became a businessman in Grand Rapids, Michigan, was benched by the late Miller Huggins to make room for the strapping youth fresh from the Hartford Eastern League club to which the Yankees had farmed him for two seasons, following his departure from Columbia University. Pipp was in the lobby of the Book Cadillac Hotel at noon when the withdrawal of Gehrig was effected.

"I don't feel equal to getting back in there," Pipp said on June 2, 1925, the day Lou replaced him at first. Lou had started his phenomenal streak the day before as a pinch hitter for Peewee Wanninger, then the Yankee shortstop.

This latest momentous development in baseball was not unexpected. There had been signs for two years that Gehrig was slowing up. Even when a sick man, however, he gamely stuck to his chores, not particularly in pursuit of his all-time record of consecutive play, although that was a big consideration, but out of a driving desire to help the Yankees.

What Lou had thought was lumbago the year before when he suffered pains in the back that more than once forced his early withdrawal from games he had started was diagnosed later as amyotrophic lateral sclerosis, a disease of the spine.

The signs of his approaching fadeout were unmistakable during spring training at St. Petersburg, Florida, yet the announcement from Manager McCarthy was something of a shock. It came at the end of a conference Gehrig arranged immediately after McCarthy's arrival by plane from his native Buffalo.

"Lou just told me he felt it would be best for the club if he took himself out of the lineup," McCarthy said following their private talk. "I asked him if he really felt that way. He told me he was serious. He feels blue. He is dejected.

"I told him it would be as he wished. Like everybody else I'm sorry to see it happen. I told him not to worry. Maybe the warm weather will bring him around.

"He's been a great ball player. Fellows like him come along once in a hundred years. I told him that. More than that, he's been a vital part of the Yankee club since he started with it. He's always been a perfect gentleman, a credit to baseball.

"We'll miss him. You can't escape that fact. But I think he's doing the proper thing."

Gehrig, visibly affected, explained his decision quite frankly.

"I decided last Sunday night on this move," said Lou. "I haven't been a bit of good to the team since the season started. It would not be fair to the boys, to Joe, or to the baseball public for me to try going on. In fact, it would not be fair to myself, and I'm the last consideration.

"It's tough to see your mates on base, have a chance to win a ball game, and not be able to do anything about it. McCarthy has been swell about it all the time. He'd let me go until the cows came home, he is that considerate of my feelings, but I knew in Sunday's game that I should get out of there.

"I went up there four times with men on base. Once there were two there. A hit would have won the ball game for the Yankees, but I missed, leaving five stranded as the Yankees lost. Maybe a rest will do me some good. Maybe it won't. Who knows? Who can tell? I'm just hoping."

When Gehrig performed his duties as Yankee captain that day, appearing at the plate to give the batting order, announcement was made through the amplifiers of his voluntary withdrawal and it was suggested he get "a big hand." A deafening cheer resounded as Lou walked to the dugout, doffed his cap and disappeared in a corner of the bench.

Open expressions of regret came from the Yankees and the Tigers. Vernon "Lefty" Gomez expressed the Yankees' feelings when he said, "It's tough to see this thing happen, even though you know it must come to us all. Lou's a great guy and he's always been a great baseball figure. I hope he'll be back in there."

Hank Greenberg, who might have been playing first for the Yanks instead of the Tigers but for Gehrig, said, "Lou's doing the right thing. He's got to use his head now instead of his legs. Maybe that Yankee dynasty is beginning to crumble."

Everett Scott, the shortstop who held the record of 1,307 consecutive games until Gehrig broke it, ended his streak on May 6, 1925, while he was a member of the Yankees. However, Scott began his string, once considered unapproachable, with the Red Sox.

By a strange coincidence, Scott gave way to Wanninger, the player for whom Gehrig batted to start his great record.

A Hail and Farewell

By JOHN DREBINGER

In perhaps as colorful and dramatic a pageant as ever was enacted on a baseball field, 61,808 fans thundered a hail and farewell to Henry Louis Gehrig at Yankee Stadium on July 4, 1939.

To be sure, it was a holiday and there would have been a big crowd in any event to see the doubleheader with the Washington Senators. But it was the spectacle staged between the games that never would be forgotten by those who saw it. For more than forty minutes there paraded in review two mighty championship hosts—the Yankees of 1927 and the current edition of Yanks who were winging their way to a fourth straight pennant and world title.

From far and wide the 1927 stalwarts came to reassemble for Lou Gehrig Appreciation Day and to pay their own tribute to their former comrade-in-arms who had carried on beyond all of them only to have his own brilliant career come to a tragic close when it was revealed that he had fallen victim of a form of infantile paralysis.

The vast gathering, sitting in absolute silence for a longer period than perhaps any baseball crowd in history, heard Gehrig himself deliver as amazing a valedictory as ever came from a ball player.

So shaken with emotion that at first it appeared he would not be able to talk at all, the mighty Iron Horse, with a rare display of that indomitable willpower that had carried him through 2,130 consecutive games, moved to the microphone at home plate to express his own appreciation.

And for the final fadeout, there stood the still burly and hearty Babe Ruth alongside of Gehrig, their arms about each other's shoulders, facing a battery of cameramen.

All through the long exercises Gehrig had tried in vain to smile, but with the irrepressible Bambino beside him he finally made it. The Babe whispered something to him and Lou chuckled. Then they both chuckled and the crowd roared and roared.

The ceremonies began directly after the debris of the first game had been cleared away. From out of a box alongside the Yankee dugout there spryly hopped more than a dozen elderly gentlemen, some gray, some shockingly baldish, but all happy to be on hand. The crowd recognized them at once, for they were the Yanks of 1927, not the first Yankee world championship team, but the first, with Gehrig an important cog in the machine, to win a World Series in four straight games.

Down the field, behind Captain Sutherland's Seventh Regiment Band, they marched—Ruth, Bob Meusel, who had come all the way from California; Waite Hoyt, alone still maintaining his boyish countenance; Wally Schang, Benny Bengough, Tony Lazzeri, Mark Koenig, Jumping Joe Dugan, Bob Shawkey, Herb Pennock, Deacon Everett Scott, whose endurance record Gehrig eventually surpassed; Wally Pipp, who faded out as the Yankee first sacker the day Columbia Lou took over the job away back in 1925, and George Pipgras, now an umpire and, in fact, actually officiating in the day's games.

At the flagpole, these old Yanks raised the World Series pennant they had won so magnificently from the Pirates in 1927, and as they paraded back, another familiar figure streaked out of the dugout, the only one still wearing a Yankee uniform. It was the silver-haired Earle Combs, now a coach.

Arriving at the infield, the old-timers strung out, facing the plate. The players of both Yankee and Senator squads also emerged from their dugouts to form a rectangle, and the first real ovation followed as Gehrig moved out to the plate to greet his colleagues, past and present.

One by one the old-timers were introduced with Sid Mercer acting as toastmaster. Clark Griffith, venerable white-haired owner of the Senators and a Yankee himself in the days when they were known as Highlanders, also joined the procession.

Gifts of all sorts followed. The Yankees presented their stricken comrade with a silver trophy measuring more than a foot and a half in height with a wooden base, supported by six silver bats with an eagle atop a silver ball. It made Gehrig weep. Yankee team president Edward G. Barrow walked out to put his arms about Lou in an effort to steady him when this presentation was made. It appeared for an instant that Gehrig was near collapse.

On one side of the trophy were the names of all his present fellow-players. On the other was the following touching inscription:

To Lou Gehrig

We've been to the wars together,
We took our foes as they came,
And always you were the leader
And ever you played the game.

Idol of cheering millions.
Records are yours by the sheaves,
Iron of frame they hailed you,
Decked you with laurel leaves.

But higher than that we hold you,
We who have known you best,

Knowing the way you came through
Every human test.

Let this be a silent token
Of lasting friendship's gleam,
And all that we've left unspoken,
Your pals of the Yankee team.

Manager Joe McCarthy, almost as visibly affected as Gehrig himself, made this presentation and hurried back to fall in line with his players. But every few minutes, when he saw that the once stalwart figure they called the Iron Horse was swaying on shaky legs, Marse Joe would come forward to give Lou an assuring word of cheer.

Mayor Fiorello H. La Guardia officially extended the city's appreciation of the services Columbia Lou had given his hometown.

"You are the greatest prototype of good sportsmanship and citizenship," said the mayor, concluding with, "Lou, we're proud of you."

When time came for Gehrig to address the gathering, it looked as if he simply would never make it. He gulped and fought to keep back the tears as he kept his eyes fastened on the ground.

But Marse Joe came forward again, said something that might have been, "Come on, Lou, just rap out another," and somehow those magical words had the same effect as in all the past fifteen years when the gallant Iron Horse would step up to the plate to "rap out another."

He spoke slowly and evenly, and stressed the appreciation that he felt for all that was being done for him. He spoke of the men with whom he had been associated in his long career with the Yankees—Colonel Jacob Ruppert, the recently deceased owner of the team; Miller Huggins, his first manager, who gave him his start in New York; President Barrow; the Yanks of old who now stood silently in front of him, as well as the players of today.

"What young man wouldn't give anything to mingle with such men for a single day as I have for all these years?" he asked.

"Fans, for the past two weeks you have been reading about a bad break I got," he said. "Yet today I consider myself the luckiest man on the face of the earth. . . . I have an awful lot to live for."

As Gehrig finished his talk, Ruth, robust, round, and sun-tanned, was nudged toward the microphone and, in his own inimitable, blustering style, snapped the tears away. He gave it as his unqualified opinion that the Yanks of 1927 were greater than the Yanks of 1939, and seemed even anxious to prove it right there.

"Anyway," he added, "that's my opinion, and while Lazzeri here pointed out to me that there are only about thirteen or fourteen of us here, my answer is, shucks, we only need nine to beat 'em."

Then, as the famous home run slugger, who also had faded into baseball retirement, stood with his arms entwined around Gehrig's shoulders, the band played "I Love You Truly" while the crowd took up the chant: "We love you, Lou."

All given spontaneously, it was without doubt one of the most touching scenes ever witnessed on a ball field and one that made even case-hardened ball players and chroniclers of the game swallow hard.

When Gehrig arrived in the Yankee dressing rooms, he was so close to a complete collapse it was feared that the strain upon him had been too great, and Dr. Robert E. Walsh, the Yankees' attending physician, hurried to his assistance. But after some refreshment, he recovered quickly, and faithful to his one remaining task, that of being the inactive captain of his team, he stuck to his post in the dugout throughout the second game.

Long after the tumult and shouting had died and the last of the crowd had filed out, Lou trudged across the field for his familiar hike to his favorite exit gate. With him walked his bosom pal and teammate, Bill Dickey, with whom he always roomed when the Yanks were on the road.

Lou walked with a slight hitch in his gait, but there was supreme confidence in his voice as he said to his friend, "Bill, I'm going to remember this day for a long time."

So, doubtless, would all the others who helped make this an unforgettable day in baseball.

Not a Dry Eye in the House
By ARTHUR DALEY

Baseball has had many a sentimental moment over the years, but it is doubtful that any produced the shattering impact of Lou Gehrig Appreciation Day at Yankee Stadium. It sent 61,000 onlookers into emotional turmoil and caused strong men to weep unashamedly, including the strongest of all, Babe Ruth. The Babe blubbered like the big kid he really was.

It was truly an occasion for tears. A short while earlier announcement had been made that the Iron Horse, the symbol of indestructability, was in the grip of a rare disease, amyotrophic lateral sclerosis. It was a progressive paralysis of sorts. Two years later he was dead. Yet in what amounted to his farewell appearance, Larruping Lou faced that future unflinching and unafraid.

"For the past two weeks," he said in his acknowledgment to the stadium fans, his voice booming clear and deep, over the loudspeakers, "you've been reading about a bad break I got. Yet today I consider myself the luckiest man on the face of the earth."

This gentle giant spoke with such fervor that he kept triggering more and more tears. Proudly he pointed to the assembled members of the 1927 Yankee team, perhaps the greatest of all baseball clubs.

"Look at these grand men," he said. "Sure, I'm lucky."

It was an unforgettable occasion and it was such a historic one that it has since been shown and reshown on television. A quarter of a century later it still brings a lump to the throat and moisture to the eyes. The return of the 1927 team that afternoon was notable in one other respect. It became the first of the Old-timers Days, now one of the most nostalgic and rewarding of all diamond promotions.

Not only do his qualities as a superathlete enrich Gehrig's memory but it is ennobled also by the distinction he imparted as a man. He was a model youth, the All-American Boy. He did not have the lavish natural talents of the Babe, but his unflagging industry and determination made him an exceptional ball player. He set an endurance record of 2,130 consecutive big league games, a mark so far-fetched that it never can be approached again.

Fate ordained that he would always be performing in the shadow of the mighty Babe. There was no escape from it, and in his painful modesty the good-natured Lou was fully aware of it. Even when the flamboyant and fantastically colorful Ruth quit the Yankees, Gehrig refused to accept the suggestion that he would get the headlines alone.

"Let's face it," said the practical Lou. "I'm not a headline guy. I always knew that as long as I was following the Babe to the plate I could have gone up there and stood on my head. No one would have noticed the difference. When the Babe was through swinging, whether he hit one or fanned, nobody paid any attention to the next hitter. They all were talking about what the Babe had done."

It almost seemed as if a conspiracy was under way to keep the burly Gehrig hidden in Ruth's shadow. In 1931 the Babe had not quite started his over-the-hill slide and the two teammates were battling for the home run championship. They tied at 46 apiece. Why?

It was an ironic jest. On Easter Sunday in Washington the powerful Gehrig hit a screamer into the concrete bleachers with Lyn Lary on base. He hit it so hard that the ball caromed back to the field of play and the center fielder retrieved it. Lary mistakenly thought the ball had been caught for the last out. So he rounded third and headed for the dugout. Gehrig jogged happily home and was automatically out for passing a base runner. His "homer" became a triple. That's how he tied Ruth with 46 instead of beating him with 47.

One of the epic batting days in baseball history came on June 3, 1932. Gehrig hit four home runs in a game, the first such output in thirty-six years. It was front-page stuff. But no big news ever received more obscure play. This was the day the immortal John McGraw resigned as manager of the Giants. McGraw drew front-page attention and column after column on the inside. Gehrig's feat was buried back with the want ads.

The Columbia strong boy was one of the greatest of all big leaguers and is properly ensconced in the Hall of Fame at Cooperstown. Somehow or other, though, he is best remembered as the No. 2 man in the most feared one, two punch baseball ever produced.

There almost is something symbolic about the fact that Ruth's career batting average was .342 while Gehrig's was .340, a mite behind the Babe, but behind him always.

LEFTY GOMEZ

1909–1989

BACK IN THE DAYS when baseball games were being played on lazy summer afternoons and the Yankees were winning more games than anybody else, few persons symbolized the sport more joyously or successfully than Vernon "Lefty" Gomez.

The light-hearted left-hander reflected the mood of the business by breezing through thirteen seasons as one of the happier, more colorful souls on the landscape—the "Singular Señor" and "El Goofy" of the Yankee pitching staff, and a wit and raconteur of the front rank.

But he also reflected the Yankees' dominance of the business in the "middle years" of the empire, starting in 1931, when Babe Ruth was king, and ending in 1942, when Joe DiMaggio reigned. During those summers, plus one post-script summer with the Boston Braves and Washington Senators in 1943, Lefty Gomez performed as one of the slickest pitchers in the big leagues.

In his fourteen major league seasons, Gomez won 189 games, lost 102, and was nearly flawless in the World Series, winning six games without losing in his seven starts. He was elected to the Baseball Hall of Fame in 1972.

Four times he won more than twenty games in a season, three times he led the American League in strikeouts, twice he led in winning percentage and earned-run average. And in 1934, when he pitched twenty-six victories with only five defeats, he led the league in shutouts, strikeouts, complete games, innings pitched, and just about everything else.

But his reputation as a "money pitcher" probably rested just as firmly on his World Series record. During his years with the Yankees, pitching in five World Series over eight years, he won six games and did not lose. He also appeared in five All-Star Games, winning three, including the first one in Chicago in 1933 and losing one.

The secret of his success? "Clean living and a fast outfield," Gomez replied on more than one occasion. Then, just as often, he would add, "I'd rather be lucky than good."

He apparently was both lucky and good because the Yankees were blessed with a full cast of power hitters in the 1930s from Ruth and Lou Gehrig to DiMaggio, Bill Dickey, Joe Gordon, and Charlie Keller as well as with a strong pitching corps that extended to the bull pen and Johnny Murphy, one of the early relief specialists.

Even when he was elected into the Hall of Fame, Gomez did not take himself too seriously. He stood at the microphone in Cooperstown, New York,

and said, "I want to thank all my teammates who scored so many runs; Joe DiMaggio, who ran down so many of my mistakes, and Johnny Murphy, without whose relief pitching I wouldn't be here."

He also could joke just as cheerfully about his anemic batting average, which added up to only .147 during his thirteen seasons, in the days when all pitchers batted for themselves.

"They throw, I swing," he once said, analyzing the problem at bat. "Every once in a while they're throwing where I'm swinging and I get a hit."

He also remembered that sometimes he would call for a bat from the Yankee batboy, who would reply, "What are you planning to do with it?"

"Remember the 1934 All-Star Game?" he once asked the late Red Smith of *The New York Times.* "Carl Hubbell struck out five great hitters in a row, Babe Ruth, Lou Gehrig, Jimmie Foxx, Al Simmons, and Joe Cronin. Then Bill Dickey singled, and I was the next hitter. Gabby Hartnett was catching, and he asked me, 'You trying to insult Hubbell, coming up here with a bat in your hand?' "

Gomez was a thin 6-footer of mixed Irish and Spanish descent who was born in Rodeo, California. He got into professional baseball in 1928 with Salt Lake City of the Utah-Idaho League, then won eighteen games with the San Francisco Seals of the Pacific Coast League the following year and was sold to the Yankees for $35,000.

In 1933, Gomez was married to June O'Dea, a Broadway showgirl who was touring in the musical *Of Thee I Sing.* Five years later, she sued for separation, and for a time the couple made headlines with charges and counter-charges that centered on the pitcher's temperament and zest for high life. Mrs. Gomez later dropped the suit, they were reconciled, and they made their home base in the San Francisco area.

At his peak, Gomez earned $20,000 with the Yankees, which was big money in baseball then. That was in 1938, when the Yankees won their third straight World Series by sweeping the Chicago Cubs. In the second game, in a typical Yankee performance, Frank Crosetti hit a home run in the eighth inning to put the Yankees ahead and DiMaggio hit one in the ninth to clinch things, 6–3. And Gomez, with the customary help from Murphy, outpitched the great Dizzy Dean.

After his career ended in 1943, Gomez worked as recreational director of the Norden Bombsight Company; later served as a manager for the Yankee farm team in Binghamton, New York, where his protégés included Whitey Ford; and eventually represented the Wilson Sporting Goods Company.

Through it all, he continued to regale baseball dinners and World Series gatherings with tales of the glory years—even his final year with the Yankees, when Manager Joe McCarthy observed, "Lefty, I don't think you're throwing as hard as you used to." And, the Singular Señor remembered dryly, he overlooked the solemnity of the warning and replied, "You're wrong, Joe. I'm throwing twice as hard, but the ball isn't going as fast."

Hard to Beat

By IRA BERKOW

In the 1931 photograph in Donald Honig's book *The American League: An Illustrated History,* three strapping young ball players, three Yankees, are smiling into the camera. In the middle is Lefty Gomez, his glove, looking as big as a cushion (baseball gloves were puffier in those days), is thrown over the right shoulder of Bill Dickey, and Gomez's left hand—the one that won all those games—rests on the left shoulder of Lou Gehrig.

And there, halted blissfully for all time, are Dickey the catcher, Gomez the hurler, Gehrig the slugger: "Three future Hall of Famers" reads the caption. Three Yankee teammates, presumably after another winning game, in slightly undone pinstripes with T-shirts exposed and wearing flattened baseball caps (baseball caps were flatter in those days).

Ten years later, Gehrig, the Iron Horse, would be dead at age thirty-seven. In 1989, at age eighty, a second in that sunny picture, Lefty Gomez, nicknamed El Goofy, and The Gay Castillion, for he was part Spanish and part Irish and part zany, died, in Larkspur, California.

The next morning, in his home on Choctaw Road in Little Rock, Arkansas, Bill Dickey, the third and last in that photograph, eighty-one years old and recovering from a broken back, recalled Lefty, whom he caught for thirteen of Gomez's fourteen big league seasons. "He was a great guy, a gentleman, and we were good friends," said Dickey. "I didn't sleep well last night, I guarantee ya."

Dickey recalled the first time he saw Gomez. "It was in spring training in St. Petersburg, in 1930, I think it was," he said. "He was tall, about six two, and very, very skinny, like a beanpole. And I saw him whizzin' that ball out there. He had the liveliest fastball I ever saw."

Dickey recalled that one batter Gomez had particular trouble with was Jimmie Foxx, the great power hitter. Gomez once said about Foxx, "He's got muscles in his hair." One time, with Foxx at bat, Dickey gave one signal after the other and Lefty shook them all off. Finally Dickey ran out to the mound.

"What do you want to throw him?"

"I don't wanna throw him nothing'," said Gomez. "Maybe he'll just get tired of waitin' and leave."

Dickey laughed when telling the story. "Actually, Lefty was always in good humor except when he was in trouble. Then he'd be so nervous he'd shake. His hand used to shake real bad. I'd go out to the mound to try to relax him. He'd say, 'Give me the ball, give me the ball!'

"But then he'd reach back and give you that extry stuff. He did it in so many games. He was awfully hard to beat."

But Gomez, despite his pitching exploits, may be better known for his quips. When, for example, he was asked the secret of his success, he replied, "Clean living and a fast outfield." Another time, asked about an inning in which three hard-hit balls were caught by his outfielders, he said, "I'd rather be lucky than good."

There were other sides to Lefty, as well.

When a dispirited Gehrig, after playing 2,130 straight games, finally had to take himself out of the lineup because of the disease that would soon claim his life, Gomez sat down beside him on the dugout bench. "Hell, Lou," he said, "it took fifteen years to get you out of a game. Sometimes I'm out in fifteen minutes."

When Jimmy DeShong heard that Gomez had died, he called June O'Dea Gomez, Lefty's widow, to offer condolences, and tell her what Lefty had meant to him. DeShong was a rookie pitcher with the Yankees in 1934 and assigned to room with Gomez. "In those days, veterans usually wouldn't give rookies the time of day," DeShong would recall. "But not Lefty. He made me feel a part of the team. Once I had a run-in with one of our veteran players, and Lefty told me, 'Don't bother with him, he's just a jerk.' I'll always be grateful to Lefty."

In 1932 Gomez fell in love and started "going with" June O'Dea, then the leading lady of the Broadway show *Of Thee I Sing*. He recalled "hanging around the theater" and seeing "the show so often I could act myself."

"February 26," said June O'Dea, "would have made fifty-six years that Lefty and I were married." In newspaper clips, there were reports early on of a stormy marriage, and possible divorce—"he could be kind of high strung in those days," she said—but they held on, and had three children and seven grandchildren.

"We had such a good time, all that laughter," she said, "even up to the end. In the hospital, the doctor leaned over his bed and said, 'Lefty, picture yourself on the mound, and rate the pain from one to ten.' And Lefty looked at him and said, 'Who's hitting, Doc?' "

RED GRANGE

1903–1991

By GERALD ESKENAZI

HAROLD (RED) GRANGE'S dramatic exploits as a football running back for the University of Illinois and the Chicago Bears in the 1920s and 1930s made him an idol of his age and a legend to later generations.

With his flaming hair and his many notable achievements on the football field—some so spectacular they still read like fiction—Red Grange fit easily into that group of superstars that helped elevate the 1920s into a golden age of sports in the United States.

The Grange legend flowered one afternoon in 1924, when his Illinois team was facing undefeated Michigan. That day was also dedication day for Illinois Memorial Stadium, and 66,609 fans turned out for the game.

While many people were still finding their seats, Grange took the opening kickoff 95 yards for a touchdown. Then, on the Illini's first play from scrimmage, he broke through for a 67-yard touchdown. He followed that with touchdown runs of 54 yards and then 44 yards. He astounded everyone present, as well as the larger football world, by rushing for 265 yards and 4 touchdowns in the first 12 minutes of the game.

"I need a breather," he reportedly told his quarterback, before going off the field to rest for five minutes. Soon after, he returned and scored his fifth touchdown of the day, on a 13-yard run. For good measure, he tossed a 20-yard scoring pass in the fourth quarter as Illinois won, 39–14. In 41 minutes of play, he was responsible for 402 yards of offense, including 64 yards as a passer.

For this performance, and for his performances on other golden afternoons, Grange became known as the Galloping Ghost, in tribute to his elusive, yet barreling running style. Damon Runyon once wrote of him: "He is three or four men rolled into one. He is Jack Dempsey, Babe Ruth, Al Jolson, Paavo Nurmi, and Man o' War."

Even while Grange was a student, his jersey number, 77, took on almost mythic proportions. He was a three-time all-American, continually producing games that seemingly could not be topped.

In his collegiate debut, for example, he ran 35 yards for a touchdown against Nebraska in the first quarter, 65 yards for another score in the second, and 12 yards for a third touchdown in the final period. In his first Big Ten game, against Iowa, he caught three passes on a drive that took Illinois to the 2-yard line. Then he scored and the Illini went on to beat the Hawkeyes for the first time in 22 games.

Grange's collegiate career mark of 2,071 yards rushing over three seasons

was actually bettered several times by other Illini runners, but he accomplished that figure with only 388 carries—an average of 5.3 yards a carry. The last of his many records at Illinois, 31 career touchdowns, was broken in 1990 when Howard Griffith ended his Illini career with 33 touchdowns. Grange also threw six scoring passes.

Grange's collegiate exploits suddenly ended in November 1925, when he was persuaded to join the Chicago Bears on Thanksgiving Day to begin a remarkable tour that helped lift pro football into the American consciousness. His abrupt shift also had a long-lasting effect on the relationship between colleges and the National Football League.

The Bears were owned and coached by George Halas, himself a former Illinois player. Coach Bob Zuppke of Illinois, angered by Halas's hiring Grange, contacted the Bear coach and told him that such actions could jeopardize the college game. Halas came to agree with Zuppke, and although Grange stayed on the Chicago team, Halas eventually persuaded the NFL to adopt a draft of collegians and not take any of them before their class graduated.

Grange's debut professional tour started with 8 games in 12 days, and by the time it ended, in February 1926, he had earned $100,000. But more important than his earnings was the fact that he almost instantly gave the NFL the credibility it had lacked in its first five years.

Grange's first tour with the Bears, orchestrated by a former theatrical magician named C. C. (Cash and Carry) Pyle, attracted big crowds, like the 66,000 fans in the Polo Grounds for a meeting with the Giants.

At one point during the tour, Babe Ruth invited himself up to Grange's hotel room to meet the celebrated young football player. "Kid," Ruth reportedly told him, "don't believe anything they write about you, and don't pick up too many dinner checks."

Grange followed that first pro season with two seasons with the New York Yankees football team, and then returned to the Bears to play from 1929 to 1934. After a brief career as an assistant coach, he left the game to try a variety of pursuits, including acting. He returned to football as a radio and television analyst and announcer, broadcasting many college games and 312 Bear games from 1947 to 1961.

Grange then retired to Indian Lake, Florida, where he owned an orange grove and an insurance agency and was involved in the real-estate business.

Grange became a charter member of the Professional Football Hall of Fame in 1963, and was also a member of the National Football Foundation's College Football Hall of Fame.

Harold Grange was born on June 13, 1903, in Forksville, Pennsylvania, but he was raised in Wheaton, Illinois. He was a perfect football figure for the age of hyperbole in American sports. It was one of that era's primary chroniclers, Grantland Rice, who labeled him the Galloping Ghost. The nickname was so widely known that Grange even made a series of cliffhanger movie serials called *The Galloping Ghost*.

Yet when he was asked once for his fondest college football memory, Grange did not cite his five-touchdown performance against Michigan or his opening-game heroics. Instead, it was a game at Iowa won when Earl Britton, his prime blocker on runs, kicked a 55-yard field goal.

"I held the ball for him," Grange explained.

In July 1990 Grange was hospitalized in Florida. Six months later he died of pneumonia at age 87.

A Conversation With the Ghost
By IRA BERKOW

Perhaps still the most famous football player ever, Harold (Red) Grange looked in wonderment at the joggers going past his home in Indian Lake, Florida. "I think they're crazy," he said in an interview before Super Bowl XVI in 1982. "If you have a car, why run?"

But once he ran like few others. He was fast and strong and so elusive that he seemed to vanish from tacklers. He was a star halfback in the 1920s for the University of Illinois—he once scored four long touchdowns in the first quarter against powerful Michigan—and then went on to play for the Chicago Bears.

Grange almost single-handedly popularized professional football. He signed with the Bears right out of college in 1925 for the then staggering sum of $100,000. The pro league had been in existence for only five years and it still had trouble getting space in newspapers and crowds to the games. Now, wherever Grange played, the stadiums were packed, and his exploits made headlines.

"People don't realize today how the colleges fought against pro ball," said Grange. "They were afraid that the pros would dominate the game. After I signed, my coach at Illinois, Bob Zuppke, wouldn't talk to me for three years. I'd have been more popular with the colleges if I had joined Capone's mob in Chicago rather than the Bears."

It was in 1933, that Grange played with the Bears in the National Football League's first title game. Chicago beat the New York Giants 23–21, at Wrigley Field.

"It had none of the atmosphere that the Super Bowl has today," he said. "Now, it's like a circus. But I don't think there's anything wrong with all the hoopla. If you follow the news, with one disaster after another, then it's a relief to turn your attention to a football game."

He was going to tune in to that year's Super Bowl game, but did not intend to watch all of it. "I just can't sit through three hours of football," he said. "I've been footballed up to my eyeballs. I'd rather spend some of that time mowing the lawn.

"I don't know much about the two teams in it this year, but I'm sure Cincinnati (Bengals) and San Francisco (Forty-Niners) are good. They have to be, once they reach this level. But I can't imagine this game being any better than the first championship game. It was tied six times.

"The players today are good, but I don't think they're any better than in my day. They're bigger, that's all. When I joined the Bears in 1925, the linemen averaged 235 poounds. Now, they go at least 260 or 270.

"People seem to try to make the game more complicated than it is. The team that blocks better and tackles better still wins."

But the current players are certainly richer. "In that first championship game," Grange said, "the winning share for each player was $210 and some change. The losers got $140 apiece."

In Super Bowl XVI, the split was $18,000 for each winning player, and $9,000 for each losing player. A few years earlier, Grange had been outspoken about the modern players who had cut off the old-timers in the pension fund. He had called them "cheap."

"I don't need the money," he had said, "but a heckuva lot of fellas do. My gosh, where do the modern guys think the league came from?" But Grange seemed to have mellowed on that point, to an extent. "If I was their age, I might not have that kind of perspective, either."

One old player he recalled with particular fondness was Jim Thorpe, whose story is still seen on late-night television in the old movie *Jim Thorpe, All-American,* with Burt Lancaster in the lead.

"Jim was a wonderful guy," said Grange, "and a friend of mine. Once, we were in Hollywood together. We were both working on football films. I had a manager—they call them agents now—named Charlie Pyle, and Charlie had some magic tricks; in fact, he once played the Orpheum circuit. Well, we went to a party, and he had Thorpe help him with a trick he often played.

"Pyle had two quarters of the same date. He gave one to Thorpe, and told him to make a small slice in an apple on the table and slip the quarter in it. When the time came with everyone at the party watching, Pyle showed his quarter, then made believe it disappeared into the apple. But of course he'd palm the quarter.

"This night he did it, but when he opened the apple, he found two dimes and a nickel. Oh, was he mad. He shouted, 'I'll kill that [Thorpe]!' "

Grange retired in 1935 when, having broken into the clear for what seemed a touchdown run, he was caught from behind by a lineman. "I knew then," he said, "that it was time to say goodbye."

After having lived in Florida for many years, he was asked what he did. "Nothing," he replied "What's wrong with that?" He did spend some time on the golf course, though. "I don't keep score anymore. I can still hit the ball long, but I have trouble around the green, like everyone else."

As for being a so-called legend, it didn't interest him very much. "They built my accomplishments way out of proportion," he said. "I never got the idea that I was a tree-men-dous big shot. I could carry a football well, but there are lot of doctors and teachers and engineers who could do their thing better than I."

He said his neighbors knew that he played football "a long time ago for some midwestern college, and I let it go at that." His hair, once a bright rust, had turned gray. He was asked whether his wife, Margaret, called him Harold or Red. "Neither," the old football player replied. "She calls me honey."

ROCKY GRAZIANO

1919–1990

By PHIL BERGER

I N THE RING, Rocky Graziano was a primal force. While he lacked finesse and did not trouble himself much with defense, he had a taste for action that made him a crowd pleaser.

"He was not a great fighter," Harry Markson, former president of Madison Square Garden Boxing, characterized him, "but he was a good puncher and a tremendous competitor. He could knock you out with either hand. And when you knocked him down, he always got up. He put on a good show."

As W. C. Heinz, a reporter who covered Graziano for the *New York Sun*, put it, "You could louse Rocky up if you wanted him to jab and move. So what you did was get him in shape and turn him loose."

With his brawling style, Graziano compiled a record of 67–10–6 from 1942 to 1952. His three bouts with Tony Zale in the years after World War II are considered classics of brutal action.

Zale knocked out Graziano in six rounds in September 1946—their first fight—but the next time they fought, in July 1947, Graziano stopped Zale in six rounds and became world middleweight champion.

"Afterward," Heinz observed, "he told the press, 'I wanted to kill him. I like him, but I wanted to kill him.' Which is so true of the fight instinct." Graziano lost his second rematch with Zale in June 1948 on a third-round knockout.

He would get one more shot at the middleweight title, but that came very late in his career, in April 1952, when Sugar Ray Robinson knocked him out in three rounds. After Graziano lost his next match, a ten-round decision to Chuck Davey, he retired.

He was elected to the Boxing Hall of Fame in 1971.

Born Thomas Rocco Barbella, Graziano grew up on the Lower East Side of Manhattan, the son of a former boxer nicknamed Fighting Nick Bob. Like his boyhood friend Jake LaMotta, who would also become middleweight champion of the world, the young Graziano frequently came into conflict with the law.

"We were the original juvenile delinquents," said LaMotta. "Always in fights. Stealing stuff. In fact, we both ended up in reform school in Coxsackie, New York, at the same time. I remember Rocky was in quarantine, so I'd set him up with comic books and candy and cigarettes."

Graziano was proud of his ability as a street battler. "I was the best street fighter in history when I was growing up on the Lower East Side," he said.

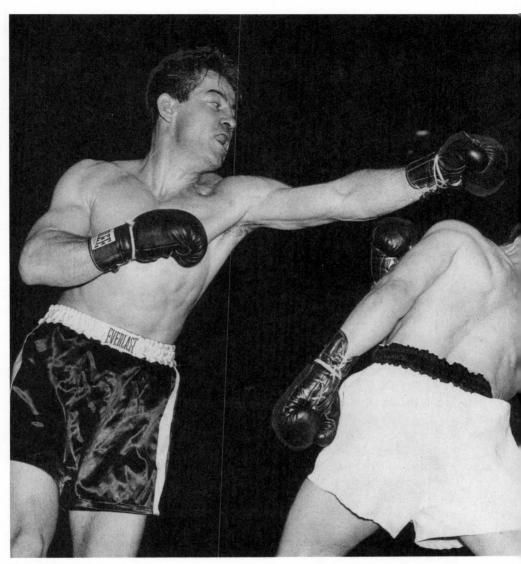

The New York Times

"Hell, I never lost a street fight. Never. I thought I could lick Jack Dempsey or Joe Louis or anybody. I was fantastic."

Graziano often made himself and his delinquent childhood the butt of jokes. "I quit school in the sixth grade because of pneumonia," he once said. "Not because I had it, but because I couldn't spell it. We stole everything that began with an *a*—a piece of fruit, a bicycle, a watch, anything that was not nailed down.

"It took me nine years to get through the fourth grade. When I got into television commercials, I had to take a crash course in reading. I was thirty-two years old and I couldn't read the cue cards."

At age twelve, he was arrested for the first time, caught breaking into a subway gum machine. While on probation, he stole a bicycle and was sent for the first of three trips to reform school.

In 1939, a friend, Jack Healy, took him to the famous Stillman's Gym in New York to see if he could put his street fighting instincts to use in the ring. When a seasoned pro named Antonio Fernandez beat him up, he swore he would never box again. Two months later, however, he was back in the ring, this time fighting under the name of his sister's boyfriend, Rocky Graziano. He won the Metropolitan Amateur Athletic Union welterweight championship.

"The AAU gave me a medal, which I hocked for fifteen dollars," Graziano recalled years later. "Maybe this is not so bad a racket after all, I think. I will give this a shake."

Graziano later served nine months in prison for going AWOL from the army. His defection, which grew out of an argument with a superior officer, led to a dishonorable discharge.

"As Rocky told it to me," said Heinz, "this captain came from behind his desk and said something like, 'You think you're so tough?'. And when the captain started to remove his jacket, Rocky hit him. He said, 'What was I supposed to do? I belted him, pow, and flattened him and took off.' "

Graziano came to be a figure beloved by the fight crowd and the public. That popularity owed as much to the good humor he showed outside the ring as to the savagery he displayed between the ropes.

"He was a natural comedian," said LaMotta. "Anything he said cracked you up. It's why he was so popular so many years. Everybody loved him 'cause he was such a nice person."

In 1956, Graziano was the subject of a film, *Somebody Up There Likes Me*, in which Paul Newman portrayed him. Later, Graziano caught on as an entertainer, his first major role being the boyfriend of the comedienne Martha Raye on her television show in the 1950s.

Graziano was unchanged by his success as an entertainer. He retained his rough-edged speech down to the "dems" and "dese," as LaMotta put it, and never put on fancy airs. He remained the Rock, ever the loveable rogue.

He died on May 22, 1990, after having suffered a stroke a month earlier. His funeral was held in St. Patrick's Cathedral in New York. He was seventy-one years old.

Leave Your Worry on the Doorstep
By IRA BERKOW

"On the Sunny Side of the Street," sung by Louis Armstrong, was playing on a tape recorder beside the laid-out body of Rocky Graziano in a room in the Frank E. Campbell Funeral Chapel in Manhattan.

It was Graziano's favorite song, and it was the wish of the family that it be played at his wake. Rocky had died of cardiopulmonary failure two nights earlier at age seventy-one. But the wake wasn't altogether a solemn occasion, because Rocky wasn't a solemn guy, even in death.

Oh, it's true that he had suffered in his last several weeks, and even months and years, from a series of ailments, but even as he lay in his coffin, in red tie and dark suit, there seemed actually to be a smile on his face.

The life had been a hard one, especially early on, in the poverty of the Lower East Side, but he had made something of himself, something even beyond the achievement he was best known for, and that was winning the middleweight championship of the world.

At that moment, when his hand was raised in the Chicago Stadium on July 16, 1947, after he knocked out the incumbent, Tony Zale, Graziano grabbed the microphone and shouted, "The bad boy done it!"

He had started off, certainly, as "a bad boy," a kid in and out of reformatories, who later joked about dropping out of school in the sixth grade because of pneumonia. "Not because I had it," he'd say, "because I couldn't spell it." He would hit an officer when he was in the army, go AWOL, and be jailed in Leavenworth for nine months.

Speaking at the wake and delivering the liturgy at the funeral Mass for Graziano in St. Patrick's Cathedral, Monsignor Anthony J. Dalla Villa called Rocky "this very good man."

There was not much from him about how hard Rocky punched, or the savage way he'd come back to knock out with that lethal right Red Cochrane twice, and Harold Green and Zale, among scores of others.

But those who came to pay their last respects to the guy with the flattened nose and the backward diction saw him as something beyond just a pug. He had made something of himself.

"He was a nice boy," said Tami Mauriello, a onetime heavyweight contender who used to work out in Stillman's Gym with Graziano, "a beautiful boy."

"Know what I learned from Rocky?" said Jake LaMotta, a boyhood friend and reform-school mate of Graziano's. "I learned you should be nice to people. He was a master at that. I had become bitter in later years from the way some people treated me, and I became like a recluse, a loner. I'd watch Rocky, and people was always comin' over to say hello. I learned that the good people overcome the bad."

"Inside the ring," said Bernie Palmer, a preliminary fighter in the 1930s, "he would do anything to win. Like when he fought Red Cochrane, a fast fighter, and both times Rocky had lost all nine rounds. But in the tenth round, the last round, of both fights he grabbed Cochrane by the throat and hit him with the right and knocked him out.

"But what I remember best about Rocky is one time a few years ago there was a banquet for old fighters and the champs were up on the dais. At that time, I'd had some problems with gambling, but I turned my life around. He said to me, 'You oughta be up on the dais. You're as much a champ as dese guys, for all you went t'rough.' "

When one of Graziano's daughters, Roxee Lifton, talked to the gathering in the funeral chapel, she recalled the advice that Rocky always gave: "Let people be who they are."

She recalled, "You would walk down the street with my father, and one block would take half an hour. Everybody wanted to shake his hand. But he wasn't doing it just for them, he was doing it for himself, too."

One old friend from the Lower East Side was talking about Rocky's wide appeal and remembered driving in a convertible with Graziano just a few years ago and stopping for red lights in Harlem and people would be shouting, "Hi, Champ! Hi, Champ!"

In 1956, Paul Newman starred as Rocky in the autobiographical film *Somebody Up There Likes Me.* At the end, Graziano, having beaten Zale for the title, comes home to New York and, in a parade, receives the applause of the multitude.

Graziano later became a television personality, doing comedy routines and commercials. Always, he played only Rocky. He was married to the same woman, the former Norma Levine, for forty-seven years. "What was the secret?" she was asked.

"I hit harder than he did," she said, smiling.

Before the Mass, a man on Fifth Avenue noticed the television cameras in front of St. Patrick's. He said to someone standing nearby, "What's going on?"

When told it was because of Rocky Graziano, the man said: "Oh, yeah. I saw the movie. Good story."

Very good story.

Champion for Life's Underdogs
By W. C. HEINZ

[EDITOR'S NOTE: *W. C. Heinz covered most of Graziano's fights as a sports columnist for the* New York Sun. *This "Views of Sport" article is reprinted here with his permission.*]

They, the participants or observers who describe a sporting event as a war, have never been in one. On the night of March 29, 1946, however, as the old Garden shook with the sound that always filled it whenever he fought, I watched from ringside as Rocky Graziano held Marty Servo's head up with his open left glove under Servo's chin and, almost in a frenzy, clubbed him again and again with his right until, finally, Servo went down for the third and last time.

It seemed to me then, and later as I tossed for hours unable to sleep, that what I had just seen emerge from man was more hate and rage and viciousness than I had ever found in those whom, months before, I had accompanied in the campaign across Northern Europe from Normandy until we met the Russians on the Elbe. Still, that wasn't the end of it.

That fight, over the weight limit, would not cost Servo his new welterweight title, but that beating would. He would give up the title, and the security it could have brought him, without ever defending it. Then, one evening two years later, Irving Cohen, who managed him, Teddy Brenner, and I were following Graziano down Eighth Avenue in Manhattan.

"Where are we going?" I asked Cohen, as ahead of us Graziano, with those quick, nervous steps, dodged pedestrians and then, crossing the street, the moving traffic.

"We're going to the place where Marty Servo tends bar," Cohen said. "Rocky likes him, and he always tries to bring business into the place."

When we walked in, Servo, in a white jacket, his arms folded across his chest, was standing behind the bar. As he saw us, his face brightened. Then he reached over the bar, and as he shook hands with Graziano, he faked as if to throw a left hook. Graziano, leaning over the bar, stuck his left hand under Servo's chin as he had that night, and he faked to start the right hand. Then the two of them dropped their hands and laughed.

That came as no surprise, but rather as an affirmation. On the night of the previous July 16, in a shower room in the bowels of the Chicago Stadium, Graziano was standing naked, the shower water still on him. In the sixth round in the second of those furious fights with Tony Zale and in that 120-degree heat under the ring lights, he had knocked out Zale to win the middleweight championship of the world.

Now a clamp held closed the cut over his left eye, there was still some swelling under his right eye, and the sportswriters were coming at him, yelling their questions.

"How did you feel in there?" one of them shouted.

"I wanted to kill him," he said. "I got nothing against him. He's a nice guy. I like him, but I wanted to kill him."

He had nothing against any of them. It always seemed to me that his opponent was not the other fighter but society, and that the punches he threw were the payback for the hurts that, admittedly, he had invited and that society had inflicted on him in reform school, jail, and finally Leavenworth after he had slugged that captain at Camp Dix.

Every fighter who makes it forever out of a ghetto is an advertisement for an endeavor ever castigated by the comfortable, who call for its abolition. Graziano, one of seven children of an emotionally and mentally disturbed mother and an alcoholic father, had a fifth-grade education and ran wild on New York's Lower East Side with some who would do twenty-to-life in Sing Sing and some who would die by gunfire on the street. What were his chances on the tennis circuit, the pro golf tour, or brokering stocks and bonds?

"I just made the Big One!" he told me about twenty-five years ago.

"The Big One?" I said.

"A million bucks," he said. "My accountant just told me. How about that?"

And how about the quarter, the two bits, that Frank Percoco, a corner-man, happened to have in his pocket that night in Chicago? At the end of the fifth round, as Graziano dropped onto the stool, blood from a cut over his left eye was seeping into it, blinding it, and the swelling under his right eye had closed it.

"I can't see no more," he said, gasping, as Whitey Bimstein, his trainer, started to work on a cut that was beyond repair. It was then that Percoco reached into his pants pocket, found the quarter, and pressing it flat against the swelling under the right eye, forced the flesh down.

"I can see now," Graziano said, and he went out and finished Zale.

With the middleweight title came all that was to follow: *Somebody Up There Likes Me,* his autobiography, from which they made the film starring Paul Newman; the Martha Raye show on television; personal appearances; and the dozens of commercials over the years.

"You and Zale were perfectly matched to make great fights," I said. "Then you and Martha Raye were another great pair."

"I go to the office," Graziano said, describing his audition for the Raye show. "I meet Marlon Brando and they give me a stupid script. Big words I can't pronounce. Nat Hiken, the writer, says, 'Don't worry. The public doesn't know what the script is.' I go on and guys are sayin', 'Great! Great!' I'm playin' myself."

He always did. The Christmas of the first year he had any money, he bought a secondhand Cadillac and filled it with $1,500 worth of toys. He drove it down to his old East Side neighborhood and unloaded the toys on the kids and another $1,500 on their parents. He never mentioned it. It came out because a trainer from Stillman's Gym saw it.

"Look, Rocky," Cohen said to him. "It's nice to do things like that, but you haven't got that kind of money, and you've got to save money. You won't be fighting forever."

"Sure, Irving," he said, "but those are poor people. They're good people. They never done no wrong. They never hurt nobody. They just never got a break."

In that shower room in Chicago Stadium, before they let the rest of the press in, there was only that uniformed fireman with us guarding the door. I had to ask the obligatory, obvious question.

"Well," I said, "the world is a big place, and how does it feel to be the middleweight champion of it?"

"I don't know," he said, bruised, exhausted, leaning back and resting an arm on the shower handles, trying to think and to talk. "I don't know. . . . I mean . . . I mean as a kid . . . I mean I was no good. . . . I mean nobody ever. . . . You know what I mean?"

"I know what you mean, Rocky," the fireman said. "You're giving a talk on democracy."

"I mean I never . . ." Graziano said, and then he turned and looked at the fireman and he said, "You're a good guy. You're all right. You know what I mean?"

Later that night, when he got back to the hotel where his wife, Norma, had waited, unable even to listen to the fight on the radio, the party had already started. The noise of it awakened their first daughter, Audrey, and she began to cry. When he went into the bedroom and bent over the crib, she looked up at that face with the bandage over one eye and with the swelling under the other one.

"Daddy, what happened?" she said.

"You see what I mean now?" he said. "Stay out of the gutter."

That was the Rocky Graziano I knew.

HANK GREENBERG

1911–1986

H ANK GREENBERG was the boy from the Bronx who grew up to become a Hall of Fame slugger.

Henry Benjamin Greenberg was born January 1, 1911, and spent his youth first in Manhattan's Greenwich Village and then in the Bronx.

After graduating from James Monroe High School, he enrolled at New York University on an athletic scholarship in 1929 but dropped out to sign a baseball contract for $9,000 a year. He thus began a long career in professional baseball as a player, executive, and team owner after refusing to listen to Paul Krichell, the Yankee scout, who tried to sign him to a contract.

"As a high school ball player," Greenberg recalled in his later years, "I turned down a chance to be part of the Yankee farm system. I was a slugging first baseman and the Yankees had the greatest in Lou Gehrig. So I chose Detroit."

By his own admission, Greenberg was "a pretty gosh-awful player in my younger days." But he became a polished player through hard work. He hired peanut vendors and park attendants every morning to help him with his hitting and fielding.

After one time at bat with the Tigers in 1930, he returned to the minors until 1933, when he rejoined the Tigers for good. He spent twelve of his thirteen seasons with Detroit as a first baseman and a left fielder. He led the American League in home runs five times and runs batted in four times.

He retired in 1947 after playing one season with the Pittsburgh Pirates, to whom he had been sold. In that one season in Pittsburgh, Greenberg became the highest-paid player in baseball.

When he threatened to retire, John Galbreath, the owner of the Pirates, signed him to a $65,000 contract, plus options. Greenberg sold back those options after the season, thus attaining what was believed to be the first $100,000 contract.

Greenberg enjoyed his best season in 1938 when, in addition to hitting 58 home runs, he drove in 146 runs. He also scored 144 runs and drew 119 walks that season, both tops in the league. The 58 home runs, at the time second best to Babe Ruth's 60, equaled the 1932 feat by Jimmie Foxx of the Philadelphia Athletics.

But Greenberg, who hit 331 homers and had a .313 lifetime batting average, counted the 1945 season as his greatest. After returning from army service to the Tigers on July 1, he hit a home run before a crowd of 47,721 and led the

96

Tigers in their pennant fight with the Washington Senators that was culminated by a grand slam on the final day of the season.

Greenberg played in four World Series with the Tigers—1934, 1935, 1940, and 1945, in which he compiled a .318 career batting average.

He was drafted into the army on May 7, 1941, the first baseball star to go into the service. He was discharged on December 5, 1941, under a rule allowing those over the age of twenty-eight to cut short their terms. When Japan attacked Pearl Harbor on December 7 he enlisted in the Army Air Corps.

After hitting only 25 homers, driving in 74 runs and batting .249 in 1947 with the Pirates, he retired. The following year he bought a share of the Cleveland Indians from Bill Veeck, one of his closest friends. He later became the club's general manager.

He was dismissed after the 1957 season, and when Veeck purchased the White Sox in 1959, Greenberg was one of the first people he brought to Chicago, naming him vice president and general manager.

Greenberg, who was the American League's Most Valuable Player in 1935 and again in 1940, was elected to the Baseball Hall of Fame in 1956, the first Jewish player to be chosen.

On September 4, 1986, he died of cancer at the age of seventy-five.

A Kind of Beacon

By IRA BERKOW

One afternoon Hank Greenberg, in tennis togs, stopped beside the pool of a Las Vegas hotel to chat with friends. Greenberg, then sixty-five years old and still vigorous at 6 feet 4 inches and 220 pounds, was there to participate in a celebrity tennis tournament.

The talk got around to 1947, when he played first base for the Pittsburgh Pirates. It was a terrible team, a team, he would recall, that in the clubhouse regularly had a record player blaring, and the favorite song was "Cigareetes, Whusky, and Wild, Wild Women."

That was in Greenberg's last season as a baseball player, the end of a thirteen-year career in which he established himself as one of baseball's greatest sluggers and catapulted himself into baseball's Hall of Fame.

"I wasn't used to this kind of team—this losing, and a lot of these guys drinking and carousing," said Greenberg. "I had been with the Tigers for twelve seasons, and we won four pennants and two World Series and everything was serious and bent on winning.

"Not the Pirates. Billy Herman was in his first year as a manager. He was a nice guy, maybe too nice, and he just locked the door of his office and didn't want to know what the players were doing.

"Well, one afternoon, one of the players got married and a bunch of the guys attended and got looped. We had a game that night. I think Kirby Higbe was pitching for us, and guys were making errors all over the place."

Now Greenberg stood, laughing, to demonstrate. "And Kirby—" Suddenly, Greenberg grabbed one leg, and began to hop around. "A cramp!" he moaned. "A cramp!"

He grimaced, yet still laughed—and was determined to finish the story. "Herman comes out to the mound to get Higbe out of there," said Greenberg. "Oh! Oh! My leg!—And Higbe—Higbe—Oh!" Greenberg's grabbing his leg and laughing as he nears the punch line. "Higbe says, 'I can't pitch when they're drunk out there.' " Greenberg is hopping here and there. "And Herman says, 'Who's drunk?' And Higbe—Higbe—Higbe says, 'Everyone!' "

And Greenberg collapsed into a chair, laughing and moaning, as he ended the story.

On September 4, 1986, Henry Benjamin Greenberg, born on Perry Street in Greenwich Village on January 1, 1911, and raised in the Bronx, came to another end. He died of cancer at age seventy-five, at his home in Beverly Hills, California. Like that story he told many years ago, his life was lived fully all the way to the end, and was filled with elements both funny and painful.

He had been a clumsy player in his youth, but with determination became a star. His high school coach at James Monroe once said, "Greenberg doesn't play baseball, he works at baseball." As a major leaguer, he hired ushers and peanut vendors to shag flies when he regularly took extra batting practice. He became a general manager with the Cleveland Indians and later part-owner of the Chicago White Sox, until his retirement from baseball in 1965. He learned the stock market so ably that he became a rich man from his investments.

I never saw Hank Greenberg play, but he was a legendary ball player to many, especially in Jewish households, like mine. He was the first truly great Jewish ball player and, ironically, a power hitter in the 1930s when the position of Jews in the world—especially, of course, in Hitler's Germany—grew weaker.

I remember my uncles talking about Greenberg's baseball exploits as if he were a kind of beacon for them—of the year he drove in a remarkable 183 runs, and of his homers. In 1938 he had 58 home runs with five games left in the season, and had a great shot to break Babe Ruth's record of 60. The rumor, said my uncles, was that because of anti-Semitism pitchers wouldn't pitch to him down the stretch.

I once asked Hank about that. Not true, he said. "I got some hits and hit some balls hard, but I couldn't get one over the fence," he said. "In fact, there were people in baseball rooting for me to break the record." He recalled trying for an inside-the-park homer late in the season in which the umpire called him safe at home, "when I was really out."

But, he would recall, there were "remarks about my being a sheenie and a Jew all the time." During the 1935 World Series, it became so vicious that Umpire George Moriarty went to the Cubs' bench and made them stop.

Greenberg said he tried to carry himself with dignity because he understood that he was a symbol for many Jews in America. There were a few times, though, when he fought with his fists to stop remarks, on one occasion even battling a teammate.

Greenberg wasn't religious, but he believed he should observe Yom Kippur. He sat out a game that day in 1934, in the heat of a September pennant drive. That day, a Detroit newspaper bore a headline in Hebrew. Above it was the English translation: "Happy New Year, Hank."

When Greenberg returned from serving in the Army Air Corps during World War II, he rejoined the Tigers midway through the 1945 season. On the last day of the season, he hit a grand slam in the ninth inning to win the pennant for the Tigers.

In 1947, when Jackie Robinson broke the color barrier in the major leagues, Greenberg was at first base when the Dodgers played the Pirates for the first time that season.

Greenberg recalled, "Guys on our team were calling Jackie, 'Coal Mine. Hey, we'll get you, Coal Mine.' He got a hit and stood beside me on first base with his chin up, like a prince. I had a feeling for him because of the way I had been treated. I remember saying to him, 'Don't let them get you down. You're doing fine. Keep it up.'" Robinson later said that Greenberg was the first opposing player in the big leagues to give him encouragement. "Hank Greenberg," said Robinson, "has class. It stands out all over him."

Hank Greenberg was a special man in special times. He would have been a special man in any time.

LEFTY GROVE

1900–1975

ROBERT MOSES "LEFTY" GROVE, a member of baseball's Hall of Fame, was a star pitcher with Connie Mack's Philadelphia Athletics in the 1920s and 1930s and won 300 major league games.

The fiery left-hander chalked up a phenomenal winning percentage of .682 with the Athletics and later the Boston Red Sox. There were eight seasons in which he won 20 or more games—once registering 31 victories, this during the 1931 season. That year was generally considered his best—he lost only four games.

In a seventeen-year major league career, Mr. Grove recorded 2,266 strikeouts and posted a lifetime earned-run average of 3.06.

He joined the Athletics in 1925 after four outstanding seasons with Baltimore of the International League.

He started a string of seven consecutive 20-victory seasons in 1927, reaching 28 wins and 5 losses in 1930. Coupled with his outstanding performance in 1931, his 59–9 won-loss record for two consecutive seasons is an achievement never since equaled.

Mr. Grove tied the American League record of 16 consecutive victories in the summer of 1931 and shared that record with Walter Johnson, Joe Wood, and Linwood "Schoolboy" Rowe.

Lefty Grove pitched only to win, and when he didn't win he could make life hard for teammates and others. He had one of the hottest tempers in the major leagues.

However, one of the biggest blows he suffered did not make him angry. Uncharacteristically, he was left speechless.

That blow fell December 9, 1941, when he received his unconditional release from the Boston Red Sox and the other fifteen major league clubs waived on the forty-year-old hurler.

Actually, the Grove pitching story ended on July 25, 1941, when he struggled to a 10–6 victory over the Cleveland Indians. This was the pitcher's 300th and last major league triumph.

Grove tried time and again before he posted his 300th.

Born March 6, 1900, Grove never cared much about baseball until he was asked to play for a company team in his hometown of Lonaconing, Maryland. He was noticed by a scout and signed in 1920 to play professional ball for the Blue Ridge League.

In 1925, Connie Mack, owner and manager of the Philadelphia Athletics,

purchased him for $100,600. At the time it was a record price. According to stories of the time, the price was made $600 higher than the price the Yanks paid for Babe Ruth just for the sake of a record.

Grove was sold to the Red Sox for $125,000 in 1934.

It was Mack who had the best success in handling the hot-tempered pitcher. Once after he had lost a 1–0 decision to the St. Louis Browns he got angry at his teammates, who had three hits. Later that night, Mack said to him, "Robert, didn't Coffman [the Browns' pitcher] pitch a wonderful game? We made only three hits and we wouldn't have scored a run if we'd been still playing."

Grove came around to his manager's way of thinking and calmed down in his attitude toward his teammates.

He had his own ideas of what were his best performances and liked to recall some. Among his favorite accomplishments was the time he struck out Lou Gehrig, Babe Ruth, and Bob Meusel on nine pitches in a game in which the Yankees had the tying run on third in the ninth inning. Another feat was his striking out of Ruth, Gehrig, and Tony Lazzeri on ten pitches, with bases loaded.

Grove, who was voted to baseball's Hall of Fame in 1947, finished his seventeen-year major league career with 300 victories and 141 defeats.

The Terrible-Tempered Mr. Grove

By RED SMITH

Lefty Grove was a pitcher who, in the classic words of Bugs Baer, "could throw a lamb chop past a wolf." One day in Yankee Stadium he threw them past three wolves named Babe Ruth, Lou Gehrig, and Bob Meusel. The Philadelphia Athletics were leading, 1–0, when Mark Koenig led off the Yankees' ninth inning with a triple. Grove threw three pitches to Ruth, three to Gehrig, and three to Meusel, all strikes. Meusel hit one of them foul. Another time Grove relieved Jack Quinn with the bases full of Yankees. That day it required ten pitches to strike out Ruth, Gehrig, and Tony Lazzeri, who hit two fouls. In still another game he relieved Roy Mahaffey in Chicago with runners on second and third and nobody out. Again he struck out the side on ten pitches. Don Honig's book *Baseball When the Grass Was Real* includes George Pipgras's account of batting against Walter Johnson for the first time. He took two strikes, stepped out of the box and said to Muddy Ruel, Johnson's catcher, "Muddy, I never saw those pitches."

"Don't let it worry you," Muddy said. "He's thrown a few that Cobb and Speaker are still looking for."

Grove's fastball was like that, but he didn't have Johnson's comforting control. (One season when Johnson won 34 games he gave up only 38 bases on balls; batters could oppose this gentleman confident that they wouldn't be hit in the head by accident or design.) Along with his blinding swift, Grove had the quality that Uncle Wilbert Robinson described as "pleasingly wild."

"But Groves wasn't a pitcher in those days," Connie Mack once said. "He was a thrower until after we sold him to Boston and he hurt his arm. Then he learned to pitch, and he got so he just knew, somehow, when the batter was going to swing."

It was typical of Connie Mack that he could pay an all-time record of $100,600 for a man, manage the guy for nine years, win three pennants and two world championships with him, and never learn to pronounce his name. To Connie, Lefty was always "Groves," Lou Boudreau was "Mr. Bordeer," and Zeke Bonura and Babe Barna were both "Bernair."

In his later years, Robert Moses Grove was a tall, genial gentleman with a head of lustrous white hair who loved to sit around at baseball gatherings cutting up old touches. Lefty Grove, who threw bullets past Ruth and Gehrig and the rest, stood 6 foot 3 and wore an expression of sulky anger stuck on top of a long, thin neck.

He was a fierce competitor who made little effort to subdue a hair-trigger temper. His natural speed had dazzled and overpowered minor league hitters, and he wasn't accustomed to adversity when he got to the American League. When things went bad, he raged blindly, blaming anybody who was handy.

One team that drove him wild was the Washington Senators. Before reaching the majors he had worked against them in an exhibition game. He was wild, and they combed him over without mercy. When Clark Griffith heard about his old friend Connie paying all that money for Grove, he said it would be a cold day in August before that busher ever beat his club, or words to that effect. Chances are some thoughtful soul relayed the remark to Grove. At any rate, the Senators whipped him the first seventeen times he worked against them.

Lefty threw his most memorable tantrum in St. Louis on August 23, 1931. He had won sixteen straight, tying the American League record shared by Smoky Joe Wood and Walter Johnson, and was going for his seventeenth against the tractable St. Louis Browns. While Dick Coffman was pitching a shutout, Goose Goslin got a bloop single off Grove and ran home when Jimmy Moore, a substitute for the injured Al Simmons in left field, misjudged an ordinary liner by Jack Burns. Beaten, 1–0, Grove took the visitors' clubhouse apart locker by locker, cursing Moore, Coffman, Goslin, Burns, and especially Simmons, who was home in Milwaukee consulting his doctor.

The press found Grove surly and laconic and put him away as a grouch, although it wouldn't have been hard to discover what made him the way he was. A product of the bituminous fields of the western Maryland mountains, he had little experience with strangers and no exposure to social graces. People who had more schooling than he or had traveled more widely made him uneasy. Retreating into a shell, he became one of the great lobby sitters of his time, a graven image shrouded in cigar smoke.

On the mound he was poetry. He would rock back until the knuckles of his left hand almost brushed the earth behind him, then come up and over with the perfect follow-through. He was the only 300-game winner between Grover Alexander and Warren Spahn, a span of thirty-seven years. He had the lowest earned-run average in the league nine different years, and nobody else ever did that more than five times. If the old records can be trusted, Alexander, Christy

Mathewson, Johnson, and Sandy Koufax each won five ERA titles. Some men would say these were the best pitchers that ever lived. Are the records trying to tell us Old Man Mose was twice as good as any of them?

Grove held at least one record that doesn't appear in the books. In 1920 Martinsburg, West Virginia, got a franchise in the Blue Ridge League and hired Grove at $125 a month. Martinsburg had no ball parks, but the team opened on the road and a little jerrybuilt grandstand was flung up before the first home game. There was no money for a fence, however, so Grove was sold to Jack Dunn's Baltimore team for $3,000. That makes Old Mose the only player ever traded for an outfield fence.

WALTER HAGEN

1892–1969

By ALDEN WHITMAN

I N THE 1920s, the "golden era of sports," Walter Charles Hagen was a giant in professional golf, a man mentioned in the same breath as Bobby Jones, the king of the amateurs.

A fabulous player, an elegant dresser, and a truly impressive bon vivant, The Haig (as Hagen was generally known) captivated the public imagination as much for his resplendent personality as for his prowess with mashie and putter.

He elevated the professional golfer from his role as a country club hireling to the status of a friend of royalty and a man of means. Former King Edward VIII of England was "Eddie" to Hagen, and, as the Prince of Wales, he delighted in being ordered to hold the flag for a Hagen putt.

Hagen made one of his last public appearances in August 1967 at a testimonial sponsored by his friends. Arnold Palmer, in a moving tribute to a man he idolized, said, "If it were not for you, Walter, this dinner tonight would be downstairs in the pro shop and not in the ballroom."

Hagen earned a lot of money—he put it at a million dollars—and he spent it as easily as he made it.

From 1914, when he won his first championship, the United States Open, until 1929, when he retired from competition, Hagen won seventeen major golf titles, gathered laurels, and entranced galleries in every country in which the game was played. He appeared in more than 2,500 exhibitions, made thousands of friends, and led a life that was the envy of and the pattern for his fellow professionals.

"He is in golf to live, not to make a living," Chick Evans, one of Hagen's contemporaries, once observed. But there was pride, too, for Hagen retired, he said, because "I couldn't stand the thought of possibly shooting an eighty."

Hagen's major championships were two United States Opens (1914 and 1919); five Professional Golf Association titles (1921, 1924, 1925, 1926, and 1927); four British Opens (1922, 1924, 1928, and 1929); five Western Opens; and one Canadian Open. He also was captain of the American Ryder Cup teams in 1927, 1929, 1931, 1933, 1935, and 1937, and was the nonplaying captain in 1948.

Of all Hagen's victories, the most satisfying was a one-sided triumph over Jones in a special 72-hole match in Florida in 1926.

"Everybody was saying Jones was the greatest golfer in the world and I was second best," Hagen recalled later. "It rankled me a bit, so I got a friend to arrange the match—36 holes over Bob's course at Sarasota and 36 over mine at St. Petersburg.

"I had an eight-hole lead leaving Sarasota and went on to win. It was my greatest thrill in golf."

But Hagen did not let his victory obscure his esteem for Jones's golf. When a sportswriters' poll in 1950 picked Jones as the greatest golfer of the half-century (Hagen was third and Ben Hogan second), Hagen remarked, "I would have voted for Jones myself. He was marvelous."

Hagen was an immaculate dresser and his attire helped to revolutionize wearing apparel on the golf course. He is credited with introducing plus fours—knickerbockers for men—to golfing. He also made the camel's hair coat standard equipment for the well-dressed golfer.

A 6-footer and trim about the waist and jowls in his prime, Hagen looked handsome in a dress suit. His sleek black hair added to the suave impression that he gave at dances and at parties. Some of these lasted all night, and Hagen, not one to go to bed while the fun was on, sometimes showed up for a morning golf engagement in a dress shirt. His game on such occasions was not noticeably affected.

Hagen was renowned for his devastating mashie shots and his marvelous putting skill. He was frequently in trouble off the tee, so that his talent with the irons was essential. A serene disposition, an almost faultless aplomb, and a knowledge of psychology were also a part of his wizardry.

An example of his guile was the PGA final at Westbury, Long Island, in 1926. Hagen began by conceding six- and eight-foot putts to his opponent, Leo Diegel. Then, late in the match, when pressure had mounted, Diegel had a simple 25-incher. He glanced at Hagen for another concession, but the Haig turned away.

"There must be a hidden roll," Diegel said nervously. He missed his putt, and Hagen went on to win.

On another occasion Hagen's ball was fifteen feet from the cup while his opponent's was half that distance. Hagen broke into a grin.

"What's the joke?" his opponent asked.

"I was just thinking how much harder your putt will look after I make mine," Hagen replied.

Hagen went on to sink his putt with ease. His opponent missed.

He unnerved his opponents still more by the way he played. He would ponder an easy shot, creating the impression that it was difficult and thereby eliciting whoops of joy from the gallery when he made it. "Impossible" shots Hagen made with debonair ease, and this, too, threw his adversaries off.

Hagen had, moreover, a Babe Ruthian confidence in himself. To win the British Open in 1924 he had to get a 4 on the last hole to nose out E. R. Whitcombe. It was a rainy day and the greens were slippery. He wound up by having to drop a six-foot putt to carry off the cup.

With scarcely a glance at the flag, Hagen hit the ball and, without waiting to see where it went, tossed his club to the caddy and started off the green. He didn't actually know what had happened to the ball until the crowd's roar told him that it had gone into the hole.

He had, too, an unmatched insouciance. Members at one golf club bet him

$3,000 he couldn't equal the course mark of 68. He reached the final green, needing only a 12-foot putt to make good.

"Step up, suckers, and pay me," he sang out. Then he holed the putt.

Hagen was often late for golf appointments. One such occasion, a match in Tokyo with Prince Konoye, gave rise to a celebrated remark. Hagen arrived two hours late, and a nervous aide to the prince said, "The prince has been waiting since ten o'clock."

"Well, he wasn't going anywhere, was he?" Hagen shot back.

The prince wasn't, and the two played amiably.

Hagen was a splendid competitor, even when he wasn't at the top of his form. His last PGA championship, at Dallas in 1927, was one example. He had at first no intention of defending the title he had won three times in succession. He was, in fact, on a fishing expedition in Wisconsin and hadn't touched a club for weeks when he decided to compete.

"Well, I just got to thinking that if I didn't play," he explained, "much of the credit would be taken away from the man who won. People would say, 'It would have been different if Hagen had played.' I didn't think I had one chance in a million to win for the fourth consecutive time."

When Hagen appeared in Dallas, it was just in time to play the qualifying round. He not only qualified, despite his rustiness, but he also went on to defeat Al Espinosa and Joe Turnesa for the title.

To win four times in a row meant that Hagen took 24 consecutive matches. Actually, he did better than that, for after losing to his archrival, Gene Sarazen, in the final round of the 1923 PGA event, he did not suffer defeat until he bowed to Diegel in the third round of the 1928 play.

Hagen disdained thrift. He once collected $3,000 on a Canadian tour and just before leaving Winnipeg for home he telephoned the hotel where he was stopping and told the manager, "Fill the bathtub with ale and champagne and break out your best Scotch. The party's on me."

When he returned to the United States he had less money than when he began the tour.

Hagen got $500 as his first British Open prize and gave it all to his caddy. His tips were rarely less than $20, and it was not all for showmanship. He was genuinely openhanded and carefree.

Hagen did a great deal to break down the caste barriers behind which golf professionals had been herded. In many country clubs here and abroad the professionals had to use the servants' entrance, and they were not permitted in the dining room or the bar.

His triumphs obliged the snobbish to seek him out, and for his friendship he insisted upon his social due. He got it, and so did professionals that followed him.

Hagen left his imprint in another way, too, in that he was a model for such caddies as Sarazen and Johnny Farrell, who rose to fame.

Caddying was how Hagen got his start. He was born in Rochester, New York, December 21, 1892, the son of William and Louise Balko Hagen. His father was a blacksmith.

When he was five years old, he began playing with a discarded golf club left at his home by a local professional. He started caddying at nine, and spent a lot of his spare time in the pro shop of the Rochester Country Club, where he swept the floor and polished clubs. He practiced whenever he could, and when he was eleven years old he broke 80.

He had a chance to play baseball for the Philadelphia Phillies, but decided against it after high school. He made his competitive golf debut at twenty at the United States Open in Brookline, Massachusetts, and he finished only three strokes away from making it a four-way tie for the championship.

From that time until he retired Hagen was not often out of the money, or out of the sports headlines. When he was not playing for titles, he was engaged in exhibition matches.

Joe Kirkwood, an Australian trick-shot artist, was a frequent companion in these matches, which contributed greatly to popularizing golf as a game for everyone, not just the wealthy and idle.

After his retirement Hagen kept only a business attachment to golf as head of the Walter Hagen Division of the Wilson Sporting Goods Company.

Living near Detroit he renewed his interest in baseball as a fan of the Detroit Tigers. He did some hunting and fishing and wrote a book, *The Walter Hagen Story*, that Simon & Schuster published in 1956.

He was elected to the Golf Hall of Fame. In 1961 he was given the Walter Hagen Award of the Golf Writers Association of America. The following year the Metropolitan Golf Writers Association bestowed its Gold Tee Award on him at a dinner in New York.

Although he was obliged to give up even friendly golf because of a heart condition, Hagen often turned up in the clubhouse at big tournaments. Older, more fleshy, and scarcely able to talk, he nonetheless liked to chat about the game and to meet those who had followed in his footsteps.

He died of cancer on October 6, 1969, at the age of seventy-six.

Such a Marvel

By WILLIAM D. RICHARDSON

What is there about him that makes Walter Hagen such a marvel when it comes to match play? Is it that he is so far superior to his fellow professionals? Was he born under a lucky star? Does he bear a charmed life?

Questions such as these were asked and discussed after Hagen won the PGA championship for the fourth year in succession in 1927. Walter was always an interesting figure in golf, but never the outstanding man he became through that triumph over men and nature at the Cedar Crest Country Club in Dallas.

Not often has it happened that in a game fraught with so many uncertainties as golf one man is able to dominate his field the way Hagen did his for those four years. In fact, never before had there been an instance where the same man has won a major title four times running, especially at match play.

Having followed Hagen's career through those four years, having been in a position to watch him play many notable matches down that stretch of years and to talk with him about them afterward, the writer feels qualified to set down a few observations that may shed some light on some of the questions that Hagen's triumph brought.

Hagen's main asset, we are inclined to think, was his head. Others, his mechanical equals, maybe superiors, had to give way to him when it came to headwork on the links. An incident that happened in the course of one of Hagen's matches in Texas will serve to illustrate the point.

He was faced with a difficult putt on a green with a double roll. It being autumn, the ground was covered with leaves, and Hagen, instead of picking up each and every one that was between his ball and the hole, as most golfers would do, left two as "markers." By so doing he knew exactly where to aim.

Robert Cruikshank, watching the match, was quick to observe the strategy. "What do you know about that?" he asked. "Did you see him use those leaves as markers? Had I been in that situation there wouldn't have been a leaf left on the green, and here The Haig uses them as sights. We live to learn new tricks every day."

Now for a second asset—confidence in himself. Hagen was a great believer in Hagen. Not that he was a braggart. He wasn't. He was a swaggerer. His swagger on the links was nothing more nor less than a pose designed to mask his own inward feelings and emotions and, if possible, to have an effect on the man he happened to be playing against. No matter how the tide of battle happened to be running, whether it was with or against, one would always see Hagen stamping forward—long, big, confident strides; chest out, head up.

We saw him at Olympia Fields in 1925 when he was three down to Diegel with four holes left to play; more recently we saw him when he was apparently beaten by young Jack Farrell in the first round at Cedar Crest and by Espinosa in the semifinal. Against Diegel and Espinosa he had every reason to believe that his end had come, but did his face show it? No. Not once in all the time we trailed after Hagen did we ever see him evince a single outward sign that betrayed doubt of his ability to pull through somehow.

In this same connection it is interesting to learn how Hagen came to defend his title at Dallas. It illustrates not only his self-confidence, but his sense of fairness.

Few persons know that up to within two weeks or so of the PGA event Hagen had definitely decided to let his title go by default. He had played little if any golf between then and the time he won the Western Open in September. He was out of shape physically and not in playing form.

"I had figured that the odds were all against my winning the championship again and decided to rest on my oars and let it go at that," he said on the way back from Dallas. "I'd won the thing four times, three years in succession, so why flirt with trouble?

"And then I happened to look at it another way. I looked at it from the point of view of the fellow who would win without me in it, and I decided it was only fair for me to come and take my medicine and let the winner take all the glory there was coming to him."

Walter was perfectly sincere about it all. With him away, the victory would be a more or less hollow one for the next champion, for there would always be those who would say, "Well, Hagen wasn't there. If he had been, So-and-So might not have won."

Having checked up and found that the facts were exactly as Hagen had stated them, we returned with a greater feeling of admiration for Hagen than we ever cherished before.

Having decided to defend his title, and as he was prepared to do, to sacrifice himself in order that the man who won might receive full credit, did Hagen repair at once to the nearest golf course and begin to practice? He did not. Instead he went up into the north woods of Wisconsin and began getting himself in shape physically.

He went to Dallas, therefore, out of practice, but decidedly keen, more keen, perhaps, than anybody else who was there. The others had spent weeks preparing for the ordeal. Hagen played only one practice round prior to the championship and then stepped out on the qualifying day and led the field by three strokes.

There is still another attribute which Hagen had in abundance—nerve. He could play the game safely if he had to or if it served his purpose best, but let the match get tight and he was as bold as a pirate. Look at those second shots he played on the last two holes against Espinosa if you don't believe it—the one at the thirty-sixth hole and the other at the thirty-seventh.

Each one was right at the flag, not below it. What mattered it to Hagen if the holes were cut on the upper side of the green and if the slightest miscalculation would send his ball into the rough and cost him the match? Not a thing. He gave the ball a chance. He always did that. The one thing that seemed to annoy him in a golf match is cowardice on a pitch or an approach putt. He knew full well that the hole, being stationary, cannot meet the ball halfway.

A great deal was written concerning Hagen's baiting his opponents. He was accused of divers acts of unsportsmanship designed to get an opponent's "goat." He was severely censured for causing Abe Mitchell to wait on the tee for such a long period in their now famous 72-hole match in England that poor Abe was in a state of nervous exhaustion when Hagen finally did appear.

Although late arrival at the tee is a breach of etiquette that cannot be condoned, we are inclined to think that the mere thought of Hagen as an opponent had as much to do with Mitchell's collapse as Walter's delay, which, it was later shown, was not his fault but that of some officials.

Last we come to Hagen's main asset—his ability to forget to remember a bad shot or a series of bad shots.

When he went out to play a round of golf, be it in match or medal play, Hagen resigned himself to the thought that he was bound to make some errors, that he was certain to miss some putts, and that all the breaks would not be in his favor. He figured the adversities first, and then, when they did come, he was not put out by them.

At a critical point in the final match of the PGA tourney, Turnesa, his opponent, hit a crooked second shot, and the ball was prevented from doing a disappearing act into the woods only because it happened to strike a spectator standing at the green. It was a good break for Turnesa, a bad one for Hagen.

It meant that instead of winning the hole he might not even get a half, for Joe's ball was closer to the hole than his was in spite of the fact that he had played a fine second.

Instead of gnashing his teeth and pulling his hair, Hagen holed the long putt for a birdie 3 and won the hole anyway.

Playing any round of golf, Hagen makes up his mind in advance that he is going to get four fives. "What does it matter," he asked, "whether they come on the first four holes, in the middle, or at the end of the round? If I happen to start out with four fives I simply figure that I've used up my quota. I forget them and start out on a new tack.

"Another mistake golfers often make is to figure their scores by nines. If they take 40 going out, they become panic-stricken over the thought that they've got to come home in 35 or less in order to get a good score. Or, if they go out in 34, they become equally panic-stricken over the thought that they may take 40 coming in.

"Why make the ninth hole the one where all reckoning takes place? If I have some good holes to start with, I figure that I have some bad ones due me and make allowance for them; if I get a bad start, I don't wait until the ninth hole to start a rally. What's the matter with the sixth or the seventh?"

What can you do with a fellow possessing such a philosophy as that?

Ask Diegel, Barnes, Espinosa, Mitchell, Jones, Watrous, Turnesa, Armour, and all the rest. Maybe they know!

GEORGE HALAS

1895–1983

F OR FIFTY YEARS, George Stanley Halas ruled as one of the pioneers
and pillars of professional football, the coach and owner of the Chicago
Bears, the mastermind of the legendary Halas U., the creator of the Monsters
of the Midway, the Papa Bear.

The son of a Czechoslovak tailor, he became one of the founders of the
National Football League, its most successful coach, and the absolute baron of
the sport in Chicago. He also was one of the men who kept football alive in the
early days when players traveled by bus or trolley car and were paid by the
game, and he lasted into the postwar era of television and $500,000 bonuses for
college seniors.

As an athlete, he endured violent careers for a time in both baseball and
football. He tried out with the New York Yankees in 1919, went to bat against
the great Rube Marquard of the Brooklyn Dodgers in spring training, hit a triple
off the center-field fence, and injured his right hip sliding into third base. He
played in only nineteen games with the Yankees after that, batted .091, retired
with a damaged hip, and as he observed later, was "replaced" in right field by
Babe Ruth.

In football, he once punched the ball out of the hands of the celebrated
Jim Thorpe, recovered the fumble, and ran 98 yards. It was 1920, and Halas
was the playing coach of the Decatur Staleys of the American Professional
Football Association; Thorpe was the president of the league. Thorpe caught
him at the goal line, and with a vicious tackle knocked him into the end zone
for a touchdown.

As a coach, Halas was a fundamentalist in strategy, a master of the
T formation, a worrier who stalked the sidelines flinging his battered hat onto
the ground, and a sentimentalist who held "alumni reunions" for graduates of
his team. His players included Red Grange, Bronko Nagurski, Jack Manders,
Sid Luckman, George McAfee, Joe Stydahar, Johnny Lujack, and Gale Sayers.
In his forty seasons of coaching, his teams won 321 regular-season games, an
NFL mark for a coach.

As a businessman, he started with little and finished with millions. The
Chicago Bears lost $71.63 the first year they played. By the time Halas retired
as the active coach in 1968, the franchise was worth millions of dollars. He also
made money in real estate, sporting goods, oil, and even in the breeding of
Shetland ponies.

He was criticized as ruthless, dictatorial, conniving, and cheap, but he

grew rich and powerful with pro football, coached seven championship teams, and became one of the institutions of modern sports.

George Halas was born February 2, 1895, in the working-class section of southwest Chicago. He was a skinny, quick-minded sort who graduated in 1918 from the University of Illinois with a degree in ceramic engineering but with a runaway desire to be an athlete. Even during his term as an ensign at the Great Lakes Naval Training Station, he played football and as a 6-foot, 170-pound end was named to the all-America second team.

After World War I, he worked briefly as a railroad engineer and played minor league baseball and semipro football. Then he accepted an offer from A. E. Staley, a corn-products manufacturer in Decatur, Illinois, to learn the business while continuing in sports. And the Decatur Staleys two years later— the Chicago Bears of the new National Football League—were born.

Halas, working fifteen to eighteen hours a day, as he did most of his career, did it all: he played end, coached the club, handled administrative details, collected tickets, wrote publicity releases, and booked games. On the side, he sold automobiles to earn money while his partner, Dutch Sternaman, pumped gas in a filling station.

They turned the corner financially in 1925 by signing Red Grange, the famed running back of Illinois, the day after his final college game. Four days later, with Grange in the Bears' lineup against the Chicago Cardinals in Wrigley Field, they drew the first sellout crowd in the team's history. For the next two months, Grange and the Bears barnstormed across the country, drawing 360,000 persons to twenty games and clearing a quarter of a million dollars.

"I knew then and there," said Halas, "that Grange was the box-office shot in the arm pro football needed. The publicity established pro football as a national sport."

It became a sport frequently dominated by the Bears. In 1934, they rolled up a winning streak of thirteen games before losing to the New York Giants in the playoff. And in 1940 they staged one of the most awesome performances in football history by stampeding the Washington Redskins, 73–0, for the league title.

The Washington owner, George Preston Marshall, had baited Chicago by ridiculing the Bears as "a bunch of crybabies." At halftime, Halas "reminded" his players of the taunt, and they added seven touchdowns to their 28–0 margin and scored the most memorable rout in the league's annals. To people who complained that he had "poured it on" the Redskins, Halas replied, "We used thirty-three men and the thirty-third scored a touchdown. Should I have rushed out and tackled him myself?"

By the time Halas had coached his last championship team in 1963, he had helped to revive the T formation to its place of eminence in football and he had helped stake football to its eminence in professional sports. He also had acquired a reputation as the Sarah Bernhardt of the game because he had "retired" several times—in 1929, in 1942 (to reenter the navy), and in 1955.

But he was never happy for long away from the stadium, and finally retired at seventy-three as coach on May 27, 1968. He was still considered a tough customer, especially after he had taken George Allen to court in 1965 to prevent his switch from the Bears' coaching staff to the Los Angeles Rams. Halas yielded that time.

In 1970 he was elected president of the NFL's National Conference and he held that position for thirteen years. He retained a firm hand on the Bears' operations throughout the 1970s. In fact, Halas was instrumental in hiring the Bears' coach, Mike Ditka, away from the Dallas Cowboys in 1982.

Before he died on November 1, 1983, Halas could look back on over sixty years of fierce football, from the golden days of the 1960s to the primitive time when a telephone call to the "night number" of the Chicago Bears would ring in the apartment of George Stanley Halas, owner, coach, and Papa Bear.

Papa Bear
By RED SMITH

The Chicago Bears, who were more cuddly than grizzly for most of the 1970s, were in Philadelphia on December 23, 1979, bucking for the half-championship of the National half of the National Football League, but Papa Bear was not with them. George Stanley Halas was the last survivor of that little group of willful men who sat on running boards in Ralph Hay's Hupmobile showroom in Canton, Ohio, on September 17, 1920, and laid the foundation of the NFL.

Six weeks short of his eighty-fifth birthday, George found travel difficult, and the preceding week was especially hard on him. The previous Sunday morning his fifty-four-year-old son Muggs, president of the Bears, died of a massive coronary. It took a lot out of George, but except when he was at the wake and the funeral, he continued to keep regular hours in the club office in the Loop.

Papa Bear was a flaming wonder. As the team he founded wound up its sixtieth season, he still functioned as owner, chairman of the board, and chief executive officer. In forty of those seasons he was also the coach. In bad weather he had twinges in the hip he injured as an outfielder in the 1919 training camp of the New York Yankees (that was a year before they got Babe Ruth), but he remained tough as a boot.

"There was never any question that George was tough," Red Grange writes in the foreword to a handsome book, *The Chicago Bears—An Illustrated History* by Richard Whittingham. "At times there were factions on the team . . . one time in 1934, before going out to practice, he said he wanted to talk to us. Instead he started to call certain players by name and told them to line up in two different groups. Then George said, 'Here are the guys who are breaking up the team into factions, and I'll fight you all, one by one or all together.' And that was the end of the factions."

George was seventy-three the last time he retired as coach. "I knew it was time to quit," he said, "when I was chewing out the referee and he walked off the penalty faster than I could keep up with him."

As with most athletes, it was the legs that went first, not the spirit, not the capacity for rage. In his foreword, Grange tells of George's clashes with his friend Jim Durfee, a referee in the 1920s:

When Halas was riding him hard one day, Jim began marching off a five-yard penalty. Halas got really hot. "What's that for?" he hollered.

"Coaching from the sideline," Jim yelled back. (You couldn't do that in those days.)

"Well," said George, "that just proves how dumb you are. That's fifteen yards, not five."

"Yeah," said Jim, "but the penalty for your kind of coaching is only five yards."

Another day Jim was penalizing the Bears fifteen yards, and Halas cupped his hands and yelled, "You stink!" Jim just marched off another fifteen yards, then turned and shouted, "How do I smell from here?"

George's eyes still flashed when he remembered how a referee robbed the Bears in 1920, when they were the Decatur Staleys. They played thirteen games that first season, and the only team that scored against them legitimately was the Hammond Pros, whom Decatur whipped, 28–7. In Chicago the Staleys were leading the Racine Cardinals, 6–0, late in the game when the Cardinals completed the sideline pass. The receiver ducked behind a knot of spectators who had crowded onto the field and with his civilian interference ran in for a touchdown. Not wishing to become suddenly dead, the referee allowed the score, and the Cardinals won, 7–6.

In 1975, W. B. Wolfan of Chicago forwarded a letter from George. And it began: "Yes, I did make an offer to now President Gerald Ford to join the Bears after the 1935 College All-Star Game against our team. I might add that the Bears' bid exceeded the $50 per game offer from Curly Lambeau of Green Bay. However, Jerry Ford turned both of us down with the explanation that he intended to go on to Yale for his law degree and wasn't interested in pro football."

The Halas memory remained keen for details like those. Eleven teams were represented when the league was formed in that Canton auto agency, and after the meeting it was announced that the franchise fee was a hundred dollars each. Actually, George says, nobody paid anything. "I doubt if there was a hundred bucks in the whole room."

Whittingham's lively history borrows an anecdote from *My Life with the Redskins* by Corinne Griffith, the star of silent films who married George Preston Marshall, the owner of the Washington club. She tells of a sidelines shouting match between Marshall and Halas during the 1937 championship game after Marshall, infuriated because a Bear had taken a punch at Sammy Baugh, stormed down to the playing field:

George [Marshall] stomped back to the box, snorted as he sat down and, of course, took it out on me.

"What's the matter with you? You look white as a sheet!"

"Oh, that was awful!"

"What was awful?"

"That horrible language. We heard every word."

"Well, you shouldn't listen."

"Oh, you. And right in front of the ladies . . . And as for that man

Halas!" Every hair of George's raccoon coat bristled. "He's positively revolt—"

"Don't you dare say anything against Halas." George was actually shaking his finger under my nose. "He's my best friend!"

GIL HODGES

1924–1972

By JOSEPH DURSO

O NE WARM SUNDAY in May of 1953, a parish priest in Brooklyn told his congregation, "It's too hot for a sermon. Keep the Commandments and say a prayer for Gil Hodges."

Gilbert Ray Hodges, the first baseman and power hitter for the Brooklyn Dodgers, was in the throes of a particularly fretful batting slump that day. But by the time the season had ended, he had hit .302 with 122 runs batted in and 31 home runs.

He also had appeared in the All-Star Game and the World Series, and had fastened his grip on the public affection to a degree that rarely was rivaled in modern baseball.

Some years later, though, in 1969, Hodges reached even greater heights of esteem when he managed the New York Mets to the first pennant in their eight-year history and a World Series triumph over the potent Baltimore Orioles.

That feat, coming with a team that only a few seasons before had been one of the most laughed at in baseball history, stood as a tribute to Hodges's managerial ability, an ability that equaled his prowess as a player.

A 6-foot-2-inch 210-pounder with a brute's physique, he was that unusual type of professional athlete—the gentle giant in private, the executioner in a baseball suit.

For sixteen seasons, he was one of the most graceful first basemen in the major leagues, and one of the most feared hitters. He started with the Dodgers in 1947, then played 2,006 games with them and 65 with the New York Mets. He hit .273 with 1,274 runs batted in and 370 home runs—14 of them with the bases loaded.

He also appeared in seven World Series and six All-Star Games, and then settled into a career as manager with the Washington Senators and the Mets.

But for all his success with the cudgels of the game, Gil Hodges became best known as the "nice guy" who finished first, the hero of Flatbush, the devoted family man, the good marine—the man for whom a congregation would say prayers.

Although he worked for years at Ebbets Field and lived for more years five miles farther down Bedford Avenue, Hodges really was a midwesterner who adopted Brooklyn as his home.

He was born April 4, 1924, in Princeton, Indiana, a town of about 8,000 persons in the mining and farm region in the southwestern part of the state. He

was the second son of Irene and Charles Hodges, a coal miner who lost several toes and his right eye in a mining accident.

The family moved to Petersburg, Indiana, where Gil won seven varsity letters in track, basketball, and baseball. He also played American Legion ball for two summers and was offered a minor league contract by the Detroit Tigers. But he declined, followed his brother Bob to St. Joseph's College nearby, and decided on a coaching career.

But in 1943, while he was a full-time drill-press operator and part-time baseball player for a company team, he was signed by the Brooklyn Dodgers.

However, except for one game at third base that summer, Hodges did not become a regular member of the Dodger carnival until 1947. He spent most of the intervening time in the Marines, where the Hodges legend quietly took form.

He served in the Pacific at Pearl Harbor, Okinawa, and Tinian until he was discharged as a sergeant early in 1946. Don Hoak, who later became his teammate with the Dodgers, recalled that "we kept hearing stories about this big guy from Indiana who killed with his bare hands."

Hodges was generally silent about his adventures as a jungle fighter, but once he returned to baseball his reputation grew as the strong, silent man with pale blue eyes who could hit balls with remarkable right-handed power.

He spent the 1946 season at Newport News, Virginia, in the Piedmont League, as a catcher. Then in 1947 he joined the Dodgers, caught twenty-eight games, gradually yielded his spot to Roy Campanella, and in 1948 took over at first base.

The switch was arranged by Leo Durocher in one of his final tactical moves as manager of the Dodgers, and Hodges rapidly established himself as one of the surest fielders in baseball history.

He hit 23 home runs the next year, then 32 in 1950 and 40 in 1951. For seven straight years he hit more than 20 home runs.

On August 31, 1950, Hodges hit four home runs and a single in one game. The same season he took part in 159 double plays at first base, and a year later he took part in 171. He hit 14 grand slam home runs for a National League career record since surpassed by Willie McCovey, who hit 18 from 1959 to 1980 while playing for the San Francisco Giants and the San Diego Padres. He finished with 1,921 hits, about 40 percent of them for extra bases.

Hodges was part of the pride of Flatbush, the flamboyantly potent Dodger teams of Campanella, Duke Snider, Pee Wee Reese, Jackie Robinson, Pete Reiser, Carl Furillo, Cookie Lavagetto, and later of Don Drysdale and the young Sandy Koufax.

Hodges suffered from some unusual lapses, but even these seemed to endear him to the public as human failings of a superman.

He sometimes had trouble hitting curveballs. He had a fast-footwork style at first base that brought complaints that "he never touched the bag." He even tied a record by going to bat 21 times without a hit in the 1952 World Series.

But Hodges always seemed to possess the serenity and the strength to be a winner. In 1953, when his World Series slump extended into the regular season, he was flooded with letters of encouragement, goodwill messages, charms, and prayers. At midseason, he started to rally, finished the season with 32 home runs and then hit .364 in the Series with eight hits, including a home run.

Hodges surpassed even that performance in 1954, when he hit .304 with 42 homers and 130 runs batted in, and the next year he helped the Dodgers win their first world championship in a seven-game Series against the Yankees.

When the Dodgers migrated to Los Angeles after the 1957 season, Hodges went with them. But his family moved back to Brooklyn after one year and reestablished its home in Flatbush. Then, when the Mets were organized in 1962, they bought Hodges for $75,000 and for part of two seasons he helped them revive memories of the Dodgers and the good old days of National League baseball in New York.

His last season was 1963. He played in only eleven games, then on May 22 started his career as a manager by taking charge of the Washington Senators. He had never played in the American League and had never managed anywhere. But in five seasons he guided the Senators from last place in the ten-team league to sixth, and then returned to the Mets in 1968 as manager where he had started—in the National League in New York.

Hodges, in his first season with the Mets, quickly renewed all the old public esteem from the Dodger days.

Even though they wound up ninth, the Mets began to play a more business-like brand of baseball, won more games than any team in Met history, and developed some of the best young pitchers in the game.

Hodges's adoring public was shocked on September 24 of that season when he suffered a heart attack during the second inning of a game in Atlanta. But the manager recovered, and one year to the day later, the Mets clinched the National League's Eastern Division championship.

Within a few weeks, the so-called Miracle Mets had added the pennant and the World Series to their collection of sudden riches.

A second heart attack, on April 2, 1972, ended his life at the age of forty-seven.

Some Baseball History

By ROSCOE McGOWEN

Gil Hodges made baseball history on August 31, 1950, as the Dodgers made merry with the Braves by beating them, 19–3, at Ebbets Field.

The big Brooklyn first baseman hit four home runs and thus became the second major leaguer and first National Leaguer in modern annals to perform the feat in a nine-inning game.

The late Lou Gehrig was the man Hodges tied. The only difference was that the Yankee Iron Man hit his consecutively, his final one in the seventh inning, against the Athletics in 1932.

Gil hit his fourth one in the eighth inning into the upper left-field stand off Johnny Antonelli. His first was in the second inning off Warren Spahn, the second in the third inning off Normie Roy, and the third off Bob Hall in the sixth. In the fourth Gil grounded to the third baseman and in the seventh he singled.

All homers save the last went into the lower left-field stand. Altogether Gil hit for seventeen total bases and he drove in nine runs, all with his homers. Carl Furillo was on base in each instance, and in the third inning Jackie Robinson also was aboard.

Before the turn of the century Bobby Lowe, Boston Nationals, hit four consecutive homers within nine innings in 1894, and Ed Delahanty hit four with the Phils in 1896.

Three moderns, Lou Gehrig in 1932, Chuck Klein with the Phils in 1936, and Pat Seerey with the White Sox in 1948, who required ten and eleven innings, respectively, to get four in one game.

In the years since Hodges accomplished the feat, it was subsequently matched by Joe Adcock of the Milwaukee Braves (1954), Rocky Colavito of the Cleveland Indians (1959), Willie Mays of the San Francisco Giants (1961), Mike Schmidt of the Philadelphia Phillies (1976), and Bob Horner of the Atlanta Braves (1986).

Hodges also tied an all-time record with his seventeen total bases, subsequently eclipsed by Adcock, who hit a double along with his quartet of homers.

There were only 14,226 cash customers present to see Hodges's almost unprecedented feat—certainly unprecedented for a Dodger—but they enjoyed every minute of the entire performance by the Brooks, who hadn't beaten any team so humiliatingly in many a moon.

They scored seven times in the third inning, with Duke Snider also tuning in with a terrific two-run homer over the scoreboard in right.

As the third player on the team to hit three or more homers in one game this season, Hodges also helped the Dodgers establish another major league record. Previously both Snider and Roy Campanella had driven for the circuit thrice in a single contest.

The most lonesome home run was struck by Sid Gordon, and believe it or not, it gave the Braves a 1–0 lead. Sid clouted his shot into the lower left-center-field stand off Carl Erskine in the second inning. Then Hodges started the Brooks on their spree in the Brooklyn half.

Erskine went all the way for his second triumph—both over the Braves—and, until Gordon singled in the seventh, personally outhit the entire Boston team. Carl made four straight singles—in the second, third, fifth, and sixth innings—and was hit by an Antonelli pitch in the seventh. They didn't get Erskine out until the eighth when he sent a long drive to Gordon in left field.

Spahn, searching for his seventeenth triumph, instead took his fifteenth setback. He would finish the season at 21–17.

The Miracle Mets

By JOSEPH DURSO

The Mets entered the promised land on October 16, 1969, after seven years of wandering through the wilderness of baseball.

In a tumultuous game before a record crowd of 57,397 in Shea Stadium, they defeated the Baltimore Orioles, 5–3, for their fourth straight victory of the sixty-sixth World Series and captured the championship of a sport that had long ranked them as comical losers.

They did it with a full and final dose of the magic that had spiced their unthinkable climb from ninth place in the National League—100-to-1 shots who scraped and scrounged their way to the pinacle as the waifs of the major leagues.

At 3:17 on a cool and often sunny afternoon, their impossible dream came true when Cleon Jones caught a fly ball hit by Dave Johnson to left field. And they immediately touched off one of the great, riotous scenes in sports history, as thousands of persons swarmed from their seats and tore up the patch of ground where the Mets had made history.

It was ten days after they had won the National League pennant in a three-game sweep of the Atlanta Braves. It was twenty-two days after they had won the Eastern title of the league over the Chicago Cubs. It was eight years after they had started business under Casey Stengel as the lovable losers of all sports.

They reached the top, moreover, in the best and most farfetched manner of Met baseball.

They spotted the Orioles three runs in the third inning when Dave McNally and Frank Robinson hit home runs off Jerry Koosman.

But then they stormed back with two runs in the sixth inning on a home run by Donn Clendenon, another in the seventh on a home run by Al Weis, and two more in the eighth on two doubles and two errors.

The deciding run was batted home by Ron Swoboda, who joined the Met mystique in 1965 when the team was losing 112 games and was finishing last for the fourth straight time.

But like most of the Mets' victories in their year to remember, the decision was a collective achievement by the youngest team in baseball, under Manager Gil Hodges—who had suffered a heart attack a year ago after the Mets "surged" into ninth place.

The wild, final chapter in the story was written against the desperate efforts of the Orioles, who had swept to the American League pennant by nineteen games as one of the most powerful teams in modern times.

The Orioles had not won since the opening game in Baltimore and needed three straight victories to survive. In the third inning, they lashed out at Koosman with three runs and erased the memory of the six no-hit innings he had pitched against them in Game Two.

Mark Belanger led off with a looping single over first base. He was nearly caught off the base by Jerry Grote, the New York catcher, who was backing up the play. But in a brief shoving contest, Belanger was called safe as he scrambled back to the base, where Grote took a throw from Swoboda.

On the next pitch, McNally hit a home run into the Baltimore bull pen in left field and the Orioles led, 2–0.

McNally, who had lost the second game to Koosman, was a twenty-seven-year-old left-hander who could hit as well as pitch. He didn't lose a game that season until August 3, then finished with twenty victories. He also hit three home runs the previous year, including a grand slam, and another in 1969.

His drive off Koosman was the first extra-base hit for Baltimore in thirty-five innings, and it cast a pall over the fans who had come to see the Mets reach the stars. Two outs later, Frank Robinson bombed Koosman's first pitch over the center-field fence, Baltimore led by 3–0, and the Mets' magic suddenly seemed remote.

But Koosman settled down after that and checkmated the Orioles on one single for the final six innings. He retired nineteen of the last twenty-one batters, closed with a five-hitter, and even swung a mean bat when the Mets began to do their "thing."

They almost revived in the third when Koosman doubled past third base. Nothing came of it because McNally knocked off the next three batters, but it was an omen: Koosman had made only four hits in eighty-four times at bat all season.

Then, in the sixth, another omen appeared. Each team argued in turn that a batter had been hit by a pitched ball. The Orioles, though, lost their argument; the Mets won theirs. And the game veered inexorably toward the "team of destiny."

The Orioles pleaded their case first. With one out in the top of the sixth, an inside fastball plunked Frank Robinson on his right thigh. The home plate umpire, Lou DiMuro, ruled that it had glanced off the bat first for strike two. Baltimore's volatile manager, Earl Weaver, who had been banished from Game Four, argued that it had simply struck Robinson, who already had started for first base.

When the Orioles were overruled, Robinson disappeared into the runway behind the dugout for five minutes while the trainer sprayed his thigh with a freezing medication and while everybody in the stadium waited. Then he returned, was greeted by a sea of waving handkerchiefs, and struck out.

In the bottom of the sixth, it was the Mets' turn to plead an identical case, and in the amazing spirit of their new fortune, they won it on an appeal.

Jones was the leadoff batter and he was struck on the right instep by a dropping curveball. The umpire called it a ball; Jones insisted he had been hit. Hodges, the old hero of Ebbets Field, retrieved the ball from the Mets' dugout, where it had bounced, and executed the old "look-at-the-ball-trick."

DiMuro duly looked at the ball, detected a swatch of shoe polish on its cover, reversed himself, and waved Jones to first base. Now Weaver shot out of the dugout to voice his indignation, but lost his point and soon his ball game.

The next batter, Clendenon, went to a count of two balls and two strikes, then whacked a home run off the auxiliary scoreboard on the facing of the left-field loge seats.

It was his third home run in three games (he had hit sixteen during the regular schedule) and it punctuated a remarkable season for the thirty-four-year-old ex-student of law.

His homer put the Mets back in business. In the next inning, Al Weis brought them even on McNally's second pitch.

Weis, the silent supersub, drove the pitch over the 371-foot sign in left-center as the crowd rocked the stadium, and the game was tied, 3–3. It marked another achievement for the right-handed platoon that Hodges deployed against left-handed pitching, and it was no mean achievement for Weis.

During Weis's two seasons with the Mets, 212 home runs had been hit in Shea Stadium—none by Al. He had hit only two all year, both in Chicago in July. But in the World Series, the quiet little infielder turned tiger with four walks, four singles, and one historic home run.

Finally, the stage was set for the last full measure of Met magic.

In the eighth, with Eddie Watt pitching for Baltimore, Jones looked at three straight balls and then a strike. Then he lined the 3-and-1 pitch off the center-field fence for a double.

Clendenon, who was voted the outstanding player in the Series, fouled off two attempts to bunt. Then he lined a long fly into the right-field corner, just foul, then bounced out to Brooks Robinson, with Jones holding second base.

The next batter was Swoboda, and with first base open, the Orioles might have walked him intentionally. But they elected to challenge him and Swoboda drilled the second pitch down the left-field line, where Don Buford almost made a brilliant backhand catch off the grass. But the ball dropped in for a double as Jones streaked for home to put the Mets in front, 4–3, and tumult broke out across Flushing Meadow.

Ed Charles lifted a fly to Buford for the second out. But Grote followed with a low line drive toward Boog Powell, and the 250-pound first baseman booted it for an error. He chased the ball, though, to his right and lobbed it to Watt, who was rushing over from the mound to cover first base.

By this time, Grote was flashing across the bag, and when Watt juggled the throw and dropped it, Swoboda was flashing across the plate with the second run of the inning.

That made it 5–3 and the Mets were three outs from fantasy. There was a brief delay when Frank Robinson opened the ninth with a walk. But then Powell forced him at second base, Brooks Robinson flied out to Swoboda in right and—at 3:17 P.M.—Johnson lifted a fly to Jones in left-center.

Jones made the catch with a flourish, then he and his old high school mate from Mobile, Tommie Agee, turned and streaked across the outfield to the Mets' bull pen in right.

They beat the avalanche by a split second, and as they ducked into the safety of the stadium's caverns, the crowd let go. Children, housewives, mature men, all swarmed onto the field where the Mets had marched. They tore up home plate, captured the bases, ripped gaping holes from the turf, set off orange flares and firecrackers, and chalked the wooden outfield fence with the signs of success.

The Mets were the champions of the world on October 16, 1969.

"I never saw anything like it," said Joe DiMaggio, the old Yankee who had thrown out the first ball.

Transformer of the Mets

By JOSEPH DURSO

"It was a colossal thing that they did," Gil Hodges said that October afternoon in 1969, while the New York Mets poured champagne and danced with Pearl Bailey in their chaotic clubhouse in Shea Stadium. "These young men showed that you can realize the most impossible dream of all." As he spoke, he had been manager of the Mets for two seasons and had led them from last place in the National League to first—a team that had lost 101 games the year before he arrived and then had swept spectacularly to the top two months after man first walked on the moon. And his own contribution to that coup, a long-time baseball man said last night, was simple: "He took the clown out of the Mets."

That is, Gilbert Ray Hodges deliberately set out to erase the "mystique" that had made the Mets rich, famous, and cuddled as a sort of national joke—and that had drawn two million customers into their ballpark.

He talked less than Casey Stengel, sermonized less than Wes Westrum, and tolerated less than either. He gambled that the boys could become men and survive in the public's affection, and he won the gamble because the boys responded with the only result that could have survived the change: success.

He took over the mammoth job of redirecting the Mets in the spring of 1968. He had powerful muscles and a gentle voice, he helped old ladies cross the street and young pitchers cross the infield. He was reverent, friendly, strong, and silent. He had a reputation for shooting straight, and he kept his hands in his back pockets when arguing with umpires. He was a kind of middle-aged Eagle Scout.

He also had the problem of following one of the great acts on the public stage—Stengel's. And he knew that Stengel had had an absolutely clear view of his mission as master of the Mets: not so much to build up the stamina of the team as to build up the stamina of the public for the team.

It was something that the interregnum of Westrum did not change from 1965 through 1967, and it was there when Hodges took over that spring day with the terse announcement to the circle of players: "My name is Hodges."

In pursuit of his own philosophy as manager of the lovable clowns of baseball, Hodges immediately laid down the law, quietly but absolutely. The curfew was midnight, the hotel bar was off limits, golf was permitted in spring training but not swimming, and everybody was expected in uniform by 9:30 in the morning.

That was an hour after he had arrived, and, during the regular season, the early-bird players who got to the park by 4:30 for a night game found the Eagle Scout already in uniform, sitting in the swivel chair in the manager's office, planning the "platoon" moves that he followed on the field.

He enforced his quiet revolution through his coaches, three of whom accompanied him to New York from Washington, where he had worked small miracles with the Senators—Rube Walker, Eddie Yost, and Joe Pignatano. He rarely stopped in the players' part of the clubhouse to chat, he levied fines but refused to discuss them publicly, and, Tom Seaver once said, "He probably hasn't talked to me directly about pitching more than three times in three years."

He was, in short, an organization man, raised on the type of organization that had surrounded him with the Brooklyn Dodgers, especially under another strong and silent manager, Walter Alston.

To most of his players, his style added up to a "lack of communication." But after he suffered his first heart attack, in September 1968, they closed ranks around him and charged to their 1969 pennant while denying that any "conspiracy of silence" had been formed in the clubhouse to protect him.

In the spring of 1972, Hodges appeared healthy and relaxed as the Mets won 15 of 23 games in Florida despite an agonizing series of injuries. He resumed smoking cigarettes, he drank coffee again, he hit grounders (one of which broke Jim Fregosi's thumb), he played golf a few times—and he had just played golf with his coaches when he collapsed in West Palm Beach.

True, he was surrounded by trouble. The team had finished third two years in a row. His key players were still injured, and all his players were on strike over pensions with the season's opening in doubt. But he was still the quiet man of baseball who had taken the clown out of the Mets and had steered them to the impossible dream of 1969.

CARL HUBBELL

1903–1988

KNOWN AFFECTIONATELY AS the Meal Ticket to appreciative players and dedicated fans of the Giants in the Depression years, Hubbell was the National League's premier left-handed pitcher of the 1930s and one of the finest in modern baseball history.

He pitched only for the Giants, winning 253 games and losing 154 from 1928 to 1943. He was the National League's Most Valuable Player in 1933 and 1936.

Pitching in the World Series of 1933, 1936, and 1937, King Carl won four games and lost two with an exceptional earned-run average of 1.79. He had an 1.66 ERA in 1933, when he enjoyed a streak of 46 consecutive scoreless innings.

He won 21 or more games each year from 1933 to 1937.

In the 1934 All-Star Game, he struck out in succession Babe Ruth, Lou Gehrig, Jimmie Foxx, Al Simmons, and Joe Cronin, all of whom are in the Hall of Fame.

Hubbell, who won 24 consecutive games in a streak that overlapped the 1936 and 1937 seasons, was elected to the Hall of Fame in 1947.

Hubbell's businesslike demeanor on and off the pitching mound contrasted with more colorful, eccentric pitchers of his era, like Lefty Gomez of the Yankees and Dizzy Dean of the St. Louis Cardinals. Hubbell won respect and attention solely from on-field performances.

Although consistency of excellence was the trademark of his pitching, he is also remembered for three particular instances of brilliance.

In his first full major league season, 1929, he pitched a no-hitter against the Pittsburgh Pirates. Then in 1933, he threw an 18-inning, 1–0 victory over St. Louis at the Polo Grounds. And his dramatic feat of striking out in order five of baseball's greatest hitters in the second All-Star Game embedded itself in the nation's sporting consciousness.

After giving up a hit and a walk to the first two batters in the game, he relied exclusively on the screwball for strikes as he struck out the American League's top sluggers (Ruth, Gehrig, and Foxx) and two of its finer contact hitters, Simmons and Cronin.

Fernando Valenzuela of the Los Angeles Dodgers matched Hubbell's feat in 1984, but his five consecutive strikeouts did not have the national impact that Hubbell's achieved.

Hubbell's success with the screwball made the pitch famous. Thrown with the wrist snapping in instead of out, the delivery broke the opposite direction

from a normal curveball—that is, down and away from a right-handed batter when thrown by a left-handed pitcher.

Controlling the enormously effective pitch was the secret to Hubbell's success. He threw it with pinpoint accuracy as he did his unexceptional fastball. In his 18-inning shutout, he did not walk a batter.

Carl Owen Hubbell was born in Carthage, Missouri, on June 22, 1903, but grew up in Meekeer, Oklahoma. Just before his twentieth birthday, he began his professional baseball career with Cushing of the Class D Oklahoma State League.

Five years later, he was still in the minor leagues, but had begun to develop his special delivery. Most successful pitchers, he noted later, had some sort of sinkerball. He tried to acquire one by starting to snap his wrist—and out came the screwball. "I didn't even know what a screwball was," he said.

In mid-1928, Hubbell was pitching for Beaumont in the Texas League when the Giants, managed by John McGraw, bought his contract and called him to New York. Before the season ended, he had won 10 games and lost 6 and was looked upon as a starter.

On May 8, 1929, he hurled his no-hitter, against Pittsburgh, and he continued as a competent but unspectacular winner as the Giants failed to win a pennant for four years. When McGraw retired in June 1932 and Bill Terry succeeded him as manager, Hubbell began his finest streak of pitching, leading the Giants to three pennants in five years.

In 1933, Hubbell turned in 10 shutouts (including the 18-inning effort against the Cardinals) and 23 victories in all. In the World Series against the Washington Senators, he won the first and last games, allowing no earned runs as the Giants prevailed in five games.

He continued to win more than 20 games each season, but the Giants did not win another pennant until 1936, when Hubbell had 26 victories, the best of his career, against 6 losses. In the first game of the World Series, he ended a Yankee streak of 12 consecutive Series victories, holding them to one run. A three-run double by Frank Crosetti led to Hubbell's defeat in his only other start as the Yankees won in six games.

Hubbell had won his final 16 regular-season decisions in 1936 and began the 1937 season with eight more consecutive victories. He continued to a 22–8 season that led the Giants to another pennant and another meeting with the Yankees. He broke even in two decisions as the Yanks prevailed again, in five games.

Hubbell developed elbow trouble in 1938 when he was thirty-five years old, his left arm bent because of his heavy use of the screwball. He won 13 games but was never again fully effective, winning 11 in each of the next four seasons before he retired in the middle of 1943 with a 4–4 record.

Although he had become affluent from oil investments with friends in Oklahoma, Hubbell accepted an appointment as director of the Giants' farm system.

He was killed in an automobile accident in Arizona on November 21, 1988. He was eighty-five years old.

The 1934 All-Star Game

By JOHN DREBINGER

Packing thrill upon thrill, the foremost professional ball players of the nation battled for two and three-quarter hours at the Polo Grounds in the 1934 edition of the ball game of the century, with the forces of the American League demonstrating for the second successive year that at this newly devised form of interleague competition they still held the edge.

For by uncorking a devastating six-run rally in the fifth inning, the All-Stars of the American League carried the day over Memphis Bill Terry and his carefully chosen National League cast by a score of 9–7.

A capacity crowd of 50,000 witnessed the struggle. It was a gathering that occupied every seat in the historic arena, jammed the aisles, and roared itself purple.

About 15,000 more roared, too, when the gates were locked fifteen minutes before game time, shutting all out who had not already purchased reserved seat tickets. The paid attendance totaled 48,363 and the receipts donated to the players' charity fund were $52,982, net.

It was a crowd, too, which at the outset seemed undecided with which side it was to align itself. The National Leaguers were the home team and they were being bossed by Bill Terry. The American circuit had Joe Cronin, boy pilot of the Senators, at the head, and this sort of gave it a renewed setting of the previous fall's World Series, in which Terry's Giants prevailed over Cronin's Senators in five games.

On the other hand, the American Leaguers also had Babe Ruth and Lou Gehrig, and no New Yorker could very well be expected to root against either of these two. Whereupon the crowd simply compromised and bellowed unreservedly for whichever side was showing to advantage for the moment.

In rather sharp contrast with the first All-Star Game in Chicago the year before, this conflict developed into a titanic struggle of hitters, during which great names in the pitching industry were rudely jostled about.

In the 1933 conflict a homer by Babe Ruth won the struggle for the American League, 4 to 2, but while the great Bambino, appearing in only five innings in this game, was held in more or less restraint, others did some thunderous walloping. Frankie Frisch and Joe Medwick hit homers for the National Leaguers, while Earl Averill banged three runs across with a triple and a double in two successive innings.

Of the eight pitchers to step to the mound, three for the American League and five for the National, only two survived with their prestige intact. One, as can readily be imagined, was the invincible Carl Hubbell, who gave a masterly exhibition of his left-handed talents during his assignment for the first three innings.

The other was Mel Harder, trim right-hander of the Cleveland Indians, who checked a National League rally in the fifth after the Americans had swept to the fore, and hurled scoreless baseball for the remainder of the distance.

Vernon "Lefty" Gomez, ace left-hander of the American circuit, who opposed Hubbell for the first three rounds, fell for four runs during his tenure of office on the wings of the homers hit by the two Cardinals, Frisch and Medwick.

His right-handed Yankee colleague, the burly Charlie "Red" Ruffing, was routed summarily from the mound in the fifth, while for the National Leaguers, Lon Warneke of the Cubs and Van Lingle Mungo of the Dodgers came down with a grand crash in the fourth and fifth as the forces of the junior circuit amassed a total of eight runs.

In the minutes before the game there was a respectful silence as a memorial tablet to John J. McGraw was unveiled in front of the center-field clubhouse. McGraw had died the previous winter. A full-throated, hearty cheer then went up as the popular Hubbell received a plaque from the Baseball Writers Association for his services as the outstanding player of the 1933 campaign.

This done, the spectators warmed quickly to the battle at hand. Nor was there much delay in providing them with plenty of provocation for exercising their vocal accomplishments. Charlie Gehringer, leading off the American League batting order, greeted Hubbell with a single to center and when Wally Berger momentarily fumbled the ball the fleet Tiger swept down to second. Came a pass to Heinie Manush and there was some uneasiness on the National bench.

Hubbell looked around to his infield, apparently awaiting the familiar Giant huddle. However, for this occasion the lean southpaw was not flanked by Blondy Ryan or Hughie Critz. True, he had his manager, Terry, on one side of him, and behind him, at short, was Travis Jackson, his ailing eye sufficiently improved to permit him to play at the last moment. But at second base was Frisch and at third Pie Traynor of the Pirates, both aliens to him during the regular campaign.

So Hubbell merely bore down to his work with renewed vigor and at this point turned on some of the most magnificent flinging seen in years as he mowed down the best of the American League's batting strength.

Ruth was called out on strikes, the Babe looking decidedly puzzled as a screwball just clipped the outside corner for the third one. Then Gehrig struck out with a grand flourish, and not even the fact that Gehringer and Manush executed a double steal right under Gabby Hartnett's nose as Lou fished for the third one perturbed the long, lean left-hander.

Amid a deafening uproar Hubbell completed the string by fanning Jimmie Foxx, who at the last moment had been inserted in the American League lineup as the third baseman in place of Frank Higgins.

Scarcely had the furor of this masterstroke subsided than the crowd was thrown into another uproar as Frisch, first up for the Nationals, caught one of Gomez's speedballs and lined it into the densely packed upper right tier. Unmindful of this, Gomez retired the next three, and then all eyes again focused on Hubbell.

And once again the famous southpaw held the crowd and American Leaguers spellbound alike as he continued his sweep down the batting order. He fanned the great Al Simmons and also Cronin, making it five in a row. Bill

Dickey, the Yankee catcher, clipped him for a single to left, but Gomez was also swept aside on strikes to make it six strikeouts for the first two innings.

For the third, Gehringer flied to Cuyler in right, Manush grounded out, Ruth drew a pass, Gehrig flied out, and as Hubbell marched to the center-field clubhouse, his afternoon's assignment completed, he was accorded a tremendous ovation from all sides of the packed arena.

JACK JOHNSON

1878–1946

J ACK JOHNSON led a madcap existence that touched the heights, hit the depths, and lingered at intermediate points in the scale.

One of the craftiest boxers known to the ring, recognized by many as one of the outstanding heavyweight champions of all time, Jack Johnson lived in the lap of luxury but died bereft of riches.

At the height of his career Johnson wore diamonds. His "golden smile" revealed a mouth full of gold. He had at one time as many as half a dozen automobiles when they were a luxury. He shook hands with royalty as he traveled the world over with a retinue of servants.

He was involved in a sensational court trial which ended in his conviction on a charge of violation of the Mann Act (which made it unlawful to transport women across state lines for immoral purposes). He fled justice, roamed the world, a man without a country, until his fortune was gone. He confessed "faking" a fight, a battle in which he admitted he let his title pass to Jess Willard in Havana in 1915.

Among the distinctions that came to him was that of having collected the largest purse ever paid a boxer to that time—$120,000 he received in 1910 when he knocked out James J. Jeffries in fourteen rounds at Reno, Nevada. For this bout Johnson collected 60 percent of the purse of $101,000—$10,000 as a bonus and $50,000 for his share of motion pictures.

He was the cause of the white hope craze that swept the country after the Reno debacle when Jeffries succumbed to his craft after being brought out of retirement "to bring the title back to the white race."

The result of that fight brought a ban on interstate commerce of motion pictures of fights. Also as a result came riots in different sections of the country, which resulted in eight deaths and injuries to many.

Johnson was arrested many times for minor law violations. He exhausted his supply of money while a fugitive in foreign lands.

He came back after seven years and served a one-year jail sentence for his Mann Act violation, tried fighting again and failed, made a precarious living as an evangelist, supporting prayer in opera and personal appearances at museums and carnivals.

John Arthur Johnson, also known as Li'l Arthur, was born in Galveston, Texas, March 31, 1878. He was one of the craftiest boxers known to the ring. He boasted a right-hand uppercut that was his greatest weapon of attack and defense.

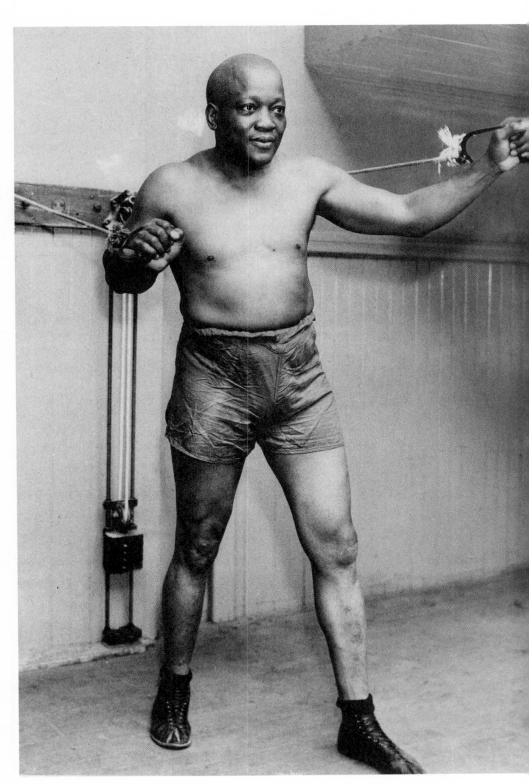

Johnson was discovered by Leo Posner, leader of the Galveston Athletic Club, quite by accident.

Charley Brooks, a ranked heavyweight who spent much time in Galveston gymnasiums, introduced Johnson to Posner. Brooks, who was looking for an easy foe, ended up being knocked out by the young man, and Johnson's ring career was launched.

In 1901 he won six bouts, one of them a two-round knockout of Brooks, and fought a draw, until he undertook a clash with Joe Choynski, another accomplished heavyweight and a good boxer. Choynski knocked out Johnson in three rounds, but the setback was temporary.

Choynski took an interest in Johnson when they were jailed as a consequence of the battle and undertook a course of instruction which started in the jail yard and formed the foundation of the ring development of Johnson.

In 1902 Johnson started a campaign in which he lost only three bouts in six years. He lost a twenty-round decision to Hank Griffin in 1902, another to Marvin Hart in 1905, and in the same year lost on a foul to Joe Jeanette in two rounds.

He was fighting all over the country, against whatever opposition was presented, and his engagements included bouts with Sam McVey, Sandy Ferguson, Sam Langford, as well as Jeanette.

It is recorded that in an early round of their bout in Boston in 1906 Langford, hardly more than a welterweight, knocked Johnson down with a left hook early in the fight, and Johnson, profiting by a count that was none too accurate, survived by calling upon all his consummate defensive boxing skill. They never fought again.

Johnson's 1907 victories included a two-round knockout of Bob Fitzsimmons, but the Cornishman at the time was at the end of his pugilistic career.

This consistent campaign established Johnson as a title threat at a time when Tommy Burns was recognized as a champion. Burns shied away from a meeting, but Johnson pressed his challenge until he finally got a match with Burns in Sydney, Australia, and then pounded Burns to such an extent that police stopped the fight in the fourteenth round, giving Johnson claim to the title.

Johnson's next battle of note, aside from a six-round no-decision affair with Philadelphia Jack O'Brien, was a twelve-round knockout of Stanley Ketchel, world middleweight champion in 1909.

This was an ill-fated undertaking by the smaller Ketchel, who nevertheless pressed Johnson hard at times before being knocked out. It was also the last bout for Johnson before he knocked out Jeffries in the fifteenth round on July 4, 1910, in Reno, a contest promoted by Tex Rickard and Jack Gleason that drew an unprecedented $270,775 in receipts.

After that bout, his claim to the title undisputed since he had knocked out the man who had gone into retirement as champion, Johnson came upon difficulties. He married two white women. One of them committed suicide in a room above his Cafe de Champion in Chicago.

The other he married while she was being interrogated as the government's chief witness in prosecution of charges that Johnson violated the Mann Act in transporting her from Pittsburgh to Chicago.

The champion was found guilty, was released from jail, pending sentence, on $30,000 bond, was sentenced to a year in jail, and released on bond of $15,000 pending appeal, and went to Canada as a member of a Negro baseball team, leaving Chicago after a game. He sailed from Montreal and arrived in Le Havre on the morning of July 10, 1913, as a fugitive.

For seven years Johnson fought on foreign soil. Barred from the music halls of London, he subsequently was expelled from the country. He fought three bouts in Paris in 1913, beating Frank Moran, Al Sproul, and Jim Johnson.

In 1915 he went to Havana, where he was knocked out in twenty-six rounds by Willard, a bout for which Johnson later said he was promised, but never collected, $50,000 for "laying down."

Gradually Johnson disappeared from the picture thereafter, fighting in Spain for the most part until in 1919 he went to Mexico City to win a fight from Captain Bob Roper.

In 1920 he arranged for his surrender to federal marshals who awaited him as he stepped across the border. Old and fleshy when he emerged from Leavenworth prison, Johnson intermittently undertook a ring comeback thereafter, with indifferent success, until in May 1926, Bob Lawson knocked him out in seven rounds of a scheduled twelve-round bout at Juarez, Mexico.

He finally retired from the ring in 1928 after a six-round bout with Bill Hartwell in Kansas City.

For the remainder of his life he maintained a livelihood mostly through personal appearances. He was killed in an automobile accident while returning to New York from such an engagement on June 10, 1946.

The Fight of the Century

By JOHN L. SULLIVAN

[EDITOR'S NOTE: *For the heavyweight championship fight between James J. Jeffries and Jack Johnson, held in Reno, Nevada, on July 4, 1910,* The New York Times *hired former champion John L. Sullivan to cover the bout. What follows is his account of the first interracial championship match.*]

The fight of the century is over and a black man is the undisputed champion of the world. It was a poor fight as fights go, this less than fifteen-round affair between James J. Jeffries and Jack Johnson. Scarcely ever has there been a championship contest that was so one-sided.

All of Jeffries's much-vaunted condition and the prodigious preparations that he went through availed him nothing. He wasn't in it from the first bell tap to the last, and as he fell bleeding, bruised, and weakened in the twenty-seventh second of the third minute of the fifteenth round no sorrier sight has ever gone to make pugilistic history. He was practically knocked out twice in this round.

Johnson's deadly left beat upon his unprotected head and neck, and he went down for the count just before the second minute had gone in the fifteenth round. As Johnson felled him the first time he was conscious, but weakened. He tactfully waited for the timekeeper's call of nine before he rose. When he did Johnson caught him flush on the jaw again, and he fell almost in the same spot, but farther out, and as he leaned against the lower rope his great bulk crashed through outside the ring.

His seconds and several newspaper men hauled him into the ring again, and he staggered weakly over to the other side. Johnson slowly followed him, measured his distance carefully, and as Jeff's head always hangs forward, struck him hard in the face, and again that terrible left hand caught him, sending him reeling around to a stooping posture.

Johnson pushed his right hand hard as Jeffries wheeled around, and quick as a flash whipped his left over again, and Jeff went down for the last time. His seconds had given it up.

They didn't wait for the ten seconds to be counted, but jumped into the ring after their man. Billy Delaney, Johnson's chief second, always watchful for the technicalities, yelled his claim for the fight for his man on the breach of the rules by Jeff's handlers. Tex Rickard, in the meantime, was trying to make himself heard, and he was saying that the fight was Johnson's.

By this time the crowd was realizing that Johnson had won out, but there was very little cheering. Jeff had been such a decided favorite they could hardly believe that he was beaten and that there wouldn't still be a chance for him to reclaim his lost laurels. The crowd was not even willing to leave the arena, and as poor old Jeff sat in his corner being sprayed with water and other resuscitating liquids he was pitied from all sides.

The Negro had few friends, but there was no real demonstration against him. They could not help but admire Johnson, because he is the type of prize fighter that is regarded highly by sportsmen. He played fairly at all times and fought fairly. He gave in wherever there was a contention and he demanded his rights only up to their limit, but never beyond them.

I have never witnessed a fight where I was in such a peculiar position. I all along refused to announce my choice as to the winner. I refused on Jeff's account, because he was sensitive and I wanted to be with him sometime during his training. I refused on Johnson's account, because of my well-known antipathy to his race, and I didn't want him to think that I was favoring him from any other motive than a purely sporting one. He might have got this impression, although since I know him better in the last few weeks, I am rather inclined to believe that he hasn't many of the petty meannesses of human character.

You will deduce from the foregoing that I really had picked Johnson as the winner. My personal friends all know it, and even Jeffries accused me of it one day, but I denied it in this way. I said, "Jeff, I have picked the winner, but I haven't done it publicly. A few personal friends know who I think will win, and I am not going to tell you before the fight. I don't want you to get any wrong impression."

However, the fact remains that three weeks ago I picked Johnson to win. It seems almost too much to say, but I did say inside of fifteen rounds. It's all over now, and it does not matter who I picked to win to either Jeff or Johnson, but the main theory I based my decision on was the old one that put me out of the game. Jeff could not come back. Jeffries was a mere shell of his former self. All the months of weight reducing, involving great feats of exercise, had come to naught.

The experts who figured that a man must receive his reward for such long, conscientious, muscle-wearing and nerve-racking work, figured that he must get it even providentially.

It seemed only just to human nature that Jeffries must win, even in the face of all the features resting on the other side of the argument. For it is true, and probably would only be denied by Johnson himself, that the big colored champion did not train conscientiously. As subsequent events proved he didn't have to train more than he did, but nevertheless he took a chance, and by his manner and deportment, seemed perfectly willing to stand the consequences, whatever they were. The result was success for him in its fullest meaning.

Johnson got scarcely a hard knock during the whole encounter, and was never bothered by Jeffries's actions one little bit. He came out of the fray without a mark, if one excepts the cut lip he got in the third round, which proved to be only the opening of the old cut that George Cotton gave him the other day when Governor Dickerson was out at his training quarters.

Never before has there been a fight for the championship of the world with so many peculiar ends to it, because never before has a black man been a real contender for the championship. Johnson, of course, was the credited champion even before today's fight by virtue of his defeat of Tommy Burns, but just the same the rank and file of sporting people never gave him the full measure of his title. Jeffries has always been the bugaboo of Johnson's championship career, and it seemed to many that if only the big boilermaker would go back into the fighting game and get himself into condition he could obliterate this so-called blot on the pugilistic map.

Jeffries was persuaded against his will, and he went to work with a willingness and determination that brought about wonderful results, but that couldn't bring back outraged old nature.

Probably never before was a championship so easily won as Johnson's victory today. He never showed the slightest concern during the fifteen rounds, and from the fourth round on his confidence was the most glaring thing I ever saw in any fighter. He was the one person in the world at that moment who knew that Jeffries's best blow was packed away in his last fight and on the road and by the running brooks from which he lured the fish during his preliminary training for his fight.

He was a perfect picnic for the big Negro, who seemed to be enjoying himself rather than fighting for 60 percent of a $101,000 purse. It could not have been all assumed, either, as his remarks during the contest to me, while I sat below and near him at the ringside, showed that he had honestly a good opinion of himself.

Once in the interval between the fifth and sixth rounds he leaned over and said, "John, I thought this fellow could hit."

I said, "I never said so, but I believe he could have six years ago."

Johnson continued with conversation when he should have been paying attention to the advice his seconds were giving him, and said, "Yes; five or six years ago ain't now, though."

By that time the bell had rung and he was up and at it again.

My, what a crafty, powerful, cunning left hand he has. He leads with it, of course, but he does most of his work in close, and some of his blows look as though he were trying to lead with his right while his left is traveling to its goal.

He is one of the craftiest, cunningest boxers that ever stepped into the ring, and poor old Jeffries could not get set or anywhere near him for an effective punch.

As a matter of fact, he didn't have any. They both fought closely all during the fifteen rounds. It was just the sort of a fight that Jeffries wanted. There was no running around and ducking like Corbett did with me in New Orleans.

Jeffries didn't miss so many blows, because he hardly started any. Johnson was on top of him all the time, and he scarcely attempted a blow that didn't land. There wasn't a full swing during the whole fifteen rounds, something unusual in this latter-day fighting.

The only thing that wasn't actual fighting today was the many clinches that occurred, and here, instead of Jeff getting in the fatal work, it was Johnson. None of the plans that all of the experts and critics have been talking about for the last six months materialized.

Jeffries's fearful rushes were not there. The awful wallops that he was going to land on Johnson's body, where were they?

Johnson didn't receive a blow during the whole encounter that would have hurt a sixteen-year-old boy. From the time Jeff got his right eye closed in the sixth round it was all over as far as I was concerned. I felt then that if Jeffries had all this power behind that had been claimed for him, he would get mad and he would at least take a desperate chance. Probably he had some such idea in mind himself, for he did step in viciously in the next round, but a gloved fist always stopped his onward way.

When I saw Johnson throw Jeffries away from him in one of the many clinches in the eighth or ninth round I was still further convinced that the Negro was the winner.

This had been one of his favorite stunts during his training, and he was expected to at least attempt it here. He didn't get gay at all with Jeffries in the beginning, and it was always the white man who clinched, but Johnson was very careful, and he backed away and took no chances, and was good-natured with it all.

There were those in the throng today who will probably say it was the greatest fight the world ever saw, but that is because it was the most peculiar fight crowd the world ever saw, for half of them never saw a fight before. It was the greatest fight this class ever saw, but, as a matter of fact, it was about the poorest fight that has ever been fought for the championship. It will probably be the last big fight in this country notwithstanding the crowd's enthusiastic reception of Billy Muldoon's sentimental speech, "Let us give three cheers for the great, broad-minded State of Nevada and its great, broad-minded governor," because it will be hard to work up the fervor that has existed all through the arrangements for this fight.

It will go down in history as the greatest fight that ever took place in some respects, and from a purely sporting point of view the very worst.

Nevertheless, the best man won, and I was one of the first to congratulate him, and also one of the first to extend my heartfelt sympathy to the beaten man.

The Willard Fight

"It was a clean knockout and the best man won. It was not a matter of luck. I have no kick coming."

Such were the words of ex-champion Jack Johnson when he had recovered from Jess Willard's terrific left jab to the heart and right swing to the jaw in the twenty-sixth round of the championship fight that restored pugilistic supremacy to the white race and made Willard champion on April 5, 1915, in Havana.

To those who watched the battle and longed for the white man to win, the day looked dark in the earlier stages because the Negro outgenerated the younger man and appeared to hit him as he willed. As Johnson's terrific blows rained on Willard he appeared to be suffering, but as the fight continued and Willard found that the champion's blows were not able to put him out he appeared to gain confidence, which he had seemed to lack when the battle started, and under the coaching of Tom Jones, he began to look more cheerful.

Johnson's old-time ring smile continued throughout these early rounds, but as time sped and he found that, although he landed his blows, they never appeared to have much effect, the smile disappeared, and from the tenth to the twentieth round Johnson exercised every art in his power to put out the challenger. After that twentieth round there was little doubt among those at the ringside as to how the fight was going. It was too plain that once more youth was showing. Johnson was tiring so fast that he tried to hold Willard in clinches, but his strength, which was able to do that earlier, was unable then, and Willard always got the best of the infighting, continually landing terrific blows to the body.

Johnson realized in the twenty-second round that his hold on the championship was growing short and asked for Jack Curley. The latter was at the gate at the time but appeared shortly before the last round.

"Tell my wife I'm tiring, and I wish you'd see her out," said Jack. Curley understood and carried out Johnson's wish.

It was only a little time after that when Willard landed his terrific body blow, followed by the blow to the jaw that spelled defeat to Johnson and turned bedlam loose among the thousands of spectators, who could hardly realize, so quickly did it happen, that Johnson was prostrate in the ring and that Jack Welsh was counting the fateful ten. The decisive blow landed about the middle of the round.

At the end Johnson made a movement as if to grab Willard, but the latter stepped back and Johnson fell full length upon the floor and lay there until his seconds had assisted him to his feet.

At first after his defeat Johnson appeared dazed, but he quickly recovered, and his smile reappeared as he explained that the best man had won.

WALTER JOHNSON

1887–1946

T HERE HAS NOT been a pitcher who had a greater hold on the American baseball public than Walter Johnson. Following the immortal Christy Mathewson, Big Barney attained popularity among the fans of the country equal virtually to that of Big Six.

In more ways than one they were alike. Both were great pitchers, both were sterling characters, and both were idols of young America. In 1936 Johnson was one of the first five men named to baseball's Hall of Fame at Cooperstown, New York, the others being Babe Ruth, Ty Cobb, Honus Wagner, and Mathewson.

Johnson, coming to the big leagues several years after Mathewson, but contemporary with him when Christy was fading and the youngster was at his peak, had a longer time to wait for his triumph. Destined to be with a second division club, Johnson waited seventeen long seasons before he played in his first World Series.

When the chance came, however, he made good, and his feat of winning for the Senators in the deciding game with the Giants in 1924, a twelve-inning classic, earned for him a place secure in baseball's Hall of Fame.

When he retired as a player in 1927, after twenty-one consecutive years with one club—a record in itself—he went for a time to the minors as a manager and then returned to Washington to become the leader of the team with which he had started as a major leaguer in 1907. He was manager of the Senators for 1929, 1930, 1931, and 1932.

He retired in 1932, willing to go back to his Maryland farm, but in midsummer of 1933 returned to the big leagues to become manager of the Cleveland team. The Big Train, as he was also called, piloted the Indians until he resigned early in August 1935.

Johnson received much publicity on February 22 of the following year when he hurled two silver dollars across the Rappahannock River—a span of 272 feet—in connection with the annual Washington's Birthday celebration at Fredericksburg, Virginia. He thus duplicated a feat said to have been performed by George Washington in the latter's boyhood days.

The presidential campaign of 1936 found Johnson taking an active interest in politics, and his Maryland farm was the scene of a Republican rally for Alf Landon, governor of Kansas, and his party's candidate for president.

In 1938 Johnson was the lone Republican elected to the Board of Commissioners in Montgomery County, Maryland, adjoining the District of Columbia.

Two years later, he was the Republican nominee to represent Maryland's Sixth Congressional District but was defeated by his Democratic opponent.

Between games of a Yankee-Washington doubleheader at Yankee Stadium on August 23, 1942, Johnson and George Herman "Babe" Ruth came out of retirement to thrill 69,136 fans in a benefit program that enriched the Army-Navy Relief Fund by more than $80,000.

The assemblage gave a tremendous ovation as Johnson walked out to the mound and the Sultan of Swat stepped to the plate. Benny Bengough was behind the plate, with Billy Evans umpiring. Then the Big Train tossed them up, perhaps not so fast, but with the same effortless motion, while Ruth swung with all his old-time fervor.

Looking over his record, one finds it a veritable mine of wonderful feats. He holds the shutout record, having registered 110 in his career. He also struck out more batters than any other pitcher of his day. His total, including his last season as a hurler, 1927, when he was ill and unable to pitch very many times, was 3,508 for 801 games. This record has since been eclipsed, and Johnson now stands seventh on the all-time list, behind Nolan Ryan, Steve Carlton, Tom Seaver, Don Sutton, Bert Blyleven, and Gaylord Perry. His high mark for a season was 313, made in 1910.

These are only a few of forty-five records. His twenty-one years with one club and his pitching 801 games for Washington constitute another. He led the American League in most complete games for the greatest number of years, six, in 1911, 1913, 1914, 1915, 1916, and 1918. He led his league in earned-run average for six years.

Johnson also held the big league record for the greatest number of consecutive scoreless innings, 56 (currently held by Orel Hershiser, who had 59 in 1988), and he once scored three consecutive shutouts in four playing days. On April 15, 1911, he struck out four men in one inning.

Not until 1920 did Johnson pitch his way into the baseball hall of fame reserved for no-hit, no-run games. On July 1 of that year he turned the trick against the Boston Red Sox. In his major league career he won 416 games and lost 279. His best season was in 1913, when he won thirty-six games and lost only seven. He led the American League in games won for six years. His longest winning streak was sixteen, in 1912. He was voted the Most Valuable Player in the American League in 1924.

Johnson was born in Humboldt, Kansas, on November 6, 1887. Drifting out to the Pacific Coast in 1906, Johnson was discovered by a Tacoma (Washington) scout and offered a job with that club, then in the old Northwestern League. For some reason Johnson did not fancy going to Tacoma, and though recorded as a member of that team, he never played with it.

Johnson died in Washington, D.C., at the age of fifty-nine, on December 10, 1946.

The Big Train

By ARTHUR DALEY

Sports writing is a trade in which the superlatives flow in easy fashion. The words "greatest pitcher" and "fastest pitcher" often are bandied about too carelessly. But when they are applied to the Big Train they fit with glove-tailored perfection. However, he was more than merely a mechanical marvel, even though his amazing records were achieved for the most part with a last-place team. The big fellow from Coffeyville, Kansas, was a gentleman of the highest type, a distinct credit to sport.

Not once did he ever question an umpire's decision in a rowdy display of temperament. Never did he throw at a batter's head in the time-honored dusting operation that is designed to "loosen up the hitters." Safe in that knowledge, they took an unfair advantage of him, but still they couldn't touch his blinding speed.

Perhaps the closest he ever came to uttering a word of complaint came in a tight game with the slugging Detroit Tigers. With two out in the ninth the bases were full and Wahoo Sam Crawford was at bat. Walter whistled two strikes past him and the mighty Sam never saw the ball. Then he fogged past a third one that split the heart of the plate, waist high!

Billy Evans was the umpire and Billy was the best arbiter in the league. For some reason he was never been able to explain, Evans called it a ball. He knew he'd booted one, but it was too late to change. All he could do was pray that Wahoo Sam wouldn't hit the next one over the fence. And Crawford came perilously close to doing just that. The Washington center fielder made a miraculous catch near the wall to end the inning.

Walter strode off the mound, a mildly reproachful look on his face. "What was the matter with that pitch?" he asked gently. Evans hedged, shifted uncomfortably, and temporized. "What do you think?" he parried.

Johnson shrugged his shoulders. "Maybe it was a little low, at that," he said in the closest he ever came to a complaint.

The Big Train was not an easy man to umpire. That effortless, graceful sidearm motion of his whipped in the ball at explosive speed. Even the arbiters had to fight hard to keep from closing their eyes instinctively when Walter's swift one rocketed in. Even as great an umpire as Evans had trouble with him.

Johnson fired away one day with Joe Gideon at bat. Much to his chagrin, Evans found that he'd closed his eyes before the ball plummeted into the catcher's glove. But it had been a strike when he last saw it and thus he called it.

"What was it, Billy?" questioned the batter, "a fastball or a curve?"

"Why ask me?" said the embarrassed but quick-thinking Evans.

"I'm asking you," replied Gideon, "because I never saw it myself. I just had to close my eyes."

It was reassuring news to the umpire. No one ever would second-guess him on Johnson. The batters were unable to follow his blinding speed themselves.

But Gideon should have known better than to inquire about the curve.

Johnson never bothered with that fancy stuff in his early days. He just blasted the ball past them, overpowering every hitter on sheer speed. Not until his later days, when that terrific fast one had lost a mite of its zip, did he develop a hook.

It was his speed, though, that made him so famous that many seasons later he still was regarded as the norm of perfection, with the expression "as fast as Johnson" held as the ultimate in fastball pitching. He was so swift that Eddie Ainsmith once puckishly suggested to him in the gathering darkness of a late inning that he merely go through the motion of pitching without throwing the ball. Walter agreed. His right arm swept around, Ainsmith thumped his mitt and the umpire shouted, "Strike!"

The batter wasn't fooled—much. "You blind buzzard!" he screamed at the Man in Blue. "You missed that one. It wuz a foot outside."

It's been an age-old axiom in baseball that you can't hit what you can't see. Yet the Big Train rolled along for most of his career without a curve or change of pace. Every batter knew that each offering was coming in straight as a string. They also knew that the gentlemanly Walter had such perfect control that they never were in danger. So they dug in at the plate and still they couldn't hit him. Even with a last-place team he was winning steadily, averaging twenty-six victories a season for one ten-year stretch and with an earned-run average as incredibly low as 1.14.

The great Ty Cobb unashamedly admitted that he took every advantage of Johnson. "He was one of the finest, most decent men in baseball," he once remarked, "and he was too much a gentleman ever to dust me off at the plate although I deserved it." Cobb crowded the plate, his toes just three inches from the rubber, his knees across it and his chin jutting over the edge. So Walter had to pitch outside to him instead of driving him back the way he should. The result was that Johnson never was too effective against the fiery Georgian, although Ty had been unable to get a loud foul off him until he had adopted the crowding strategy.

The Big Train has reached the end of the line. Not only will he be remembered for his pitching feats but for his nobility of character, a perfect model for American youth.

BOBBY JONES

1902–1971

By FRANK LITSKY

I N THE DECADE following World War I, America luxuriated in the golden era of sports and its greatest collection of superathletes: Babe Ruth and Ty Cobb in baseball, Jack Dempsey and Gene Tunney in boxing, Bill Tilden in tennis, Red Grange in football, and Bobby Jones in golf.

Jones, an intense, unspoiled young man, started early on the road to success. At the age of ten, he shot a 90 for 18 holes. At eleven he was down to 80, and at twelve he shot a 70. At nine he played against men, at fourteen he won a major men's tournament, and at twenty-one he was United States Open champion.

At twenty-eight he achieved the grand slam—victories in one year in the United States Open, British Open, United States Amateur, and British Amateur championships. (Today, the grand slam of golf is winning the Masters, U.S. Open, British Open, and PGA championship in the same year. No golfer had accomplished that feat as of 1990.) At that point, he retired from tournament golf.

A nation that idolized him for his success grew to respect him even more for his decision to treat golf as a game rather than a way of life. He competed only as an amateur.

"First come my wife and children," he once explained. "Next comes my profession—the law. Finally, and never as a life in itself, comes golf."

His record, aside from the grand slam, was magnificent. He won the United States Open championship four times (1923, 1926, 1929, and 1930), the British Open three times (1926, 1927, and 1930), and the United States Amateur five times (1924, 1925, 1927, 1928, and 1930).

"Jones is as truly the supreme artist of golf as Paderewski is the supreme artist of the piano," George H. Greenfield wrote in *The New York Times* in 1930.

Success did not come easily. Though Jones was cool and calculating outwardly, he seethed inside. He could never eat properly during a major tournament. The best his stomach would hold was dry toast and tea.

The pressure of tournament competition manifested itself in other ways, too. Everyone expected Jones to win every time he played, including Atlanta friends who often bet heavily on him. He escaped the unending pressure by retiring from competition.

"Why should I punish myself like this over a golf tournament?" he once asked. "Sometimes I'd pass my mother and dad on the course, look at them and

not even see them because I was so concentrated on the game. Afterward, it made a fellow feel a little silly."

The quality of the man projected itself, too. He was worshipped as a national hero in Scotland, the birthplace of golf. Scots would come for miles around to watch him play.

In 1936, on a visit, he made an unannounced trip to the Royal and Ancient Golf Club at St. Andrews for a quiet morning round with friends. There were 5,000 spectators at the first tee and 7,000 at the eighteenth. Businesses closed as word spread that "Our Bobby is back."

In 1927, when he tapped in his final putt to win the British Open there, an old Scot stood by the green and muttered, "The man canna be human."

Off the course, Jones was convivial in a quiet way. He was a good friend and always the gentleman, though he had full command of strong language when desired. He had a fine sense of humor, and he laughed easily. He smoked cigarettes and drank bourbon.

He was besieged by people who wanted to play a social round of golf with him. When they talked with him, it was always golf. He managed to tolerate their one-sided approach to life. He also learned to put up with the name of Bobby, which he hated (he preferred Bob).

He was not always so serene. As a youngster, he had a reputation for throwing clubs when everything was not going right. When Jim Barnes, the 1921 United States Open champion, watched him let off steam, he said, "Never mind that club throwing and the beatings he's taking. Defeat will make him great. He's not satisfied now with a pretty good shot. He has to be perfect. That's the way a good artist must feel."

The defeats Barnes spoke of were frequent in the early years. For young Jones, though he had the game of a man, had the emotions of a growing boy. He never won the big tournaments until he got his temper under control.

At eighteen, he learned that his greatest opponent was himself. He was playing at Toledo one day with Harry Vardon, the great English professional, and was his usual brash self. They were about even when Jones dribbled a shot into a bunker. Hoping to ease his embarrassment, he turned to Vardon and asked, "Did you ever see a worse shot?"

"No," replied the crusty Vardon. It was the only word he spoke to Jones all day.

He also had the dream of every golfer—a picture swing. No one taught it to him, for he never took a golf lesson in his life. He learned the swing by watching Stewart Maiden, a Scottish professional at the Atlanta Athletic Club course. He would follow Maiden for a few holes, then run home and mimic the swing.

His putting was famous. So was his putter, a rusty, goose-necked club known as Calamity Jane. His strength was driving, putting, and an ability to get out of trouble. He was an imaginative player, and he never hesitated to take a chance. In fact, he seldom hesitated on any shot, and he earned an unfair reputation as a mechanical golfer. The game often baffled him. "There are times," he once said, "when I feel that I know less about what I'm doing on a golf course than anyone else in the world."

When he was an infant, doctors were not sure that he would survive, let alone play golf. He had a serious digestive ailment until he was five, and he stayed home while other children played. In his later years, he was crippled by syringomyelia, a chronic disease of the spinal cord, and he had circulation and heart trouble.

Robert Tyre Jones, Jr. (named for his grandfather), was born on St. Patrick's Day, 1902, in Atlanta. His father was a star outfielder at the University of Georgia, and the youngster's first love was baseball. He also tried tennis. At the age of nine he settled down to golf.

His parents had taken up the game after moving to a cottage near the East Lake course of the Atlanta Athletic Club. Young Bobby would walk around the course, watch the older folk play, and learn by example. He was only six years old, a scrubby youngster with skinny arms and legs, when he won a six-hole tournament. At nine he was the club's junior champion.

He was fourteen when he journeyed to the Merion Cricket Club near Philadelphia for his first United States Amateur championship. He was a chunky lad of 5 feet 4 inches and 165 pounds and somewhat knock-kneed. He was wearing his first pair of long trousers.

After qualifying for match play, he defeated Eben M. Byers, a former champion, in the first round. He beat Frank Dyer, a noted player at the time, in the second round, after losing five of the first six holes. Then he lost to Robert A. Gardner, the defending champion.

In 1922 he reached the semifinals of the United States Amateur before losing. That ended what he called his seven lean years. Next came what Keeler called "the eight fat years" as Jones finally achieved the heights.

All this time, golf was a sidelight to education. Jones wanted to be an engineer, and he earned bachelor's and master's degrees in engineering at Georgia Tech. Then he decided to become a lawyer. He went to Harvard and earned another bachelor's degree, then to Emory University in Atlanta for a Bachelor of Laws degree. In 1928, he joined his father's law firm in Atlanta.

In 1924, Jones decided that he was worrying too much about his opponent in match-play (man against man) competition. He vowed to play for pars and forget about his opponent.

This was a turning point in his career. He started to win match-play competition. That year, at Merion, he won the United States Amateur for the first time. In the final, he defeated George von Elm by the overwhelming score of 9 and 8.

Also in 1924, he married Mary Malone, his high school sweetheart.

In 1929 Jones had a close call in the United States Open at the Winged Foot Golf Club, Mamaroneck, New York He sank a 12-foot sloping, sidehill putt on the last green to tie Al Espinosa. The next day, Jones won their thirty-six-hole title playoff by 23 strokes.

Then came 1930 and the grand slam. Lloyds of London quoted odds of 50 to 1 that Jones wouldn't win the world's four major tournaments that year. He won them.

First came the British Amateur. Next was the British Open at Hoylake, England, and his 72-hole score of 291 won that championship.

Back home, Jones got his sternest test of the year in the United States Open at Interlachen, near Minneapolis. There were 15,000 spectators in the gallery as he played the par-4 eighteenth hole. He got a birdie 3 by sinking a 40-foot undulating putt, and his 287 won by two strokes.

He had become the first man to win three of the four major titles in one year. The last of the grand slam tournaments, the United States Amateur, at Merion, was almost anticlimactic.

No one doubted for the moment that Jones would win. And when he did, the crowd surged around him so wildly that it took a detachment of United States Marines to get him out safely.

Soon after, he retired from tournament play and made a series of golf motion pictures, the only time he ever made money from the game. Later, he became a vice president of A. G. Spalding & Bros., the sporting goods manufacturer. He became a wealthy lawyer and soft-drink bottler and a business and social leader in Atlanta.

He never played serious tournament golf again. He didn't seem to mind.

"Golf is like eating peanuts," he said. "You can play too much or too little. I've become reconciled to the fact that I'll never play as well as I used to."

A few years later, Jones and the late architect, Alister Mackensie, designed the Augusta National Golf Course in Georgia. In 1934 the Masters tournament was started there, and in Jones's lifetime many golf people considered it the most important tournament of all.

Jones played in the first Masters and in several thereafter, but he was never among the leaders. He always wore his green jacket, signifying club membership, at victory ceremonies, and he served as club president.

He became strong enough to rip a pack of playing cards across the middle, but his health deteriorated. He underwent spinal surgery in 1948 and 1950. He was forced to use one cane, then two canes, and then a wheelchair, and his weight dropped to less than a hundred pounds. He last saw the Masters in 1967.

He was a close friend of Dwight D. Eisenhower, and the president often used his cottage adjacent to the Augusta National course for golfing vacations. During his first term in office, the president painted a 40-by-32-inch oil portrait of Jones at the peak of his game. On the back was printed by hand:

"Bob—from his friend D.D.E. 1953."

In January of 1953, three months after a heart attack, Jones was honored at Golf House, the United States Golf Association headquarters in Manhattan. Augusta National members, including General Eisenhower, had donated another oil portrait to be hung at Golf House. A highlight of the ceremony was the reading of a letter from the president.

"Those who have been fortunate enough to know him," the letter said, "realize that his fame as a golfer is transcended by his inestimable qualities as a human being. . . . His gift to his friends is the warmth that comes from unselfishness, superb judgment, nobility of character, unwavering loyalty to principle."

Bobby Jones listened and cried.

He died on December 18, 1971, at the age of sixty-nine.

Bobby's "Grand Slam"

By WILLIAM D. RICHARDSON

When Gene Homans's ball grazed the side of the cup on the twenty-ninth hole at the Merion Cricket Club, Bobby Jones not only became the national amateur champion for 1930 but the holder of a record that probably will survive through the ages.

At twenty-eight, this rarely gifted golfer from Atlanta, who defeated Homans 8 up and 7 to play in the final and who came closer to mastering the intricacies of the game than anyone else, performed a feat that no one hitherto had considered possible.

Within the short span of five months, Bobby played in the four major golf events—the British Amateur and Open championships and the American Open and Amateur—and won them all, outscoring the professionals at their own game in the two open tournaments and outstripping all his fellow amateurs in the others.

Moreover he became the first man in the history of American golf to win the National amateur five times, he and Jerry Travers, who was in the gallery that followed the marvelous Atlantan today, having previously been tied at four victories each.

It was no more than appropriate that all these honors should be spread at Bobby's feet on the same golf course where, as a boy of fourteen, he made his debut in championship golf in 1916 and where, eight years later, he broke his spell of failures in the Amateur by beating George von Elm, 9 and 8.

No one in the great throng of fully 18,000 spectators, who made a great human fringe around the green and a solid mass packed in the fairway that Jones had just played from, could help but feel that here was golf history being made.

Regret for Homans, who had put up a resistance that looked weak beside the finished golf of the world's greatest golfer, was overbalanced by the joy of seeing the southerner make his record.

It was an epochal moment, and the demonstration that came after it was one that will never be forgotten. Playing the hole, a two-shotter with two level fairways and an island green tucked away back in the woods, Jones was dormie 8. But a moment before he had missed a chance to close out the match on the previous hole by misjudging a little pitch shot out of the rough and putting his ball into a bunker alongside Homans's.

Both sides of the fairway were lined with persons ten and twelve rows deep as he and Homans drove off. It was Gene's honor, Bobby having conceded him a birdie 2 on the No. 9 hole. The ex-Princeton star, realizing by now, of course, that it was all over, drove to the left.

Having nothing to lose, Bobby lit into his drive and sent his ball flying down the fairway. It was a long drive, almost reaching the edge of the little stream that runs across the fairway near the 300-yard mark. Homans had to play first and sent a beautiful mashie shot onto the green, a trifle beyond the hole. A moment later Bobby's ball came sailing on, stopping short of the pin.

Despite the fact that all those thousands were standing as close as they could get, the dropping of a pin in the grass would have been heard as Bobby, looking a little haggard and drawn, walked over to his ball after his caddie had handed him his pet putter, known the world over as Calamity Jane. One of those quizzical glances that he gives the hole, the familiar cocking of the Jones head, a slight movement of the wrists as they brought the club back and then forward.

The ball started on its journey up to the hole over the closely cropped grass. He didn't quite have the line, but it stopped so close to the side of the hole that Homans would have had to sink his in order to prevent the match from ending there and then. Knowing full well that it was all over, Gene took comparatively little time over his own putt, hit the ball, and almost before it passed by the side of the hole he was over wringing Bobby's hand.

Immediately a great shout was sent up, then the tumult that reverberated for miles. It lasted for several minutes. There was a wild rush toward Jones who, had it not been for the presence of a squad of marines, would have been crushed.

It was some moments before order was restored and an opening made through which Jones and Homans could walk over to the No. 12 fairway and begin their journey back to the clubhouse. And over the entire distance Jones was cheered on as triumphant a journey as any man ever traveled in sport.

The match was far more of a spectacle than it was a contest. As a matter of fact there was not much contest to it. It was merely an exhibition on Jones's part, a parade to victory.

Approached Perfection

By ARTHUR DALEY

Bobby Jones was buried in the red clay of his native Georgia in December 1971 and it would seem indecent not to add one more fond farewell to a man who was one of the most admired and beloved figures in sports. It was more than four decades since Bobby retired from the excitements of major golf tournaments, and yet his magic endured. Nor will the legend of Robert Tyre Jones, Jr., ever grow less. He truly belongs to the ages.

Some day, perhaps, someone will break the Jones record of winning thirteen major tournaments, but all it will amount to will be an exercise in arithmetic. It will not supersede Bobby's feats. It will merely enhance them. The sweet-swinging Georgian not only dominated the sport during his seven-year tenure but he did it as an amateur. Four times he won the United States Open and three times he won the British Open, outplaying the best professionals in the world in order to achieve so phenomenal an accomplishment. At the age of twenty-eight he retired, and it boggles the mind to think what else he might have done had he elected to continue with the same high degree of intensity.

Of all the rounds of golf that Bobby shot over the years, though, the one that has always held me in a grip of utter fascination was one he fashioned at Sunningdale during the British Open championship of 1926. This was an era, mind you, when par figures were considered reasonably sacred, especially in Britain. Furthermore, play was with wooden-shafted clubs and the wedge had not been invented. So Bobby had none of today's stroke-savers.

At Sunningdale on that extraordinary day the Emperor Jones came about as close to perfection as ever can be achieved on a golf course. Par was 72. He left the gallery stunned with a 66.

But the details are what put such a strain on credulity. On the outgoing nine Bobby scored a 33. He therefore also had a 33 on the trip in. He had exactly 33 putts and 33 other strokes. He did not have a 2 or a 5 on his card. He had six 4's and three 3's on each nine.

Ever since I read about that spectacular round, I was itching to catch up with the Emperor Jones and get a firsthand report from him. Ordinary golfers usually get so swept away by the might-have-been that their judgment becomes warped. But when I finally corraled Bobby Jones, I discovered that he recognized this round for exactly what it was.

"It was as perfect a round as I ever played in my life," he said with that delightful drawl.

A smile of satisfaction lighted up that handsome face and his eyes were twinkling. Without even trying, he snowed everyone with his overwhelming charm and appeal. No wonder he was so popular an idol, one of the glittering showpieces of the golden age of sports.

"Even when I shoot a good round of golf," he related, "I doubt that I put six shots exactly where I want. But this was uncanny. I holed one putt of 18 feet, but I didn't have another difficult putt all day. I made two mistakes on the entire round. Both proved trifling. On the short thirteenth I hooked my tee shot into the bunker but I blew out to within three feet of the cup. On the seventeenth I twisted my drive some five feet off the fairway. But the grass wasn't deep and I put the ball on the green. What a round that was!"

When Bobby won the British Amateur championship in 1930, the germ of an idea took root in his mind. This had always been his jinx tournament, one he couldn't even come close to winning. But now that he had triumphed he wondered out loud for the first time if he might have a chance at golfdom's Grand Slam, once described in George Trevor's purple prose as the Impregnable Quadrilateral.

A fortnight later the Emperor Jones was in the British Open. He was not sharp and seemed to be in constant trouble. Doggedly he scrambled out of difficulty after difficulty. It's a sign of greatness, though, when a man can win even when not at his best. Bobby won and he was halfway there.

It was in the United States Open that Bobby accepted help from Lady Luck. Surging galleries barely gave him room to swing his clubs and his idolators almost did him in. Just as he was on the downswing for a delicate loft over a lake to an island green, two little girls broke through the lines for his autograph.

The startled Bobby half-topped the ball. It rocketed toward the lake. Historians have since been calling it the lily pad shot. The ball skipped across the lake like a skipping stone and came to rest on dry land, 30 yards short of the green. He won the United States Open. He won the United States Amateur. He had his Grand Slam. Many years later Sammy Snead asked the Emperor Jones which championship he most wanted to win.

"Whatever one I was in at the time," said Bobby. That told it all.

JOE LAPCHICK

1900–1970

By GEORGE VECSEY

J OE LAPCHICK began his career in the dance-hall days of basketball, a gangly young man with a grade school education who was trying to keep away from the factories.

He ended his career as a respected educator, a basketball coach at St. John's University who supervised his players' study habits and warned them of the dangers of associating with gamblers.

Lapchick, a gentle man, honest and smart, had a nervous stomach and jangled nerves, souvenirs of too many close games. Yet he endured in basketball and retired in 1965 only because of a mandatory retirement rule at St. John's.

Joseph Bohomiel Lapchick was born on April 12, 1900, to a Czechoslovak immigrant family in Yonkers. The family was poor, and young Joe helped out by collecting coal from the railroad tracks.

Basketball was just working its way down from Springfield, Massachusetts, where it had been invented in 1890 by Dr. James Naismith of Springfield College. Young Lapchick, already 6 feet 2 inches tall at the age of twelve, was playing on a number of club teams, in a uniform his mother had made.

One day Mrs. Lapchick hung out the uniform on the clothesline of their tenement. When her husband came home, he spotted the skimpy outfit.

"What is that?" Mr. Lapchick roared.

"That's my basketball uniform, Dad," the young man replied.

"You mean you get in front of people dressed like that?" shouted the father.

At fourteen, after graduation from Public School 20 in Yonkers, young Lapchick went to work, first as a golf caddy, later in a factory, working a ten-hour day for about fifteen dollars a week.

But he found it more profitable to hang around the information booth at Grand Central Terminal juggling offers from the Holyoke Reds, the Brooklyn Visitations, and other clubs. A good negotiator, he worked his way up to seventy-five dollars a game.

Finally, Lapchick got to play against the best team in the area, the New York Celtics, and their experienced center, Horse Haggerty. When Haggerty wore out in the early 1920s, Lapchick joined the Celtics.

They were the finest team of that day, not big by today's standards, but rough and smart. Nat Holman, Dutch Dehnerg, Chris Leonard, Pete Barry, Johnny Beckman, and the 6-foot-5-inch Lapchick toured the East.

The tour was a succession of one-night stands, automobile rides, and

third-rate accommodations. There was no such thing as medical aid. If a man was hurt, his teammates treated him.

Once Lapchick had a nasty cut on his wrist that became infected from the green dye of the uniforms. Johnny Beckman, the leading medical authority of the Celtics, knotted a towel, rubbed off the scab, and poured whisky on the wound. The whisky killed the infection; Lapchick survived.

The Celtics dominated the American Basketball League until the other teams insisted they disband. Lapchick was assigned to Cleveland, where he helped win two straight championships before the Depression ended the league.

From 1930 to 1935, Lapchick pulled his old teammates together and toured as the Original Celtics, backed by Kate Smith, the singer.

In 1936 Lapchick took the coaching job at St. John's College of Brooklyn. He was nervous about facing young men with better educations than his own. For a while he merely let them shoot baskets in practice, but eventually he paced off the old Celtic plays, showing how Nat Holman used to work the "give-and-go."

St. John's soon became a prominent team, winning the National Invitation Tournament in 1943 and 1944. In the 1944 finals, Lapchick fainted early in the second half but woke up to see his players holding a 12-point lead just before the final buzzer.

After the 1947 season, Lapchick accepted the coaching job of the New York Knickerbockers in the National Basketball Association. Pro ball had grown up considerably in Lapchick's absence, but there was still a 70-game grind, one-night stands, strange travel connections, and constant pressure.

Lapchick was a peaceful man, enjoying his home and three children, working in his flower garden: pro basketball made a nervous wreck of him.

Sometimes he would rip off his jacket, pull the sleeves inside out, and stomp on it. Once he threw a water tray in the air and it fell on his head, drenching him. Another time he smashed a chair against a wall. Sometimes he feared that his team would not score a single point that night.

"The trouble with you," a doctor told him, "is that day after day, you're suffering what the average person suffers once or twice in a lifetime."

One thing Lapchick particularly hated was cutting a player from the squad. Once he had to give the bad news to young Tommy Byrne, just out of Seton Hall College. A few minutes, later, Lapchick collapsed on the floor. He spent a week in the hospital before his system calmed down.

For all his suffering, Lapchick was a good coach, patient and knowledgeable. The Knicks did not have a superstar, but they worked together and in three straight years—1951, 1952, and 1953—they reached the finals of the playoffs, only to lose.

When the Knicks began to fade, Lapchick began to feel pressure from his boss, Ned Irish, and in 1956 he resigned. At the age of fifty-six he started all over again at St. John's.

This time Lapchick knew the right words and the techniques of coaching. But the angular, bald man was more than a coach. He lectured his young players on the value of a college degree, sometimes looming over them in study hall.

The coach had another message for his players. He had kept newspaper clippings about several basketball gambling scandals and pasted them in a scrapbook. Before each season, he made each player read the clippings—and sign his name after reading it.

The young players responded well to the coach. Perhaps Lapchick's greatest asset was his ability to inspire his players. They may have laughed at his speeches—but then they ran out on the court and "gave 110 percent," just as he had asked.

The players knew he was being forced to retire after the 1964–65 season because of the university rule, so they dedicated themselves to "win for the coach."

They responded by clawing past a superior Michigan team, with Cazzie Russell, to win the Holiday Festival in December 1964. Then in March of 1965 they beat Villanova, 55–51, in the finals of the NIT.

"What a way to go," Lapchick shouted as his players hoisted him on their shoulders.

He died of a heart attack on August 10, 1970, in Monticello, New York, where he was serving as sports coordinator of Kutsher's Country Club.

A Place with Rockne and McGraw

By LEONARD KOPPETT

Pride was the mainspring of Joe Lapchick's character and philosophy. That he had a philosophy, in the most unpretentious way, was the aspect of his personality that made the most lasting impression on the thousands of people who had direct dealings with him through the half-century he lived in the sports limelight. He preached pride—pride in oneself, pride in accomplishment, pride in being a true professional who delivers all the effort he is paid for, pride in being able to win without gloating and to lose without whining.

As a basketball coach, he never presented himself as a tactical genius or master technician. He taught attitudes rather than mechanics, and he had one of the rarest and least definable qualities a leader can have: the capacity for bringing out the best in the men who played for him, not "for the coach," but out of the sense of obligation he could make them feel toward themselves.

His career went through four stages, all marked by success. In his twenties, he became one of the best professional basketball players in his day. In his mid-thirties, with no college education and no teaching experience, he became coach of St. John's and took a key role in the process that built basketball from a localized to a national mass spectator sport.

In his mid-forties, he returned to the pros as coach of the newly formed New York Knickerbockers and played a vital part in building the stability and success of the National Basketball Association.

Finally, approaching sixty, he returned to St. John's, to a college basketball world in which recruiting competition was far more extensive than any he had faced. Once again he produced championship teams whose main characteristic was fighting spirit. When he retired in 1965, he remained a familiar and gregarious figure on the basketball scene, an elder statesman whose advice was always sought and freely given.

In each stage, he had an important effect on the basketball world. As a player, he was a "giant" at 6 feet 5 inches in a day of few 6-footers, skinny and tough. He won most fame as a member of the Original Celtics, the team that dominated the sport so thoroughly in the 1920s that no effective league could be formed around it.

His more famous teammate, Nat Holman, was already coaching City College and was accepted as the greatest player. But Lapchick, even then, had started to learn and to prove the basic fact of basketball's future: the overwhelming importance of getting the ball, and therefore the inescapable supremacy of the big man.

In his first tour at St. John's, college basketball blossomed through the Madison Square Garden doubleheaders, and four coaches and their teams took the lead in selling the game to the public: Lapchick, Holman, Clair Bee, at Long Island University, and Howard Cann, of New York University.

Cann was basically shy, reserved; Holman aloof; Bee and Lapchick were the gregarious ones, but Bee was busier and more erratic. In educating the press and public about basketball's inner dramas, Lapchick was of supreme importance.

When he went to the Knicks, he performed the same function for the NBA. His reputation made him the most sought after figure connected with the league, and he used his position to promote pride, dignity (despite lost battles with himself about referee baiting), and maximum honest effort.

It's not a coincidence that so many of his players became coaches. He can be compared, in this way, to Knute Rockne in football and to John McGraw in baseball. When he returned to St. John's, he cemented the bonds between college and professional basketball, helping to make them, in the minds of the public, more than ever two parts of one attractive sport.

His legacy, and his philosophy, were often expressed in one sentence: "Anyone can walk with kings if he walks straight." Belief in yourself, he felt, was what mattered—and one had to try to behave so that the belief would be justified.

You might fail, and the exceedingly human Lapchick did at times, but you had to try. Few major sports figures went through so long a career generating so much affection in so many places, and that's something no statistic can match.

VINCE LOMBARDI

1913–1970

V INCE LOMBARDI was the professional football coach who symbolized toughness and dedication in sports.

He guided the Green Bay Packers to the premier position in the National Football League in the 1960s and sought to do the same with the Washington Redskins in the 1970s.

The Redskins had long been losers. But Vincent Thomas Lombardi had never associated with losers in his thirty-one years as a football coach.

His first year in Washington, the Redskins had their first winning record in fourteen seasons.

"Winning isn't everything," Lombardi once insisted. "It is the only thing."

Under his direction the Green Bay Packers won six division titles and five National Football League championships in nine seasons between 1959 and 1967. This was professional football's best winning record, and Lombardi was acclaimed as the sport's best coach.

He retired from coaching after the 1967 season, when he was fifty-four years old. But his wife and his close friends wondered how long he could stay away from the sidelines. The answer: one year. Most pro football games are played on Sunday afternoons, and during the season that Lombardi confined himself to the duties of the Packers' general manager he said, "I miss the fire on Sunday."

Lombardi was a symbol of authority.

"When he says 'Sit down,' I don't even bother to look for a chair," one of the Packer players explained.

"He's fair. He treats us all the same—like dogs," said Henry Jordan, another Packer.

"He coaches through fear," said Bill Curry, a sensitive player Lombardi let go.

Most of his athletes accepted his demanding ways and biting criticisms. His primary target was a player named Marvin Fleming, who said in reflection, "I didn't mind. When I came to him, I didn't have anything. He taught me how to be a winner."

Another Packer, Jerry Kramer, said, "His whippings, his cussings, and his driving all fade: his good qualities endure."

Lombardi admitted that his scoldings sometimes were merely for effect. During his last season at Green Bay, when he was goading an aging team to

another championship, he said, "I have to go on that field every day and whip people. It's for them, not just me. I'm getting to be an animal."

Lombardi was always a hard man when it came to football. In college, at Fordham, where he graduated with honors in 1937, he played guard on a famous line called the Seven Blocks of Granite. He was the smallest of the group at 5 feet 8 inches and 175 pounds. "But he hit like 250," a teammate said.

The son of an immigrant Italian butcher, Lombardi was born June 11, 1913, and grew up in the Sheepshead Bay section of Brooklyn. He went to Cathedral High School and St. Francis Preparatory School before Fordham. He had ambitions to study for the Roman Catholic priesthood for a while, but after graduation he went to law school for a year.

He supported himself by playing for a minor league football team, the Brooklyn Eagles, and serving as an insurance investigator. But a coaching career was calling and in 1939 he joined the faculty at St. Cecilia High School in Englewood, New Jersey. For an annual salary of $1,700 he was an assistant football coach and a teacher of physics, chemistry, algebra, and Latin.

Lombardi stayed at St. Cecilia for seven years. He soon was head coach of the football, basketball, and baseball squads. His football teams won six state championships and had a string of thirty-six victories in a row.

He returned to Fordham to coach the freshmen in 1947 and served as an assistant in 1948. When Ed Danowski was reappointed head coach for the 1949 season, Lombardi left and joined Colonel Earl Blaik's staff at the United States Military Academy.

Life at West Point suited Lombardi and he was strongly influenced by Colonel Blaik, who had his own hero, General Douglas MacArthur. Lombardi, too, became a disciple of General MacArthur, and in ensuing years he attempted to inspire his teams by quoting one or the other of the military men with sayings such as "If you can walk, you can run."

Pro football beckoned in 1954 when the New York Giants put together a new coaching staff under Jim Lee Howell, who delegated the offense to Lombardi.

"Vince didn't understand our game," said Frank Gifford, one of his stars. "At first we players were showing him. But by the end of the season he was showing us."

Lombardi's opportunity to be a head coach did not come until 1959, when he was forty-six, which is considered old in that line of work. The Green Bay Packers, a community-owned team in a city of only 70,000, were losers and troubled financially.

The directors offered Lombardi the job as coach and general manager. He insisted upon full authority and they gave it to him. The prior coach, Ray McLean, had a team that won only one game in twelve. With a nucleus of the same players, Lombardi's first Packer team won seven of twelve games and tied for third place in the western division of the NFL.

The next season they were first but lost the league championship to the Philadelphia Eagles. Then the parade began, with league titles in 1961, 1962, 1965, 1966, and 1967, plus Super Bowl victories over the American League champion in 1967 and 1968.

During his span of nine seasons as head coach, Lombardi saw his teams win 141 games, lose 39, and tie 4. He insisted that the Packers never lost. Time merely ran out on them.

Green Bay, the smallest city in the league, became nationally known, and the citizens adulated Lombardi. They named the street outside the stadium Lombardi Avenue.

One year when the Los Angeles Rams were striving to woo him away, the directors gave Lombardi 320 acres of apple orchards in nearby Door County.

Under the rules of their incorporation, the Packers could not pay their 1,700 stockholders any dividends. The money piled up and Lombardi spent it in enlarging the stadium and building a magnificent field house. After the winning of the first championship, he bought the players' wives mink stoles.

To keep a touted rookie from Texas, Donny Anderson, from signing with the rival American Football League, Lombardi agreed to pay the young man the highest bonus in pro football's history, $600,000.

Lombardi, who had a keen appreciation for money, related winning to business success in pro football. "The teams that win the most make the most money," he said.

Although the Packers had annual profits as high as $800,000, Lombardi insisted upon keeping players' salaries "in line." Jim Ringo, a center who once played a game for Lombardi with fourteen painful boils, held out for more money one season. He was traded the next.

The Packer fullback star, Jim Taylor, exercised the option clause in his contract and became a free agent so he could sign for more money with another team. The other running star, Paul Hornung, retired the same year. "We'll miss Hornung," Lombardi said. "The other fellow we'll replace."

Hornung was a favorite of the coach. Lombardi was deeply hurt when Hornung was suspended for the 1963 season for gambling in violation of his contract, but Lombardi quickly forgave him.

The Catholic and military influences upon Lombardi were strong. After the assassination of Senator Robert F. Kennedy, whom he knew, Lombardi said, "What's the matter with the world? There has been a complete breakdown of mental discipline."

In speaking before an audience of businessmen, Lombardi said, "There is an abuse of freedom in our society—freedom without responsibility."

He deplored the long hair, sideburns, mustaches of youth. He told a Redskin rookie, Trenton Jackson, "You could run faster if you didn't have that thing on your lip." Jackson shaved off the mustache at lunchtime.

Lombardi maintained there was no mystery to the Packer success. "Coaches who can outline plays on a blackboard are a dime a dozen," he once said. "The ones who win get inside their players and motivate them."

Perhaps there was no mystery. But the Packers had a losing record the first season after he retired as coach.

Lombardi believed in attacking strength. "Hit them at their strongest point," he said. Before their first regular season game in his first year at Green Bay, Lombardi told the Packers in the locker room, "Go through that door and bring back victory."

Bill Forester, a tackle, said, "I jumped up and hit my arm on my locker. It was the worst injury I had all year."

Lombardi loved to laugh, and his friends delighted in his company. But he put off strangers, and the public regarded him with both awe and fear.

René Carpenter, the former wife of the astronaut Scott Carpenter, described a reception held for Lombardi when he first came to Washington. "All of a sudden my skirt was too short and my back too bare," she said. "We were reduced to feeling like children."

In 1970, Lombardi was found to be suffering from an extraordinarily virulent form of cancer.

He underwent two operations. After the first, on June 27, he appeared to be recovering and was released on July 14. However, his condition deteriorated and he had to be operated on a second time, on July 27.

He died on September 3 at the age of fifty-seven.

The First Super Bowl

By WILLIAM N. WALLACE

Bryan Bartlett "Bart" Starr, the quarterback for the Green Bay Packers, led his team to a 35–10 victory over the Kansas City Chiefs on January 15, 1967, in the first professional football game between the champions of the National and American Football Leagues.

Doubt about the outcome disappeared in the third quarter when Starr's pretty passes made mere Indians out of the AFL Chiefs and Green Bay scored twice.

Those fourteen points stretched Green Bay's lead to 28–10, and during the final quarter many of the spectators in the crowd of 63,036 left the Los Angeles Memorial Coliseum, which had been only two-thirds filled.

The outcome served to settle the curiosity of the customers, who paid from five to twelve dollars for tickets, and a television audience estimated at 60 million, regarding the worth of the Chiefs.

The final score was an honest one, meaning it correctly reflected what went on during the game. The great interest had led to naming the event the Super Bowl, but the contest was more ordinary than super.

Starr, methodical and unruffled as ever, completed 16 of 23 passes, six producing first downs on key third-down plays. Seven completions went to Max McGee, a thirty-four-year-old substitute end who was in action only because Boyd Dowler, the regular, was hurt on the game's sixth play.

McGee scored two of Green Bay's five touchdowns, the first one after an outstanding one-handed, hip-high catch of a pass thrown slightly behind him.

The Packers, who had been favored by two touchdowns, knew they were in a challenging game for at least half of the 2½-hour contest.

Kansas City played very well in the first two quarters and the halftime score, 14–10, made the teams just about even. Green Bay's offense was sluggish. Kansas City had stopped the Packer rushing game and Starr had not exploited the Chiefs' defensive men—Fred Williamson and Willie Mitchell—who looked vulnerable. Bart was to take care of that matter in the second half.

The Chiefs, with Len Dawson running the offense at quarterback, had found they could pass on Green Bay, so three times the team was in scoring range. Out of that came one touchdown, scored by the fullback, Curtis McClinton, on a 7-yard pass from Dawson, and a 31-yard field goal by Mike Mercer.

But that was all for Kansas City. In the second half the mighty Packer defense shut out the Chiefs, who were in the Green Bay half of the field only once—for one play. And they were only four yards into Packer territory.

The Packers changed their defensive tactics for the second half. They had not blitzed their linebackers during the first two periods, and the four rushing linemen were unable to get at Dawson.

But the blitz came in the third period and Dawson found himself harassed.

Three times he was dropped for losses and once, under blitzing pressure, he threw a weak pass that Willie Wood intercepted for Green Bay and ran back 50 yards to the Kansas City 5-yard line.

Elijah Pitts, the halfback, scored on first down from the 5, running off left tackle behind a power block from Bob Skoronski, a tackle. That gave the Packers a 21–10 lead, and they were in command for good.

The pass rush that led to Wood's interception was the key play. The Chiefs and Dawson never recovered. The Kansas City quarterback later left the field and Pete Beathard took his place in the fourth quarter.

For their efforts the forty Packer players won $15,000 each, with $7,500 going to each Chief. Gate receipts were estimated at $750,000, and two television networks—the Columbia Broadcasting System and the National Broadcasting Company—paid $1 million apiece for the TV rights. So this was a $2,750,000 event, the richest for any American team sports event up to that time.

Starr was worth every cent of his $15,000. In the first period he took his team 80 yards in six quick plays for the opening score. The sixth play, on third down, was the 37-yard pass to McGee on which Max made his great catch.

Kansas City tied the score at 7–7 in the second quarter with a six-play, 66-yard drive featuring three passes by Dawson to Mike Garrett, Otis Taylor, and McClinton, the one to McClinton for a touchdown.

Starr connected on a 64-yard touchdown pass play to Carroll Dale (on third down), but a Packer lineman was illegally in motion and the play was called back. That failed to bother Starr, who after eleven subsequent plays had the Packers over the Kansas City goal line.

It was a beautiful series of plays. On four third-down situations, Starr passed successfully for the first down. The score was made from 14 yards out by hard-running Jim Taylor on a sweep behind blocking by the guards, Fred Thurston and Jerry Kramer.

Just before the half, Kansas City drove to the Green Bay 31, but a pass to Garrett failed to pick up a first down and Mercer kicked a field goal that cut the NFL team's lead to 14–10.

In the second half Starr concentrated on Mitchell, the cornerback who had had so much trouble covering McGee and Dale. Bart had great protection, and on two touchdown drives that featured the pass, he probed at Mitchell's position successfully five times.

On these drives, one of 56 yards in the third quarter and one of 80 yards in the fourth, Starr completed seven of eight passes with cool precision. The Chiefs were helpless to stop him.

The first score was made by McGee from 13 yards out. He casually bobbled the ball, then caught it for six points, performing as if he were back in Green Bay during a routine practice on a Wednesday afternoon. McGee had caught only four passes during Green Bay's regular 14-game season.

The second touchdown went to Pitts, who slid off left tackle from a yard out as the Packer line closed down to the inside.

The Green Bay execution was as impeccable as ever. The only mistake was a harmless interception by Mitchell of a pass by Starr. It was the first interception against Starr since last October 16. He had thrown 173 passes without an interception.

The Packer defense held the elusive Garrett to only 17 yards and Kansas City's offense had a net gain of only 239 yards. At the end the Packers were playing substitutes, but Paul Hornung never got in the game.

The Super Bowl games would go on year after year, but the AFL would not win its first until after the Green Bay dynasty had ended.

A Farewell
By ARTHUR DALEY

In the swirling, emotional frenzy that engulfed the Green Bay Packers after their outrageously dramatic victory over the Dallas Cowboys in the final thirteen seconds of the 1967 championship playoff, the heroes were interviewed endlessly. No statement struck with more impact than that delivered by Jerry Kramer, whose thunderous block had cleared the path for Bart Starr's winning touchdown.

In his role as the Packer intellectual, big Jerry reached all the way to Camelot to find a parallel to the one-for-all spirit of the Green Bay team. Then he spoke of his coach, Vince Lombardi.

"This is one beautiful man," said Jerry.

It was a strange choice of words, almost jarring in their incongruity. Vince was one of the least beautiful of men—on the outside. But Kramer was looking deeper. He saw what also had been seen by the Lombardi friends, players, associates, and others closely connected with him over the years—a beautiful man.

That's why there had been so much apprehension in sports circles in the summer of 1970 as the whispers kept spreading that Vince had been victimized by cancer. It was to be the same race-horse type that mowed down five years ago another beautiful man, Jack Mara of the football Giants, Vinnie's close friend. Each had a nobility of character, although the Lombardi personality was far more complex than Mara's.

No one could possibly have offered a more penetrating description of

Vince than did Kramer in his best-selling book, *Instant Replay.* It also will do as an epitaph. Here it is:

"Vincent Thomas Lombardi, a cruel, kind, tough, gentle, miserable, wonderful man whom I often hate and often love and always respect."

It was fascinating for me to watch Vinnie gain that respect and that stature because I first knew him when he was one of the Seven Blocks of Granite at Fordham. True friendship was to come later.

A stay at West Point under Red Blaik was to have a profound influence on Vinnie's life and career. Lombardi learned from his idol, Blaik, what Blaik had learned from his idol, General MacArthur: "There is no substitute for victory."

That's the way Vince coached. He was demanding, but the rewards were great as he took a moribund Packer franchise and built a dynasty, climaxing it with two successive Super Bowl victories. Sure, he was a slave driver of uncompromising intensity.

"He treats all of us the same—like dogs," once remarked the flippant Henry Jordan.

But they were repaid with the winning shares of championship games and Super Bowl games. Like Kramer, they had a love-hate syndrome working for them and they respected him to an ultimate degree.

If he coached through fear, as one of his players once remarked, it has to be a left-handed tribute to the overwhelming strength of the man that he could command such iron discipline in an era when men sneered contemptuously at authority, including such once impregnable strongholds as the army, the courts, and the church.

Vince was so strong that he just couldn't comprehend the situation when he first was ordered to the hospital only weeks before his death. It was impossible, he thought, that anyone with his vigor could be ill. It was almost as if he expected to wish it away by sheer will power.

When he left the hospital the first time, the player-owner battle was raging so heatedly that there was no indication that it would be settled in time to start the regular season, much less the exhibition season. Vince showed up at one session, pale and a trifle gaunt. But the old fires were still blazing within him.

"Gentlemen," he said to the owners, "don't give away your game to a bunch of twenty-two-year-old kids."

It was the voice of management, which he had become. It was not heeded too strictly in the panic of a quick settlement. But the Lombardi words made a more lasting impression than he thought when he spoke them. They are likely to be remembered in the years to come. Many owners have since repeated them as if they were something to be treasured.

There was nothing esoteric about the football Vince taught. It was straightaway stuff, based on those two key fundamentals, good blocking and good tackling. He taught them so well in his demanding reach toward perfection that he has been acclaimed as the most successful coach of his era.

He has become a football legend and his place in history is secure. But the vital, vibrant force of Vince Lombardi has been stilled and the game will be that much the poorer for it.

JOE LOUIS

1914–1981

By DEANE McGOWEN

S LOW OF FOOT but redeemingly fast of hands, Joe Louis dominated heavyweight boxing in a long reign. As world champion, he defended his title twenty-five times, facing all challengers and fighting the best that the world could offer. In the opinion of many experts, the plain, simple, unobtrusive Brown Bomber—as he was known—with his rushing left jab and hook, was one of the best heavyweight fighters of all time.

The 6-foot, 1½-inch, 197-pound Louis won his title June 22, 1937, in Chicago by knocking out James J. Braddock in eight rounds, thus becoming the first black heavyweight champion since Jack Johnson, who had reigned earlier in the century. Before Louis retired undefeated as champion on March 1, 1949, his last title defense was against Jersey Joe Walcott. Louis knocked him out in New York on June 25, 1948.

As the titleholder, his fights had grossed more than $4.6 million, of which he received about $800,000.

A fighter who wasted little time in dispatching his opponents, Louis's earnings per round were extraordinarily high. Of the twenty-five defenses, only three went the full 15 rounds. Tony Galento, for example, survived four rounds in 1939, and Buddy Baer managed one round in 1942.

Excluding exhibitions, Louis won 68 professional fights and lost only 3. He scored 54 knockouts, including five in the first round. After retiring, he continued to appear in exhibitions, and in 1950 he decided to make a comeback but was beaten by Ezzard Charles in 15 rounds. His final professional bout took place on October 26, 1951, when he lost to Rocky Marciano in New York.

The most spectacular victim of Louis's robust punches was Max Schmeling, the German fighter who was personally hailed by Adolf Hitler as a paragon of Teutonic manhood. Schmeling, who had knocked out Louis in 12 rounds in 1936, was given a return bout on June 22, 1938, in Yankee Stadium. He was knocked out in 2 minutes 4 seconds of the first round.

Describing the bout in *The New York Times*, John Kieran wrote:

Well, of all things! It's on and it's over. Just as Joe promised. He stepped in and started a lightning attack. Lefts and rights—Bang! Bang! Bang! Schmeling reeled into the ropes on the first-base side of the ring and clung like a ship-wrecked soldier to a lifeline.

Swaying on the ropes, Max peered out in a bewildered manner. He pushed himself off and Louis struck like dark lightning again. A ripping left

and a smashing right. The right was the crusher. Schmeling went down. He was up again and then, under another fusillade, down again. Once more, and barely able to stand, and then down for the third and final time.

Not all of Louis's fights were so savage. Many of his adversaries entered the ring already quaking and his task of finishing them off was thus a matter of a half-dozen solid punches at the proper moment.

There was no Joe Louis behind any facade. He was the same slow-spoken, considerate person in a close social group as he was to the vast crowds that surged in on him to clutch his every word when he was at the apogee of the boxing world.

A simple dignity was characteristic of Louis, who never pretended that his sharecropper origins in Alabama were more than humble.

Louis was born Joseph Louis Barrow on May 13, 1914, in the cotton field country near Lafayette, Alabama, the eighth child of Munn and Lilly Barrow. His boyhood was one of want and little schooling.

In his teens, he did odd jobs to help his family until they moved to Detroit. He worked as a laborer there in the River Rouge plant of the Ford Company.

The future champion attended Bronson Vocational School for a time to learn cabinetmaking, before turning to amateur boxing at the request of a schoolmate. He made his boxing debut in an amateur tournament in Detroit, where he was then making his home, as a light-heavyweight.

He lost the decision, getting knocked down three times by Johnny Miller in a three-rounder. However, he persevered and in 1934 won the national Amateur Athletic Union light-heavyweight title. That ended his career as an amateur. His record included 43 knockout victories in 54 bouts.

On July 4, 1934, Louis appeared as a professional fighter for the first time and knocked out Jack Kracken in one round in Chicago.

Much of Louis's success was because of the capable manner in which he was handled as a professional. His amateur record brought him to the attention of Julian Black and John Roxborough, who engaged the late Jack Blackburn, one of the ring's great competitors, to polish the rough spots in the young fighter's style and to get the maximum results out of his tremendous strength and punching power.

Louis had 11 more fights in 1934 and 14 in 1935. By then his prowess had attracted the attention of Mike Jacobs in New York.

Jacobs was competing against Madison Square Garden for the right to promote boxing. He went to Detroit to see Louis fight Natie Brown in March 1935.

After outpointing Brown, Louis soon joined the New York promoter.

On June 25, 1935, Louis appeared for the first time before New York fans and was an immediate success, knocking out Primo Carnera in six rounds. He was so impressive that fans clamored for a match between him and Max Baer. Baer had lost the heavyweight championship to Braddock only two weeks before Louis stopped Carnera.

Louis and Baer met on September 24 of that year, and the young fighter, already recognized as a punching machine, pounded Baer into helplessness in four rounds.

Altogether Louis had 14 bouts in 1935 and earned a total of $368,037, an almost incredible sum then for a fighter in his second year as a professional.

On June 19, 1936, Louis had his first meeting with Schmeling in New York and suffered his first professional defeat, a twelfth-round knockout.

Schmeling told reporters before the bout that he had seen faults in Louis's style. After the bout, Schmeling disclosed that Louis had a habit of lowering his left shoulder and arm, leaving his chin open for a right-hand counterpunch.

Schmeling floored Louis with that weapon in the fourth round and finally knocked him out with more of the right-hand blows in the twelfth.

Schmeling was promised a title bout against Braddock after he stopped Louis, but Mr. Jacobs wanted Louis to get the chance. After stalling Schmeling, Braddock agreed to meet Louis.

They fought in Chicago and Louis knocked out Braddock in the eighth round to win the heavyweight title.

In 1938 the new champion had only three bouts, but one of those was his second against Schmeling.

Germany was then expounding its superman propaganda to the world, and Hitler had made it known that Schmeling was one of those supermen.

Schmeling made the mistake of believing Hitler and made some disparaging remarks about Americans in general and blacks in particular.

When Louis and the challenger met on June 22, 1938, in New York, the champion was in a rage. Louis cut his opponent down with terrific head and body punches. Schmeling went to a local hospital to recuperate before he returned to Germany.

The 2-minute-4-second time span was a record for turning back a challenger in a heavyweight title bout. The bout was the first million-dollar gate Louis attracted during his career.

After that Louis had things pretty much his own way in the ring. Tony Galento had him on the canvas briefly in 1939, Arturo Godoy's crouching nose-to-the-floor tactics puzzled Louis the full 15 rounds in 1940, and Buddy Baer, brother of Max, knocked Louis out of the ring for a nine-count in 1941 before losing.

That last event came during Louis's so-called bum-of-the-month campaign. During it, beginning in December 1940, he met challengers at the rate of one a month, a performance that no other heavyweight champion ever attempted.

Louis came close to losing his crown in the first fight with Billy Conn of Pittsburgh on June 18, 1941, at the Polo Grounds. Conn, the light-heavyweight king, relinquished his title to meet Louis.

Before that fight many boxing writers had said that Conn would be too speedy and would outbox Louis. The champion had the perfect answer when he said, "He can run but he can't hide."

For twelve rounds Louis received a lesson in boxing from the stylish challenger. However, in the thirteenth, Conn dropped his successful tactics and attempted to slug it out with Louis. The move cost him the championship. Louis knocked him out with two seconds left in the round.

Three months later Louis stopped Lou Nova, and in January 1942 he defeated Buddy Baer again, in two minutes and fifty-six seconds of the first round. That bout in Madison Square Garden was for the Naval Relief Fund, which received $47,000.

Two months later Louis knocked out Abe Simon in the sixth round of a fight in New York. The Army Relief Society gained by $36,146. He then went into the army as a private.

As a soldier, Louis traveled more than 21,000 miles and staged 96 boxing exhibitions before 2 million soldiers.

Louis came out of the army on October 1, 1945, and shortly after signed to defend his title against Conn. The bout was the second million-dollar gate Louis drew and earned him the largest purse of his career, $625,916.44. The champion stopped Conn in the eighth round at Yankee Stadium on June 19, 1946.

The champion defended his title three more times after the Conn fight, knocking out Tami Mauriello and Jersey Joe Walcott twice. After the second Walcott bout on June 25, 1948, Louis retired—officially on March 1, 1949.

He later tried a comeback but failed to regain his championship form. Ezzard Charles outpointed him in 15 rounds at Yankee Stadium on September 27, 1950. A year later Louis's ring career came to an end when Rocky Marciano knocked him out in the eighth round of their bout at Madison Square Garden on October 26, 1951.

Although he made a lot of money, it passed through his fingers quickly—and without the sort of accounting that the Internal Revenue Service expects. As a result, the government calculated that his delinquent taxes—after penalties and interest—amounted to $1.25 million, a sum that Louis found staggering. "I liked the good life," Louis said. "I just don't know where the money went. I wish I did. I got 50 percent of each purse and all kinds of expenses came out of my cut." In the mid-1960s, an accommodation was reached with the government and the boxer was able to pay off his obligations.

In 1965, Dana Latham, the commissioner of the Internal Revenue Service, informed Congress: "We have gotten all we could possibly get from Mr. Louis, leaving him with some hope that he can live. His earning days are over."

Louis was not officially forgiven by the tax collectors, but attempts at getting the money he owed ceased, according to a close friend of the boxer.

Out of the ring for good, Louis tried to establish himself in a variety of careers. He wrestled briefly and engaged in various sports and commercial promotions. In 1969, he and Billy Conn, who had lost twice to Louis in title fights, set up the Joe Louis Food Franchise Corporation in the hope of operating an interracial chain of food shops.

In 1969, he collapsed on a lower Manhattan street, and was rushed to Beekman-Downtown Hospital for treatment of what was then described as "a physical breakdown."

And in 1970, he spent five months at the Colorado Psychiatric Hospital and the Veterans Administration Hospital in Denver. He was hospitalized by his wife, Martha, and his son, Joe Louis Barrow, Jr., suffering from paranoia. Because of his confinement he was unable to attend a tribute to him in Detroit that was attended by more than 8,000 people.

Louis disclosed the truth about some of his problems in 1971 in a book, *Brown Bomber: The Pilgrimage of Joe Louis,* by Barney Nagler. He said that his collapse in 1969 had been caused by cocaine. And he admitted that his hospitalization had been prompted by his fear of a plot to destroy him.

Louis's son once said of his father, "I couldn't help thinking of Arthur Miller's play *Death of a Salesman.* In the play, the man's name was Willy Loman, wasn't it? Well, there's a correlation between them. Wasn't Willy a grand guy, just like my father, and then he started growing old and losing his customers? He was never really aware that he had lost his territory. That's the tragedy of it, just like my father's."

Louis's third wife, Martha, said during her husband's troubles, "Joe's not broke. He's rich—rich with friends. If he said he needed a dollar, a million people would send him a dollar and he'd be a millionaire."

Joe Louis was more than just a boxing champion. He also had a role in the social history of the United States. In a 1970 article about Louis in *Ebony* magazine, Chester Higgins wrote:

He gave inspiration to downtrodden and despised people. When Joe Louis fought, blacks in ghettos across the land were indoors glued to their radios, and when Louis won, as he nearly always did, they hit the streets whooping and hollering in celebration. For Joe's victory was their victory, a means of striking back at an oppressive and hateful environment. Louis was the black Atlas on whose broad shoulders blacks were lifted, for in those days, there were few authentic black heroes.

In 1974 he took time off from his job as a "greeter" at Caesars Palace in Las Vegas, Nevada, to referee the heavyweight fight between Joe Frazier and Jerry Quarry, proclaiming Frazier the winner after the fifth round because of heavy cuts on Quarry's face.

Louis and Marva Trotter, a nineteen-year-old Chicago secretary, were married on September 24, 1935. The marriage took place in a Harlem apartment just a few hours before Louis stepped into the ring and knocked out Max Baer.

The couple were divorced in March 1945, but remarried a year later. They were divorced a second time in February 1949. A daughter, Jacqueline, was born to the couple on February 8, 1943, and a son, Joe Jr., on May 28, 1947.

Mr. Louis's third marriage was to Rose Morgan, a New York cosmetics manufacturer, on Christmas Day 1955.

His fourth marriage was to Martha Jackson, a Los Angeles lawyer. It took place March 17, 1959, after his union with Rose Morgan Louis was terminated by annulment.

In 1977, Louis was confined to a wheelchair following surgery to correct an aortic aneurysm. His health over his last decade was poor, beset with heart problems, emotional disorders, and strokes.

Louis died of cardiac arrest in Las Vegas on April 12, 1981. He was sixty-six years old.

Louis's death came only a few hours after he had attended the heavyweight championship fight on Saturday night between Larry Holmes and Trevor Berbick at Caesars Palace.

A Sense of Dignity

By RED SMITH

When Joe Louis's tax troubles were still making headlines, a man told him, "You were fifteen years ahead of your time. You should have been around today to cut in on these multimillion-dollar closed-circuit shows." "No," Joe said, "when I was boxing I made five million and wound up broke, owing the government a million. If I was boxing today I'd make ten million and wind up broke, owing the government two million."

Joe Louis Barrow lived a month less than sixty-seven years. He was heavyweight champion of the world in an era when the heavyweight champion was, in the view of many, the greatest man in the world. He held the title for 12 years, defended it 25 times, and retired undefeated as a champion.

Not once in sixty-six years was he known to utter a word of complaint or bitterness or offer an excuse for anything. To be sure, he had nothing to make excuses about. In 71 recorded fights he lost three times, on a knockout by Max Schmeling before he won the championship, on a decision to Ezzard Charles when he tried to regain the title, and finally on a knockout by Rocky Marciano when that young man was on his way to the top.

Joe had just celebrated his twenty-first birthday when he came to New York the first time. This was 1935, not a long time ago, yet some people still saw any black man as the stereotype darky, who loved dancing and watermelon. Some news photographers bought a watermelon and asked Joe to pose eating a slice. He refused, saying he didn't like watermelon.

"And the funny thing is," said Harry Markson, telling the story, "Joe loves watermelon."

At twenty-one, this unlettered son of Alabama sharecroppers had the perception to realize what the pictures would imply and the quiet dignity to have no part of the charade. Dignity was always a word that applied to him. Dignity and candor.

Early in Muhammad Ali's splendacious reign as heavyweight champion, he hired Joe as an "adviser" and they appeared on television together.

"Joe, you really think you coulda whupped me?" Ali said.

"When I had the title," Joe said, "I went on what they called a bum-of-the-month tour."

Ali's voice rose three octaves. "You mean I'm a bum?"

"You woulda been on the tour," Joe told his new employer.

During World War II, Joe defended his championship against Buddy Baer for the benefit of the Naval Relief Fund. Wendell Willkie, defeated candidate for president of the United States, made a resounding speech in the ring. "And you, Max Baer," he said, "and you, Joe Louee . . ." Earlier that day Harry Markson, then doing publicity on Mike Jacob's promotions in Madison Square Garden, offered to write a few words for Joe in case he was called on to speak. Joe said no, thanks, he wouldn't be invited.

To his surprise, he was asked to address the crowd. Unprepared though he was, he said a few altogether appropriate words, assuring listeners that we would win the war "because we're on God's side." Dignity. If memory serves, Buddy Bear wasn't called on. Before the first round ended, he couldn't speak, being unconscious.

This story has been told here before but perhaps it will bear repeating. Before Floyd Patterson's second match with Sonny Liston, the one in Las Vegas, a visitor remarked to Joe that every time Floyd talked with the press he spoke of losing. "If I lose, if I lose bad, if I'm humiliated," he would start over again at the bottom and work his way back to main events.

"A fighter can't think that way," Joe said, "and he can't talk that way."

"It seems to me," his companion said, "that any time a man of intelligence goes into an athletic contest, he realizes that he stands a chance of losing."

"Oh, I think I reckanized it," Joe said. "Especially when I was just starting out and scared. After I won the title I didn't think about it no more. Oh, I knew that if I kept on fighting, some guy would come along and take the title away from me, but not this guy, never tonight."

Joe Louis may very well have been the greatest fighter who ever lived. Comparisons with Jack Dempsey and Gene Tunney and others are foolish, though there is no shadow of doubt here that he would have caught and destroyed Muhammad Ali as he caught Billy Conn and other skillful boxers.

At the top of his game he would have outboxed Rocky Marciano and perhaps have taken him out, though after 49 fights without a defeat or draw, Rocky said he had never been dazed by a punch, even the punches that floored him. Joe's aging legs betrayed him when he finally fought Marciano.

That was his last competitive match, though he boxed a few exhibitions afterward. Marciano knocked him out of the ring in the eighth round, and afterward Joe lay on his stomach on a rubbing table with his right ear pillowed on a towel. He wore his faded dressing gown of blue and red, with a raincoat spread over it. His left hand was in a bucket of ice on the floor and a handler massaged his left ear with ice. With his face squashed against the padding of the table, newspapermen had to kneel with their heads close to his lips to hear his words.

He said the best man had won. Asked whether Marciano could hit harder than Schmeling, who had knocked him out fifteen years earlier, Joe said, "This kid knocked me out with what? Two punches. Schmeling knocked me out with—musta been a hundred punches. But I was twenty-two years old then. You can take more then than later on."

"Did age count tonight, Joe?"

"Ugh," Joe said, and bobbed his head.

The Louis-Schmeling Rematch

By JAMES P. DAWSON

The exploding fists of Joe Louis crushed Max Schmeling on June 22, 1938, in the ring at Yankee Stadium and kept sacred that time-worn legend of boxing that no former heavyweight champion has ever regained the title.

The Brown Bomber from Detroit, with the most furious early assault he had ever exhibited before, knocked out Schmeling in the first round of what was to have been a 15-round battle to retain the title he won the previous year from James J. Braddock.

In exactly 2 minutes and 4 seconds of fighting Louis polished off the Black Uhlan from the Rhine, but, though the battle was short, it was furious and savage while it lasted, packed with thrills that held three knockdowns of the ambitious ex-champion, every moment tense for a crowd of about 80,000.

This gathering, truly representative and comparing favorably with the largest crowds in boxing's history, paid receipts estimated at between $900,000 and $1 million to see whether Schmeling could repeat the knockout he administered to Louis just two years earlier and be the first ex-heavyweight champion to come back into the title, or whether the Bomber could avenge this defeat as he promised.

As far as the length of the battle was concerned, the investment in seats, which ran to thirty dollars each, was a poor one. But for excitement, for drama, for pulse throbs, those who came from near and far felt themselves well repaid because they saw a fight that, though it was one of the shortest heavyweight championships on record, was surpassed by few for thrills.

With the right hand that Schmeling held in contempt Louis knocked out his foe. Three times under its impact the German fighter hit the ring floor. The first time Schmeling regained his feet laboriously at the count of three. From the second knockdown Schmeling, dazed but game, bounced up instinctively before the count had gone beyond one.

On the third knockdown Schmeling's trainer and closest friend, Max Machon, hurled a towel into the ring, European fashion, admitting defeat for his man. The towel sailed through the air when the count on the prostrate Max had reached three.

The signal is ignored in American boxing, and Referee Arthur Donovan, before he had a chance to pick up the count in unison with knockdown time-keeper Eddie Josephs, who was outside the ring, gathered the white emblem in a ball and hurled it through the ropes.

Returning to Schmeling's crumpled figure, Donovan took one look and signaled an end of the battle. The count at that time was five on the third knockdown. Further counting was useless. Donovan could have counted off a century and Max could not have regained his feet. The German was thoroughly "out."

It was as if he had been poleaxed. His brain was awhirl, his body, his head, his jaws ached and pained, his senses were numbed from that furious, paralyzing punching he had taken even in the short space of time the battle consumed.

Following the bout, Schmeling claimed he was fouled. He said that he was hit a kidney punch, a devastating right, which so shocked his nervous system that he was dazed and his vision was blurred. To observers at the ringside, however, with all due respect to Schmeling's thoughts on the subject, the punches that dazed him were thundering blows to the head, jaw, and body in bewildering succession, blows of the old Alabama Assassin reincarnate for a special occasion.

Louis wanted to erase the memory of that 1936 knockout he suffered in 12 rounds. It was the one blot on his brilliant record. He aimed to square the account and he did.

Because of the excitement attending the finish, Louis, in the records, will be deprived of a clean-cut knockout. It will appear as a technical knockout because Referee Donovan didn't complete the full 10-second count over Schmeling. But this is merely a technicality. No fighter ever was more thoroughly knocked out than was Max that night.

Thrilling to the spectacle of this short, savage victory that held so much significance was a gathering that included a member of President Roosevelt's cabinet; Postmaster General James A. Farley; governors of several states; mayors of cities in the East, South, and Midwest; representatives and senators; judges and lawyers; politicians; doctors; figures of prominence in the professional world; leaders of banking, industry, and commerce; stars of the stage and screen; ring champions of the past and present; leaders in other sports and other fields—all assembled eagerly awaiting the struggle whose appeal drew them from distant parts of the country and from Europe.

In addition to those looking on at the spectacle, there were millions virtually all over the world listening in, for this battle was broadcast in four languages, English, German, Spanish, and Portuguese, so intense was the interest in its outcome.

Louis, hero of one of the greatest stories ever written in the ring, owner of a record of 38 victories in 39 bouts spread over four years, entered the ring the favorite to win at odds of 1 to 2. He won like a 1-to-10 shot. The knockout betting was at even money, take your pick. It could have been on Louis at 1 to 10, for Schmeling never had a chance. His number was up from the clang of the opening gong.

Schmeling, thirty-two-year-old campaigner over a period of fourteen years, aspired to the unparalleled distinction of being the first man to regain the heavyweight crown. He suffered, instead, the fate that overtook Jim Corbett, Bob Fitzsimmons, Jim Jeffries, and Jack Dempsey, ring immortals all, who tried and failed.

The fury of Louis's attack explains the result in a nutshell. The defending champion came into the ring geared on high. He never stopped punching until his rival was a crumpled, inert, helpless figure, diving headlong into the resined canvas, rolling over there spasmodically, instinctively, trying to come erect, his spirit willing to return to the attack, his flesh weak, for mind and muscle could not be expected to function harmoniously under the terrific battering Schmeling absorbed in those fleeting two minutes.

Emphasizing the savagery with which Louis went after this victory was

Schmeling's feeble effort at retaliation. The German ex-champion threw exactly two punches. That is how completely the Bomber established his mastery in this second struggle with the Black Uhlan.

With the opening gong, Louis crept softly out of his corner, pantherlike, eyes alert, arms poised, fists cocked to strike from any angle as he met Schmeling short of the ring's center. Max backed carefully toward his own corner, watching Louis intently, his right, the right that thudded so punishingly against Joe's jaw and temple two years ago, ready to strike over or under a left guard. At least, that was Schmeling's prearranged plan.

But Louis wasted only a few seconds in studying his foe, menacing Max meanwhile with a spearing left, before quickly going to work.

Like flashes from the blue, the Bomber's sharp, powerful left started suddenly pumping into Schmeling's face. The blows tilted Max's head back, made his eyes blink, unquestionably stung him. The German's head was going backward as if on hinges.

Max's face was exposed to a left hook attack, and Louis interspersed his onslaught with a few of these blows, gradually forcing Schmeling back to the ropes and preventing the German from making an offensive or countermove, so fast and sharp and true was the opening fire of the defending champion.

Schmeling suddenly shot a right over Louis's left for the jaw, but the blow was short and they went close. At long range again, Joe stuck and stabbed with his left to the face and head, trying to open a lane through Schmeling's protecting arms and gloves for a more forceful shot from the right.

But the opening didn't come immediately. Instead, Schmeling again lunged forward, his right arching as it drove for Louis's jaw, and it landed on the champion's head as the Schmeling admirers in the tremendous crowd roared encouragement.

Louis, however, only scowled and stepped forward, this time with a terrific right to Schmeling's jaw that banged Max against the ropes, his body partly turned toward the right from Louis.

Schmeling shook to his heels under the impact of that blow, but he gave no sign of toppling. And Joe, like a tiger, leaped upon him, driving a right to the ribs as Schmeling half turned—apparently the blow Schmeling later claimed was foul—swinging with might and main, lefts and rights that thudded against Schmeling's bobbing head, grazed or cracked on Max's jaw and swishing murderous-looking left hooks into Schmeling's stomach as the crumpling ex-champion grimaced in pain, his face wearing the expression of a fighter protesting "foul."

Shaken when he first landed against the ropes, Schmeling was rendered groggy under the furious assault to which Louis subjected him while he stood there trying unsuccessfully to avoid the blows or grasp a chance to clinch.

Suddenly the Bomber's right, sharp and true with the weight of his 198¾ pounds back of it as well as his knack of driving it home, landed cleanly on Schmeling's jaw. Max toppled forward and down. He was hurt and stunned, but gamely the German came erect at the count of three.

Louis was on him in a jiffy, with the fury of a jungle beast. After propping the tottering Schmeling with a jolting left to the face, the Bomber's deadly right fist again exploded in Max's face, and under another crack on the jaw, Schmeling went down. This time, however, the German regained his feet before the count progressed beyond one.

But Schmeling was helpless. He staggered drunkenly for a few backward steps, the crowd in an uproar as Louis stealthily followed and measured his man. Max was an open target. His jaw was unprotected and inviting. His midsection was a mark for punches. The kill was within Louis's grasp. He lost no time in ceremony.

Spearing Schmeling with blinding straight lefts, numbing Max with powerful left hooks that were sharp, true, and destructive, Louis set the stage for one finishing right to the jaw, released the blow and landed in a flash, and the German toppled over in a headlong dive, completely unconscious.

The din of the crowd echoed over the arena, cheers for the conquering Louis, shrieks of entreaty and shouts of advice for Schmeling. But this thunderous roar was unheard by the befogged Schmeling and was ignored by the Bomber, intent only on the destruction of his foe.

In routine fashion, Eddie Josephs, a licensed referee converted into a knockdown timekeeper, started the count over the stricken Schmeling. He counted one, then two, as Referee Donovan went about the duty of signaling Louis to the farthest neutral corner.

At "three" a white towel sailed aloft from Schmeling's corner, hurled by the ever-faithful Machon, who realized, as did everyone else in the vast gathering, that Schmeling was knocked out, if he was not, indeed, badly hurt.

The towel fell in the ring a few feet from Schmeling. It was the custom in European rings at the time to recognize this gesture as a concession of defeat. But for many years now it had been banned in America, and Referee Donovan, disregarding the emblem of surrender, tossed it through the ropes and out of the ring.

When he returned to the prostrate figure of Schmeling, moving convulsively on the ring floor doubtless with that instinctive impulse to arise, the count had reached "five." One look was enough for Donovan. Instantly he spread his arms in a signal that meant the end of the bout, although Timekeeper Josephs, as he is duty-bound to do, continued counting outside the ring.

This led to confusion at the finish. Some thought the third knockdown count was eight. Actually, the bout was ended at the count of five, the three seconds beyond that time being a gesture against emergency that was superfluous. Schmeling could not have arisen inside the legal 10-second stretch. His hopes were blasted. He was a thoroughly beaten man.

In a few moments, however, as police swarmed into the ring and his handlers worked over him in the corner to which he was assisted, Schmeling returned to consciousness. He was able to smile bravely as he walked across the ring to shake the hand of the conquering Louis, a gesture that carried the impression, somehow, that Max realized at long last that Louis is his master now and for all time.

"Now I feel like the champion."

These were Joe Louis's first words on his arrival in his dressing room.

"I've been waiting a long time for this night," he added, "and I sure do feel pretty glad about everything. I was a little bit sore at some of the things Max said. Maybe he didn't say them, maybe they put those words in his mouth, but he didn't deny them, and that's what made me mad."

What Louis referred to, probably, was the statement attributed to Schmeling a month ago, to the effect that the Negro would always be afraid of him. Something must have rankled Joe, for the savagery with which he battered down the German was never displayed in his other bouts here.

Most of Louis's remarks were addressed to Governor Frank Murphy of Michigan, one of the first admitted to the champion's dressing room.

The governor admittedly was "full of hero worship" as he shook hands with the Detroit boxer who, on his own account, was immeasurably pleased with Murphy's visit.

"You'll never know how my heart thumped during that round, Joe," said the governor.

"I'm glad I made it short for you, sir," responded the champion, who looked exactly like a wool-gathering youngster standing in awe of royalty, instead of a young man who had just earned about $400,000 in 124 seconds.

Louis's managers, Julian Black and John Roxborough, were incensed at Schmeling's claim of foul at first, then laughed it off, saying, "That's for German consumption."

Asked if Schmeling would be considered for a return fight, Black replied, "Certainly not. We've demonstrated tonight that Joe is just too good for Schmeling. We've had enough of him, and he certainly has had enough of us!"

CONNIE MACK

1862–1956

C ONNIE MACK was the master builder of baseball teams. No other manager in the history of the game ever handled more young players and brought more of them to stardom and on to fortune. But it is probable that he will be best remembered for his sensational scrapping of championship machines, the tearing apart of teams that other men would have been eager to lead.

No man in the history of organized baseball served as a manager longer than Mack—he began as a team leader in 1894—and no manager ever directed one team as long. He assumed the leadership of the Philadelphia Athletics in 1901 and held it until 1950. With them he won nine American League pennants and five world championships.

He was famous for waving a scorecard to and fro as he stood in the dugout directing his team. But it was more than a white plume of Navarre in the battlefront, as more than one pitcher or infielder or outfielder discovered after the dust had settled. The manager kept accurate records of what ball the batter had hit, that the hurler should not have thrown, and the direction of every hit that had escaped a fielder. It was this constant drilling of small details that made his teams mechanically perfect.

Through the years, Mack was one of the most respected men in baseball. He received many honors and was considered one of the pillars of the sport. His exit from the game in 1954 was tinged with pathos as he signed the Athletics away to Arnold Johnson of Chicago, who transferred the club to Kansas City. Mack put his signature on the agreement from a sickbed.

He was baptized Cornelius McGillicuddy soon after his birth on December 22, 1862, in East Brookfield, Massachusetts. His name was shortened in his playing days so that it would fit in the printed box scores of that period. Mack learned to play baseball while working in a shoe factory to help support a widowed mother. He became a catcher and first attracted notice in 1883, when East Brookfield won the championship of Central Massachusetts.

The next season he became a professional with the Meriden, Connecticut, club and played in that city and in Hartford until the Washington team of the old National League bought his release on September 9, 1886.

By that time he had become known as a smart catcher and a reliable batter in the clutch, though he never was a heavy hitter. He was in Washington three years, left to join the Players (Brotherhood) League in Buffalo, where he played

one year, and then joined Pittsburgh, where he remained for six years, becoming manager in 1894.

He was a new type of manager. The old-time leaders ruled by force, often thrashing players who disobeyed orders, committed blunders on the field, or broke club rules off the field. One of the kindliest and most softspoken of men, he always insisted that he could get better results by kindness. He never humiliated a player by public criticism.

From Pittsburgh he went to the Milwaukee club of the Western Association. In 1901, when Ban Johnson organized the American League, Mack became manager and a part owner of the Philadelphia franchise. He had given up catching by this time, and did not even appear on the coaching lines. He was well over six feet tall and thin, and he said that he realized he was not an impressive figure in a baseball uniform.

But he knew good ball players, and he quickly assembled a team of stars, at the same time devoting much of his time, apart from the actual directing of games, to learning the business phases of baseball.

He won his first pennant in 1902. There was no World Series that year because the National League refused to recognize the American. But in 1905 Mack won again, and his team faced the Giants under John J. McGraw in what was the second World Series.

Mack had three brilliant pitchers, Chief Bender, Eddie Plank, and Rube Waddell. The last one was injured and did not play in the Series, and the Athletics were beaten, four games to one, chiefly because of the wonderful pitching of Christy Mathewson. He beat the Athletics three times, all shutouts. Bender won the only game for Philadelphia.

Mack began his first rebuilding job after this defeat. He kept Bender and Plank, his veteran pitchers, but assembled youngsters in the field. One of them was second baseman Eddie Collins. Another was Frank "Home Run" Baker, a powerful hitter.

In 1910 the Athletics won the American League pennant again and faced the Chicago Cubs, under Frank Chance. The Cubs had won the National League championship in 1906, 1907, and 1908 and were the favorites in the Series, but the Mack youngsters won in one of the biggest upsets ever scored in the classic, four games to one.

The Athletics won again in 1911 and Mr. Mack had his revenge, for his team defeated the McGraw Giants, four games to two, Mathewson being beaten twice, though he defeated Bender in the opening game.

The same teams came together in 1913, and the Athletics won again. When they captured another American League pennant in 1914 and were slated to face the Boston Braves, it seemed that the Mackmen could not lose.

They did, however, in four straight games, a crushing setback. And here Mack electrified the baseball world by scrapping the championship array, selling Collins, Baker, and Jack Barry of his famous $100,000 infield, and keeping only Stuffy McInnis, the star first baseman. In less than two seasons his team was at the bottom of the American League and he was starting all over again with a group of youngsters. He was at the bottom eight years in one stretch.

It was a long, hard struggle. He spent six seasons building and spoiling—

and then building again. Then came the rush of the Yankees and Babe Ruth, and it seemed harder than ever to reach the top. He made a masterstroke when he obtained Robert Moses "Lefty" Grove, one of the greatest left-handers of all time—almost as powerful, Mack always said, as Waddell in his prime—and in 1927 he finished second.

In 1928 he was second again. By this time he had Al Simmons and Jimmie Foxx, powerful hitters; Cochrane, a superb catcher; Jimmy Dykes, Joe Boley, and Max Bishop, skillful infielders—a combination considered almost as great as the Baker-Barry-Collins-McInnis machine of fifteen years before.

Then came 1929, and the Athletics made a runaway of the American League race. They beat the Cubs in the World Series. In 1930 they won again and defeated the Cardinals. Grove and George Earnshaw, Mack's star hurlers, performed in stunning fashion.

In 1931 the Mackmen won the ninth pennant for their manager but were balked in the attempt to place a sixth world's championship at his feet. The Cardinals won, four games to two. The Athletics finished second to the Yankees in 1932 and third in 1933.

Being third did not suit Mack. At seventy-one, and after thirty years of toiling with one club, he again shocked the fans by demolishing his machine.

He kept one of his stars, Foxx, first baseman and home run leader of the previous season, but the following year sold him also to the Red Sox, with Johnny Marcum, a pitcher, for $150,000 and two players. Then he began rebuilding, making a specialty of reaching into the colleges for pitching talent.

In 1937 Mack was among the first thirteen pioneers of the game enshrined in the Hall of Fame.

Mack acquired financial control of the Athletics in December 1940. His purchase of stock from Mrs. Ethyl M. Shibe gave him a majority interest in the club.

"My greatest thrill," he recalled on his seventy-ninth birthday, "was starting Howard Ehmke as surprise pitcher against the Cubs in the first game of the 1929 World Series. My biggest disappointment was the 1914 team that lost four in a row to the Braves in the World Series."

A bust of Mack has been enshrined in Cooperstown, New York, commemorating his long service to baseball. The bust was entitled Mr. Baseball.

He died at the age of ninety-three on February 8, 1956.

Baseball's Oldest Inhabitant

By ARTHUR DALEY

The Kid had not the slightest intention of quitting at the end of the season. No, siree. There almost was a defiant gleam in his pale blue eyes when he made the statement. "I hope to manage the Athletics next year and for many years to come," said Connie Mack, a trim, sprightly, and agile-minded eighty-seven-year-old during spring training in 1950. "Attaboy, Connie!" exclaimed his listener and then stopped abruptly, appalled by such irreverence.

It merely happened to be the fiftieth campaign as the boss of the Athletics for baseball's Oldest Inhabitant. He was their first and only manager. Connie chuckled softly. "Don't be so impressed by a mere fifty years, young man," he said. "By golly, do you realize when I made my first spring training trip? It was in 1888 and we went to Jacksonville. I was with Washington then and Ted Sullivan was our manager. We lived in shacks at one dollar a day, American plan. Baseball was in such disrepute those days that only a third-class hotel would take us—providing we didn't mingle with the guests."

The ancient Cornelius McGillicuddy sat in his chair, straight as a ramrod. His eyes were peering into the distance, down memory lane. "In my first year with the Athletics," he continued, "only our pitchers went to spring training. Dave Fultz took them down to North Carolina. That was in 1901 and by 1904 we had the whole team in camp, at Spartanburg."

By the way, which was his best team?

"I've always thought," he said without the slightest hesitation, "that my best team was the one from 1910 through 1914. We won pennants in 1910, 1911, 1913, and 1914. We should have won pennants—and this was a great disappointment to me—for five straight seasons because I've always thought that our 1912 club, which failed, was the best of them all. But we finished third behind Boston and Washington.

"I guess we could have won if I hadn't suspended Chief Bender and Rube Oldring for breaking training. I sent them ahead of the rest of the squad from Washington to New York and they never did show up. That happened in mid-August and ruined our chances. So the next year I sent Bender a contract for only $1,200. Goodness gracious, but that was mean of me. His wife tore it up so he couldn't sign it."

Connie smiled shyly and resumed.

"A few days later he came to see me. 'I don't know anything else but baseball,' he blurted out, 'I'll sign and I'll behave.' So he signed at that ridiculous figure." Those pale blue eyes suddenly took on warmth. "The odd part about it," said the gentle Mr. Mack, "is that I wound up paying him more money than I'd paid any ball player.

"Just before we were to play the Giants in the World Series of 1913 I asked him, 'How much of a mortgage is there on your house?' He answered, 'Twenty-five hundred dollars.' So I told him, 'If you beat the Giants I'll pay it off for you.' He won and I paid it. In fact I gave him something like $12,000 instead of the $1,200 he signed for. The Chief had kept his promise and had been outstanding.

"There was one thing about the 1912 season that I've never been able to forget. Washington came into Philadelphia with a nineteen-game winning streak and we brought it to an end. But we wouldn't have if what's-his-name had caught that foul ball. What was his name, anyway?" Connie snapped his fingers in annoyance. "Never mind, I'll think of it later.

"By golly, that was a close one. Washington had us beaten, one to nothing, with two out in the ninth and with two strikes on Home Run Baker. He hit a foul and the game would have ended if what's-his-name had caught the ball. But he didn't and Baker hit a home run to tie it up. We won in the tenth."

The amazing thing about that little story is that the eighty-seven-year-old Mack could remember with uncanny clarity every detail of a game that took place thirty-eight years earlier except the identity of "what's-his-name."

He sat silently for a few minutes, began to talk, hesitated and started all over again in a somewhat apologetic fashion. "Perhaps I shouldn't even mention this," he said, "but it's been on my mind ever since I read about Branch Rickey's claim, that the hit-and-run is baseball's most overrated play. I agree with him fully. I met John McGraw in the World Series three times and I beat him"—Connie gulped hard in embarrassment—"two times out of three.

"Do you know why? McGraw was too much of a gambler. In a World Series it's imperative that you play conservatively for one run. But John was never content with one. He gambled for more by ordering the hit-and-run much too recklessly. I don't think I ever admitted this before, but that's the way I always saw it.

"The Giants beat the Athletics only once and that was in 1905 when McGraw and his team wore those awful black uniforms. Every game was a shutout, and I've often wondered what might have happened if Andy Coakley hadn't worn the straw hat that day. It was late September when Andy wore the straw hat and Rube Waddell appointed himself a committee of one to smash the hat. They wrestled for the hat on a station platform and in the horseplay Waddell wrenched his pitching shoulder.

"The Rube had won twenty-seven games that season and he never did get into the World Series. There were stories circulated at the time that gamblers had reached him. Goodness gracious, that was ridiculous! No one loved winning more than Waddell and he'd have given his arm to have been able to pitch in that Series. If he had pitched—who knows? Maybe there would have been seven shutouts instead of five. Maybe we'd have won."

No one in baseball could ever spin back the years as gracefully as the Oldest Inhabitant. He was always in a class by himself.

PETE MARAVICH

1947–1988

By THOMAS ROGERS

P ETE MARAVICH was the leading career and single-season scorer in major college basketball history.

In May of 1987, he was inducted into the Basketball Hall of Fame, a tribute to his efforts as a pro that included a 24.2 scoring average and one league-scoring championship. But it was as a player at Louisiana State University that he truly sparkled.

For three straight seasons, between 1967 and 1970, he led the nation in scoring while performing under the coaching of his father, Press Maravich. In acquiring the nickname Pistol for his penchant for shooting the ball, he amassed 3,667 points in college for an average of 44.2 over 83 games, a National Collegiate Athletic Association record. In his senior year, the 1969–70 season, he scored 1,381 points for a 44.5 average.

He scored more than 50 points in a game 28 times and hit 69 points against Alabama in 1970, his collegiate high point. As a loose-limbed, floppy-haired 6-foot-5-inch guard with sagging gray socks as his trademark, he was an enormous drawing card.

He averaged 38 shots a game, of which about 17 hit the mark, but he also had a knack for brilliant ball handling, dribbling, and passing.

"Shooting is nothing," he once said. "Anybody can shoot. The big charge is putting on a show for the crowd."

Peter Press Maravich was born on June 22, 1947, at Aliquippa, Pennsylvania, while his father was playing professional basketball for the Pittsburgh Ironmen. He grew up in the Carolinas while his father coached at Clemson and at North Carolina State before moving on to Louisiana State.

After his college career, Maravich took advantage of a bidding war between the Atlanta Hawks of the National Basketball Association and the Carolina Cougars of the American Basketball Association to get a five-year contract with Atlanta worth a reported $1.6 million, the richest contract for a rookie to that time.

As in college, he never played for a championship team in the pros, and his ten pro seasons never surpassed the ones at LSU. Still, he won the NBA scoring championship in 1977 when he averaged 31.1 points a game for the New Orleans Jazz. The next season he suffered a knee injury that dogged him until his retirement in the fall of 1980 after he was released by the Boston Celtics.

After leaving basketball, Maravich was involved in work within the reli-

gious community and as a basketball broadcaster. He also ran basketball camps in Clearwater, Florida, and near his home in Covington, Louisiana.

"Most of my career was negative," he once said. "I accomplished what I set out to do, but I lost my discipline and my career. I got involved in going out. I got by on talent. That was my fatal mistake."

On January 5, 1988, at the age of forty, Maravich collapsed after suffering a heart attack during a half-court pickup game with friends. He died about an hour later. A member of the group playing said that just before collapsing, Maravich had told him he had played only once in a year but felt "really good."

They Called Him Pistol

By GEORGE VECSEY

The first thing you noticed were the eyes, sad eyes, moist eyes, unfulfilled eyes. Bil Keane has made a career of painting sad-eyed clowns, waifs who have seen too much, but Pete Maravich was not merely a Keane painting, he was a man trying to go straight.

He would describe his career in terms of the championship ring he never won, but behind that was the respect he never gained, the friends that came and went, the wild times he tried to forget.

When it was over, Pete Maravich tried to live by disciplines as demanding as the inspired anarchy he once practiced on the court. He became a vegetarian, then a Christian, and his family was everything to him. The eyes stayed sad, but the commitment was there. He was not a preacher but he was a practitioner.

He said he was not hooked on basketball, but he surfaced in 1984 to play in his first Old-timers Game at the age of thirty-six. He didn't need this, he said. He had his camps but they were mostly to teach nutrition and religion and the fun of playing ball.

He would show up for subsequent old-timers gatherings, lean, almost scrawny, the result of lengthy fasts and limited diets. His eyes looked haunted above the ancient mariner mustache, but he could still look one way and flick a soft lead pass the other way. Playing for fun at the Church of the Nazarene in Pasadena, California, Pete Maravich fell dead of a heart attack at the age of forty. His mother, Helen, had been an apparent suicide in 1974, and his father, Press, who was also his college coach, had died the previous April, a month before Pete was inducted into the Basketball Hall of Fame in Springfield, Massachusetts.

The basketball was with him nearly all of those forty years. He even carried the ball to the movies, sitting on the aisle so he could bounce the ball at intermission.

"Pete carried a basketball around like some kids carry a teddy bear," Helen Maravich once said.

Little Pete, Pistol Pete, was such a prodigy that he was placed on the high school team while he was an eighth-grader to get the ball to his older brother, Ronnie. The team went to the state semifinals but the pressure got to the child.

"I can't remember the nightmare," he said years later, "but I remember I felt we were all in great danger. Our whole family. I got my basketball and climbed out of the window and started running. I must have run two miles. Finally I came to this place in the woods . . . and, I remember, I laid down on some stones and pulled my basketball up against me and went to sleep."

In his waking hours, Pistol Pete was fearless. None of the coaches at his three high schools could control him, and his college coach didn't try. Press, a rugged old bomber pilot and pro basketball player from the coal mine country of western Pennsylvania, moved over to LSU and more or less told his son to sign the grant-in-aid to LSU. As a coach, Press Maravich told the other players to let the boy with the long hair and the floppy socks do whatever he felt like.

Pistol Pete led the nation in scoring for three straight seasons, and he later led the National Basketball Association in scoring, too. He was expected to save the Atlanta franchise, and then the New Orleans franchise, but he could not even stabilize himself. Maravich admitted he had been out of control during much of his professional career. He knew other players resented him because he was allowed to do things on the court that they were not allowed to try. Gifted black players were urged, compelled, to play within a system but Maravich was the great white hope of two southern franchises.

The combination of freedom and responsibility made him old before his time. He once suffered from Bell's palsy, a disturbance of the facial nerves. He moved from Atlanta to New Orleans to Utah to Boston. He was willing to subordinate himself to the Boston Celtics' way of doing things, but they cut him in training camp of 1980. He was thirty-three.

"I was always sick when I played," he said four years later. "I'd have a drink and stay up late. One year in camp I had something wrong with me, and my roommate, I don't even remember his name, said, 'You have to change the way you eat.' I didn't know what he was talking about. I figured you could eat anything. He had fifty bottles of vitamins on his dresser. He didn't make the team—but he'll probably live to be a hundred." Maravich had quietly given up eating red meat in 1976–77 when he led the league in scoring. Later he gave up chicken and fish and dairy products, too. He began running basketball camps with his father, taping up the water taps and making the children drink only bottled spring water and serving them salads instead of hot dogs.

Then he got religion, although he shied away from the subject of his conversion, unless pressed. For the first time in his life, Pistol Pete was subdued, cautious. He had set too many bonfires in his life. Now he was trying to be one small, steady candle for his wife, Jackie, and their two sons, Jaeson and Joshua.

He once described waking up at 5:30 A.M. and hearing a voice say to him, "Be strong. Lift thine own heart." He said he woke up and asked Jackie, "Did you hear that?" Afterward, he said, he felt "an unbelievable peace."

In the years before his death, he ran his basketball camps without regard to profit, saying he had salted away some money from his playing days. He made the campers dribble and pass the ball behind their backs. He once said these moves were "fundamentals." In his final years, there was still room for a gaudy pass in the fundamental vision of Pistol Pete.

The Heart of Pistol Pete

By IRA BERKOW

Too many times, said Atlanta Hawks coach Richie Guerin in 1970, Pete Maravich gets himself "stuck up there in the air." It's a great trait for a moon, but not necessarily for a basketball player.

Pistol Pete Maravich was then a rookie in the National Basketball Association, and finding that his $2 million contract and his all-America press clippings and his great one-man show replete with feathery touch, blind passes, and slick dribbling—all done with long hair flopping and gray socks sagging—did not entitle him to immediate success in the league.

At Louisiana State University, where he averaged 44.2 points a game during three seasons (he remains college basketball's scoring leader), Maravich could go up for a jump shot and remain for a while, taking his good time, until he decided to pass or pop the shot. But then, there weren't many other 6-foot-5-inch guards.

When he soared in the NBA, he discovered he had company. The guards there could hang from a roof beam or a moonbeam with as much perseverance as Pete. He soon adjusted his game and generally soared only when it was most propitious. He went on to play a decade in the NBA, twice making first-team All-Pro and eventually making the Basketball Hall of Fame.

This was recalled when an autopsy of Maravich revealed that he suffered from a rare, natural heart defect that had gone undetected during his life. He had no left coronary artery. Normally, humans have two.

"All those years," noted Earl Ubell, a science reporter on CBS-TV in New York, "his life hung by a thread."

Most people with the kind of heart condition Maravich had die before they are twenty; a relative few may live to thirty. Maravich, who had been retired as an athlete for seven years, died at forty.

"For a guy to go ten years in the NBA and have a congenital anomaly like that is, to say the least, very unusual," said Dr. Paul Thompson of Brown University, an expert on sudden death. "How could a guy like that run up and down the court for twenty years?"

The question is provocative. We often talk about someone having heart. That their heart was in it. Songs tell us we gotta have heart. Could it be that Maravich, although with less physical heart than most, metaphorically had more? Could it be that he actually strengthened his heart because of his passionate involvement in the game? And was it this fulfillment that possibly contributed to his living virtually twice the expected lifetime? What did Dr. Thompson think?

"I often tell my patients, the heart bone is connected to the head bone," he said. "There is no scientific proof that emotions and feelings and desire affect how we feel, but I think most physicians believe there is a correlation. It's entirely possible that Maravich's drive to excel and love for the game kept him alive."

Did Pistol Pete have heart? "Oh yes, oh sure," said Butch van Breda Kolff, who coached Maravich for two years with the New Orleans Jazz. "No one learns to handle the ball the way Pete did and not love the game. The hours that he spent on it. I remember one trick he did that I've never seen before. He would take a ball and slam it on the floor with two hands and have it bounce between his legs and he'd catch it behind him."

Maravich would recall that, as a boy, he dribbled a basketball wherever he went. In the movie theater, he once said, he'd sit on the aisle so he could keep bouncing the ball.

He played with a clear love of the game, sometimes even to his detriment, for as someone recently pointed out, he was an individual in a team sport. And early in his pro career, with two southern franchises, Atlanta and New Orleans, he was also a "white hope," it was said, in a black-dominated sport.

When he was derided early on by fans, and even by teammates, Maravich persevered, just as he had in college, when he was the whole show, playing for his father, Press, which was a kind of burden as well.

He had dreams and strivings, perfectionist's dreams and strivings. "One of these nights," he said, after a game at LSU, "one of these nights I'm going to hit all my shots. Forty shots, maybe. I'll hit 'em all. I don't know when that night will be. I just know it's coming."

It never came, not that kind of night, although he had many brilliant ones, like the February night in 1977 when he scored 68 points against the Knicks, on 26 for 43 from the field and 16 for 19 from the free-throw line. Only three players have ever scored more in an NBA game. His heart never showed signs of weakness, although he proved physically vulnerable. He came down with mononucleosis, and separated his shoulder. In 1972, he suffered from Bell's palsy, a temporary nerve disorder that caused headaches and a partial paralysis of the right side of his face.

"Heart" may also mean conquering adversity. Maravich came back from illness and injury. He became a strong enough team player to twice make first-team all-NBA. He had problems with alcoholism during his playing days, but beat that, and became a health-food enthusiast. In retirement, he was active as a born-again Christian.

Then, after not having played the game he loved for nearly a year, he entered a halfcourt pickup basketball game in Pasadena, California, with a chance to once again soar and hang in the air.

"I feel great," Maravich said, breaking a sweat. A few minutes later, the concealed thread from which his life had been hanging since birth, snapped. Pistol Pete Maravich collapsed and died on the basketball court, where, for so many years, his heart had been.

ROCKY MARCIANO

1923–1969

ROCKY MARCIANO was a fighter in the proper sense of the word. The blocky, short-armed, aptly nicknamed Brockton Blockbuster was a boxer in name only.

Actually, his greatness was based on his aggressiveness, his willingness to trade punches and to brawl at close range, and his ability to withstand punishment in long exchanges. The sharp left jab, the clever footwork, and the sense of timing that could make an opponent miss punches by narrow, calculated margins were not part of Marciano's makeup. But he certainly could hit, 43 of his 49 victories ending by knockout.

In contrast to the "bruiser" qualities that he displayed in the ring, Marciano was a gentle, affable, and pleasant companion in his everyday activities. His constant alertness was evident by the quick movements of his large brown eyes, which were able to pick out shy acquaintances in the jubilant crowds that gathered around him in moments of victory.

His gaze could become still and, intent as he participated in conversation, in which he was articulate and, in professional interviews, most cooperative. His high-pitched speech, bearing the trace of his native Massachusetts, was soft and reminiscent of that of a parish priest or family counselor.

With a record of 49 victories in 49 professional fights, Marciano, of necessity, was counted among the best of heavyweights.

Ring buffs generally place him with the top three champions in the division until his time: Jack Dempsey, his conqueror Gene Tunney, and Joe Louis.

But there was animated discussion as to which of these was the best, at his fighting peak. Some hold for Dempsey of the flashing and murderous left hook, others for Tunney of the cool, methodical, calculated battle plan. Still others for Louis, the young Joe Louis with power and crushing speed in each hand.

Marciano's adherents concede all these points, but they also maintain that their champion performed so well against each of these types. Of the three, Marciano fought only Louis, whom he knocked out in eight rounds on October 26, 1951. However, at that time there was the age difference in Marciano's favor. He was born on September 1, 1923, and Louis on May 13, 1914.

His fight with Louis was the thirty-eighth of Marciano's professional career, and the outcome stamped him as having championship potential. His manager, Al Weill, carefully "picked spots" for him after that, selecting oppo-

nents that were acceptable as box office attractions but hardly powerful enough to sidetrack Rocky on the road to the title.

One of these opponents was Harry Matthews, a "built up" light-heavyweight whose manager, Jack Hurley, had ballyhooed into a heavyweight championship contender. Marciano knocked out Matthews in two rounds on July 28, 1952, and assured himself of a match with Jersey Joe Walcott, who was then the champion.

That fight took place in Philadelphia two months later, on September 23, and it developed into what has come to be regarded as the archetype of a duel between a boxer and a bruiser. Walcott, a superb ring workman, was almost nine years older than Marciano, and therefore he was on the short end of the betting at odds of 8 to 5.

But Walcott, in the first round, took command by ripping a left hook to the head and knocking Marciano down for a count of four. It was the first time that Rocky had ever been knocked down, and when he got back to the corner he asked his handler, "Who did that?"

Craftily outpunching his foe at the long exchanges, and giving Marciano little chance to get in close where he could deal out devastating punishment, Walcott enjoyed a comfortable edge on the score sheets going into the thirteenth round of the scheduled fifteen-round contest. Contributing in a great measure to Walcott's lead was the fact that Marciano had been cut on the nose by a punch in the fifth round.

In the rest period, medication was applied to the cut, but it spilled over into his eyes, and for the next three rounds Marciano was almost completely blind as he sought to grapple with the elusive Walcott. The effects of the medication wore off, but the plodding Marciano still found it difficult to catch up with the champion.

But in the thirteenth round, as the highly skillful Walcott bounced off the ropes Marciano let fly with a straight, solid right that caught Walcott flush on the chin. Down he went, for the full count, and Marciano became champion. In a return bout, a year later, Marciano had little trouble with Walcott, knocking him out in one round.

A loose comparison with Marciano's first fight against Walcott could be made with the Brockton Blockbuster's scrap with Archie Moore, which took place on September 21, 1955, and which was Marciano's last fight. Moore, who was born in 1913, had experienced a resurgence that had brought him to the forefront of challengers for the crown.

Like Walcott, Moore was a consummate boxer, and also like Walcott, Moore scored an early knockdown, in the second round, for the only other time in his career that Marciano was on the floor. After that, though, Marciano dominated his smaller rival, and finally stopped him in nine rounds.

At the time there seemed no indication that Marciano was about to end his fighting career, if for no other reason than that he would try to win an even fifty fights.

But in the months following the Moore fight word came down from Brockton that Rocky's wife, the former Barbara Cousens, and his mother, Pasqualina, were trying to persuade him to stop fighting. Their main reasons were that he had accumulated enough money and that they would like to be able to see more of him. The long training grinds and the personal appearances that went with being champion kept him away from home too long, they felt.

So, on April 27, 1956, he announced his retirement. He had held the title three and a half years and had defended it six times.

In his fighting career, Marciano's gross earnings, before taxes and manager's shares, amounted to $1.7 million. Like most successful boxers, he discovered it was difficult to stay out of the limelight and the action, and in 1959 he went through a secret training session of a month in contemplation of a comeback, but he decided against it. At his best, Marciano weighed 185 pounds, standing 5 feet 11 inches.

After he definitely retired, Marciano tried several business activities, some with indifferent success and others good enough to prevent a drain on his savings, if nothing else.

Marciano, who was born and reared in Brockton, was christened Rocco Francis Marchegiano. His father came to the United States in World War I from Italy to become a shoemaker in the famous Massachusetts shoe center.

Marciano's boyhood was the typical one of a sports-loving American youngster, with his main interests being baseball and football. Indeed, while playing center for the Brockton High School eleven, he might have made a bid for an athletic scholarship at Holy Cross or Harvard. In baseball his chunky build made him an ideal catcher, and he was even tried out by the Chicago Cubs, who turned him down because he could not make the big-league throw to second base.

It was while he was in the Army—in Fort Lewis, Washington—that Marciano was introduced to boxing. He participated in a number of tournament matches, and when he was released, he entered the amateur ranks, losing only one fight.

He turned pro in 1947 and won his first sixteen fights by knockouts, mostly in Providence, Rhode Island. An interruption to the knockout skein came when Don Mogard went the scheduled ten rounds with him, although losing the decision, in 1949. Marciano's first New York fight, also in 1949, was against Pat Richards, whom he stopped in two rounds.

Among the good fighters that Marciano beat on the way up were Ted Lowery, Red Applegate, Rex Layne, and Bernie Reynolds. In his early days Marciano's tutelage came, more or less, from a close friend, Allie Colombo, who died in an auto accident in 1968.

Weill, the sharpest boxing manager of the era, was finally persuaded to guide Marciano's career, and Weill was a strict, if not tyrannical, boss. He insisted that Marciano learn the ring rudiments from the late Charley Goldman, a veteran of the barge fighting days, and Goldman was shrewd enough to mold Marciano's strength and durability in the fighter's ring education.

The retired champion was killed in a plane crash on August 31, 1969, near Des Moines, Iowa.

The Dreaded Moment

By ARTHUR DALEY

The moment everyone had been dreading finally arrived on October 26, 1951. Joe Louis lay flat on his back under the still-quivering ring ropes in Madison Square Garden, eyes staring unseeingly at the blinding glare of the arc lamps. Old age and Rocky Marciano had simultaneously caught up with the old champion. He was champion, no longer, though. But he was, oh, so old.

The once-feared Brown Bomber came to the end that even the mightiest sometime reach. He was knocked out by a younger and stronger man. No longer was he fighting on the borrowed time that he had been stretching and stretching in the hope of regaining his heavyweight championship. The usurers had come to demand instant repayment. Reluctantly the Jolter paid the big price.

The finish was relatively unexpected. Marciano had been crowding him more and more for three rounds. But Joe's jab had Rocky missing so frequently that it almost seemed the Brown Bomber might escape. But in the eighth a left hook sent Louis reeling to the canvas. He took the count of 8 on one knee and didn't seem unduly hurt.

But as he clinched and twisted around with his back to the ropes, it happened. Rocky fired two thunderous left hooks. That impassive Louis face showed no pain. But a vacant look entered his eyes. He was about to take the journey down Dream Street.

Rocky crossed with his right and Louis went bouncing to the end of a glorious career. He hit the middle strand with his shoulders, bounced up, and caromed off the taut bottom strand. He seemed to slide like a loose sack of wheat under the rope half out on the ring apron. Referee Ruby Goldstein didn't bother to count.

Ruby took one look and waved his hands in a downward motion. The knockout was official. Rocky's handlers poured joyously into the ring, doing a dance of insensate joy. Joe's handlers stepped sadly into the ring for what they knew was the absolute end.

The referee had done his usual competent and unbiased job. But this was no ordinary occasion. Ruby tried hard not to show any emotions, but this ringsider watched him curiously. He walked away with head bowed. He wiped his hand across his face, almost as if he wished to banish from his memory what he had just seen. He gulped unconsciously, swallowing hard. A great champion had reached the end of the trail.

This was a dramatic moment. It even affected the referee and it bowled over the ringsiders. Ever since Louis ended his "retirement" some thirteen months earlier, they knew that he would eventually resemble the proverbial pitcher that had gone to the well once too often. Rocky was the well on which he was shattered.

The Jolter had worked with diligent persistency during his comeback. He had shown steady improvement. But Rocky was the first fighter of the lot who had a punch, a punch which was to carry him through thirty-two knockout victories in thirty-seven bouts. Now the box score is thirty-three in thirty-eight. Joe Louis had become just another line in the record book.

Only in the early stages of the fight did he show well. But then his old uncertainties began to creep up upon him. His reflexes, which had responded so well, failed to answer the call from his brain. In the seventh he had Marciano pinned in a corner.

The Louis of old would have finished him with a punch. But the old Louis let him escape. Perhaps it was the tip-off, because the twenty-seven-year-old gladiator with the strength of a young bull was in command from that point on.

Sure, he was missing his looping rights. Often. But he was also connecting with his target with glancing blows. Then he got the range. Down went Louis. Down sank the hearts of his admirers. It had to happen sometime and it happened that night.

Walcott and the Championship

By JAMES P. DAWSON

Rocky Marciano, undefeated Brockton, Massachusetts, fighter, knocked out Jersey Joe Walcott, thirty-eight-year-old ring warrior from Camden, New Jersey, on September 23, 1952, to become the world heavyweight champion.

With a devastating right to the jaw, Marciano ended the reign of the old champion after forty-three seconds of the thirteenth round. Until that moment it was a bruising battle that thrilled 40,379 fans from all over America in Philadelphia's Municipal Stadium. The receipts were $504,645.

Under the impact of that one terrific blow Walcott sank against the ropes, then slid headfirst to the canvas, while Referee Charley Daggert counted him out of the title he had won after much desperate effort slightly more than a year before.

The knockout was the cue for a tremendous demonstration. Fans swarmed into the ring as the unbeaten Bay State boxer with the paralyzing punch stood in his corner, winner of the ring's richest prize after a battle that he could have lost as early as the first round. He was the first white heavyweight to hold the title since Jim Braddock was stopped by Joe Louis in Chicago in 1937. Here was the new champion and nothing could halt the crowd in its eagerness to acclaim him.

From all sections of the vast arena, where Gene Tunney had lifted the title from Jack Dempsey just twenty-six long years ago, fans rushed on the ring to greet the conqueror.

Many were trampled in the rush, which started in the lower-priced seats in the permanent stands and under increasing momentum, moved across and through the seats at the ringside.

When Walcott had been counted out, his stricken handlers leaped through the ropes to the side of their fallen idol and carried him to his corner. It was several minutes before he could be revived sufficiently to leave the ring, with the assistance of Trainer Dan Florio and his brother Nick, and his manager Felix Bocchicchio.

Marciano, on the other hand, was virtually a prisoner in the ring, in more danger of injury at the hands of the crowd than he had been against Walcott through twelve bruising rounds of fighting.

It was at least fifteen minutes before the ring was cleared and order restored. Then Marciano was taken through the crowd under protection of a flying wedge of police and his handlers. Hundreds followed the conqueror to his dressing quarters, singing his praises, yelling themselves hoarse.

Marciano pulled victory from imminent defeat with that one paralyzing punch to the jaw. He didn't know it, but the three bout officials all had Walcott in front on a round basis for the twelve completed sessions.

Referee Daggert had Walcott leading, seven rounds to four, with one even. Zach Clayton, one of the judges, called it eight rounds for Walcott and four for Marciano. Pete Tomasco, the other judge, had Walcott leading, seven rounds to five. The writer had it even at six rounds apiece, giving Marciano the third, fourth, fifth, sixth, and seventh, and Walcott the first, second, eighth, ninth, eleventh, and twelfth.

Marciano came on to win after being knocked down in the first round, the first knockdown of his career. He rallied courageously, shook off the best punches of Walcott, and gradually wore down his thirty-eight-year-old rival with blistering blows. And, finally, to the stage where Walcott exposed his jaw for the finishing wallop.

Fighting before the largest crowd of his career, Rocky proved himself every inch a fighting man. He was crude and awkward so far as ring finesse is concerned but amazing in his resistance to punishment and altogether destructive in administering it.

A less hardy soul would have been finished in the first round. Rocky took an unmerciful beating then, and went to the canvas under a short left hook to the jaw.

Marciano arose at the count of three, infuriated, enraged at having been floored for this first time in an undefeated record of forty-two engagements that held thirty-seven knockouts. He was determined not only to avenge the indignity but to accomplish the complete destruction of his foe.

So Marciano plodded on, though buffeted about at times like a cork on an angry sea, until he had registered his thirty-eighth knockout. This was the big one.

Marciano was bruised and bleeding at the finish. He bled from a cut on the crown of his head, suffered in the sixth round when he accidentally bumped heads with Walcott. Joe got a severe cut over the left eye. Marciano had a puffed left eye and he bled from a cut above the right eye.

Walcott had only the cut over his left eye to show for the fifth knockout in a career that extends back over twenty-two years. His ribs must have been sore, his body must have been weary, and his nervous system certainly was upset under the pounding to which he had been subjected. But he had made a gallant stand, one that came near to completely upsetting the dope.

Marciano entered the ring a favorite to take the crown, at odds of 8 to 5.

It was forecast in advance of the fight that he must score a knockout to win. He won just as had the majority predicted, but with greater contention than had been anticipated. It did not seem possible that the aging Walcott legs could carry Joe on the long journey he traveled before going down for the count.

Walcott surprised all but his own supporters by the crafty, perfectly paced battle he waged until Marciano broke through with the crusher.

The finishing blow was a surprise. It was the first really clean punch of the fight landed by Marciano. Bewildered and confused earlier by the strategy of his more experienced and heavier rival, Rocky floundered badly through most of the battle, while winning some of the rounds principally through his fiery offense.

It was a short punch, straight and true to the mark, delivered as Walcott backed into the ropes near a neutral corner. Walcott appeared to be taking it easy at the time, boxing superbly, retreating cagily, letting Marciano fight himself out, as he had done earlier.

In the twelfth round, Walcott had the challenger befuddled by his clever defensive fighting followed by furious slugging. In the eleventh Walcott hurt Marciano with a right under the heart and, volleying furious lefts and rights to the head, face, and jaw, had Rocky sagging.

The thirteenth had opened as had many of the rounds preceding, with Marciano pressing forward on the attack, half-crouched on his toes, boring in, fists and arms poised to strike, Walcott backing away carefully, pecking and pawing with straight lefts, circling about the ring. A rush by Rocky and a wild left and right sent Walcott to the ropes.

Walcott parried a left for the head and blocked a left for the body. Walcott swayed slightly. His left arm and shoulder were down. Marciano swung with a right that didn't travel more than eighteen inches, and the fight was over.

ROGER MARIS

1934–1985

By JOSEPH DURSO

URING THE EARLY 1960s when the New York Yankees reigned for five straight pennant-winning seasons, Roger Maris was all things to all people. But baseball history will remember him as the home run twin to Mickey Mantle, and generations of fans will remember him as the man with the asterisk in the record books: hit 61 home runs in 1961 in a 162-game season.

The asterisk was inserted to distinguish Maris's home run record from the one set in 1927 by the greatest Yankee of them all: Babe Ruth, who hit 60 in the days of the 154-game season.

It was inserted into the record books by Ford C. Frick, the commissioner of baseball, who apparently reflected the traditionalist view of many fans that the Olympian feats of Babe Ruth must be defended against long seasons, short fences, and newly arrived sluggers—even one who eventually played in seven World Series and hit 275 home runs in twelve seasons in the big leagues.

But on October 1, 1961, asterisk or no asterisk, Roger Maris made history when he hit his sixty-first home run of the season in his 161st game on the final day of the 162-game season in Yankee Stadium against Tracy Stallard of the Boston Red Sox.

It was the rousing end to a rousing season, and it ended with the Yankees winning the pennant race before roaring sellout crowds and swarms of writers and broadcasters drawn by Mantle and Maris, the power hitters on yet another great Yankee team. Mantle, who was injured in September, still managed to hit 54 home runs, so the "twins" combined for an awesome total of 115. But Maris, an accomplished outfielder with a powerful arm and bat, was besieged as he pursued the memory and the record of Ruth.

And yet Maris was not universally embraced for his achievement. The Yankees received 3,000 messages a day during the final weeks of the season, many of them cheering him on. But the commissioner announced that any record would have to be set in 154 games. And Rogers Hornsby, the Hall of Fame slugger, who also had been a contemporary of Ruth, said in the passion of the day, "Maris has no right to break Ruth's record."

Maris had no "right" to break Ruth's record ostensibly because he was none of the things that had made Babe Ruth renowned as the Bambino. He was imported to the Yankees from the Kansas City Athletics, a stocky figure with a blond crewcut, and he was playing only his second season in the celebrated pinstripes. He was considered an upstart in the House That Ruth Built, and the

house that Mantle dominated. He was dour, aloof, sometimes arch, and in no way the flamboyant bear portrayed by Babe Ruth.

His manager in 1960, Casey Stengel, once said, "You ask Maris a question, and he stares at you for a week before he answers."

"I was born surly," Maris acknowledged in 1961 when the home run race had ended, "and I'm going to stay that way. Everything in life is tough.

"Even the Yankee clubhouse attendants think I'm tough to live with. I guess they're right. I'm miffed most of the time, regardless of how I'm doing. But regardless of my faults, I'll never take abuse from anybody—big or small, important or unimportant—if I think it's undeserved."

Roger Eugene Maris was born in Hibbing, Minnesota, on September 10, 1934, but was still an infant when his family moved to Fargo, North Dakota. The family name was Maras, but he changed it legally in 1955 to Maris.

He was an outstanding athlete at Shanley High School, a star in basketball and track and an all-state halfback in football. The school had no baseball team, but he played American Legion ball and became a star there, too.

When he graduated from high school, the University of Oklahoma offered Maris a football scholarship, but a scout for the Cleveland Indians persuaded him to try for a baseball career. He offered a $5,000 bonus and $10,000 more if Maris made the big leagues, and Maris signed.

It didn't take him long to redeem the full bonus. He broke into professional ball in 1954 in Keokuk, advanced in 1955 to Reading, then in 1956 to Indianapolis in the American Association, one notch below the majors. One year later, in 1957, he was playing outfield for the Indians.

But on June 15, 1958, he was traded to the Kansas City Athletics with Dick Tomanek and Preston Ward for Vic Power and Woodie Held. And a year and a half later, on December 11, 1959, with some recognition as a blooming power hitter, he was traded to New York with Joe DeMaestri and Kent Hadley for Don Larsen, Hank Bauer, Norm Siebern, and Marv Throneberry. He was twenty-five years old and a Yankee.

It didn't take Maris long to "join the club." In his debut in 1960, he hit a single, double, and two home runs. He finished the season with 39 home runs, and the Yankees won the American League pennant and began a streak of five straight pennants.

In 1961, the season that made him both famous and controversial, he posted these numbers: 161 games, 590 times at bat, 159 hits, 94 walks, 67 strikeouts, 132 runs scored, 142 runs batted in, a batting average of .269—and 61 home runs.

But if 1961 was a difficult time for Maris, he soon found that 1962 was an ordeal. He was engulfed wherever he went, cheerleaders asking if he could hit more than 61 home runs, critics asking why not. He hit 33.

After 1964, the Yankees stopped winning pennants after an extraordinary run of 14 in 16 years. Maris, meanwhile, endured several seasons of injuries to his back, hand, and legs, and said later that he was outraged by intimations that he had been exaggerating his ailments. On December 8, 1966, he was traded to the St. Louis Cardinals, where he again distinguished himself as a professional with a strong right-handed throwing arm from right field and a strong left-handed swing at the plate.

He played in the World Series of 1967 and 1968 for the Cardinals, and then retired at the close of the 1968 season. His career line, with no asterisk, read: twelve years in the big leagues, 1,463 games, 5,101 times at bat, 1,325 hits, 275 home runs, 826 runs, 851 runs batted in and an average of .260. In seven World Series, he hit six home runs.

For many years, Maris lived in Independence, Missouri, with his wife, the former Patricia Carvell, and their seven children. After retiring from baseball, he lived in Gainesville, Florida, where he owned a beer distributorship.

For a while, he shunned Old-timers Games, because he resented the criticism and controversy from his playing days. But he began to appear at reunions later, and he remained close friends with Mantle, Whitey Ford, Yogi Berra, Tony Kubek, and his other teammates from the time when the Yankees ruled the day.

He died of cancer on December 15, 1985, at the age of fifty-one.

The Sixty-first Home Run

By JOHN DREBINGER

Roger Maris on October 1, 1961, became the first major league player in history to hit more than 60 home runs in a season.

The twenty-seven-year-old Yankee outfielder hit his sixty-first at Yankee Stadium before a roaring crowd of 23,154 in the Bombers' final game of the regular campaign.

That surpassed by one the 60 that Babe Ruth hit in 1927. Ruth's mark stood in the record book for thirty-four years.

Artistically enough, Maris's homer also produced the only run of the game as Ralph Houk's 1961 American League champions defeated the Red Sox, 1 to 0, in their final tuneup for the World Series against the Cincinnati Reds.

Maris hit his fourth-inning homer in his second time at bat. The victim of the blow was Tracy Stallard, a twenty-four-year-old Boston rookie right-hander. Stallard's name would in time gain as much renown as that of Tom Zachary, who delivered the pitch that Ruth slammed into the stadium's right-field bleachers for No. 60 on the next to the last day of the 1927 season.

Along with Stallard, still another name was bandied about at the stadium after Maris's drive. Sal Durante, a nineteen-year-old truck driver from Coney Island, was the fellow who caught the ball as it dropped into the lower right-field stand, some ten rows back and about ten feet to the right of the Yankee bull pen.

For this achievement the young man won a $5,000 award and a round trip to Sacramento, California, offered by a Sacramento restaurant proprietor, as well as a round trip to the 1962 World's Fair in Seattle.

Maris was fooled by Stallard on an outside pitch that he stroked to left field for an out in the first inning. He let two pitches go by when he came to bat in the fourth with one out and the bases empty. The first one was high and outside. The second one was low and appeared to be inside.

The crowd, interested in only one thing, a home run, greeted both pitches with a chorus of boos. Then came the moment for which fans from coast to coast had been waiting since September 26, when Maris hit his sixtieth.

Stallard's next pitch was a fastball that appeared to be about waist high and right down the middle. In a flash, Roger's rhythmic swing, long the envy of left-handed pull hitters, connected with the ball.

Almost at once, the crowd sensed that this was it. An earsplitting roar went up as Maris, standing spellbound for just an instant at the plate, started his triumphant jog around the bases. As he came down the third-base line, he shook hands joyously with a young fan who had rushed onto the field to congratulate him.

Crossing the plate and arriving at the Yankee dugout, he was met by a solid phalanx of teammates. This time they made certain the modest country lad from Raytown, Missouri, acknowledged the crowd's plaudits.

He had been reluctant to do so when he hit No. 60, but this time the Yankee players wouldn't let Roger come down the dugout steps. Smiling broadly, the usually unemotional player lifted his cap from his blond close-cropped thatch and waved it to the cheering fans. Not until he had taken four bows did his colleagues allow him to retire to the bench.

Ruth's record, of course, will not be erased. On July 17, Commissioner Ford C. Frick ruled that Ruth's record would stand unless bettered within a 154-game limit, since that was the schedule in 1927. Maris hit 59 homers in the Yanks' first 154 games to a decision. He hit his sixtieth four games later.

However, Maris will go into the record book as having hit the sixty-first in a 162-game schedule.

Maris finished the season with 590 official times at bat. Ruth, in 1927, had 540 official times at bat. Their total appearances at the plate, however, were nearly identical—698 for Maris and 692 for Ruth.

According to the official baseball rules, a batter is not charged with an official time at bat when "he hits a sacrifice bunt or sacrifice fly, is awarded first base on four called balls, is hit by a pitched ball, or is awarded first base because of interference or obstruction."

Though it had taken 162 games (actually 163, since the Yankees played one tie) a player finally had risen from the ranks to pass Ruth's majestic record.

An Angry Young Man

American League pitchers were not alone in their judgment that Roger Eugene Maris was a difficult man to get along with. The Yankee had a demeanor that could be as intimidating as his big bat.

"Even the Yankee clubhouse attendants think I'm tough to live with," said Maris during his record-breaking 1961 season. "I guess they're right. I'm miffed most of the time, regardless of how I'm doing. But regardless of my faults, I'll never take abuse from anybody—big or small, important or unimportant—if I think it's undeserved."

As his own severest critic, Maris apparently felt that he did not need additional second-guessers. Like Mickey Mantle, his henchman in the harassment of hurlers, Roger directed most of his anger at himself.

"Maybe I'm a lot of things people say I am," the Mad Bomber admitted. "I just don't like to lose. When I think I'm not doing the best I can, I get steamed."

During a doubleheader with the Chicago White Sox during the 1961 season, the twenty-seven-year-old outfielder belted four home runs and then popped out.

"Roger was mad as hell," a teammate recalled. "He reacted like a guy who'd gone zero for twenty."

Again like Mantle, Maris was known to express his disappointments in phrases that would make a drill sergeant blush, and to swing from his heels at water coolers and dugout posts. He later learned to curb such tendencies—perhaps because he did not have a really prolonged slump during the 1961 season.

While with the Kansas City Athletics, he was described by Manager Harry Craft this way:

"He's a very confused young ball player when he's not hitting."

Later, when Roger was apprised of Craft's comment, he said, "I don't know how confused I was then, but I do know that when I'm not hitting, my wife could pitch and get me out."

As that quote suggests, Maris was by no means lacking in a sense of humor. As a general rule, however, the 200-pound Yankee star kept the punch lines to a minimum. A player who had been traded by the Athletics, along with Maris, to the Yanks put it this way:

"Roger doesn't kid around too much. He takes the game more seriously than lots of other players."

The Athletics traded Maris to the Yankees in December of 1959. In his debut as a Yankee in 1960, he clouted two homers, a double, and a single.

Even on the day of his greatest triumph, Maris insisted that he would have been just as happy with the lowly Athletics. The main reason was that his family lived in Raytown, Missouri, a suburb of Kansas City. His wife, the former Patricia Carvell, had recently given birth to their fourth child.

"I don't see them enough," said Maris. "I sure miss the children and my wife. That's why I miss K.C. so much."

As any sidewalk psychologist could plainly see, that statement probably was the real key to Roger's perpetual anger. He was unhappy over the long separation and said, "I don't intend to start moving young children around."

A Kansas City executive said of Maris, "This is a clean-living kid. He's not interested in bright lights. Prefers country life and barbecue pits. It's like people say: You can take the boy out of the country, but you can't take the country out of the boy."

The "country," in Maris's case, is Fargo, North Dakota. He was born in Hibbing, Minnesota, on September 10, 1934. His father, Rudie Maras (Roger changed his name legally), was a railroad man who had been transferred there. He moved the family to Fargo when Roger was an infant.

Roger was an all-round athlete at Shanley High School in Fargo, starring in football, basketball, and track. Shanley didn't have a baseball team.

He had been discouraged by the Chicago Cubs after his first workout with a major league team. Roger was only seventeen at the time and scouts from other teams had been on his trail because of his exploits in American Legion ball.

Roger seriously considered accepting a football scholarship at Oklahoma. A scout for the Cleveland Indians changed his mind.

"I guess I wasn't smart enough to go to college," said Maris. "I never had the patience for schoolwork, or even now for writing letters. I'm too fidgety. I always have to be doing something."

While in the Cleveland farm system, Maris played under Manager Jo Jo White at Keokuk in 1954 and at Reading in 1955.

"He was one of the great influences I've had in baseball," said Maris. "He advised me to stick to pull hitting because of my power."

The wisdom of that advice now is baseball history.

During his unsuccessful assault on Babe Ruth's record of 60 homers in a 154-game span, Roger demonstrated several times that he was a team player. He often tried to bunt his way to first base if the third baseman played him deep. In 1956, when he was with Indianapolis in the American Association, he beat out eighteen of nineteen drag bunts for hits.

Maris was philosophical about his feats. He said, "I don't claim to be a student of hitting. I just concentrate on my timing and my swing. If some of my hits are homers, so much the better."

CHRISTY MATHEWSON

1880–1925

C HRISTY MATHEWSON, idol of the nation's baseball fans over a span of more than two decades, and one of the greatest pitchers the game has ever known, was a symbol of the highest type of American sportsmanship.

Running the full gamut of baseball fame, first as a playing star, later as a coach and manager, Mathewson left the game to answer the call during World War I, subsequently fought and won a battle for his life, threatened by after-effects of his service, and then capped the climax of his diamond career by returning as part owner and president of a major league club.

But after all the remarkable achievements of Mathewson's career are recounted, the greatest tribute of all will be paid to his wonderful pitching skill. For on the mound he was a master craftsman, one of the most consummate and brilliant artists of all time, in the opinion of many of the game's closest students. Mathewson finished his career with a record of 373 wins and 188 losses, matching Grover Cleveland Alexander for the most career victories by a National League pitcher.

Big Six—a sobriquet contracted from Big Six Footer—started his major league career with the New York Giants in 1901, and it was during his seventeen seasons with that club that he carved a lasting niche for himself in pitching annals. Later he became manager for two and a half years of the Cincinnati Reds, served as a captain in the chemical warfare arm of the American Expeditionary Force, returned from the service to rejoin his old teammates, the Giants, as a coach, and retired from the game temporarily in 1920, when his health was dangerously impaired. He came back, again hale and hearty, in February 1923, to accept the presidency and part ownership of the Boston Nationals.

A graduate of Bucknell, where he was both a football and baseball star, Mathewson broke into the professional game with the Taunton, Massachusetts, club of the New England League in 1899, receiving a salary of eighty dollars a month for his first season. He lost his first start by a score of 6–5. During the season he won but two and lost nine games, lack of control—a fault he did not overcome for several years—handicapping his effectiveness.

Mathewson, however, was not long in attracting major league attention. Playing with Norfolk, in the Virginia League, in 1900 he won 21 out of 23 games, and was obtained by the Giants, who sent him down again. Later the same year he was drafted by Cincinnati, but soon afterward was sent to the Giants in a deal with the Reds.

Matty's first major league appearance was in the role of relief pitcher in

a game lost by the Giants to Brooklyn. He had but indifferent success as a pitcher and utility player until 1902, when John McGraw succeeded Horace Fogel as manager of the Giants. Big Six was playing first base at the time, but McGraw quickly recognized his pitching ability and took him in hand. His strides toward greatness dated from that period.

Feats of pitching brilliance too numerous to catalogue filled Matty's record during the dozen years in which he ranked consistently among the most effective hurlers in the major leagues.

He was a prominent factor in the pennant victories of the Giants in 1904, 1905, 1911, 1912, and 1913; he threw two no-hit games, one against the St. Louis Cardinals, in 1901, and the second against the Chicago Cubs, in 1905. He held jointly with Cy Young and Grover Cleveland Alexander a major league record of winning more than thirty games three seasons in a row; but his greatest achievement was in the World Series of 1905, when he pitched three shutout victories against the Philadelphia Athletics.

McGraw ranked Mathewson's feat in the 1905 Series as the greatest in his memory. All five games in that series were shutouts: Joe McGinnity pitched the fourth victory for the Giants, while Chief Bender blanked the Giants for the only triumph scored by the Mackmen.

Mathewson had the misfortune to lose two of the most important games of his career, the play-off contest with the Chicago Cubs for the pennant in 1908 and the deciding game of the World Series with the Boston Red Sox in 1912. Breaks of the game played a big part in both defeats. Misjudgment of a fly by Cy Seymour, Giant outfielder, was blamed for the defeat by the Cubs, while a costly error by Fred Snodgrass turned the tide against the Giants and Matty in the struggle with the Red Sox.

Mordecai "Three Finger" Brown of the Cubs was Matty's greatest rival on the mound, and the two had many stirring duels. Brown was Matty's opponent when the latter pitched his no-hit game against the Cubs in 1905 but conquered his New York rival in the famous 1908 play-off game. One season when the Giants and Cubs were battling for first place, President William Howard Taft, an ardent fan, had his private car attached to the train bearing the New York team to Chicago in order to see Mathewson and Brown oppose each other in the opening game of a series.

Oddly enough, both of these great pitchers closed their major league careers as players by opposing each other in a game on September 4, 1916. Mathewson then was manager of Cincinnati, and the Reds won, 10–8, both "old masters" being hit freely.

Mathewson suffered a shoulder injury in 1914 that virtually ended his career as a regular on the mound. He pitched infrequently thereafter and persuaded McGraw to let him go to Cincinnati during the middle of 1916 to fulfill his managerial ambition.

The Reds finished last in 1916 but improved rapidly under Matty's leadership, landing fourth place in 1917 and third place the following year, his last with the club.

Mathewson responded to the call to World War I at the close of the abbreviated season of 1918 and served with distinction overseas. He returned to become a coach with the Giants, holding that post until 1920, when he became seriously ill from the effects of being "gassed" during the war, and faced a battle for his life with tuberculosis.

Displaying the courage that won him many diamond victories. Matty fought and won the battle for his health during nearly three years of treatment at Saranac Lake, New York. Pronounced practically cured, he returned to New York in the fall of 1922 to witness the World Series triumph of his old teammates, the Giants, over the New York Yankees.

Restored in health, Mathewson was eager to get back into the game, and when early in 1923 an old friend and admirer, Emil E. Fuchs, prominent New York attorney, engineered a deal by which a New York syndicate obtained control of the Boston Braves from George W. Grant, "Big Six" was persuaded to take the club presidency.

Mathewson thus took his place among the few playing stars who rose to executive power in the game, a list that included Charles Comiskey, of the Chicago White Sox, Clark Griffith, of the Washington Senators, Branch Rickey, of the St. Louis Cardinals, John McGraw, of the New York Giants, Jimmy McAleer, A. G. Spalding, and John M. Ward.

Mathewson, baseball experts agreed, possessed all the attributes of a brilliant moundsman as well as those of a great athlete—natural skill, keen knowledge of the sport, generalship, and coolness under fire. One of the most popular figures in the history of the game, among players and fans alike, Big Six also was a hero and idol to the army of youthful followers of the national pastime.

"Matty was without a peer, either before or since the days he was at the height of his greatness," declared McGraw at one time in paying tribute to the pitcher.

"He had a greater variety of stuff than any pitcher I ever knew or handled."

Mathewson died of tuberculosis on October 7, 1925. Eleven years later, he would be named one of the first five members of the Baseball Hall of Fame.

JOHN J. McGRAW

1873–1934

FROM THE EARLY 1890s John J. McGraw was one of the greatest figures in baseball. In his playing days he was a brilliant third baseman, whose efforts were not confined to the mere mechanics of the sport, but a player who brought a keen, incisive mind to the national game. A fighter of the old school whose aggressiveness inspired his teammates on the famous old Baltimore Orioles, McGraw became one of the most successful figures in baseball history. His record—ten pennants and three World Series victories—speaks eloquently of McGraw, the molder of championship clubs, a stickler for discipline, and a martinet who saw that his orders were rigidly enforced both on and off the field.

Connie Mack, Joe McCarthy, and Casey Stengel are the only other leaders whose accomplishments are in any way comparable with those of the fiery McGraw. Mack won nine flags for the Philadelphia Athletics; McCarthy, nine for the Chicago Cubs and New York Yankees; and Stengel—a former player under McGraw—matched his erstwhile skipper with ten.

John Joseph McGraw was born in the rural community of Truxton, New York, on April 7, 1873, and gained his first knowledge of the game on the sandlots of that tiny village of upstate New York. There were not many boys in the little hamlet of some 300 persons, and decidedly few of any special baseball-playing ability. So it was significant of McGraw's persistency and close application to the task in hand that he was able to attain so much proficiency as a player that in 1890, at the age of seventeen, he obtained an engagement with the Olean, New York, club, then a member of the original New York and Pennsylvania League.

The next season, 1891, found McGraw transplanted to a far distant field. He had journeyed westward to Iowa, where he signed a contract with the Cedar Rapids club of the Illinois-Iowa League.

Reports of McGraw's rapid-fire fielding, his speed on the bases, and his solid hitting reached the ears of the officials of the Baltimore team of the old American Association, and in midsummer of that year, August 26, to be exact, McGraw, following his purchase, donned the uniform of the famous Orioles.

McGraw played in thirty-one games during the remainder of the season and showed enough ability to warrant retention. The next year Baltimore became a member of the twelve-club National League. The Orioles had been doing badly, and Ned Hanlon, who had shown an exceptional faculty for organization and leadership as well as playing ability, was obtained to manage the team.

Hanlon made a number of player deals during the winter, and in one of them he acquired a youth whose name was to be linked inseparably with McGraw ever thereafter. The new acquisition was a redheaded youngster from Louisville, Hughey Jennings.

Jennings and McGraw met on the Orioles' spring training trip of 1893. The conditioning campaign took the Baltimore club to New Orleans. The year before, the Orioles had descended to last place in the twelve-club circuit, and Hanlon was determined to lift the club out of the rut. He set to work with the fixed idea of weeding out some of the slipping veterans and replacing them with new blood. McGraw and Jennings got the chance to show what they could do at third base and shortstop and came through with flying colors and clinched these positions.

The Orioles of that period included many exceptional players, men like Wilbert Robinson, then rated as one of the finest catchers in baseball. His battery mate was the noted pitcher John "Sadie" McMahon. Joe Kelley roamed the outfield.

Hanlon welded the club into a formidable and close-knit unit in the season of 1894 and brought it home in front of the rest of the field, a remarkable performance. By this time, however, the wily pilot had obtained Wee Willie Keeler, Walter Brodie, Kid Gleason, and others to supplement the nucleus remaining.

McGraw and Jennings in the winter previous to the Orioles' first pennant-winning achievement had advanced themselves along another line of endeavor. In one of their long and frank talks they came to the conclusion that their education had largely been neglected and they resolved to overcome the deficiency.

McGraw proposed taking a course at St. Bonaventure College in Allegany, New York, not far from his home and the scene of his first professional baseball experience, and Jennings quickly fell in line with the idea. They were not in a position financially to afford much of an outlay for the education they sought, but with real business acumen arranged with the college authorities to serve as coaches, exchanging their knowledge of baseball for an education.

The Orioles from 1894 to 1899 were one of the most formidable and widely discussed clubs in baseball history. Under Hanlon's magic guidance this dashing, aggressive combination captured three National League pennants in succession, then finished second two years in a row, and in 1899, the last year of Baltimore's connection with the older major circuit, the club, many of whose famed veteran players had been replaced by that time, dropped to fourth.

Four times the Orioles played for the Temple Cup, the premier trophy of baseball of that period, which was annually contended for by the first- and second-place clubs in the National League. Twice McGraw and his mates captured the annual classic. Many of McGraw's Oriole teammates would accompany him into the managerial ranks: Robinson with the Brooklyn Dodgers, Jennings with the Detroit Tigers, and Gleason with the Chicago White Sox.

McGraw gained his first managerial experience in 1899, taking the helm at Baltimore for part of the season, Wilbert Robinson succeeding him. The end of that season witnessed the sale of these two stars to the St. Louis National

League club. However, they preferred to cast their lot with the American League, then in the process of organization.

McGraw and Robinson took over the Baltimore franchise in the new circuit.

In the meantime, Andrew Freedman, then president of the New York Giants, had taken a fancy to McGraw and offered him the post of manager. The Giants had been going from bad to worse under several different regimes, and Freedman believed that McGraw was the man to put the club on its feet.

On July 19, 1902, McGraw, then a rather stocky, black-haired little fellow, twenty-nine years old, walked out on the old Polo Grounds to take command of the hapless, disorganized Giants. This date is a significant one in the annals of the diamond, and in 1927 was enthusiastically celebrated by a great army of fans plus baseball and city officials on the occasion of the twenty-fifth anniversary of McGraw's leadership of the New York franchise.

McGraw undertook the reconstruction of the team, and the success of his efforts is evidenced by the fact that in 1903, his first full year at the helm, the Giants finished in second place. McGraw brought Joe McGinnity, Dan McGann, and Roger Bresnahan, three bright young stars, with him from Baltimore. He signed Arthur Devlin as his third baseman, Billy Gilbert as his second-sacker. The immortal Christy Mathewson already had joined the club from Bucknell University.

He was remarkably successful in the development of Mathewson, George Wiltse, Leon Ames, and Dummy Taylor to aid McGinnity, and the Giants were made. The attendance figures increased tremendously, and the advent of the New York Highlanders (later, the Yankees), an opposition club placed in the metropolis by the American League, was scarcely noticed.

In 1904 McGraw's Giants swept through the league, bowling over all opposition and rolling up the huge total of 106 victories. McGraw was hailed as the Little Napoleon of organized baseball, and baseball followers heaped encomiums on his head as the organizer of one of baseball's most powerful machines.

The previous year the Pittsburgh club, champion of the National League, and the Boston club, title winner in the American League, had met in the first Series for the world's championship. But much to the fans' disappointment, John T. Brush, who had succeeded Freedman as president of the Giants, stubbornly refused to let his club meet the Boston club, which had captured another pennant. He had been one of the stanch supporters of the National League and could not see that anything was to be gained by recognizing and playing against the champion team of a rival circuit.

The following year the Giants repeated, and this year Brush finally consented to allow his club to contend against the champions of the American League, the Philadelphia Athletics. The most brilliantly pitched World Series of all time ensued.

Connie Mack's Athletics were a formidable team, but were no match for the Giants with Mathewson and McGinnity pitching all five games for the National Leaguers. Mathewson established a record by shutting out the opposition in three of the battles. McGinnity blanked the Athletics in another contest, and in the other battle, the only one that Philadelphia won, Chief Bender shut out the Giants. All five games were shutouts, another record for the annual classic.

The Giants then finished second to Frank Chance's sensational Chicago Cubs for the next three years, dropping to third in 1909 but rising to second in 1910. McGraw made many bold moves to strengthen his club and invariably had his nine in the running. In 1908 the Giants came within an ace of taking the flag, losing it through defeat in a play-off with the Cubs. The blunder by Fred Merkle in not touching second base and thus giving the Cubs another chance to win out ultimately was one of the most discussed diamond happenings of that decade.

McGraw forgave Merkle and instead of censuring him condoned the fatal oversight and, moreover, raised his salary for the sake of encouraging the downcast player. Merkle repaid his boss by playing stellar ball for years thereafter and was ranked as one of the most mentally alert players in the game.

In 1911 McGraw finally passed the fighting Cubs and brought his third flag to the metropolis. In that year he had Herzog, Fletcher, Doyle, and Merkle in his infield; Devore, Snodgrass, and Murray in the outfield; Meyers behind the bat and Mathewson, Ames, and Wiltse, sole survivors of the 1905 champions, and Marquard and Crandall in the box. The Athletics boasted their "$100,000 infield," whose valuation would have been increased tenfold just a few years later, and Frank Baker's bat, more than any other factor, laid the Giants low in four out of six games.

The Giants repeated in 1912 and this year encountered the Boston Red Sox in the annual classic. The Series went to the limit of seven games (actually eight games, as one contest ended in a tie) before Boston pulled out the Series, winning the deciding game in the tenth inning after a costly error by the Giants' left fielder, Fred Snodgrass.

The Giants captured their third straight pennant in 1913 and again faced Connie Mack's great Athletics. The latter were too much for the Giants once more and took four out of five games. The Giants still had Mathewson, and Big Six pitched the only game the New Yorkers won, but McGraw's hitters could not cope with their opponents' brilliant pitching.

McGraw built over again, and in 1917, the Giants' next pennant-winning year, many new players were members of the combination that faced the Chicago White Sox. Again the Giants were doomed to defeat, the White Sox taking four contests of the six-game series.

The jinx that persistently pursued the Giants in World Series was put to rout in 1921, the next year McGraw's club finished on top, and Miller Huggins's Yankees, with Babe Ruth cast in the heavy slugging role, could not stop the Giants' dashing, crushing attack.

Again, in 1922, they routed the Yankees, again winners of the American League flag, in five games, the one game the clan of McGraw did not capture being a tie.

For the third consecutive year the two New York clubs clashed in 1923, and this time the Yankees, thanks to a savage batting attack, came out on top, winning the world title by scoring four victories in six starts.

McGraw set a record by leading his club to its fourth consecutive pennant in 1924. That year the Giants engaged in an exciting and hard-fought struggle with Bucky Harris's Washington Senators, whose pitching mainstay was the redoubtable Walter Johnson. There was little to choose between the two clubs, but the Senators finally emerged triumphant, winning in seven games, Johnson stemming the Giants' attack in the late innings of the crucial contest.

That year marked the Giants' last surge to the top in the National League under McGraw's leadership. In 1925 the club finished second after a hard battle with the Pittsburgh Pirates, and again in 1927 McGraw's team, after a slow start, finished with a burst of speed that nearly carried it into another championship but finally finishing two games behind the Pirates.

Again rebuilding after falling to fifth place in 1926 and finishing third in 1927, McGraw almost scaled the heights in 1928. Building around the hitting of Bill Terry, Melvin Ott, and Fred Lindstrom and with a pitching staff led by Larry Benton, the Giants carried the fight almost to the last day of the season, only to finish two games behind the St. Louis Cardinals.

In fact, with the season ending on Sunday, September 30, it took defeats at the hands of the Cubs on Friday and Saturday, with a victory by St. Louis on Saturday, to decide the race. McGraw drove his team with all his old-time skill, winning ten and losing five in his last home stand. In 1929 he finished third because Benton failed, and in 1930 he was in the same place, practically for the same reason.

The last real effort came in 1931, when he finished second, but far behind the Cardinals, who that year had a super team, which went on to beat the Athletics for the world championship. The Giants won eighty-seven games, good enough in some years for pennants, but the Cardinals went over the hundred mark.

Then came 1932. McGraw made a few changes, and in the training season in California seemed again to have exercised his magic. On the Coast and on the way east his men could not lose, compiling one of the best preseason records ever made. But when the games came that counted, they could not win. Through April and May they went, luckless.

Their failure weighed on their leader, and illnesses that he had laughed off and fought off in former years brought him down. He was a sick man, sicker than most people ever knew, when he electrified the baseball world by resigning on June 3 and turning the club over to Bill Terry, whom he had recommended to the officials of the club.

After his resignation he acted in an advisory capacity in the selection of young players, something at which his wide acquaintance with baseball club owners and managers had made him invaluable, and gave much counsel to Terry in the campaign that resulted in the pennant and world titles in 1933.

There were turbulent chapters in McGraw's career. Several times he became embroiled in altercations with the umpire and once lost an impromptu bout to an arbiter following a heated dispute over the umpire's decision.

McGraw was once charged with engaging in fisticuffs at the Lambs Club, of which he was a member. John C. Slavin, a comedian, and Wilton Lackaye and William H. Boyd, actors, both received hospital attention and McGraw was expelled from membership in the organization. Later the club reinstated him following the circulation of a petition to which the names of several hundred members were appended.

McGraw also was a baseball missionary to foreign lands, spreading the gospel of baseball to many countries abroad. In 1913, after the Giants and Athletics had met for the World Series, McGraw and Charles Comiskey, owner of the Chicago White Sox, led two teams on a world tour, embarking at San Francisco and terminating their long journey in New York. The two clubs toured Japan, China, Australia, Egypt, Italy, France, and England, playing their final contest before the king and 35,000 other Britons at London.

In 1924, at the close of the regular season, McGraw and Comiskey again took two teams abroad, visiting England and France. Interest in America's national game was kindled anew and many teams were organized abroad as the direct result of this second invasion. The trip, however, was said to have been a financial failure. McGraw always said that he did not object to incurring the financial losses his tours abroad cost him provided the journeys had added to the general interest in baseball.

Besides directing the playing of the Giants, from 1919 until shortly before his death he was associated in the business management and ownership of the club. In that year Harry Hempstead sold his interests to Charles A. Stoneham, Judge Francis X. McQuade, and McGraw, and the Giants' pilot became vice president of the club. While the club was owned by John T. Brush, McGraw was reputed to be drawing a salary of $30,000 a year. When he became an official it was generally accepted that he was drawing $65,000.

During his long management of the Giants McGraw was often accused of buying pennants, meaning that he purchased stars of other clubs to strengthen the Giants and aid them in their pennant fights. The club, however, was in a financial position to acquire players developed by other teams who readily parted with their stars for needed cash.

McGraw always played the game fairly and his integrity was shown by his prompt dismissal of players who were found to have been involved in sharp practices, no matter how much this weakened the club.

His silver jubilee at the Polo Grounds in 1927 brought back many memories of his long and successful career. The general feeling of admiration and respect was in Mayor Jimmy Walker's voice when he presented a huge silver loving cup to baseball's Little Napoleon. Commander Richard E. Byrd and Clarence D. Chamberlin, transatlantic airmen, stood by the mayor's side as he eulogized the veteran silver-haired leader.

McGraw's playing days undoubtedly would have been extended had it not been for a bad spike wound he suffered as a member of the Orioles. He played only ten years and during this time compiled a grand batting average of .334, while he scored 1,016 runs and stole 443 bases, an excellent offensive record.

The Rogers Hornsby episode was still fresh in the minds of the Giants' fans at the time of McGraw's death. McGraw had brought the celebrated Rajah to New York in the spring of 1927 and he played brilliantly for the Giants, only to be traded to the Braves at the close of the season. Rumor had it that enmity had arisen between Hornsby and McGraw, but the claim was never substantiated.

Hornsby himself said after he had been traded that he still esteemed McGraw highly and considered him the greatest manager in the major leagues. McGraw denied there was anything but the most cordial relations between him and the slugging infielder. Later President Stoneham assumed full responsibility for the disposal of the star player, asserting he had been traded "for the good of the club."

When McGraw took his Giants to Olean for an exhibition contest against St. Bonaventure in the summer of 1927, he was enthusiastically greeted after thirty-seven years' absence from that town. McGraw's homecoming was one of the biggest events that ever happened in the little city, and flags waved from almost every building while the whole population turned out with several bands to greet him.

McGraw died on February 25, 1934. His funeral was held at St. Patrick's Cathedral and he was buried in Baltimore.

His Silver Jubilee

By JAMES R. HARRISON

John J. McGraw's silver jubilee celebration at the Polo Grounds on July 19, 1927, resulted in an even break. Mr. McGraw got a mammoth silver loving cup and a tumultuous ovation from 25,000 fans; Mr. McGraw's team got a rude spanking from the Chicago Cubs, who won going away by 8–5.

If the Little Napoleon sat in a corner of the bench and daydreamed of other years and other teams, who could have blamed him? Put Matty in the box and Roger Bresnahan behind the plate, scatter a few of the old, glorious Giants here and there in the field, stick McGraw himself out on the coaching line barking at the umpires—and would the Cubs have won by 8 to 5? Echoes answer, Nay, nay!

It was an afternoon of reminiscences, of happy memories, of a turning back of the clock to the good old bygone days. There was many a fan there who was present twenty-five years earlier when young McGraw, a managerial nobody, walked out on the field to pilot his tail-end Giants for the first time. On this day they saw the same McGraw, now a managerial marvel, stride out to receive honors from two transatlantic air heroes, the mayor of New York, the commissioner of baseball, and from dignitaries in a half-dozen other walks of life.

In between those two occasions lay a service of twenty-five years, bedecked with ten pennants and three world championships, studded with great teams and great players, great successes and few failures.

There was something of that in Mayor Jimmy Walker's voice as he stood near the home plate and presented to John McGraw a huge silver cup, surmounted by a statuette of McGraw as he was when he wore the uniform of a Baltimore Oriole. Ranged around the mayor as he spoke were Commander

Richard E. Byrd and Clarence D. Chamberlin, successful leaders of two American air voyages across the Atlantic, who a few minutes before had been wildly cheered by the crowd.

Near the aviators stood the white-haired commissioner of baseball, Kenesaw Mountain Landis, and the president of the National League, John A. Heydler. Nearby, also, were George M. Cohan, one of the many representatives present from the theater; James J. Corbett, the man who licked John L. Sullivan; officials of the Giants, Colonel Jacob Ruppert of the Yankees, club owners of the National League, city officials and others.

And yet, aside from McGraw, the greatest ovation from this baseball crowd went to a man who was not in that circle of celebrities, whose name did not even appear on the program. He was Hughey Jennings, lifetime pal of John McGraw and his late lieutenant on the Giants. In response to the vociferous demands of the crowd, old Hughey, grown thinner from illness and limping along on a cane, came down from a seat in the grandstand and outbyrded Byrd in the size of his ovation.

There was something lacking in this jubilee day of McGraw, the crowd decided, and that something was the man who had been with him through thick and thin for more than twenty-five years. The call for Jennings, the appearance of the freckled, smiling, battle-scarred veteran, limping out to shake hands with McGraw—these struck the high sentimental note at the jubilee.

At the beginning there was comedy. Two teams of Broadway actors played a game of what they had nicknamed baseball. Eddie Cantor, Leon Errol, Louis Mann, Jim Corbett, Bert Wheeler, and other alleged baseball players were introduced by Joe Humphries, the silver-throated announcer. At one time there were three runners on one base. The big laugh came when some vile wretch sneaked in an orange and Mr. Cantor smacked it right on the proboscis, spattering the contents over his not unhandsome features.

It was beginning to rain at this point, and the rest of the program was cut short to hasten the presentation ceremony. Joe Humphries made a neat little speech in his inimitable way on the subject of John J. McGraw, and then the manager and his convoy of notables were summoned to the home plate. A few minutes before they had marched in from center field, led by the Fire Department Band and followed by both teams. The procession was behind schedule in starting; the mayor, it was said, was late again, and the crowd had been waiting long when Byrd, Chamberlin, Mr. Walker, Judge Landis, McGraw, and the other dignitaries paraded in to receive the cheers of the populace.

Humphries introduced McGraw to the crowd as the "champion of champions," and held the Little Napoleon's right hand up in the air, as he has done for scores of other champions in the past. By the same token of the ring was Commander Byrd acclaimed "a winner and still the champion," and in turn came Chamberlin, Mayor Walker, Judge Landis, Colonel Ruppert, and, finally, Hughey Jennings.

In a speech that could not be heard in the stands but was generously applauded nevertheless, Mayor Walker presented to McGraw the silver jubilee cup on behalf of the mayor's McGraw Jubilee Committee. After that Bresnahan gave his chief a silver service—the gift of the Giant players. Then came two other presents—a silver platter from the Lamb's Club, presented by Gene Buck (president of ASCAP), and a silver cane from the ushers of the Polo Grounds.

The rain, which was coming down rather briskly now, drenched the gay flags and bunting and sent the spectators to cover, but it failed to dampen the spirit and enthusiasm of a spontaneous tribute to New York's greatest baseball figure.

One of the interesting sights of the afternoon was a detachment of McGraw's old-time stars who turned out for the jubilee. They sat in a box near the Giant bench, and McGraw was not so busy shaking hands with heroes and celebrities that he could not spare a few minutes to come out and greet his former players with a smile or a handshake.

Thousands of crippled war veterans, orphans, and other shut-ins were brought to the game as guests of the jubilee committee. The youngsters made more noise than one of those record-breaking crowds at Yankee Stadium.

Oh, yes, the ball game. It was even for six innings and very uneven after that. Bill Clarkson went to pieces in the seventh and retired on the bad end of a 4–2 score. Fay Thomas attempted to pitch the eighth. Gabby Hartnett, who would rather talk than eat, slapped a homer into the upper left-field stands with two on, and a second later young Woody English, a .200 hitter, rammed another four-baser into the right-field sector. Four runs came in and the Giants passed out. The Cubs, incidentally, again stepped out in front of the National League procession.

It was this one rally, later events proved, that upset the McGraw apple cart, for in their half of the eighth the Giants scored three runs on Bob Osborn and drove the Cub right-hander from the mound, Guy Bush stemming the flood.

The choice of Clarkson for the jubilee joust was a surprise, but for six innings the young fellow did all right. The Giants encouraged him with a two-run lead. Rogers Hornsby walked to open the second and Bill Terry cheered the crowd by singling solidly to center, sending the Rajah to third, whence it was no trick to score on Harper's fly to Webb.

In the second Hornsby opened the throttle again and blasted one of his old-time hits to the distant precincts. Nobody was near it and the ball fell for a triple. Terry walked and was forced by Jackson, and during this incident Hornsby slipped in.

The Cubs opened operations in the fifth. Riggs Stephenson's double started the trouble. Riggs went to third on Charlie Grimm's fly and tried to score when Hartnett grounded to Travis Jackson at shortstop. He was run down, but Zack Taylor and Andy Reese effected it so clumsily that Hartnett got to second and thus was able to score on English's hit down the midway.

Hack Wilson's double behind Eddie Pick's single tied the game in a pink bowknot an inning later, and the ruination of Clarkson came in the seventh. Grimm walked, Hartnett doubled, and English and Osborn—yes, Osborn— singled. This is generally good for two runs in any league.

Thomas was no blooming, ruddy success in the eighth. Singles by Wilson and Stephenson moved Hartnett so mightily that he hammered the pill into the left-field attic. The next pitched ball English golfed into the right-field seats. Ouch!

The Giants rallied around in their half, but they were six runs behind and it was raining, and everybody was blue. This was no way to end a silver jubilee.

The Little Round Man Goes Out
By JOHN KIERAN
(Excerpt from "A Ballad of Baseball")

Who was it fought them, sword and lance?
John J. McGraw, ere his hair was gray,
Shouting his war-cry: "Go to-France!"
Ready to cut and thrust and slay;
Ready to fight and no delay;
Dahlen and Gilbert, Bresnahan,
Matty, McGinnity—come what may,
Those were the days for the baseball fan.

The Little Round Man has gone out and thus the curtain came down on the leader, the last and the greatest of the old Giants. It was some ten or more years before his death, when the fiery, peppery, trim McGraw of other days had changed to the portly genius of the high chair on the left end of the Giant bench, that such players as Pop Young, Frank Frisch, Highpockets Kelly, Casey Stengel, Heinie Groh, and Zeke Barnes began calling him the Little Round Man. But not to his face! Ah, no! The biggest of them still shivered in his boots when "Mister" McGraw began to snap out his biting phrases.

The "Mister," used by all except a few of the older regulars, was the sign of the gradually widening gap between the Little Napoleon and the troops under his command. Eventually the gap widened so much that the old, firm grasp that McGraw had on his great clubs was weakened. The ruling power became something like remote control. John J. McGraw was no longer in the thick of the diamond fray.

It wasn't like that when J. J. McGraw first came to the Polo Grounds, offered to toss the then owner of the Giants, Andrew Freedman, out of his own office window, called all his plays from the coaching lines, led his players by hand in fights on the field and frolics off the field and was "Mac" or "John" to Matty, McGinnity, Bad Bill Dahlen, Billy Gilbert, the chorister, and other vanished figures of the great old days.

He was the fiery leader in those campaigns, but the boys were on his right and left, close to him, shoulder to shoulder or arm in arm. That was the real McGraw. He was the real McGraw for two full decades, during which he established himself as the great genius of baseball.

All through his "Thirty Years War" as commander of the Giants he was an absolute monarch. In the forepart of his reign he was also guide, philosopher, and friend to his players. But there came a change in the mid-1920s.

There were three things that combined to bring about this change: the increasing age of the Little Napoleon, the introduction of the lively ball into the game, and the Florida real estate boom.

On some of his early Giant teams there were half a dozen players who were as old as John McGraw. With his zest for the game and his natural energy, he could keep up with "the boys" for many years after that. But increasing age and added weight finally took him off the field to the shadows of the dugout. When he took off the spangles and stopped his old habit of taking a regular turn in fielding practice, he knew that something had been lost, something that had been part of his equipment as a leader and something that never could be regained.

Then the lively ball came in and any hillbilly, hay shaker, or plow jockey might walk up there with a blundering bludgeon to ruin a whole afternoon of fine strategy by slapping the jackrabbit ball over a distant fence. It made a new game, a slam-bang affair in which stolen bases didn't count, inside stuff ran for Sweeney, and the hit-and-run gave way to the hit-and-walk style of play; hit one into the bleachers and walk around the bases. That wasn't McGraw's type of game. He was smart enough to meet it, but he had no enthusiasm for it. He didn't sit up nights figuring it out as he sat up nights with Hughey Jennings in his old Oriole days, doping out trick plays for a coming series.

On top of that, McGraw took his team to Sarasota to train in the early days of the Florida land boom. He went into a real estate proposition, a resort development plan. He put his money into it, and he got his friends in with him. In a few years the whole thing blew up in his face. He lost his money. His friends lost their money, and the second part worried John more than the first part. One of the great things in McGraw's character was his loyalty to his friends.

Coming at that period of his life and at that stage of a great career, it was a tremendous blow. He should have been sitting on top of the world, and suddenly it seemed that everything was crumbling around him. He was getting old. They had changed the game he knew so well to a series of slugging matches that he viewed with increasing scorn and futile protest. He could still call the plays, but he was no longer close to the players. They were getting away from him. Then came the financial shock, and it was a severe one.

It wasn't so much the money. He could still make plenty of money. But his pride was hurt, badly. Some of his old spirit died away in the collapse of the Florida land boom.

The followers of the Giants and the admirers of John J. McGraw were wondering what was the matter with the Giants in his later years. In the career of the Little Napoleon of the diamond this was the retreat from Russia. Fighting to the bitter end, John wouldn't admit it until June of 1932 when, bent in spirit and broken in health, he turned over the reins to Bill Terry.

He fought too long against losing odds, but the disappointments of his later days couldn't dim the great record that John J. McGraw made in baseball. Connie Mack said that John McGraw was the greatest leader the diamond ever knew. John McGraw was also one of the great players of the game. But going beyond the cold figures that placed him at the top of his profession, it was his fiery spirit, his fertile brain, his driving force, and his amazing energy that carried him, his team, and the whole game of baseball to a high peak.

The Little Round Man has gone out, and baseball was left mourning a tremendous loss.

BRONKO NAGURSKI

1908–1990

By THOMAS ROGERS

WITH AWESOME STRENGTH as a running back and tackler, Bronko Nagurski was to football fans of the 1920s and 1930s the epitome of bone-crushing power.

He won all-America recognition from 1927 to 1929 at the University of Minnesota and in 1929 became the only football player to be honored as an all-American at two positions in a single season: defensive tackle and fullback.

Upon leaving Minnesota, he was signed in 1930 by George Halas, the owner and coach of the Chicago Bears of the National Football League, who saw him as a power runner to complement the outside scoring dashes of Red Grange.

In 1963 he became a charter member of the Pro Football Hall of Fame.

"I was a straight downfield runner; I wouldn't, or rather couldn't, dodge anybody," said Nagurski, who was known as a man who could run interference for himself. "If somebody got in my way, I ran through them."

He helped the Bears win championships in 1932 and 1933 and was voted All-Pro three times. He was paid $5,000 in his first season, but his salary then dipped for several seasons before rising again to $5,000. When Halas refused to pay him $6,000 for the 1938 season, Nagurski retired and became a professional wrestler.

"We used to say Coach Halas tossed nickels around like they were man-hole covers," he recalled in a 1972 interview. "People told me I could get into wrestling and make millions. I did it for about twelve or fourteen years. It was tough work, and I didn't make millions."

After being rejected for military service during World War II because of damaged knees and ankles, Nagurski returned to the Bears for one last season in 1943, essentially as a defensive tackle, and again helped them to a championship.

Having gained 2,778 yards rushing in nine professional seasons as he played on both offense and defense, he once again retired and alternated between wrestling and operating a filling station near his home in International Falls, Minnesota. Following his retirement from wrestling in 1960, physical movement was so painful that he became a virtual recluse and spent most of his time fishing, gardening, or watching television.

"I want people to remember the way I was and not the way I am," he said.

Bronislau Nagurski was born in Rainy River, Ontario, just over the United States border, to Ukrainian immigrants in 1908 and grew up in International

The New York Times

Falls. He was given the nickname Bronko by his first teacher, who was unable to understand his mother's pronunciation of his first name.

Nagurski inspired stories akin to those about the legendary Paul Bunyan. He was supposedly recruited to play at Minnesota after the football coach, Clarence "Doc" Spears, saw him plowing in a field—without a horse. When asked directions, Nagurski, the story goes, pointed out the correct path while holding the plow in his hand.

On another occasion, an overflow crowd was kept under control by a squadron of mounted police. With the Bears near the goal line, Nagurski supposedly crashed into and through the end zone with such determined power that he knocked over one of the horses and its rider.

Perhaps the most familiar tale about the 6-foot-2-inch, 230-pound Nagurski concerns a scoring run he made for the Bears at Wrigley Field. On a touchdown gallop against the Redskins, he is said to have knocked two linebackers in opposite directions, stomped over a defensive halfback, and crushed an interferring safety man before caroming off the goalposts and finally crashing into the stadium's brick walls.

"That last guy hit me awfully hard," were the words attributed to him as he ran back to the huddle.

Nagurski seemed to lose most of his interest in football after his retirement.

"I sometimes think there is less enjoyment in the game now," he said in the early 1970s. "The quarterback always handles the ball. The games all seem so much alike. Only the faces and numbers change. And of course, the platoons. We had eighteen men on a team and you played sixty minutes, sometimes twice a week.

"If some of the big boys today played sixty minutes, they might not be so big. They'd sweat more."

He died on January 8, 1990, at the age of eighty-one.

Bronko's Press Conference
By IRA BERKOW

"If Bronko Nagurski shows up," said Sid Hartman, sports columnist for the *Minneapolis Tribune*, "it'll be a miracle."

Hartman said that over the years a number of feature writers had traveled to Rainy Lake, Minnesota, four miles from International Falls at the Canadian border, where Nagurski lives, to interview the old football player. "But they all come back without a story," said Hartman. "He's refused to see anyone."

On a Thursday afternoon in January 1984, Hartman and about seventy other journalists gathered in a room in a downtown hotel in Tampa, Florida, waiting for Nagurski.

Bronislau "Bronko" Nagurski was scheduled to appear at a news conference for him at 2:30 P.M., called by the National Football League. He was supposed to have been flown in from his home to be the honorary coin flipper at Super Bowl XVIII between the Los Angeles Raiders and the Washington Redskins.

Nagurski is famous as one of the best, if not the best, football players ever. His strength and prowess as a fullback, end, tackle, and linebacker in the 1920s, 1930s, and 1940s, for the University of Minnesota and the Chicago Bears, created an aura about him that rivals that of another from his region, Paul Bunyan.

"They used to say that Bronko was the only man who could run interference for himself," said one reporter.

Someone else mentioned that Grantland Rice wrote, "Eleven Bronko Nagurskis could beat eleven Red Granges or eleven Jim Thorpes."

Another remembered the legend that he was recruited by Minnesota when the football coach, Doc Spears, saw Nagurski lift a farm plow.

Nagurski did not show up for the news conference at 2:30. At 2:45, no Nagurski. People checked their watches.

At about a little after 3:00, the double doors opened and an elderly man, accompanied by a few others, entered the room. The man walked with an aluminum cane and a steel elbow brace. He wore very thick glasses and the cane seemed to have a dual purpose, to aid his balance and to help him feel where he was walking. He was rather hunched and his legs were broadly bowed.

"Hello, Bronk," someone said.

Nagurski, who is seventy-five years old, craned his neck and looked at the seated reporters. "What am I in here for?" he asked with a smile. It drew a nice laugh from the journalists.

Nagurski moved slowly to a desk on a little platform in a corner of the large room and sat down. His gray hair had receded on his forehead, and his face was lined, but his cleft jaw was still prominent and looked firm. He wore a white knit shirt with a brown unbuttoned sweater over it, patterned gray slacks, white socks and brown corrective shoes, size 13.

He seemed surprised that there might still be such interest in him, and he appeared a little shy.

By today's football standards, he would not seem particularly big, but in his time he was a huge player at 6 feet 2 inches and 235 pounds.

"I'm still about the same weight," he said in a husky voice. But he stood only about 6 feet tall. "I've shrunk some," he said. "From the arthritis. I've got arthritis in about every joint, in my shoulders, legs, ankles. They're from the football injuries and the wrestling."

Nagurski took up wrestling in 1938, after eight seasons as a pro football player, when the Bears' owner, George Halas, refused to pay him a requested $6,000 for the season.

"People told me I could get into wrestling and make millions," said Nagurski. He wrestled many of the standouts at the time, like Jim Londos and Strangler Lewis. "I did it for about twelve, thirteen, fourteen years. It was tough work, and I didn't make millions."

In 1943 the Bears asked him to return, and at age thirty-five—after having been out of the game for five years—he helped them win a championship. Then he quit again. "I had other interests," he said.

He would eventually open a filling station, and for many years pump gas in International Falls. "It's a great tourist country, and that was good," he said.

For the last several years, however, he said he has spent most of his time sitting at home because moving about is too painful.

Later, he would say why he hasn't seen many people. "I wanted people to remember me the way I was," he said, "and not the way I am. I became sort of a recluse. But I come out on special occasions."

In his house there was a reminder of the old days: photographs of him in his Bears' uniform, wearing No. 3, hang on a wall.

"Is it true, Bronko, that you hit a wall in Wrigley Field so hard you cracked it?" someone asked.

"I hit a wall right behind the goal line because I couldn't put the brakes on in time after scoring a touchdown. I don't know if I cracked the wall. I have a feeling it was cracked before, but I did hit it pretty hard."

"Did you really lift up a plow?"

"If I did," he said, "it would have to have been a small one."

He said that he thought the teams of old were more "close-knit" than they are now. "We had eighteen players on a team and then twenty-two," he said. They have forty-nine today."

Nagurski also said that in his day players didn't jump up and down after scoring a touchdown as they do now. "We were too tired," he said, "we used to play on offense and defense."

He did watch some football on television.

"I'm very impressed with, oh, what's his name, the great back with the Redskins—I'm a little slow on names," he said.

"Riggins?" someone suggested.

"Who?"

Louder, respectfully: "Riggins."

"Yes, Riggins," he said.

From the audience, Augie Lio introduced himself. Lio, a onetime football player, was a reporter for the *Herald-News* in Passaic, New Jersey.

"Bronko, I played against you in New Jersey, when I was with the Lions," said Lio. "I was a guard on the right side and you were on the right side on defense. When I saw the size of your neck, I was glad I was on the opposite side of you."

When the news conference ended, some of the reporters gathered around Nagurski.

"Hello, Bronko, I'm Sid Hartman," said Hartman.

Nagurski looked at him.

"You're not Sid Hartman; I've known Sid Hartman a long time," said Nagurski.

"No, I'm Sid Hartman."

Nagurski looked closer. His glasses glinted from the lights in the room.

"You are Sid Hartman!" Nagurski threw his arm around him. "Good to see you, Sid, good to see you! It's been years."

JESSE OWENS

1913–1980

J ESSE OWENS'S four gold medals at the 1936 Olympic Games in Berlin made him perhaps the greatest and most famous athlete in track and field history.

In Berlin, Owens scored a triumph that would come to be regarded as not only athletic but also political. Adolf Hitler had intended the Berlin Games to be a showcase for the Nazi doctrine of Aryan supremacy.

A member of what the Nazis mockingly called America's "black auxiliaries," Owens achieved a feat unmatched in modern times in Olympic track competition. The year before, with a wrenched back so painful that he could not dress or undress without help, he broke five world records and equaled a sixth, all within forty-five minutes.

But the Jesse Owens also remembered by many Americans was a public speaker with the ringing, inspirational delivery of an evangelist. Later in his life, he traveled 200,000 miles a year making two or three speeches a week, mostly to sales meetings and conventions. With his own public relations and marketing concern, he earned more than $100,000 a year.

James Cleveland Owens was born September 12, 1913, in Danville, Alabama, the son of a sharecropper and the grandson of slaves. The youngster picked cotton until he and his family moved to Cleveland when he was nine. There, a schoolteacher asked the youth his name.

"J.C." he replied.

She thought he had said "Jesse," and he had a new name.

He ran his first race at age thirteen. He became a nationally known sprinter at East Technical High School in Cleveland, slim and lithe at 163 pounds. He ran with fluid grace. There were no starting blocks then; sprinters merely dug holes at the starting line in tracks of cinder or dirt.

After high school, he went to Ohio State University, paying his way as a hundred-dollar-a-month night elevator operator because he had no athletic scholarship. As a sophomore, in his first Big Ten championships, he achieved a harvest of records even greater than the Olympic glory he would attain a year later.

A week before the Big Ten meet, which was held in Ann Arbor, Michigan, Owens and a fraternity brother were wrestling playfully when they tumbled down a flight of stairs. Owens's back hurt so much that he could not work out all week. Coach Larry Snyder and teammates had to help him in and out of the car that drove him to the track for the meet.

There, in a vain attempt to lessen the back pain, he sat for half an hour in a hot tub. He did not warm up or even stretch. At the last minute, he rejected suggestions that he withdraw from the meet and said he would try, event by event.

He tried, and the results are in the record book. On May 25, 1935, from 3:15 to 4:00 P.M., Jesse Owens successively equaled the world record for the 100-yard dash (9.4 seconds), broke the world record for the broad jump, now called the long jump, with his only attempt (26 feet 8¼ inches, which remained the record for twenty-five years), broke the world record for the 220-yard dash (20.3 seconds, which also bettered the record for 200 meters), and broke the world record for the 220-yard low hurdles (22.6 seconds, which also bettered the record for the 200-meter low hurdles).

Kenneth L. "Tug" Wilson, the Big Ten commissioner, watched in awe and said, "He is a floating wonder, just like he had wings."

The next year, with the Italians occupying Ethiopia, the Japanese in Manchuria, the Germans moving into the Rhineland, and a civil war starting in Spain, the Olympic Games were held in Berlin. Despite pleas that the United States boycott the Olympics to protest Nazi racial policies, American officials voted to participate.

The United States Olympic track team, of sixty-six athletes, included ten blacks. The Nazis derided the Americans for relying on what the Nazis called an inferior race, but of the eleven individual gold medals in track won by the American men, six were won by blacks.

The hero was Owens. He won the 100-meter dash in 10.3 seconds, the 200-meter dash in 20.7 seconds, and the broad jump at 26 feet ½ inch, and he led off for the United States team that won the 400-meter relay in 39.8 seconds.

His individual performances broke two Olympic records and, except for an excessive following wind, would have broken the third. The relay team broke the world record. His 100-meter and 200-meter times would have won Olympic medals through 1964, his broad jump performance through 1968.

Actually, Owens had not been scheduled to run in the relay. Marty Glickman and Sam Stoller were, but American Olympic officials, led by Avery Brundage, wanted to avoid offending the Nazis. They replaced Glickman and Stoller, both Jews, with Owens and Ralph Metcalfe, both blacks.

Hitler did not congratulate any of the American black winners, a subject to which Owens addressed himself for the rest of his life.

"It was all right with me," he said years later. "I didn't go to Berlin to shake hands with him, anyway. All I know is that I'm here now, and Hitler isn't.

"When I came back, after all those stories about Hitler and his snub, I came back to my native country, and I couldn't ride in the front of the bus. I had to go to the back door. I couldn't live where I wanted. Now what's the difference?"

Having returned from Berlin, he received no telephone call from President Franklin D. Roosevelt and was not asked to visit the White House. Official recognition from his own country did not come until 1976, when President Gerald R. Ford presented him with the Presidential Medal of Freedom. Three years later, President Jimmy Carter gave him the Living Legends Award.

Nor were there any lucrative contracts for an Olympic hero after the 1936 games. Owens became a playground janitor because he could not find a better job. He ended his career as an amateur runner and accepted money to race against cars, trucks, motorcycles, horses, and dogs. He toured with the Harlem Globetrotters basketball team.

"Sure, it bothered me," he said later. "But at least it was an honest living. I had to eat."

In time, the four gold medals changed his life.

"They have kept me alive over the years," he once said. "Time has stood still for me. That golden moment dies hard."

He became a disk jockey, then ran his public relations and marketing concern, first in Chicago and then in Phoenix.

He also became celebrated as a speaker, using about five basic speeches with interchangeable parts. Each speech praised the virtues of patriotism, clean living, and fair play. His delivery was old-fashioned spellbinding, a far cry from the days when he stuttered. Even in casual conversations, he spoke in sweeping tones.

"When he enters a room," wrote Jon Hendershott in *Track and Field News*, "he doesn't so much take it over as envelop it."

William Oscar Johnson, writing in *Sports Illustrated*, described him as "a kind of all-round super combination of nineteenth-century spellbinder and twentieth-century plastic p.r. man, full-time banquet guest, eternal glad-hander, evangelistic small-talker . . . what you might call a professional good example."

Not everyone agreed. During the 1968 Olympics in Mexico City, when Owens attempted to mediate with militant American black athletes on behalf of the United States Olympic Committee, critics called him "Uncle Tom." He wrote a 1970 book, *Blackthink*, decrying racial militancy, and a 1972 book, *I Have Changed*, saying the ideas in his first book were wrong.

In his later years, Owens walked two miles every morning and swam and lifted weights at the Phoenix YMCA. He weighed 180 pounds.

"I don't jog," he said, "because I can't run flat-footed. And at sixty years old you're crazy to be out there running."

Owens, a pack-a-day cigarette smoker for thirty-five years, died of lung cancer on March 31, 1980, at the age of sixty-six.

The Führer's Furor

By ARTHUR DALEY

Jesse Owens stepped into his destined role in the 1936 Olympics in Berlin as 100-meter sprint champion. On August 3, the second day of competition, he ran amid the thunderous acclaim of a magnificent crowd of 110,000 at the Reich Sports Field Stadium. Owens, gliding over the red-clay track with the grace of a streamlined express flying over the open prairie, equaled the world and Olympic mark of 0:10.3 in a smashing one-yard victory over Ralph Metcalfe, a fellow American, as the United States registered a one-two "small slam" in the event.

German nationalism and the prejudice that seems to go with it revealed themselves somewhat disagreeably that afternoon. On the surface all was serene. The Führer apparently played no favorites. He did not publicly receive the winning Germans, nor did he greet the decidedly non-Aryan American Negroes, Owens and Metcalfe.

But an investigation was made by some who had taken his departure the day before as meaning he wished to avoid shaking hands with the Negro high jumpers, Cornelius Johnson and David Albritton. This investigation produced information that seemed corroborative. In the seclusion of his quarters under the stands the Reich's dictator did congratulate Karl Hein and Erwin Blask, Germans who won the gold and silver medals in the hammer throw. Perhaps two and two do make four, after all.

If Hitler is going to avoid the African-Americans, he is going to have his work cut out for him. John Woodruff spread-eagled the field in his 800-meter semifinal. He loafed in the home stretch and still won by twenty yards in the fine time of 1:52.7.

In administering a sound drubbing to Kazimiers Kucharski of Poland, he defeated the Europeans' best. The other two Americans, Chuck Hornbostel, of Indiana, and Harry Williamson, of North Carolina, also were semifinal winners.

From a general sporting standpoint, however, there could be no taking the play away from Owens. Jesse left the stadium in the belief he had broken the world record with his 0:10.3 feat. But the usually efficient Germans had an annoying roundabout way of getting news to the newspapermen and the athletes.

It was discovered the following morning that Owens's new mark had been disallowed because of a following wind. Whether he will have the same experience in future events cannot even be guessed. From the stands the breeze looked like a crosswind, but one can never tell about those things.

Owens won his race because he was in truth the world's fastest human. No one ever ran a more perfect race. His start was perfect, his in-between running perfect, and his finish perfect.

The Buckeye Bullet ripped out of his starting holes as though slung by a giant catapult. He was ahead in his first stride and let Osendarp and Wykoff battle behind him for what was left of the race.

Metcalfe, hardly the best starter in the world, was off in atrocious fashion. He was sixth in the six-man field at the getaway, but once in his stride he certainly moved. By sixty meters he had drawn up even with the Hollander and begun to cut down the two-yard advantage Owens had on him.

It was then a speed dual between a streamlined express and an old-fashioned steam engine that exuded sheer, rugged power. Metcalfe cut those two yards to one at the wire, but it was as close as he could get, losing by a yard a championship that had eluded him four years before by a hair.

An Owens Sampler

On American black athletes who question the value of their gold medals:
Any black who strives to achieve in this country should think in terms of not
only himself but also how he can reach down and grab another black child and
pull him to the top of the mountain where he is. This is what a gold medal does
to you.

On dignity: Regardless of his color, a man who becomes a recognized
athlete has to learn to walk ten feet tall. But he must have his dignity off the
athletic field.

On material rewards: Material reward is not all there is. How many meals
can a man eat? How many cars can he drive? In how many beds can he sleep?
All of life's wonders are not reflected in material wealth.

On the value of sport: We all have dreams. But in order to make dreams
into reality, it takes an awful lot of determination, dedication, self-discipline,
and effort. These things apply to everyday life. You learn not only the sport but
things like respect of others, ethics in life, how you are going to live, how you
treat your fellow man, how you live with your fellow man.

On the moment before Olympic competition: You think about the number
of years you have worked to the point where you are able to stand on that day
to represent your nation. It's a nervous, a terrible feeling. You feel, as you stand
there, as if your legs can't carry the weight of your body. Your stomach isn't
there, and your mouth is dry, and your hands are wet with perspiration. And
you begin to think in terms of all those years that you have worked. In my
particular case, the 100 meters, as you look down the field 109 yards 2 feet away,
and recognizing that after eight years of hard work that this is the point that
I had reached and that all was going to be over in ten seconds. Those are great
moments in the lives of individuals.

SATCHEL PAIGE

1906–1982

LEROY "SATCHEL" PAIGE was a hero of baseball's old Negro leagues who became a rookie pitcher in the major leagues at the age of forty-two or thereabouts. His exact age was one of the mysteries in the legend that accompanied him into the big leagues in 1948 with the Cleveland Indians, and it was still a mystery when he pitched his final three innings for the Kansas City A's in 1965 when he was admitting to fifty-nine.

That was the end of what he laughingly called "my hundred-year career in baseball." He was celebrated for his homespun wit as well as for his fastball and stamina, and most especially for his admonition: "Don't look back. Something might be gaining on you."

By then, he was viewing the world from a rocking chair in the Kansas City bull pen, a tall, thin man with a thin mustache who had lived one of the phenomenal careers in sports: twenty-two years as a barnstorming pitcher in the era before black players were admitted to the big leagues, then five seasons with three clubs in the American League, including the World Series of 1948.

In the barnstorming days, he pitched perhaps 2,500 games, completed 55 no-hitters, and performed before crowds estimated at 10 million persons in the United States, the Caribbean, and Central America. He once started 29 games in one month in Bismarck, North Dakota, and he said later that he won 104 of the 105 games he pitched in 1934.

By the time Jackie Robinson signed with the Brooklyn Dodgers in 1947 as the first black player in the majors, Mr. Paige was past forty. But Bill Veeck, the impresario of the Cleveland club, signed him to a contract the following summer, and he promptly drew crowds of 72,000 in his first game and 78,000 in his third game.

His career in the big leagues was spread over eighteen years, but because he retired twice during that span, it totaled only five seasons with these statistics: 28 victories, 31 defeats, 476 innings, 290 strikeouts, and an earned-run average of 3.29. But by then, he already occupied a special rank as a showman and country philosopher who advised people to "avoid running at all times," and who once reflected, "There never was a man on earth who pitched as much as me. But the more I pitched, the stronger my arm would get."

Despite the uncertainty about his age, there was general agreement that he was the oldest player ever to appear in a major league game when he pitched three innings against the Boston Red Sox on September 25, 1965. And, two

239

years later, clearly enjoying his role as an athletic phenomenon, he wrote an autobiography with the title *Maybe I'll Pitch Forever.*

In 1971, he was elected to the Baseball Hall of Fame as the first of the stars of the old Negro leagues to be enshrined.

Leroy Robert Paige was born in Mobile, Alabama, the son of John and Lula Page. The family name became "Paige," he remembered, because "my folks later stuck in the 'i' to make themselves sound more high-toned."

He teased people about the date of his birth, saying that the certificate had been placed between the pages of a Bible that was eaten by the family's goat. But later he did not argue with evidence that he had been born on July 7, 1906.

He was specific, though, about his nickname. He got it as a seven-year-old while hustling baggage at the railroad depot in Mobile after he had invented a contraption for carrying more bags.

"I rigged up ropes around my shoulders and my waist, and I carried a satchel in each hand and one under each arm," he said. "I carried so many satchels that all you could see were satchels. You couldn't see no Leroy Paige."

He took up pitching during four years spent at the Alabama Reform School for Boys, and became exceptional. In 1924, he presented himself to Candy Jim Taylor, the manager of the Mobile Tigers, a black semiprofessional team, and fired ten fastballs past the manager in an audition. He had a job, and soon a career.

For the next two decades, he traveled around the hemisphere with black teams, pitching across the seasons and the borders of countries. He also pitched in exhibition games against white major league stars. Once he outpitched Dizzy Dean, 1–0. Another time, he struck out Rogers Hornsby five times in one game. Joe DiMaggio called him "the best I've ever faced, and the fastest."

He was a lean but imposing figure on the mound, 6 feet 3½ inches tall and 180 pounds, with thin legs and a mean fastball, numerous curveballs, and pinpoint control. And one year after Jackie Robinson broke the color line, Veeck signed him as a drawing card and pitcher on a Cleveland team headed for the championship. The date was July 7, 1948.

Many baseball people derided the signing as a box office gimmick, since the rookie was past forty and probably past his prime. But Lou Boudreau, the Indians' manager, introduced his new pitcher carefully, using him six times in relief before starting him in a game. In his first start, he defeated the Washington Senators, 5–3, before 72,434 fans in Cleveland's Municipal Stadium. Then he pitched two shutouts against the Chicago White Sox, and by then had pitched before combined crowds of 201,829 in three starts.

His record after less than three months showed six victories and one loss, and he made one brief appearance in the World Series that October against the Boston Braves. But after one more season with Cleveland, he was released after Veeck sold his controlling interest in the team. However, two years later, Veeck bought the St. Louis Browns and promptly signed his former rookie, who now was at least forty-five years old. But in his most flamboyant defiance to age, Paige won twelve games in 1952 and was selected for the league's All-Star team.

After the 1953 season, he was released once more, but once more refused to quit baseball. He pitched in the minor leagues, then took the barnstorming route again and even appeared with the Harlem Globetrotters basketball team as a guest celebrity. He played the part of a cavalry sergeant in a 1958 motion picture, *The Wonderful Country*.

Then another baseball showman, Charles O. Finley, drew him back to the big leagues briefly in 1965 with the Kansas City A's. The theme was revival, and Paige was provided with a rocking chair in the bull pen and a nurse who massaged his right arm with liniment. He pretended that the compound was based on a secret formula and, continuing the tease, sparred with persons who asked whether he perhaps relied on "doctored" pitches.

"I never threw an illegal pitch," he replied. "The trouble is, once in a while I toss one that ain't never been seen by this generation."

Reviewing his forty years on the public baseball scene, he once said that the toughest hitters he had ever faced were Josh Gibson, the celebrated catcher from the Negro leagues, and Charley Gehringer of the Detroit Tigers.

"They said I was the greatest pitcher they ever saw," he remarked, reflecting on the segregation that had cost him a full career in the major leagues. "I couldn't understand why they couldn't give me no justice."

Paige made his last public appearance a few days before his death on June 8, 1982, in ceremonies at a Kansas City baseball park that had been named for him. He attended in a wheelchair, and said, "Nobody on earth could feel as good as I do now."

Paige's Guide to Longevity

To a world that marveled at his stamina as a fifty-nine-year-old pitcher, Satchel Paige often offered these "master's maxims" as his guide to longevity:

1. Avoid fried meats, which angry up the blood.
2. If your stomach disputes you, lie down and pacify it with cool thoughts.
3. Keep the juices flowing by jangling around gently as you move.
4. Go very light on the vices, such as carrying on in society. The social rumble ain't restful.
5. Avoid running at all times.
6. Don't look back. Something might be gaining on you.

A Little Rusted Up
By ROBERT LIPSYTE

"I never figured I'd be some kind of symbol. Well, if I was, I had to admit I was a little rusted up. You get rusted when you got to come all the way from the slums of Mobile, Alabama, from hiding from truant officers and cops, from reform school. And while I was coming all that way, I guess I'd been a lot of things people said I was—a no-good kid, a guy who left his team when money looked better some place else, a chaser. I'd been those things, but I'd also been a fine pitcher—one of the best." The event that stimulated those thoughts, which are from Satchel Paige's 1967 autobiography, *Maybe I'll Pitch Forever*, was his promotion in 1948 to the major leagues. In an action *The Sporting News* called "a publicity stunt," Bill Veeck signed Paige to a Cleveland Indian contract, and the forty-two-year-old superstar pitcher of the Negro leagues offered all America what was left of his bloopers, loopers, and droopers, his jumpballs, screwballs, wobbly balls, hurry-up balls, nothin' balls, and bat-badgers.

In 1971 the rusted-up symbol was presented in a downstairs room of Toots Shor's noisy Manhattan restaurant as "the first player to receive special recognition for outstanding achievements in the Negro baseball leagues." A bronze likeness of Paige would be hung somewhere in the National Baseball Hall of Fame and Museum at Cooperstown, New York. He would not be "technically" enshrined in the Hall of Fame, according to Commissioner Bowie Kuhn, who added, "Realistically, I agree that the Hall of Fame is a state of mind, and what's important here is how sports fans view Satchel Paige."

Athletic halls of fame tend to be eerie crypts: the powerful and gifted youth who stretched our possibilities lies dead here with his hat and number and statistics, and this short-breath, weepy, grateful, middle-aged man accepting congratulations seems as much a stranger to glory as you and I. Paige was even further removed: he had been introduced to most of America as a legend, and now was being recognized in an apology.

It was an awkward little ceremony. A dais was filled with members of the special selection committee—some black stars of the Negro leagues, a white Negro league owner—and they glowered and looked sad as white and black interviewers asked Paige if he felt "bitter" about his exclusion from major league baseball through his prime, if he was unhappy at being enshrined in separate facilities.

A little of the pleasure of his day seemed to drain out of Paige as he stood awkwardly at the microphone, but his wife held her smile, and he finally managed to bend his answers around the questions with a sly humor that depended a great deal on jokes about his age, which he said was sixty-four.

Baseball's recognition of Paige, apparently prodded by the Baseball Writers Association of America, was a gesture more meaningful for baseball than for sports fans or even for Paige. The integration of baseball was a great deal more public and spectacular than the integration of almost any other aspect of American life, and so baseball has been made to feel particularly defensive about its segregated years.

With Paige's "induction," baseball was trying to pay up some back dues. The effort seemed a little lame and the price cut-rate to many fans. But the basic fault was certainly not with Kuhn and the men who conceived and executed the ceremony, but with those long-gone founders and builders and managers and stars, many of whom are "technically" in the Hall of Fame.

Paige said, "I was satisfied with my world out there." And Larry Doby, who played against Paige in the Negro leagues and roomed with him on the Cleveland Indians, nodded from a corner of the room. "He never missed anything in money or life or baseball," said Doby. "He was a superstar. He was making $250 a month playing baseball in 1927, and he was making $40,000 a year some years."

Doby, the first black player in the American League, said he thought everyone should "rally around this decision as a good thing and not look for the bad in it." He went on: "The people who did wrong are not here. The only thing I'd be against is a separate wing. Everyone should be together now."

If there was any injustice in all of this, Doby agreed, it might just be the feeling that Paige and other Negro leaguers are pathetic figures of history, and that there was true joy and fulfillment only in the white leagues.

"We had our good times," said Doby. "The Negro league players were dedicated athletes playing a game they loved. There was laughter and songs in the bus, new people, fans in every town. When you come down to it, all the major leagues offered was more: more money, more bars, more women, more friends, more opportunities."

BRANCH RICKEY

1881–1965

BRANCH RICKEY was a dominant figure in baseball for half a century. He broke the color barrier in the major leagues, developed the farm system, and created baseball dynasties with the St. Louis Cardinals and Brooklyn Dodgers.

The cigar-chomping Rickey was a religious person who, throughout his career, declined to attend Sunday baseball games because of a promise to his mother, and was seldom known to say anything stronger than his famous "Judas Priest."

An owlish, rumpled man who gave flowery speeches in answer to simple questions, Rickey had, by his own count, more than a thousand folksy stories to illustrate his points, and most of these had been told to him by his mother.

One of them summed up his philosophy of life:

"My father was eighty-six when he died. As an old man he was still planting peach and apple trees on our farm near Portsmouth, Ohio. When I asked who would take in the fruit he said, 'That's not important. I just want to live every day as if I were going to live forever.' "

Jackie Robinson, the player Rickey picked to become the first black in the major leagues, recalled their first meeting:

"The hand holding mine was hard, gnarled, with the often broken fingers of an ex-baseball catcher. His hair was thick, deep brown. Heavy, bushy eyebrows flapped like twin crows from side to side as he talked."

This description was included in a *Reader's Digest* article by Robinson in 1961. He wrote of Rickey:

> He was taking off his coat, rolling up his sleeves. His mobile face had suddenly taken on a droll, cunning look.
>
> "Let's say I'm a hotel clerk. You come in with the rest of your team. I look up from the register and snarl, 'We don't let niggers sleep here.' What do you do then?"
>
> Again, before I could answer, the smudgy cigar shot toward my chin, and he was an umpire waving his huge fist too close under my nose, banishing me from the game. As a race-baiting fan he hurled pop bottles and insults. When the performance was over his shirt was soggy with sweat, his hair matted.
>
> His curtain line explained everything. It was the most dramatic I have ever heard, before or since:
>
> "Jackie, this talk of organizing a Negro team in Brooklyn was only a

coverup for my real plans. I want you to be the first Negro player in the major leagues. I've been trying to give you some idea of the kind of punishment you'll have to absorb. Can you take it?"

Rickey brought the young Robinson to Montreal in the International League in 1946 and then to the Dodgers the following season, opening the way for black players into the major leagues.

Rickey had been a farm boy, teacher, college athletic director, college trustee, college board member, prohibitionist, ball player, manager, general manager, club president, part owner, and even president of a baseball league.

The sport is indebted to him for the "knothole gang" idea, which helped promote the interest of youngsters in baseball. With this movement he developed the fans who would in the future pay the salaries of the players. Blackboard talks, sliding pits, plays developed exclusively to catch runners off base—all these were Rickey's innovations.

Rickey, who was never known to play, direct, or attend a ball game on Sunday, came from a devout Methodist family. In his later years he was an inveterate cigar smoker, but he never drank or used profane language. He had a reputation as a lay preacher and sometimes spoke at religious meetings.

Notable players whose development was made possible by Rickey, or with whose success he was associated, included the Dean brothers, Dizzy and Paul, whose place in St. Louis baseball will long be remembered, and Joe Medwick, a star of the Gashouse Gang era.

Rickey, known as the "master trader," used shrewd judgment in swapping many top stars, often when they had passed their peak as performers but could still draw a high price.

His most famous deal was the sale of Dizzy Dean to the Chicago Cubs in 1937. In exchange for the once-great pitcher, who was suffering from a sore arm, he obtained the pitchers Curt Davis and Clyde Shoun in addition to a reported sum of $185,000.

He even traded the incomparable Rogers Hornsby, who had been the playing manager of the Cardinals.

Rickey always looked for what he called the "young, hungry player with the basic attributes of youth and speed plus strength of arm." The result was a Rickey dynasty of great young players who repeatedly won pennants for the Cardinals and later the Dodgers.

Branch Wesley Rickey was born on a farm at Stockdale, Ohio, on December 20, 1881, the second of three sons, to Jacob Franklin and Emily Rickey, who were known for their piety.

After receiving an elementary school education, Rickey became a country school teacher. He taught himself Latin, higher mathematics, and other subjects, and was able to enter Ohio Wesleyan University. Later he obtained a law degree from the University of Michigan.

The young Rickey earned his way through Ohio Wesleyan by playing both baseball and football. He was a catcher throughout his major league career. As a big league player, Rickey did not amount to much. In one game in 1907 there were thirteen stolen bases charged against him. In eleven games he had nine errors.

He entered the big leagues in 1903 with the Cincinnati Reds but was released because of his scruples against playing on Sundays. He returned the next year from Dallas to the St. Louis Browns, by way of the Chicago White Sox. Meanwhile he earned his bachelor's degree at Ohio Wesleyan in 1905, the year in which he married Jane Moulton, after having proposed "more than a hundred times," as he later recounted.

In the off-season of 1908, he toured as a prohibition advocate. The same year he entered the University of Michigan, where he served as baseball coach while getting his law degree.

The strain of work, play, and study had its effect, and a touch of tuberculosis sent him to Saranac Lake, New York. His health regained, Rickey went to Boise, Idaho, to practice law. However, in 1913, he accepted the invitation of Robert Lee Hedges, president of the St. Louis Browns, to become a scout for the club.

Rickey later became club secretary and then field manager. He had Burt Shotton manage the club on Sundays. He was vice president and general manager by 1917, when he was hired as president of the impoverished St. Louis Cardinals. Under the terms of his contract, he was the highest-paid executive in baseball at the time.

After a hitch as a major in the Chemical Warfare Service during World War I, he returned to the Cardinals in 1918. Rickey assumed the field management and started the "farm" idea. It had its origin in 1919, when the Cardinals bought an 18 percent interest in the Houston club of the Texas League.

In 1920 Sam Breadon replaced Rickey as president, but Rickey continued to develop his chain-store idea until at one time he controlled the players of two minor leagues and had interests in, or agreements with, a number of others.

Violently opposed to the Rickey idea from the outset, Judge Kenesaw Mountain Landis, the commissioner of baseball, shook the Cardinal farm structure with a decree that limited the club to only one affiliation in each minor league.

The reign of Rickey as manager of the Cardinals ended in 1925, when Breadon replaced him with Rogers Hornsby. Rickey was retained as vice president and business manager. This arrangement continued until 1942, when, after the Cardinals had won the World Series, reports of a rift between the executives brought an announcement by Breadon that Rickey's contract would not be renewed.

Rickey had taken the Cardinals when the club was $175,000 in debt, and by spending only enough for a railroad ticket at times, had developed players who brought the club the National League pennant in 1926, 1928, 1930, 1931, 1934, and 1942, along with World Series victories in four of those years.

Shortly after leaving the Cardinals, Rickey was made president of the Brooklyn Dodgers.

A storm ensued in Brooklyn when Rickey sold Dolph Camilli and Joe Medwick, Dodger favorites. It did not diminish when there were recurrent reports of friction between him and his club manager, Leo Durocher.

He rehired Durocher as his manager shortly before spring training of 1948, thus ending much wild speculation on that score. But he drew more resentment from the fans when he traded the beloved Dixie Walker to Pittsburgh and later, when the Dodgers were in spring training, he traded Eddie Stanky, the Dodgers' sparkplug second baseman, to Boston.

Rickey's biggest baseball deal after coming to Brooklyn was the sale of Kirby Higbe and others to Frank McKinney, the new president and part owner of the Pirates. It was revealed long after the deal was made that McKinney had parted with almost $300,000 in the deal.

In November 1950, Rickey signed a five-year contract as executive vice president and general manager of the Pirates. When he left Brooklyn, he was reported to have sold his Dodger stock for $1 million.

He served for nine years in the Pittsburgh front office, serving as chairman until his resignation in 1959. The next year, however, his rebuilding program paid off: the Pirates, under field manager Danny Murtaugh, won the National League pennant and went on to take the World Series from the New York Yankees.

After leaving the Pirates, Rickey was appointed president of the newly formed Continental League. An hour after his appointment, he was conducting the league's first meeting. The eight teams constituting the league were New York, Buffalo, Toronto, Minneapolis–St. Paul, Houston, Dallas–Fort Worth, Atlanta, and Denver.

For nearly two years, it appeared that Rickey's "dream" of a third major league would be realized, but he was never able to get the league out of the dugout. The final blow was struck by the two existing major leagues.

At the end of 1960, the American League issued franchises to the Los Angeles (now the California) Angels and a new Washington Senator club (the old one moved and became the Minnesota Twins), while the National League made plans to become a ten-team league in 1962 with the admission of the New York Mets and the Houston Colt 45s (now the Astros).

Rickey returned to the Cardinals late in 1962 as a "consultant on player personnel." He held that position for two years, leaving after a shake-up of the club's executives. The aging, ailing Rickey was critical of Manager Johnny Keane and other Cardinal executives.

The Rickey influence wrought revolutions in baseball—notably his developing the farm system and breaking the color barrier—that profoundly changed the game.

He died in Columbia, Missouri, on December 9, 1965, at the age of eighty-three.

A Memorial

By DAVE ANDERSON

He's virtually forgotten now, but he shouldn't be. Branch Rickey has been dead since 1965 and major league baseball doesn't have an award or a stadium or anything named in his memory. But in 1976, Ohio Wesleyan University completed the Branch Rickey Physical Education Center in honor of its famous alumnus. The site of the modern structure is on land where Branch Rickey played and coached baseball as a student, where his relationship with a black player influenced his eventual signing of Jackie Robinson, where his innovative philosophy of baseball organization was developed. Branch Rickey, now in the Baseball Hall of Fame, was primarily responsible for building the St. Louis Cardinals, the Brooklyn Dodgers, and the Pittsburgh Pirates into dominating teams over a span of nearly four decades. But when Ohio Wesleyan was searching for donors to its $3 million physical education center, the Cardinals, the Dodgers and the Pirates couldn't spare a dime. The only major league team that contributed was the nearby Cincinnati Reds with a $10,000 gift. Bob Howsam, then the Reds' president, revered Branch Rickey and was the Cardinals' general manager in 1964 when Branch Rickey was their consulting genius.

"We tried to see Bowie Kuhn, hoping that he would make a formal proposal to the twenty-four teams," Bob Holm, the director of development at Ohio Wesleyan, was saying in his office. "But the commissioner referred me to his public relations people."

Bob Holm didn't sound bitter, only disappointed. Maybe he expected too much of baseball people. Mrs. John Eckler didn't. Mrs. John Eckler was Mary Rickey, the oldest of Branch Rickey's five daughters. Their only brother, Branch Jr., died not long after their father died.

"I wasn't surprised that baseball teams didn't contribute," she said. "Many things are much more personal to them now. I don't think their failure to contribute means they're unkind or uncaring in regard to my father's memory."

But at Ohio Wesleyan, on a grassy campus with mostly old brick or stone buildings that dominate Delaware, Ohio, a town of about 20,000 residents, the memory of Branch Rickey is alive. To some students Branch Rickey is merely a name on a building, but many students have learned who he was and what he did. They have learned of his relationship with Charles Thomas, the black outfielder and catcher who became a New Mexico dentist. When the Ohio Wesleyan team arrived at a hotel in South Bend, Indiana, in 1904, the hotel manager refused to admit the black player.

"Black skin," Thomas told Rickey while rubbing his hands from wrists to fingertips. "Black skin, oh, if I could only make it white."

That scene is part of the Rickey lore that permeates baseball history. But another scene, recalled by Bob Holm, is not so well known.

"At the burial for Mr. Rickey in Portsmouth, Ohio," said Holm, "suddenly eight members of the Harlem Globetrotters and Satchel Paige arrived. Satchel was traveling with the basketball team. They were traveling between games, but they had driven 200 miles out of their way to pay their respects."

When the Rickey Center was being constructed, the curator of Rickey lore at the university was eighty-eight-year-old Herman Shipps, a retired Ohio Wesleyan vice president.

"His first day in college," Shipps wrote, "Branch Rickey had a Latin class with Professor Grove as the teacher. In the Duck Run High School in Portsmouth, where he grew up, he had used Grove's Latin Grammar, but when he recited that first day, he didn't do well. Professor Grove asked him, 'Whose Latin grammar did you study?' and he replied, 'Yours, sir.' He told me later that it took several minutes for Professor Grove to restore order and that one big boy fell out of his seat laughing. He thought that when Professor Grove asked to see him after class that he was through at Ohio Wesleyan, but the professor asked him to explain the difference between a gerundive and a verbal noun. When he knew the difference, Professor Grove told him, 'You know, Rickey, I think you can learn Latin all right. Come down here tomorrow morning at seven o'clock and we'll do some reviewing.' And that's what Branch Rickey did every morning half an hour before class for six weeks."

Such tutelage usually commands a fee now, but Branch Rickey, known for his thrift, never considered that.

"Branch once told me," Shipps remembered, "that he never owed the professor anything except eternal gratitude."

Another time, Rickey, who favored prohibition of alcoholic beverages, made a "dry" speech on a street corner in Delaware that prompted the Anti-Saloon League to put him on their payroll at ten dollars an appearance. Rickey's first speech was in nearby Chillicothe, but when he attempted to register in a hotel there with a bar, he was refused. At another hotel, he also was refused.

"On the street," Herman Shipps recalled, "he met an old friend from Duck Run High School, and when he asked his friend what he was doing now, his friend replied, 'I'm tending bar, what are you doing?' Branch told him that he had come to make a "dry" speech but couldn't find a place to stay. His friend told him, 'Come down and stay with me,' so Branch stayed with the bartender and made a good 'dry' speech."

In later years, Branch Rickey didn't forget Ohio Wesleyan. He was a trustee and returned to the campus regularly. His son and three of his daughters attended Ohio Wesleyan, as have six of his nineteen grandchildren. And with its physical education center, Ohio Wesleyan hasn't forgotten Branch Rickey, but baseball seems to have had a lapse of memory.

JACKIE ROBINSON

1919–1972

By DAVE ANDERSON

F OR SOCIOLOGICAL IMPACT, Jack Roosevelt Robinson was perhaps America's most significant athlete. His accomplishments resulted in the acceptance of blacks in other major sports, notably professional football and professional basketball. In later years, while a prosperous New York businessman, he emerged as an influential member of the Republican party.

His dominant characteristic, as an athlete and as a black man, was a competitive flame. Outspoken, controversial, combative, he created critics as well as loyalists. But he never deviated from his opinions.

In his autobiography, *I Never Had It Made*, he recalled the scene in 1947 when he stood for the National Anthem at his debut with the Brooklyn Dodgers. He wrote: "But as I write these words now I cannot stand and sing the National Anthem. I have learned that I remain a black in a white world."

Describing his struggle, he wrote: "I had to fight hard against loneliness, abuse and the knowledge that any mistake I made would be magnified because I was the only black man out there. Many people resented my impatience and honesty, but I never cared about acceptance as much as I cared about respect."

His belligerence flared throughout his career in baseball, business, and politics.

"I was told that it would cost me some awards," he recalled. "But if I had to keep quiet to get an award, it wasn't worth it. Awards are great, but if I got one for being a nice kid, what good is it?"

To other black ball players, though, he was most often saluted as the first to run the gauntlet. Monte Irvin, who played for the New York Giants while Robinson was with the Dodgers and who served as an assistant to the commissioner of baseball, said the day he died, "Jackie Robinson opened the door of baseball to all men. He was the first to get the opportunity, but if he had not done such a great job, the path would have been so much more difficult.

"Bill Russell says if it hadn't been for Jackie, he might not ever have become a professional basketball player. Jack was the trailblazer, and we are all deeply grateful. We say, thank you, Jackie; it was a job well done."

"He meant everything to a black ball player," said Elston Howard, the first black member of the New York Yankees. "I don't think the young players would go through what he did. He did it for all of us, for Willie Mays, Henry Aaron, Maury Wills, myself.

After a versatile career as a clutch hitter and daring base runner while playing first base, second base, third base, and left field at various stages of his

ten seasons with the Brooklyn Dodgers, he was elected to baseball's Hall of Fame in 1962, his first year of eligibility for the Cooperstown, New York, shrine.

Despite his success, he minimized himself as an "instrument, a tool." He credited Branch Rickey, the Brooklyn Dodger owner who broke professional baseball's color line. Rickey signed him for the 1946 season, which he spent with the Dodgers' leading farm, the Montreal Royals of the International League.

"I think the Rickey Experiment, as I call it, the original idea, would not have come about as successfully with anybody other than Mr. Rickey," he often said. "The most important results of it are that it produced understanding among whites and it gave black people the idea that if I could do it, they could do it, too, that blackness wasn't subservient to anything."

Among his disappointments was the fact that he never was afforded an opportunity to be a major league manager. The first black manager would not be hired until 1974, two years after Robinson's death, when Frank Robinson assumed the helm of the Cleveland Indians. As of 1990, four blacks have held managerial posts in the major leagues.

"I had no future with the Dodgers because I was too closely identified with Branch Rickey," he once said. "After the club was taken over by Walter O'Malley, you couldn't even mention Mr. Rickey's name in front of him. I considered Mr. Rickey the greatest human being I had ever known."

Robinson kept baseball in perspective. Ebbets Field, the Brooklyn ballpark that was the stage for his drama, was leveled shortly after O'Malley moved the Dodger franchise to Los Angeles in 1958. Apartment houses replaced it. Years later, asked what he felt about Ebbets Field, he replied, "I don't feel anything. They need those apartments more than they need a monument to the memory of baseball. I've had my thrills."

He also had his heartbreak. His older son, Jackie Jr., died in 1971 at the age of twenty-four in an automobile accident on the Merritt Parkway, not far from the family's home in Stamford, Connecticut.

Three years earlier, Jackie Jr. had been arrested for heroin possession. His addiction had begun while he served in the army in Vietnam, where he was wounded. He was convicted and ordered to undergo treatment at the Daytop drug abuse center in Seymour, Connecticut. Cured, he worked at Daytop helping other addicts, until his fatal accident.

Robinson and his wife, Rachel, had two other children—David and Sharon.

"You don't know what it's like," Robinson said at the time, "to lose a son, find him, and lose him again. My problem was my inability to spend much time at home. I thought my family was secure, so I went running around everyplace else. I guess I had more of an effect on other people's kids than I did on my own."

With the Dodgers, he had other problems. His arrival in 1947 prompted racial insults from some opponents, an aborted strike by the St. Louis Cardinals, an alleged deliberate spiking by Enos Slaughter of the Cardinals, and stiffness from a few teammates, notably Fred "Dixie" Walker, a popular star from Georgia.

"Dixie was very difficult at the start," Robinson acknowledged, "but he was the first guy on the ball club to come to me with advice and help for my hitting. I knew why—if I helped the ball club, it put money in his pocket. I knew he didn't like me any more in those few short months, but he did come forward."

As a rookie, Robinson had been warned by Rickey of the insults that would occur. He also was urged by Rickey to hold his temper. He complied. But the following season, as an established player, he began to argue with the umpires and duel verbally with opponents in the traditional give-and-take of baseball.

As the years passed, Robinson developed a close relationship with many teammates. "After the game we went our separate ways," he explained. "But on the field, there was that understanding. No one can convince me that the things that happened on the ball club didn't affect people. The old Dodgers were something special, but of my teammates, overall, there was nobody like Pee Wee Reese for me."

In Boston once, some Braves players were taunting Robinson during infield practice. Reese, the popular shortstop, who came from Louisville, moved to the rescue.

"Pee Wee walked over and put his arm on my shoulder, as if to say, 'This is my teammate, whether you like it or not,' " Robinson said. "Another time, all our white players got letters, saying if they don't do something, the whole team will be black and they'll lose their jobs. On the bus to the ballpark that night, Pee Wee brought it up and we discussed it. Pretty soon, we were all laughing about it."

In clubhouse debates, Robinson's voice had a sharp, angry tone that rose with his emotional involvement.

"Robinson," he once was told by Don Newcombe, a star pitcher, who was also black, "not only are you wrong, you're loud wrong."

As a competitor, Robinson was the Dodgers' leader. In his ten seasons, they won six National League pennants—1947, 1949, 1952, 1953, 1955, and 1956. They lost another in the 1951 playoff with the New York Giants, and another to the Philadelphia Phillies on the last day of the 1950 season.

In 1949, when he batted .342 to win the league title and drove in 124 runs, he was voted the league's Most Valuable Player award. In 1947, he had been voted the Rookie of the Year.

"The only way to beat the Dodgers," said Warren Giles, then the president of the Cincinnati Reds, later the National League president, "is to keep Robinson off the bases."

He had a career batting average of .311. Primarily a line drive hitter, he accumulated only 137 home runs, with a high of 19 in both 1951 and 1952.

But on a team with such famous sluggers as Duke Snider, Gil Hodges, and Roy Campanella, who was also black, he was the cleanup hitter, fourth in the batting order, a tribute to his ability to move along teammates on base.

But his personality flared best as a base runner. He had a total of 197 stolen bases. He stole home 11 times, the most by any player in the post–World War II era.

"I think the most symbolic part of Jackie Robinson, ball player," he once reflected, "was making the pitcher believe he was going to the next base. I think he enjoyed that the most, too. I think my value to the Dodgers was disruption—making the pitcher concentrate on me instead of on my teammate who was at bat at the time."

In the 1955 World Series, he stole home against the New York Yankees in the opening game of Brooklyn's only World Series triumph.

Pigeon-toed and muscular, wearing No. 42, he ran aggressively, typical of his college football training as a star runner and passer at the University of California at Los Angeles in 1939 and 1940. He ranked second in the Pacific Coast Conference in total offense in 1940 with 875 yards—440 rushing and 435 passing.

Born in Cairo, Georgia, on January 31, 1919, he was soon taken to Pasadena, California, by his mother with her four other children after his father had deserted them. He developed into an all-round athlete, competing in basketball and track in addition to baseball and football. After attending UCLA, he entered the army.

He was commissioned a second lieutenant. After his discharge, he joined the Kansas City Monarchs of the Negro National League as a shortstop.

"But if Mr. Rickey hadn't signed me, I wouldn't have played another year in the black league," he said. "It was too difficult. The travel was brutal. Financially, there was no reward. It took everything you made to live off."

If he had quit the black leagues without having been signed by Rickey, what would he have done?

"I more than likely would have gone to coach baseball at Sam Houston College. My minister had gone down there to Texas as president of the college. That was about the only thing a black athlete had left then, a chance to coach somewhere at a small black college."

Instead, his presence turned the Dodgers into the favorite of black people throughout the nation.

"They picked up twenty million fans instantly," said Bill Russell, the famous center of the Boston Celtics who was professional basketball's first black coach. "But to most black people, Jackie was a man, not a ball player. He did more for baseball than baseball did for him. He was someone that young black athletes could look up to."

As the Dodgers toured the National League, they set attendance records. But the essence of Robinson's competitive fury occurred in a 1954 game at Ebbets Field with the rival Giants.

Sal Maglie, the Giants' ace who was known as "The Barber" because of his tendency to "shave" a batter's head with his fastball and sharp-breaking curve, was intimidating the Dodger hitters. In the Dodger dugout, Reese, the team captain, spoke to the 6-foot 195-pound Robinson.

"Jack," said Reese "we got to do something about this."

Robinson soon was kneeling in the on-deck circle as the next Dodger batter. With him was Charlie DiGiovanna, the team's adult batboy, who was a confidant of the players.

"Let somebody else do it, Jack," DiGiovanna implored. "Every time something comes up, they call on you."

Robinson agreed, but once in the batter's box, he changed his mind.

Hoping to draw Maglie toward the first-base line, Robinson bunted. The ball was fielded by Whitey Lockman, the first baseman, but Maglie didn't move off the mound. Davey Williams, the second baseman, covered the base for Lockman's throw.

"Maglie wouldn't cover," Robinson recalled. "Williams got in the way. He had a chance to get out of the way, but he just stood there right on the base. It was just too bad, but I knocked him over. He had a Giant uniform on. That's what happens."

In the collision, Williams suffered a spinal injury that virtually ended his career. Two innings later, Alvin Dark, the Giants' captain and shortstop, retaliated by trying to stretch a double into a third-base collision with Robinson.

Realizing that Dark hoped to avenge the Williams incident, Robinson stepped aside and tagged him in the face. But his grip on the ball wasn't secure. The ball bounced away. Dark was safe.

"I would've torn his face up," Robinson once recalled. "But as it turned out, I'm glad it didn't happen that way. I admired Al for what he did after I had run down Williams. I've always admired Al, despite his racial stands. I think he really believed that white people were put on this earth to take care of black people."

Ironically, after the 1956 season, Robinson was traded to the rival Giants, but he announced his retirement in *Look* magazine. Any chance of his changing his mind ended when Emil "Buzzy" Bavasi, then a Dodger vice president, implied that after Robinson had been paid for the byline article he would accept the Giants' offer.

"After Buzzy said that," Robinson later acknowledged, "there was no way I'd ever play again."

He joined Chock Full O'Nuts, the lunch-counter chain, as an executive. He later had a succession of executive posts with an insurance firm, a food-franchising firm, and an interracial construction firm. He also was chairman of the board of the Freedom National Bank in Harlem and a member of the New York State Athletic Commission.

In politics Robinson remained outspoken. He supported Richard M. Nixon in the 1960 presidential election. When Nixon and Spiro T. Agnew formed the 1968 presidential ticket, however, he resigned from New York Governor Nelson A. Rockefeller's staff, where he was a special assistant for community affairs, to campaign for Hubert H. Humphrey, the Democratic nominee.

Robinson described Nixon's stand on civil rights in 1960 as "forthright" but denounced the Nixon-Agnew ticket as "racist."

His niche in American history is secure—his struggle predated the emergence of "the first black who" in many areas of the American society. Even though he understandably needed a Branch Rickey to open the door for him, Branch Rickey needed a Jackie Robinson to lead other blacks through that door.

Robinson died of a heart attack at his home in Stamford on October 24, 1972.

A Hero's Funeral

By STEVE CADY

Jackie Robinson received a hero's burial in New York on October 28, 1972, mourned as a man of courage by those who knew him and solemnly saluted as a legend by strangers who never saw him play. "Today we must balance the tears of sorrow with tears of joy," the Reverend Jesse L. Jackson told a celebrity-laden congregation of 2,500 at the Riverside Church in his eulogy to major league baseball's first black player.

Jackson noted that the body corrodes and fades away, but the deeds live on: "When Jackie took the field, something reminded us of our birthright to be free."

These words, delivered over a silver-blue coffin draped with red roses, accurately reflected the mood of what amounted to an outpouring of interracial respect that softened grief with pride and hope.

Governor Nelson Rockefeller, Mayor John Lindsay, and hundreds of other dignitaries and sports figures attended the interdenominational services at the Gothic church with its thirty-story tower overlooking Grant's Tomb and the Hudson River. Family mourners included Robinson's mother, his widow, Rachel, and their two surviving children, Sharon and David.

Also in attendance were Bowie Kuhn, commissioner of baseball; Roy Wilkins, executive director of the National Association for the Advancement of Colored People; and A. Philip Randolph, labor union executive.

Later, thousands of persons lined the streets of Harlem and Bedford-Stuyvesant in bright sunshine to watch a mile-long funeral cortege carry Robinson back to Brooklyn, the borough where he made baseball history twenty-five years earlier as a second baseman for the Dodgers.

Three daughters and the grandson of Branch Rickey, the late Dodger president who gave Robinson his chance to break the color barrier in major league baseball, also were in the gathering, as were such diverse celebrities as Joe Louis, Dick Gregory, Hank Aaron, and Vida Blue.

In his eulogy, Jackson appeared at times to be rebutting any notions that Robinson was merely a pawn of the white establishment, that he was nothing more than the first black man to expose himself to American bigotry through baseball.

"Jackie was neither a puppet of God nor one of other men," he said. "Progress does not roll in on the wheels of inevitability. In order for an ideal to become a reality, there must be a person, a personality, to translate it. He had options. He didn't have to do what he did."

Even the children seemed to sense what Robinson meant to them.

"They made fun of him, teased him," said Floyd Branch, one of a number of youngsters excused from eighth-grade classes at Joan of Arc Junior High School on Ninety-third Street so they could attend the services. "We talked about him in school, they said he meant history to the black people."

Across the street in the Union Theological Seminary, where the dignitaries began gathering two hours before the funeral, Wilson Woodbeck quietly explained why he was there.

"Jackie was a few years ahead of his time," said Woodbeck, public relations director for the National Association of Negro Musicians. "It's always time to do what's right, but the power structure does not always see it that way. Jackie carried so many burdens, took so much abuse. So many times, he lost sight of himself for others."

More celebrities crowded into the waiting rooms as Bayard Rustin, the civil rights leader, tried to smooth out the logistical problems. There were too many important people to count or keep track of: Willie Mays, Bill Russell, Hank Greenberg, Bill Veeck, Howard J. Samuels, Ernie Banks, Warren Giles, Ed Sullivan, Mike Burke, Peter O'Malley. Larry Doby, the American League's first black player, was there. So were Carl Erskine, Gene Hermanski, and Billy Loes, Dodger teammates.

"You know what Jackie would have said?" somebody asked. "He'd have said, 'We need some umpires in here to straighten this traffic out.' "

They did have umpires, like Tom Gorman, but not in uniform on this occasion.

The baseball men, from ex-players to league presidents and club presidents, waited for the signal to go over to the church and talked of Robinson's magic, of days like the one when Russ Meyer of the Chicago Cubs challenged him to steal home at Ebbets Field.

"Jackie was bouncing up and down on the base path," somebody said, "and Meyer waved his arm toward the plate. Jackie took off and stole home."

Later, toward the end of his long eulogy, Jackson would bring tears and sobs from many in the church with another reference to baserunning.

"His feet danced on the base paths," said the speaker, and a woman's voice in the congregation answered, "Yes, sir, that's right."

"But it was more than a game."

"Yes, it was."

"Jackie began playing a chess game, he was the black knight."

"Yes, sir, all right, go ahead."

"In his last dash, Jackie stole home and Jackie is safe."

"Yes, sir, you're right."

"His enemies can rest assured of that."

"Yes they can, hallelujah."

"Call me nigger, call me black boy, I don't care."

"Hallelujah!"

The eulogy was over and Roberta Flack, the pop recording artist, closed the musical part of the services by singing "I Told Jesus," a traditional Negro spiritual.

Then it was time for Robinson to go back to Brooklyn, a legend borne through the tenement-lined streets of Harlem and Bedford-Stuyvesant.

What Jackie Robinson Meant to an Old Friend

By PEE WEE REESE

It was October, maybe November, in 1945 and I was on a navy transport ship coming back from overseas, from Guam. I'd played shortstop for the Brooklyn Dodgers for three seasons, then into the navy "for the duration," as they used to say during the war. Now I was finally coming home and somebody on board told me that the Dodgers had signed a black ball player. And that was the first time I can remember being aware of Jackie Robinson's arrival on the baseball scene. Actually, I had heard of Jack before—as a football player at UCLA. But now when his name came up in a baseball context, I didn't give it a whole lot of thought. You know, I reacted kind of instinctively to the news, something like "You've got to be kidding," because the color line was still keeping black players out of the major leagues.

But, except for that initial reaction, I didn't give it too much thought. I had been away for three years and was more concerned at the moment with getting myself back to work. Then I realized that Robinson could run and hit and play shortstop, and some of the guys started kidding me about my job. Welcome home, Pee Wee.

After that, it was more than a year before I saw him in a baseball uniform—a year that Jackie spent at Montreal in the International League and that I spent in Brooklyn with the Dodgers. Then in spring training in 1947, we had our camp in Santo Domingo in the Dominican Republic that year, and I finally got my first look at him. What was my first impression? That he was big, awfully big. And fast, awfully fast.

Anyway, Jack was there that year; and, once we realized he was there to stay, I began to realize that there were more problems facing him than I'd thought at first.

One thing I remember was the petition some guys passed around. But I wouldn't sign it. I wasn't trying to think of myself as being the Great White Father, really, I just wanted to play the game, especially after being in the navy for three years and needing the money, and it didn't matter to me whether he was black or green, he had a right to be there, too.

Then you'd hear a lot of insults from the opposing benches during games, guys calling him things like "nigger" and "watermelon eater," trying to rile him. But that was when Jackie Robinson started to turn the tables: you saw how he stood there at the plate and dared them to hit him with the ball, and you began to put yourself in his shoes. You'd think of yourself trying to break into the black leagues, maybe, and what it would be like—and I know that I couldn't have done it.

In a word, he was winning respect.

That was the decisive thing about Jack: he had all kinds of class. That's the reason he was selected by Branch Rickey, and that's the best way to remember him.

Playing alongside him for so many years—ten years, actually—I realized his impact. For one thing, he was one of the best pressure players I ever saw and he became instrumental in those Dodger pennants because of it. The old saying applied to him perfectly—"When the going gets tough, the tough get going." And when the chips were down, he was at his best. So after a while, I didn't pay the slightest attention to his being black. At first, he'd been a big black guy who came into a white man's game. But after two or three years, with all that class and talent, he was just a great ball player alongside me.

He had a big impact on all the Dodgers, too. In Birmingham and some other southern towns, traveling up from Florida, it was rough. Even during the season, I remember we got to St. Louis for a series, and that might've been the last place in the league where the black players were segregated, where they stayed in one hotel in the black section and the other guys stayed in the regular hotel.

Jack got off the train one day there and said, "I'm going to the hotel with you." Roy Campanella and some of the other black guys told him not to do it, they said they were doing OK and so don't rock the boat. But Jackie joined us on the team bus, went right into the hotel and registered, and Campy and the others followed. That was Jack—he got the job done.

Finally, Jack had a big impact on me personally. We had many conversations about things, and I'd ask, "Do you think blacks and whites will ever get along smoothly?" And he'd say, "Yes, it'll work, give it some time."

I used to say to him later, "You know, I didn't particularly go out of my way just to be nice to you." And Jack would say, "Pee Wee, maybe that's what I appreciated most—that you didn't."

As a ball player? Super. Jack was super. For a guy his size, well over 6 feet and maybe 215 pounds, he had the quickness of a guy 5 foot 10. In a rundown, you couldn't run him down. I don't know how many bases he would have stolen if our club ran more. . . . He didn't have the greatest arm in the world, but making the double play, he'd straddle the bag and dare you to hit him.

For all that, he was a fun guy. Sure, he could be a little nasty at times, but who couldn't? I never saw him take a drink in my life. He was just a great friend, a great baseball player, and a great influence on our lives—a lot greater than I ever could have guessed that day on the ship coming home from Guam when somebody told me the Dodgers had signed a black ball player.

Death of an Unconquerable Man

By RED SMITH

In the scene that doesn't fade, the Brooklyn Dodgers are tied with the Phillies in the bottom of the twelfth inning. It is 6:00 P.M. on a late September Sunday, but the gloom in Philadelphia's Shibe Park is only partly due to oncoming evening. The Dodgers, champions-elect in August, have frittered away a lead of 13½ games, and there is bitterness in the dusk of this last day of the 1951 baseball season. Two days ago, the New York Giants drew even with Brooklyn in the pennant race. Two hours ago, the numbers went up on the scoreboard:

New York 3, Boston 2. The pennant belongs to the Giants unless the Dodgers can snatch it back.

With two out and the bases full of Phillies, Eddie Waitkus smashes a low, malevolent drive toward center field. The ball is a blur passing second base, difficult to follow in the half light, impossible to catch. Jackie Robinson catches it. He flings himself headlong at right angles to the flight of the ball, for an instant his body is suspended in midair, then somehow the outstretched glove intercepts the ball inches off the ground.

He falls heavily, the crash drives an elbow into his side, he collapses. But the Phillies are out, the score is still tied.

Now it is the fourteenth inning. It is too dark to play baseball, but the rules forbid turning on lights for a game begun at two o'clock. Pee Wee Reese pops up. So does Duke Snider. Robin Roberts throws a ball and a strike to Robinson. Jackie hits the next pitch upstairs in left field for the run that sets up baseball's most memorable playoff.

Of all the pictures left upon memory, the one that will always flash back first shows him stretched at full length in the insubstantial twilight, the unconquerable doing the impossible.

The word for Jackie Robinson is *unconquerable.* In *The Boys of Summer,* Roger Kahn sums it up: "In two seasons, 1962 and 1965, Maury Wills stole more bases than Robinson did in all of a ten-year career. Ted Williams' lifetime batting average, .344, is two points higher than Robinson's best for any season. Robinson never hit 20 home runs in a year, never batted in 125 runs. Stan Musial consistently scored more often. Having said those things, one has not said much because troops of people who were there believe that in his prime Jackie Robinson was a better ball player than any of the others."

The point is, he would not be defeated. Not by the other team and not by life.

Another picture comes back. Robinson has taken a lead off first base and he crouches, facing the pitcher, feet fairly wide apart, knees bent, hands held well out from his sides to help him balance, teetering on the balls of his feet. Would he be running? His average was 20 stolen bases a year, and the columnist Bugs Baer wrote that "John McGraw demanded more than that from the baseball writers."

Yet he was the only base runner of his time who could bring a game to a stop just by getting on base. When he walked to first, all other action ceased. For Robinson, television introduced the split screen so the viewer at home as well as the fan in the park could watch both the runner on first and the pitcher standing irresolute, wishing he didn't have to throw.

Jackie Robinson established the black man's right to play second base. He fought for the black man's right to a place in the white community, and he never lost sight of that goal. After he left baseball, almost everything he did was directed toward that goal. He was involved in foundation of the Freedom National Bank. He tried to get an insurance company started with black capital, and when he died he was head of a construction company building housing for blacks. Years ago a friend, talking of the needs of blacks, said, "Good schooling comes first."

"No," Jackie said, "housing is the first thing. Unless he's got a home he wants to come back to, it doesn't matter what kind of school he goes to."

There was anger in him, and when he was a young man he tended to raise his falsetto voice. "But my demands were modest enough," he said, and he spoke the truth. The very last demand he made publicly was delivered in the mildest of terms during the 1972 World Series. There was a ceremony in Cincinnati saluting him for his work in drug addiction, and in his response he mentioned a wish that he could look down to third base and see a black manager on the coaching line.

Seeing him in Cincinnati recalled the Dylan Thomas line that Roger Kahn borrowed for a title: "I see the Boys of Summer in their ruin." At fifty-three Jackie was sick of body, white of hair. He had survived one heart attack, he had diabetes and high blood pressure and he was going blind as a result of retinal bleeding in spite of efforts to cauterize the ruptured blood vessels with laser beams. With him were his wife, Rachel, their son, David, and daughter, Sharon. Everybody was remembering Jack Jr., an addict who beat the heroin habit and died at twenty-four in an auto accident.

"I've lost the sight in one eye," Jackie had told Kahn a day or so earlier, "but they think they can save the other. I've got nothing to complain about."

Unconquerable is the word.

SUGAR RAY ROBINSON

1921–1989

By DAVE ANDERSON

W ITH HIS BOXING ARTISTRY and knock-out power in either fist, Sugar Ray Robinson inspired the description "pound for pound, the best," a phrase designed to transcend the various weight divisions.

In a 1984 book, *The Hundred Greatest Boxers of All Time*, the five-time world middleweight and welterweight champion was ranked No.1 by Bert Randolph Sugar, then the editor of *The Ring* magazine. In the author's opinion, Henry Armstrong was second, Harry Greb third, Jack Dempsey fourth, Benny Leonard fifth, Joe Louis sixth, and Muhammad Ali tenth.

"Robinson could deliver a knockout blow going backward," Sugar wrote. "His footwork was superior to any that had been seen in boxing up to that time. His hand speed and leverage were unmatchable."

"I agree with those who say Sugar Ray Robinson was the greatest," said Don Dunphy, the longtime ringside broadcaster. "He's my choice for number one."

Ali, who described himself as the Greatest, acknowledged that Robinson's "matador" style had been his inspiration in dethroning Sonny Liston as the heavyweight champion in 1964. Ali, then known as Cassius Clay, had asked Robinson to be his manager.

"You are the king, the master, my idol," Ali was fond of saying to Robinson.

Over a quarter of a century, from 1940 to 1965, Robinson recorded 175 victories against 19 losses. Five of those losses occurred in the last six months of his career, after he turned forty-four years old. He registered 110 knockouts, but he was never knocked out and he was stopped only once. In 1952, in a light-heavyweight title bout with Joey Maxim, he was far ahead on the judging cards and needed only to finish the fifteenth round to be awarded the decision. But he collapsed after the thirteenth round in 100-degree heat at Yankee Stadium and Maxim was credited with a knockout victory in the fourteenth round.

"Boxing is the art of self-defense," Robinson often said. "You have to pattern your style for each fight against the style of the man you're fighting."

Robinson was undefeated in his first 40 bouts, with 29 knockouts. He lost a 10-round decision to Jake LaMotta in 1943, then extended his record to 128–1–2, with 84 knockouts, while ruling the welterweight division and later the middleweight division.

He earned the 160-pound middleweight title in 1951, stopping LaMotta in the thirteenth round. Five months later he lost the title for the first time, on

a 15-round decision, to Randy Turpin in London. Two months later he regained the title from Turpin in a desperate and dramatic tenth-round knockout, although he was bleeding from a cut above the left eye.

After his loss to Maxim the next year, Robinson spent twenty-two months in show business as a tap dancer before regaining the middleweight title with a second-round knockout of Carl "Bobo" Olson in the seventh bout of his comeback, on December 9, 1955.

Robinson was dethroned in 1957 by Gene Fullmer, but four months later he won the title for the fourth time, knocking out Fullmer in the fifth round with what boxing historians called a perfect left hook.

Later that year he lost the title to Carmen Basilio in a 15-round decision, but regained it in 1958 in a 15-round decision over Basilio. Two years later he lost the title to Paul Pender, who also won their rematch, and four and a half years after that, on December 10, 1965, Robinson announced his retirement for good. He was elected to the Boxing Hall of Fame in 1967.

Robinson won the welterweight title late in 1946 in a 15-round decision over Tommy Bell. In his first title defense, his opponent, Jimmy Doyle, suffered fatal brain injuries in an eighth-round knockout at Cleveland. In his sorrow, Robinson defined his brutal profession when he was asked during the Cleveland coroner's inquest if he had intended to get Doyle "in trouble."

"Mister," said Robinson, "it's my business to get him in trouble."

At his peak, Robinson was as flashy out of the ring as he was in it. He owned a nightclub in Harlem called Sugar Ray's, and also a dry cleaning shop, a lingerie shop, and a barber shop. He drove a flamingo-pink Cadillac convertible. On his boxing tours of Europe, his entourage included his valet, his barber, who doubled as his golf pro, several members of his family, and George Gainford, his trainer throughout his career.

"Money is for spending," Robinson once said. "Money is for having a good time."

To Robinson, money was also for haggling. Except for his early years in boxing, he negotiated his own contracts, developing a reputation as a hard businessman who would threaten to ignore an offer if he was not completely satisfied with the financial terms. In a tax dispute with the Internal Revenue Service, his victory eventually contributed to the tax rule that allowed income averaging over a period of years.

Eventually, Robinson's spending sprees proved so costly that he was forced to continue boxing long beyond his best years.

"I went through four million dollars, but I have no regrets," he once said. "If I had the chance to do it over again, I'd do it the same way. I didn't gamble away my money. I used it to let people live. I took my family and my friends on trips with me. I loaned it to strangers to pay their bills, and sometimes I didn't get it back."

After his boxing career ended, Robinson moved to Los Angeles, where he lived comfortably but simply with his wife, Millie, until his death from Alzheimer's disease and diabetes on April 18, 1989.

In 1969 he founded the Sugar Ray Robinson Youth Foundation for inner-city children in the Los Angeles area. But the foundation did not sponsor a boxing program.

Robinson, of course, was boxing's original Sugar Ray, a nickname that has been usurped by several other athletes named Ray, notably Sugar Ray Leonard, also a middleweight and welterweight champion in recent years. But the original Sugar Ray never complained about Leonard being called Sugar Ray.

"Ray Leonard asked me in 1977 when he was starting out if I minded him using my name," Robinson once said. "I told him, 'No, go ahead.'"

Robinson's given name was Walker Smith, Jr. He was born in Detroit on May 3, 1921. He moved with his family to New York, where he grew up in Harlem. As a teenage amateur boxer representing the Salem-Crescent gym, he borrowed the Amateur Athletic Union card of another Harlem youngster named Ray Robinson. Once his Sugar Ray nickname stuck, he never used his real name.

"Sugar Ray Robinson had a nice ring to it," he once said. "Sugar Walker Smith wouldn't have been the same."

During World War II, he served in the army, primarily boxing on exhibition tours of military bases along with Joe Louis, then the heavyweight champion, who had been his Detroit neighbor and his inspiration.

Before one show, Robinson refused to appear until black soldiers were allowed to attend. In another incident, Robinson scuffled with an army military policeman who had threatened to club Louis for using a phone booth in a whites-only area.

When the two boxers were scheduled to embark from the Brooklyn Army Terminal in 1944 for a European tour, Robinson disappeared, creating a controversy that has never been completely clarified.

In his 1969 autobiography, *Sugar Ray*, Robinson contended that he suffered amnesia after a fall down a barracks stairs and woke up in Halloran Army Hospital on Staten Island. Robinson received an honorable discharge two months later.

But in the ring, Sugar Ray Robinson's stature has never been cloudy. According to many boxing historians, he was, pound for pound, the best.

The Original Never Lost

By DAVE ANDERSON

Shortly before the first round that night in 1950, the referee called the two boxers together. But rather than listen to the instructions, Sugar Ray Robinson stared at his opponent, a tough puncher named George Costner who had begun to use Sugar as a nickname. Costner had bragged that he would be the only Sugar in boxing. But now, in the center of the ring, Robinson's elegant ego flashed.

"We better touch gloves, because this is the only round," Robinson said. "Your name ain't Sugar, mine is."

Two minutes and forty-nine seconds later, Ray Robinson was the only

Sugar standing. And when boxing old-timers talk about the great fighters, Sugar Ray Robinson is still the only Sugar standing. But instead of defending his nickname, he should have copyrighted it. For those who think Sugar Ray Leonard a sweet fighter, the original Sugar Ray would have flattened him with either hand.

"I was a gladiator," he once said. "And like a true gladiator, I never lost. Something just happened to keep me from winning."

Not often.

"Your rhythm should set the pace," he once said. "If it does, then you penetrate your opponent's rhythm. You make him fight your fight. That's what boxing is all about."

Handsome and nattily dressed, he basked in that elegant ego. Before a 1955 comeback bout in San Francisco, he was doing roadwork along the beach when he passed Carl "Bobo" Olson, then the holder of the middleweight title.

"Hi, Carl," he called.

As they passed each other, Olson responded, "Hi, Ray," and they each kept running. But later Robinson's trainer, George Gainford, asked him why he hadn't called Olson "champ."

"He's not the champ," Robinson said. "He's just got my title."

Five months later, Robinson knocked out Olson to regain his title. He had also regained it in 1951 at the Polo Grounds when, bleeding from a head butt, he suddenly knocked out Randy Turpin with a desperate barrage.

"Somebody later counted my punches," he once said. "They counted thirty-one punches in twenty-five seconds."

He won the middleweight title for the fourth time with his most famous single punch: a left hook that dethroned Gene Fullmer.

"Fullmer liked to throw a right hand to the body," he explained. "And when he did, his jaw was open for a left hook."

Slender with supple muscles, Sugar Ray Robinson had 110 knockouts in his 175–19–6 record over more than a quarter of a century. In those years before the multimillion purses, he earned about four million dollars. He also spent that much. When he sailed to Europe on the *Liberté*, his barber and his golf pro were among his entourage of nearly a dozen family and friends. He parked his flamingo-pink Cadillac convertible outside his Harlem nightclub on Seventh Avenue alongside his dry cleaning shop, a barber shop, and a lingerie shop.

"I'm a blessed man," he liked to say. "A chosen man."

Sugar Ray Robinson was even chosen by Muhammad Ali, then known as Cassius Clay, to be one of the young heavyweight's advisers. But according to Robinson, the offer demanded that he join the Black Muslims.

"I told Cassius I don't believe in the Black Muslim religion," he once remembered saying. "I'm a Christian believer in God."

But as happened with the finances of so many other boxers, Robinson's money disappeared in taxes and bad investments. He continued to box until he was forty-four, when Joey Archer, a gentle puncher, knocked him down in winning a 10-round decision in Pittsburgh in 1965. Several months later, Robinson was honored at the old Madison Square Garden with, among other presents, a huge trophy inscribed "the world's greatest fighter." That night he and his third wife, Millie, returned to their Riverside Drive apartment.

"I had to put that trophy on the floor," he once recalled. "The only table was a metal card table with thin legs. The only other piece of furniture in the apartment was an old scratched wooden bed. But I knew it wasn't supposed to end that way for me."

It didn't. He and Millie moved to Los Angeles, where he had bit parts in movies and television shows. He also founded and operated the Sugar Ray Robinson Youth Foundation until he was afflicted with Alzheimer's disease a few years ago. Until his death, he existed almost as if his memory were in a cotton cocoon.

But now, as before, in boxing, the phrase "pound for pound, the best" will always endure as a tribute to the only Sugar standing.

The LaMotta Fight

By JAMES P. DAWSON

Ray Robinson battered Jake LaMotta into submission in thirteen rounds of gruelling fighting in Chicago on February 14, 1951, and won the world middleweight championship.

Hammering the famed Bronx Bull into a state of utter helplessness in a struggle that developed into a slaughter, Robinson won the 160-pound title when the referee, Frank Sikora, stepped between the combatants and ended the battle after the thirteenth round had gone 2 minutes 4 seconds.

Referee Sikora acted upon a signal from Dr. J. M. Houston, physician for the Illinois State Athletic Commission, who was in charge of the battle from a medical standpoint. Through the thirteenth round, the referee had been watching for the signal, aware of the distressing condition to which LaMotta had been rendered by the damaging blows of one who is recognized as the greatest boxer in the ring today.

When the referee intervened, LaMotta was being pounded on the ropes near a neutral corner, helpless to defend himself and powerless to fight back. Only his indomitable courage kept him from toppling to the canvas for the first time in his career.

Under Illinois boxing rules, the finish will go into the records as a "technical knockout." They make the distinction here between a knockout where the victim is counted out, and a knockout where intervention comes from the referee.

But, to the crowd of 14,802, which paid gross receipts of $180,619 and net of $138,938, no cleaner knockout ever was scored than the triumph of Robinson. It ended the middleweight reign LaMotta started on June 16, 1949, when he stopped Marcel Cerdan at Detroit and brought the second knockout charged against the Bronx Bull, who, even on this night, a pitiful excuse for a fighting man under the bludgeoning blows of a savage foe, left the ring with his boast untarnished—that he had never been knocked off his feet and had never been counted out.

Never in his life had the Bronx strong boy been subjected to such a hammering. In this sixth meeting of these bitter ring rivals, Robinson, the master craftsman, did everything short of battering LaMotta unconscious as he registered his fifth triumph of the series.

That LaMotta did not collapse will always be a testimonial to the amazing resistance to punishment that has always been his greatest recommendation; this, and a grim determination to go down fighting with his face to the foe.

When it was over, and frantic ministrations of his handlers had restored his faculties, a disillusioned LaMotta disdained the willing hands that reached up to assist his descent from the ring. Instead, he went down the steps under his own power, stopping several times with a wide-open gesture of the hands, which spoke louder than words of his keen disappointment and the complete futility he felt through the vital part of the night.

It was 1 hour 55 minutes after the fight before LaMotta was able to leave the stadium, and he was assisted by a trainer under each arm. He gave the customary interview after the bout and then, near collapse, received oxygen for nearly forty minutes.

With his victory, Robinson abdicated the world welterweight throne he had occupied since December 20, 1946, when he pounded out a victory over Tommy Bell. This was a condition of the battle when contracts were signed, since boxing's ruling bodies have frowned upon double titleholders since the confusion produced by Henry Armstrong's triple championship reign in the featherweight, lightweight, and welterweight classes.

Combining superlative skill with damaging punching power, Robinson excelled LaMotta in every boxing essential.

Robinson permitted himself to be outrushed by a bull-like LaMotta in the first round. He proceeded to outbox and outpunch LaMotta through the second, third, and fourth rounds. Then Robinson held back through the fifth, sixth, and seventh as LaMotta plunged and swung from all angles with his best blows to the body and head in what looked like a resurgent LaMotta in action agaisnt a tiring Robinson.

But only briefly did the illusion last. For with the eighth Robinson went back into action with a clever exhibition of boxing skill against an overeager adversary who was like a pupil against the master.

With the eleventh, Robinson cut loose with a savage fury that proved the beginning of the end. Through most of the round he hammered LaMotta all over the ring. He did the same in the twelfth. He was on the verge of battering LaMotta down and into an unqualified knockout when the thirteenth had gone 2 minutes 4 seconds.

It was a sudden spurt by LaMotta that hastened his own downfall. He had gone through ten rounds of bruising fighting in which his own face was puffed under the sting and stab of his foe's blows, and Robinson's nose and mouth were bloodied under the drive in the LaMotta jab and swing and hook. The tenth ended with the count six rounds to four in Robinson's favor.

LaMotta had been the aggressor all through the mill. He walked in fearlessly, foolishly, it seemed, at times, against the stinging jabs and left hooks, the right uppercuts and sharp right crosses of Robinson, blazing away with both hands for the body.

LaMotta made the championship poundage of 160 right on the nose at the weighing-in this morning. Robinson weighed 155½, heavier than he ever has been in action against LaMotta.

KNUTE ROCKNE

1889–1931

By ROBERT F. KELLEY

FROM HIS DAYS as a player Knute Rockne made his influence felt on how college football is played. As captain of the 1913 Notre Dame team, he figured at end in the most successful exhibition of forward passing the game had seen up to that time; and from that date on the forward pass grew steadily to its present importance in the game.

As a coach he brought the shift play to its highest state of perfection and made it such an important factor in offensive football that the rules committee finally passed legislation designed to take some of its power away.

That shift development, the backfield hop, was the most important of his contributions to the coaching of the game, but he added others, notably the reshaping of the line. Prior to Rockne, linemen were big men inevitably. Rockne brought the idea of using linemen, particularly guards, in interference, and demonstrated that the small, fast lineman could hold his own with the big man and outplay him where the big man was not as fast.

He worked for the perfection of a team as a whole, and his last two teams won game after game through the successful application of what came to be called "the perfect plays." In these every individual carried out a part of the blocking, and when no man failed to carry out his job the play often went for a touchdown.

This perfect play did a great deal to wipe away the idea of aiming first for scoring territory and then the score. Rockne always said that every play, if perfectly carried out, would go for a touchdown from wherever it was started. His last two teams usually started their scoring with long runs from scrimmage.

In coaching he tried always for perfection and spent hours in teaching the art of blocking. Simple plays, well executed, were his idea of the way to win football games. He had small use for any so-called trick plays. There were only seven places in a line to send a man with a ball, he said, and there ought not to be many more than seven plays.

Hard work was another of his slogans. "The best thing I ever learned in life," he said, "was that things have to be worked for. A lot of people seem to think there is some sort of magic in making a winning football team. There isn't, but there's plenty of work."

When Rockne first went to Notre Dame as a freshman in 1910, he explained later, he was "looking only for an education—to my mind, college players were supermen to whose heights I could never aspire."

He had been about six years getting to the college at South Bend, Indiana,

after he was graduated from Northwestern Division High School in Chicago. He had to earn the money first. By working as a railroad brakeman and later as a mail clerk in Chicago he accumulated $1,000 and reached the age of twenty-two.

His original intention was to go to the University of Illinois when he had saved this much, but two of his friends were going to Notre Dame at the time and they urged him to go with them. According to his own explanation of his decision, the chief inducement was the possibility of living more cheaply at South Bend.

Since his father brought him to this country at the age of six from Voss, Norway, where he was born in 1889, the cost of living was the chief thing that affected Knute Rockne's life.

Notre Dame made him a chemist, good enough to be an instructor during his last undergraduate year, and it also made him an end and captain of the football team.

As a player on the 1913 Notre Dame team, the first ever to beat the Army, Rockne began his shaping of football's destinies by bringing the forward pass suddenly and dramatically into the front of the game. Army that season had scheduled Notre Dame as a "breather" game on its schedule. Only a small crowd turned out, and they stood amazed as Notre Dame defeated Army, 35 to 13. Gus Dorais threw seventeen passes in that game and thirteen were completed, and a great majority of these went to the short, chunky end, Knute Rockne.

The forward pass had been more or less a haphazard thing until that time. The success of this midwestern team with it amazed the football world. Dorais and Rockne remained behind at West Point for a few days after that game to show the Army how it was done.

In that first success was an indication of Rockne's capacity for taking pains. That game was the direct result of how he spent the summer before. Dorais and Rockne had obtained vacation jobs together at a midwestern resort. All that summer they got out on the beach and threw passes. The success against Army was no accident. It had been carefully planned.

After he was graduated from Notre Dame in 1914, Rockne returned there that fall as assistant football coach and chemistry instructor. He became head coach in 1918, succeeding Jesse C. Harper.

As a coach, of course, Rockne's record of 105 wins, 12 losses, and 5 ties is one of the most remarkable that any coach of any sport has ever piled up. Nearly all of his teams were in the front rank of the game, despite the fact that they always played hard schedules. Five of them were undefeated: 1919, 1920, 1924, 1929, and 1930.

To the game in general Rockne brought the high development of the backfield shift and a new conception of line play. He never claimed the invention of the shift play. But there can be small argument with the idea that under him Notre Dame's players brought it to its highest perfection.

So successful were his teams with shift plays that the football rules committee created rules against them. He said this was like taking the feinting out of boxing, and leaving only the slugging.

Rockne organized coaching schools in which coaches might gather during the off-seasons and study the methods of others. He assisted with summer schools all over the country and in 1928 even conducted one at sea when he chartered a ship and took a party of coaches and athletes to the Olympic Games in Amsterdam that year.

Perhaps his greatest teams came in 1920, 1924, 1929, and 1930. On the first was George Gipp, who was named by Rockne as the greatest player he ever had. The coach told the story of seeing Gipp, who was not trying for the team, throwing a ball and kicking on the campus and of inducing him to join the squad. Gipp died a few weeks after the close of the 1920 season of a throat infection, with Rockne at his bedside.

The 1924 team was the one of the famous Four Horsemen: Harry Stuhldreher, Jimmy Crowley, Don Miller, and Elmer Layden. As a combination, they were the premier backfield of their day, and they had a great line in front of them, led by the famous Adam Walsh at center. That team of the Four Horsemen won all over the country, beating Princeton at Princeton with a temperature of 10 above zero, and several weeks later journeying to the West Coast to defeat Stanford in a temperature of 70 degrees.

The 1930 team came very near to being the best. Northwestern, Army, and Southern California were played on successive Saturdays. One Saturday in Chicago, Army was turned back in ice and cold rain and the following week the highly regarded Southern California team was badly beaten on the Coast.

His tenure at South Bend was uncertain only once, in 1925, when J. R. Knapp, chairman of the Columbia football committee, obtained his agreement to come to New York if a release could be secured from Notre Dame on a ten-year contract that Rockne had signed the previous year. His salary would have gone from $10,000 a year to $25,000.

Premature publicity disturbed the negotiations, and Rockne traveled back from New York to South Bend, wondering publicly if he still had a job. In testimonial of the undiminished esteem of Notre Dame, a group of alumni in Chicago collected $3,000 and bought him a new automobile.

If there was any doubt of the influence of Rockne on football, the list of head coaches he produced might remove it. One year there were, through the country, twenty-three head coaches who came from Notre Dame without naming the assistants here and there.

The mere record of his work fails to bring out for those who did not know him the biting, incisive, clear-cut character and personality of the man. Dramatic in everything he did, even to his death, Rockne became a sort of god to the boys who played for him. A great talker, a keen wit, he had a balanced, sane philosophy of life and a keen knowledge of psychology.

There are numerous instances in the near legends that have sprung up about him of his use of the latter element in dealing with his boys. The year that Army and Navy played in Chicago, in 1926, he went to Chicago to watch the game, confident his strong team would beat Carnegie Tech without too much trouble in his absence. They did not.

The coach returned to South Bend. The next week the team was to play on the Pacific Coast. All week, Rockne coached without mentioning the defeat.

The players kept waiting for him to say something. He did not. But when they boarded the train and opened their baggage, each player found a carefully clipped account of the lost game in his baggage. They won on the next game.

Before the Army game of 1930, Rockne sat in the dressing room with his players, waiting for the time to go out on the field. The players sat silently, waiting for him to say something. The minutes ticked off in the quiet room, and finally an official came to tell them to come out. Rockne nodded, stood up and said, "Come on, boys." That was all.

He has given words to the vocabulary of the sport as well, some of which fit exactly the army of people who criticize the players and coaches after a defeat, waiting until the day after to display their wisdom. "Sunday morning coaches" was Rockne's name for this class.

A polished storyteller and a constantly interesting companion, Rockne made friends wherever he went, and was almost as much at home at the colleges he played against on his numerous visits as he was at his own.

Rockne was killed in a plane crash on March 31, 1931.

The Forward Pass

The Notre Dame eleven swept the Army off its feet on the plains on November 1, 1913, and buried the soldiers under a 35 to 13 score. The Westerners flashed the most sensational football that has been seen in the East this year, baffling the cadets with a style of open play and a perfectly developed forward pass, which carried the victors down the field thirty yards at a clip. The Eastern gridiron has not seen such a master of the forward pass as Charley Dorais, the Notre Dame quarterback. A frail youth of 145 pounds, as agile as a cat and as restless as a jumping jack, Dorais shot forward passes with accuracy into the outstretched arms of his ends, Captain Knute Rockne and Fred "Gus" Gushurst, as they stood poised for the ball, often as far as thirty-five yards away.

The yellow leather egg was in the air half the time, with the Notre Dame team spread out in all directions over the field waiting for it. The Army players were hopelessly confused and chagrined before Notre Dame's great playing, and their style of old-fashioned, close, line-smashing play was no match for the spectacular and highly perfected attack of the Indiana collegians. All five of Notre Dame's touchdowns came as the result of forward passes. They sprang the play on the Army seventeen times, and only missed four. In all they gained 243 yards with the forward pass alone.

The topnotch forward pass performance of the game happened in the second period when Notre Dame carried the ball nearly the entire length of the field in four plays for a touchdown. Rockne took the kickoff and was downed on the 15-yard line. Little Dorais then got five on a quarterback run. He then hurled a long pass to Joe Pliska that netted thirty yards. Dorais followed this with a beautifully placed heave of thirty-five yards to Rockne. Another forward pass to Rockne carried the ball to the 5-yard line, and then Pliska was jammed through the Army forwards for a touchdown.

Football men marveled at this startling display of open football. Bill

Roper, former head coach at Princeton, who was one of the officials of the game, said that he had always believed that such playing was possible under the new rules, but that he had never seen the forward pass developed to such a state of perfection.

Except for a short time in the second period, when the Army team got going and hammered out two touchdowns by driving, back-straining work, the cadets looked like novices compared with the big Indiana team. Just before West Point's second touchdown, Notre Dame made a great stand under the shadow of its own goal. The cadets had the ball on the 1-yard line and hurled themselves at the line, but it would not move. A penalty gave the soldiers their first down and again the Army backs punched the rigid wall of giant Westerners. Five times they hammered at the line and on the sixth crash, got through for the touchdown.

This was the first time Notre Dame had ever been on the Army schedule, and a crowd of 5,000 came to the reservation that day to witness the game. Report had the Indiana team strong, but no one imagined that it knew so much football. Dorais ran the team at top speed all the time. The Westerners were on the jump from the start, and handled the ball with few muffs. The little quarterback displayed great judgment at all times and was never at a loss to take the cadets by surprise. He got around as if on springs, and was as cool as a cucumber on ice when shooting the forward pass. Half a dozen Army tacklers bearing down on him in full charge didn't disconcert the quarterback one bit. He got his passes away accurately, every one before the cadets could reach him. He tossed the football on a straight line for thirty yards time and again.

The Army folks from General Leonard Wood down to the youngest substitute on the scrubs were shocked at the way the Army team was put to rout. Head Coach Charley Daly paraded up and down the sidelines nervously as he watched the depressing spectacle of the giant fullback, Ray Eichenlaub, tearing the Army line to shreds. The cadet corps in the stands yelled encouragement at the soldiers until they were hoarse, but it was a losing fight from the start.

There was little of encouragement in the Army's showing with the Navy game four weeks away. Their best playing was shown only in streaks. At times the Army backs punched through the Notre Dame line with genuine power behind their driving charge, but after they had hammered out two touchdowns, much of the snap was gone from their attack. In the last period the Notre Dame team also was pretty well played out. Going at top speed all the time slowed them up considerably at the end. But the wonder of it all was that covering all the ground they did didn't tire them earlier. They had the ball most of the time, and were always eating up the distance that separated them from the Army goal line.

Rockne's Twenty-five Commandments
By DAVE ANDERSON

Rockne. The name itself provides strength—character as well as muscle. Until his death in a 1931 plane crash, Knute Rockne projected the image of Notre Dame football that all its other coaches have been burdened to maintain. Even now he remains college football's most famous coach. In the late 1970s, Rockne Jr., browsing through belongings stored at his home in Stevensville, Michigan, discovered a list of what the famous coach identified as "the correct mental qualifications of an athlete," what might be called Knute Rockne's twenty-five commandments.

Scholarship: The player should first be a good student. Do not neglect your studies. Your first purpose should be to get an education.

Cooperation: Everyone should work for the common good of the school and the squad. Everyone should boost everyone else; a disorganizer has no place on the squad.

Obedience: The public holds the coach responsible for the team; his orders must be obeyed. He is responsible for the system and the carrying out of the system, not necessarily the winning of the game.

Habits: Good habits are only doing those things which help and not doing those things that will harm or hinder.

Ambition: Keeping an eye on the future, always trying to improve oneself. Interest and spirit sometimes outweigh natural ability.

Attendance: Anything worth doing is worth doing well. Try not to miss a day of school or practice.

Earnestness: The desire to make every minute count, always wanting to do the right thing for the team and the school.

Morals: A high standard of living and thinking.

Sportsmanship: Good sportsmanship means clean and fair play. Treat your opponent with respect.

Conduct: Your school, family, town, community and yourself are judged by your conduct; you can make or break them.

Unity: Actions on the part of every member of the squad for the common good.

Service: Students should always consider that they are receiving far more than they are giving. Their best efforts for their school are none too good.

Leadership: The willingness to help, guide or direct, in the right way, by example, words or actions.

Patience: The willingness to take and profit by the instructions received, although not a member of the first team.

Loyalty: To give your best service to the team, school, game and coach.

Self-sacrifice: Giving up some of the present things for the future.

Determination: The mental quality of strong determination is very necessary to win in the face of strong opposition.

Confidence: The belief in oneself, teammates, team and plays.

Remarks: Be careful of your remarks about anyone; if you cannot say something good, say nothing. Talking too much is bad policy.

Responsibility: Being dependable, the performing of one's duties, the desire to be known as responsible.

Concentration: During school hours, think and prepare your studies; they must be of first importance. During practice, think only of playing; if you have studied, you will not have to worry about your schoolwork.

Losing: You can be a hard but good loser. Any coach or team that cannot lose and treat their opponents with respect has no right to win; a poor sportsman generally tries to amuse the spectators with his self-styled clever wit by making abusive remarks, which act as a boomerang by intelligent spectators.

Winning: If you are the rightful winner, be willing to take credit for it, but keep in mind that it was only your time to win and that your winning was probably due to conditions or a reward for your sacrifices; a kind word or a handshake goes a long way toward forming a lasting friendship, and does not change the score.

The Past: It is history. Make the present good, and the past will take care of itself.

The Present and Future: Give to your school the best that you have, and the best will come back to you. Your success in the future depends on the present. Build well.

ADOLPH RUPP

1901–1977

I N KENTUCKY, Adolph Rupp was not only the dean of basketball coaches, but also for more than forty years he was the only "Baron" in a land of honorary colonels.

No more rabid enthusiast for the state of Kentucky existed than Rupp, a Kansas boy who traded a midwestern twang for a soft-spoken drawl. He had a true Chamber of Commerce outlook on life in Kentucky and delighted in reciting the glories of the state.

A heavyset man, and a pleasant one when he wasn't coaching, Rupp was dynamic, controversial, and colorful. Because of his estate in the rolling farm country outside Lexington, where he tended to his prize Herefords and crops of burley tobacco, he was known to all as the Baron of Bluegrass Country.

Since his favorite coaching attire, out of superstition, was usually a double-breasted brown suit, he also picked up the nickname the Man in the Brown Suit. At other times he was referred to as Mr. Basketball and Ol' Rupp and Ready.

In the first college basketball game he coached in 1930, his fast-breaking Wildcats raced to a 67–19 victory over Georgetown (Kentucky) College. In the forty-two seasons that followed, he took his teams into tiny, old gymnasiums, new field houses, and big-city arenas, where he was often hooted and despised, but always respected.

Unlike some coaches, Rupp rarely played the role of a substitute father to his players. He was not the chummy sort. He had stern and demanding qualities, inherited from his German immigrant father. He had reverence for order and precision and demanded it from his players. To some persons, he appeared to be a mean old man.

"A lot of people think we run a Marine Corps outfit," he once said. "Fine, if they think that, that's fine. I knew when I came here that the only way I could be successful would be to go out and win these basketball games."

Joe Hall, the Kentucky coach who succeeded Rupp and for many years was his assistant and chief recruiter, once said, "Coach operates from an extreme competitive desire and has a strong dread of losing."

Regardless of the reason, he always put forth this kind of effort. On his weekly television shows he often said, "We have to win, we just have to win. Goodness knows, no one wants to win any more than we do."

Winning was Rupp's passion. Someone once recited to him the famed Grantland Rice line: "When the one Great Scorer comes to write against your name, he marks not that you won or lost, but how you played the game."

To this, Rupp answered, "Well now, I just don't know about that. If winning isn't so important, why do you keep score?"

Rupp's achievements were endless. His 875 victories are the most by any other basketball coach. Under his leadership, Kentucky won four National Collegiate Athletic Association championships and was the runner-up twice. The Wildcats also won twenty-seven Southeastern Conference titles. Rupp was honored for his achievements by election to the Helms Athletic Foundation Hall of Fame and the Basketball Hall of Fame in Springfield, Massachusetts.

During his fight to remain as the Kentucky coach after he reached the mandatory retirement age of seventy in 1972, he said, "If they don't let me coach, they might as well take me to the Lexington cemetery."

Rupp remained in basketball until his death. After his retirement, he was president of the Memphis Tams of the now-defunct American Basketball Association and vice chairman of the board of directors of the Kentucky Colonels.

His 1948 championship team and the Phillips Oilers of the Amateur Athletic Union combined to represent the United States in the Olympics. Kentucky also won National Collegiate titles in 1949, 1951, and 1958.

During the 1969–70 season, Rupp started to show the effect of his age and poor health, but he refused to retire. That season, looking ghastly and with his voice raspy, he spent five weeks in bed, arising only to go to games, practice sessions, or to his doctor.

During Kentucky's first few games, he sat with his foot supported by a cushion on a chair. His foot ailment was complicated by his diabetic condition.

On December 26, 1967, when Kentucky defeated Notre Dame, 81–73, the victory—No. 772—established Rupp as college basketball's leading winning coach. The honor previously belonged to Forrest "Phog" Allen of Kansas, who retired with 771 victories after forty-six seasons of coaching.

During Rupp's winning habit, he became a victim of his success. He never heeded criticism, and his recruitment of players was said to have reached every hamlet in Kentucky and its adjoining states.

But with all his success, Rupp had trying moments, especially in October 1951, when three of his former players admitted they had accepted $1,500 in bribes to lose deliberately a National Invitation Tournament game at Madison Square Garden on March 14, 1949.

The Kentucky players were involved in a national basketball scandal that touched many college players throughout the nation.

During the trial in New York, in which the three former Kentucky players were placed on indefinite probation, Judge Saul S. Streit in General Sessions Court condemned the athletic practices of the University of Kentucky.

He described them as "the acme of commercialism and overemphasis."

In August 1952, the Southeastern Conference suspended Kentucky from basketball competition. Three months later the NCAA penalized the university for rules violations and Kentucky canceled its 1952–53 basketball season.

The following season, Rupp and his team, the Wildcats, were back. They won all twenty-five games.

Rupp was born on September 2, 1901, in Halstead, Kansas, where his father homesteaded a 163-acre farm.

He died of cancer on December 10, 1977, in Lexington.

Rupp and New York

By GERALD ESKENAZI

He was an old man in a rumpled brown suit and a thousand people walked past him at Madison Square Garden that March day in 1976 without looking twice.

It was a return, sort of, for Adolph Rupp, but he was no longer the coach of those muscular, disciplined Kentucky basketball teams that invariably would overpower the opposition.

He was a seventy-four-year-old former coach, who hadn't been to the Garden since 1951, before the college basketball scandals erupted. After that year Kentucky decided to go to the National Collegiate championship instead of the National Invitational Tournament.

The Baron, as he was known, saw his teams win 875 games from 1930 until 1972, when, five years past the retirement age for most professors, he was reluctantly dropped by the school. No other coach has won as many games.

"I was never afraid of New York," he said as he waited for the start of the Kentucky-Niagara game, which opened the NIT program. "I always believed in doing things on the road just like at home. I took my boys out to see Sophie Tucker at that club—what's the name?—the Copacabana. Do they still have that place?"

Some persons, though, were afraid of the big city, Rupp recalled.

"There was that coach at Rhode Island State, Frank Keaney," he said. "You know how he would practice in his gymnasium? He'd put a smudge pot in there so his boys could get used to the smoke and smell of Madison Square Garden."

Persons who were around during the scandals have a vague recollection that Rupp gloated when some players at City College and other schools were unmasked as point shavers. Then most of the Kentucky starters in an NIT game held two years before—March 14, 1949—admitted having taken $1,500 apiece to fix that contest.

"People told me I should have known what was going on," said Rupp. "Hell, we won the NCAA and the NIT and we sent the team to the Olympics with those same players. If I was supposed to know what was going on when a team like that is winning, then why doesn't a coach of a losing team think his players are fixing games?"

It was the only time that day that Rupp raised his voice. Watching his team play Niagara, he sat quietly, almost stonily.

Once though, he held up three fingers, inadvertently sending in a play. And a few times he applauded. Never, though, did he permit himself the beginning of a grin.

"No, I haven't been to the Garden since," he said. "But I knew my way around New York better than most people. Hell, from 1925 to 1929 I went to Columbia University. I took two advanced degrees there.

"You know next year we're opening a new building that's going to hold more people than Madison Square Garden—23,600 seats. It'll be called Rupp Arena."

Little wonder. For Rupp brought the city of Lexington, where the university is located, the national championship in 1948, 1949, 1951, and 1958. A pro franchise was created around one of his teams. His Wildcat fives won twenty-seven Southeastern Conference titles.

"I was the most vicious recruiter in the world," he said with irony. "Well, 87 percent of my players came from Kentucky."

Why was he so successful?

"I had a different practice schedule from anyone else," he said. "My players knew exactly how long it was. When that minute hand was up, the practice was up. So they couldn't fool around. Every day—every day, you understand—we had thirty minutes of shooting drills. The first seven minutes were free-lancing. Then fourteen minutes in dribbling and hook shots under the baskets. Then drills for the centers and forwards, then drills for the guards.

"I rate only the players my teams went against," he said. "First, I put Jerry West. Then Tom Gola. Then Guy Rodgers. We never played Wilt or Oscar Robertson.

"The greatest coaches? I have them in no special order. They include Nat Holman, Clair Bee, Joe Lapchick, John Wooden, Hank Iba.

"The greatest games? The triple overtime with Temple in 1968, when Vernon Hatton threw from beyond the center line in second overtime at the buzzer. And then Bill Bradley, Princeton, in the NCAA semifinals in Portland. He did everything in that game that a player can do."

He noted that many of his "all-time" coaches came from New York.

"Most of them worked with Jewish ball players in those days," he said. "They were all very smart ball handlers, the best I've ever seen. Now the game's complexion has changed, and I'm not talking in terms of color. I mean in style.

"We have all the smart coaches in Ohio and Indiana and Kentucky now."

Some of that dominance was evident as Rupp watched the Wildcats score a 67–61 victory, which brought Kentucky's overall Garden record to 25 victories and 10 defeats.

Word of his appearance apparently had spread. Fans of all ages walked up to him, forming a receiving line. They included ten-year-olds asking for his autograph and thirty-year-olds asking if the old man remembered their cousin "from the 1946 team."

"Sure, I used to get into a lot of arguments," said the Baron. "I was blunt. But was I right? Time is the greatest proof."

The Baron of Bluegrass

By TONY KORNHEISER

On this particular day the pumps at this particular gas station in Lexington, Kentucky, were occupied. At one, the chairman of the department of mathematics at the University of Kentucky filled his Ford, at the other, Adolph Rupp, the university's basketball coach, filled his Cadillac.

"Coach Rupp," the professor said, "I'm the chairman of the math department at one of the country's great academic institutions, and I drive a Ford. You're the basketball coach, and you drive a Cadillac. How can that be?"

"Professor," Rupp said, "if you could square the hypotenuse before 14,000 people a night, you'd be driving a Caddy, too."

In locker rooms, in taverns, in airport terminals, wherever basketball coaches gather, people still tell Adolph Rupp stories. The Baron's legend lives on, fueled by 875 lifetime victories and four national championships. In his forty-two seasons as a coach Rupp won more games than any other college basketball coach. He may well have been the best coach in history; at the very least, he ranks with Clair Bee, Hank Iba, Nat Holman, Phog Allen, Joe Lapchick, and John Wooden.

"He could've been governor of Kentucky," said Lou Carnesecca, the St. John's coach. "He was more than a Kentucky Colonel, he was the General, the Commander-in-Chief. He could've been a czar, or a don. He sat on that bench like a chairman of the board. Hey, down in Kentucky, he's as famous as the Derby."

Dave Gavitt, then the Providence coach, remembered the time when he was lecturing at a boys' basketball camp and Rupp agreed to speak to the boys. "Some little kid asked him. 'Are you the greatest coach ever?' Well, Adolph lowered his head a bit and said, 'I don't know how you judge that. I do have 800 wins, and although I haven't given it the slightest thought, a man would have to start coaching at age twenty-five, then win twenty games a season for the next forty years. . . .' Adolph was really something, he never thought about it, sure," Gavitt said, shaking his head and chuckling respectfully.

It is said that no coach ever prepared his team as well as Rupp did, that no coach ever got more from his players. On the night after he died, the tributes from his former players and coaches began pouring in like Kentucky moonshine. Bear Bryant called him "a legend." Nat Holman called him "a wonderful man." John Wooden called him "an amazing man." And Tommy Kron, one of his former players, said, "There will never be another like him."

But there was another side to Adolph Rupp, just as there is another side to all men of great power and influence. It is too easy to remember Rupp's brown suits and his victories and let it go at that. There was his rush to judgment during the basketball scandals of the early 1950s, his failure to recruit a black player until the late 1960s, his egotism, his iron fist. Great men are not immune to great mistakes.

When the point-shaving scandals broke, Rupp was quick to identify the site of the crimes as New York City. He said he wasn't surprised that it happened here because "the newspapers . . . quote odds and play directly into the hands of the gamblers."

Rupp went one step further, one step too many as it turned out. He said, "They couldn't touch my boys with a ten-foot pole."

When it came out that three starters on Rupp's 1948–49 national champions—Alex Groza, Ralph Beard, and Dale Barnstable—had, indeed, shaved points, Rupp changed his stance. "The Chicago Black Sox threw games," Rupp said, "but these kids only shaved points." He did not say, "my boys."

It wasn't until years later that Groza saw Rupp again. As Groza recalled it: "I offered Adolph my hand and he shook it. He was one of the most knowledgeable and finest coaches I've ever known. People said he didn't like blacks, or Jews, or Catholics, but I'm a Catholic and he never showed me any prejudice. He was a perfectionist, and that overshadows what a great sense of humor he had. In 1944 we came to the Garden to play, and we had a reserve center named Ernest Sparkman from Carr Creek, Kentucky. Well, Ernie was having a terrible practice, and Adolph called us all to the center of the court and said to Sparkman, 'Ernie, you see that corner of the floor? I want you to go to that corner and spit. Then you can go back to Carr Creek and tell the folks back home you did something in Madison Square Garden.' "

Some people, however, don't remember the Baron quite so fondly. Nevil Shed, an assistant basketball coach at Wisconsin-Milwaukee, is one. Shed played on the 1965–66 Texas Western team that beat Kentucky, 72–65, in a nationally televised championship game. Kentucky's players were all white; all of Texas Western's players that night were black. That game was the college basketball equivalent of the *Brown* v. *Board of Education* segregation suit. Kentucky's defeat changed the recruiting practices of college basketball forever.

Within five years every team in the previously all-white Southeastern and Atlantic Coast conferences was fully integrated. Those last barriers fell like paper fences in a windstorm.

"We heard before the game that Mr. Rupp didn't believe that five blacks could beat his team," Shed said. "Well, we showed him just how tough five niggers could be. Don't get me wrong, Mr. Rupp was a great coach; he knew his X's and O's, and we respected him for that. But after the game he didn't shake any of our hands, not a one of us, he didn't say a kind word about us. A couple of years later he started recruiting black players, he had to confess. . . . I've walked past him plenty of times at coaching clinics, but I've never introduced myself. I've never said a word. Just to myself I said, 'I'm glad I kicked your tail.' "

Shed did not use the word *racist.* That would be an unfair judgment. Adolph Rupp was a product of his time and environment. He was not the only coach to refrain from recruiting blacks, just the most prominent one. All accounts say that he wanted to recruit Wilt Chamberlain in the 1950s, but Rupp wasn't certain that he could safely take Chamberlain on road trips in the SEC. Those were vicious times in the Deep South, and Rupp shouldered more than his share of the blame for Kentucky's tardy integration. When he did start courting black players, the years of benign neglect hurt his effort. He retired in 1972 without reaching the championship game again.

"He didn't feel blacks could do it for him," said Cecil Watkins, a black leader in New York City scholastic basketball circles. "By the time he went after them, what could he sell them?"

Adolph Rupp won 875 games. He casts a giant shadow. The irony is that his most famous loss may have done more for college basketball than any of his victories.

BABE RUTH

1895–1948

PROBABLY NOWHERE in all the imaginative field of fiction could one find a career more dramatic and bizarre than that portrayed in real life by George Herman Ruth. Known the world over, even in foreign lands where baseball is never played, as the Babe, he was the boy who rose from the obscurity of a charitable institution in Baltimore to a position as the leading figure in professional baseball. He was also its greatest drawing card, its highest salaried performer—at least of his day—and the idol of millions of youngsters throughout the land.

A creation of the times, he seemed to embody all the qualities that a sport-loving nation demanded of its outstanding hero. For it has always been debatable whether Ruth owed his fame and the fortune it made for him more to his ability to smash home runs in greater quantity than any other player of his time or to a strange personality that at all times was intensely real and "regular," which was the one fixed code by which he lived.

He made friends by the thousands and rarely, if ever, lost any of them. Affable, boisterous, and good-natured to a fault, he was always as accessible to the newsboy on the corner as to the most dignified personage in worldly affairs. More, he could be very much at ease with both.

He could scarcely recall a name, even of certain intimates with whom he frequently came in contact, but this at no time interfered with the sincerity of his greeting. Indeed, by a singular display of craft, he overcame this slight deficiency with consummate skill. If you looked under forty it was "Hello, kid, how are you?" And if you appeared above that line of demarcation it was "Hello, doc, how's everything going?"

The story is told of the case of Johnny Sylvester, a youngster whose life doctors had despaired of unless something unusual happened to shock him out of a peculiar malady. The boy's uncle, recalling how fond he always had been of baseball, conceived the idea of sending word to Babe Ruth and asking his aid.

The next day, so the story goes, the Babe, armed with bat, glove, and half a dozen signed baseballs, made one of his frequent pilgrimages to a hospital. The boy, unexpectedly meeting his idol face-to-face, was so overjoyed that he was cured—almost miraculously.

A year later an elderly man accosted the Babe in a hotel lobby and, after receiving the customary wholehearted greeting of "Hello, doc," said, "Babe, I don't know whether you remember me, but I'm Johnny Sylvester's uncle and

I want to tell you the family will never forget what you did for us. Johnny is getting along fine."

"That's great," replied the Babe. "Sure, I remember you. Glad to hear Johnny is doing so well. Bring him around some time."

After a few more words they parted and no sooner had the man removed himself from earshot than the Babe turned to a baseball writer at his elbow and asked, "Now, who the devil was Johnny Sylvester?"

Nor must this be mistaken for affectation, for there was never a doubt that the Babe at all times was tremendously sincere in his desire to appear on friendly terms with all the world. And though in later years he acquired a certain polish that he lacked utterly in his early career, he never lost his natural self nor his flamboyant, carefree mannerisms, which at all times made him a show apart from the ball field.

Single-handed, he tore the final game of the 1928 World's Series in St. Louis to shreds with his mighty bat by hitting three home runs over the right-field pavilion. That night, returning to New York, he went on a boisterous rampage and no one on the train got any sleep, including his employer, Colonel Jacob Ruppert.

Such was the blending of qualities that made Babe Ruth a figure unprecedented in American life. A born showman off the field and a marvelous performer on it, he had an amazing flair for doing the spectacular at the most dramatic moment.

Of his early days in Baltimore even Babe himself was, or pretended to be, somewhat vague during his major league baseball career. Thus various versions of his childhood were printed over the years with neither denial nor confirmation from Ruth as to their accuracy.

However, the following account of his boyhood years appeared in a national magazine under Ruth's own "byline":

In the first place I was not an orphan. . . . My mother, whose maiden name was Schanberg, lived until I was thirteen. My father, George Herman Ruth, lived until my second year in the majors. Few fathers ever looked more like their sons than my pop and I. My mother was mainly Irish, and was called Kate. My father was of German extraction. It is not true that our family name was Erhardt, as has been repeatedly written. Or Ehrhardt, or Gearhardt.

But I hardly knew my parents. I don't want to make any excuses or place the blame for my shortcomings as a kid completely on persons or places. . . . Yet I probably was a victim of circumstances. I spent most of the first seven years of my life living over my father's saloon at 426 West Camden Street, Baltimore. . . .

On June 13, 1902, when I was seven years old my father and mother placed me in St. Mary's Industrial School in Baltimore. It has since been called an orphanage and a reform school. It was, in fact, a training school for orphans, incorrigibles, delinquents, boys whose homes had been broken by divorce, runaways picked up on the streets of Baltimore, and children of poor parents who had no other means of providing an education for them.

I was listed as an incorrigible, and I guess I was. . . . I chewed tobacco when I was seven, not that I enjoyed it especially, but, from my observation around the saloon it seemed the normal thing to do.

I was released from St. Mary's in July 1902, but my parents returned me there in November of the same year. My people moved to a new neighborhood just before Christmas 1902, and I was released to them again. This time I stayed 'out' until 1904, but then they put me back again and I was not released again until 1908. Shortly after my mother died I was returned to St. Mary's once more by my father. He took me back home in 1911 and returned me in 1912. I stayed in school—learning to be a tailor and shirtmaker—until February 27, 1914. The last item on my "record" at St. Mary's was a single sentence, written in the flowing hand of one of the teachers. It read:

"He is going to join the Balt. Baseball Team."

Ruth said he played in the band at St. Mary's and always pointed with pride to this accomplishment, frequently reminding friends that he also was a musician as well as a ball player. Curiously enough, however, no one ever discovered what instrument the Babe played, although he always stoutly denied that it was the bass drum.

But baseball captivated his fancy most, and now began a train of circumstances that was to carry this black-haired, raw-boned youngster to fame and a fortune that was estimated as close to $1 million. It also happened that Brother Benedict, one of the instructors at St. Mary's, was a great lover of the national pastime.

Using baseball, therefore, as the most plausible means to a laudable end in keeping the Babe out of mischief as much as possible, the good brother encouraged the youngster to play as much as he could. The Babe scarcely needed encouragement. Every hour he was allowed to spare from his classrooms found him on the ball field.

He batted left-handed and threw left-handed. He played on his school team, also on a semiprofessional team. He also played pretty nearly every position on the field. At the age of nineteen he astounded even his sponsor, Brother Benedict, who now saw a real means of livelihood ahead for the young man, though little dreaming at the time to what heights he would soar.

He recommended the Babe to his friend, Jack Dunn, then owner of the Baltimore Orioles of the International League, and Ruth received a trial, alternating in the outfield and in the pitcher's box. That was in 1914. The same summer he was sold to the Boston Red Sox for $2,900, and after a brief period of farming out with Providence, was recalled to become a regular.

Under the direction of Bill Carrigan, then manager of the Red Sox, Ruth rapidly developed into one of the most talented left-handed pitchers ever in the majors. He had tremendous speed and a baffling cross-fire curve, which greatly impressed Ed Barrow, later to become associated with Colonel Ruppert as general manager of the Yankees. Barrow became the leader of the Red Sox in 1918 and gave much time to Ruth's development.

But even then he also displayed unmistakable talent for batting a ball with tremendous power and with unusual frequency, and Barrow, one of baseball's greatest men of vision, decided to convert Ruth permanently into an outfielder on the theory that a great hitter could be built into a greater attraction than a great pitcher.

It was quite a momentous decision, for in the 1918 World Series against the Cubs Ruth had turned in two masterful performances on the mound for the Red Sox, winning both his games. He had also turned in one victory for the Red Sox against Brooklyn in the World Series of 1916.

But Barrow had also seen Ruth, in 1918, hit eleven home runs, an astonishing number for that era, particularly for a pitcher, and his mind was made up.

The next year—1919—Ruth, pitching only occasionally, now and then helping out at first base, but performing mostly in the outfield, cracked twenty-nine home runs, and the baseball world began to buzz as it hadn't since the advent of Ty Cobb and the immortal Christy Mathewson. This total surpassed by four the then accepted major league record for home runs in a season, set by Buck Freeman with the Washington club in 1899.

But it was the following year—1920—that was to mark the turning point, not only in Babe Ruth's career but in the entire course of organized baseball. Indeed, baseball men are almost in accord in the belief that Babe Ruth, more than any individual, and practically single-handed, rescued the game from what threatened to be one of its darkest periods following the "Black Sox" scandal of 1919.

The first sensation came early that winter when Ruth was sold by Harry Frazee, then owner of the Red Sox, to the Yankees, owned jointly by the two colonels, Jacob Ruppert and Tillinghast L'Hommedieu Huston, for a reported price of $125,000. It may even have been more, for in making the purchase the Yankee owners also assumed numerous financial obligations then harassing the Boston owner, and the matter was very involved. But whatever the price, it was a record sum, and New York prepared to welcome its latest hero prospect.

The Babe did not disappoint. The Yankees were then playing their home games at the Polo Grounds, home of the Giants, and before the close of the 1920 season they were already giving their more affluent rivals and landlords a stiff run for the city's baseball patronage.

Ruth surpassed all expectations by crashing out the unheard-of total of fifty-four home runs, and crowds that hitherto had lavished their attention on the Giants now jammed the historic Polo Grounds to see the marvelous Bambino hit a homer.

But scarcely had the echoes from the thunderous roars that greeted the Ruthian batting feats subsided than another explosion was touched off that rattled the entire structure of baseball down to its subcellar. The scandal of the World Series of 1919 broke into print, and through the winter of 1920–21 the "throwing" of that series by certain White Sox players to the Reds was on every tongue.

The baseball owners of both major leagues were in a panic, fearful that the public's confidence in what they had so proudly called America's national pastime had been shaken beyond repair. True, they had induced the late Kenesaw Mountain Landis, a federal judge, to assume the position of commissioner with unlimited powers to safeguard against a repetition of such a calamity, but they feared it was not enough.

With considerable misgivings they saw the 1921 season get under way, and then, as the popular song of the day ran, "Along Came Ruth."

Inside of a fortnight the fans of the nation had forgotten all about the Black Sox, as they had come to be called, as its attention became centered in an even greater demonstration of superlative batting skill by the amazing Babe Ruth. Home runs began to scale off his bat in droves, crowds jammed ball parks in every city in which he appeared, and when he closed the season with a total of fifty-nine circuit clouts, surpassing by five his own record of the year before, the baseball world lay at his feet.

In addition to that, the Yankees that year captured the first pennant ever won by New York in the American League, and Ruth was now fairly launched upon the first chapter of the golden harvest. With the help of his towering war club, the Yankees won again in 1922 and repeated in 1923, in addition to winning the world's championship that year.

Also in 1923 came into being the "House That Ruth Built," meaning the great Yankee Stadium with its seating capacity of more than 70,000, which Colonel Ruppert decided to erect the previous year in order to make himself clear and independent of the Giants, whose tenant he had been at the Polo Grounds. The right-field bleachers became "Ruthville." Homers soared into them in great abundance and the exploitation of Babe Ruth, the greatest slugger of all times, was at its height.

But now there crept in a dark episode, decidedly less glamorous, though spectacular enough, and which must be chronicled in order to appreciate more fully the second chapter of the golden harvest. Money was now pouring upon the Babe and was being poured out as speedily. In 1921 he had drawn $20,000, and the following season he signed a five-year contract at $52,000 a season. In addition to this he was collecting royalties on all sorts of ventures.

But money meant nothing to the Babe, except as a convenient means for lavish entertainment. He gambled recklessly, lost, and laughed uproariously. The Ruthian waistline began to assume alarming proportions. He still took his baseball seriously enough on the field, but training had become a horrible bore.

Of such phenomenal strength, there seemed to be no limits to his vitality or stamina. It was no trick at all for him to spend an evening rositering with convivial companions right through sunup and until game time the next afternoon and then pound a home run.

Along in the 1924 season Colonel Ruppert began to fear he had made a mistake in having signed the Babe to that long-term contract. The Yankees lost the pennant that year and there came ominous rumblings that Miller Huggins, the diminutive manager who had just piloted the Yankees through three successful pennant years, was not in harmony with the Babe at all.

There even had been trouble back in 1921 when Ruth openly flouted Commissioner Landis by playing on a barnstorming tour that fall after the limit date set by the commissioner. The following spring Landis, in order to demonstrate his authority, suspended Ruth for thirty days from the opening of the season.

But it was not until 1925 that the real crash came and high living proved as exacting in collecting its toll as the high commissioner. Coming north at the end of the training season Ruth collapsed at the railroad station at Asheville, North Carolina, from a complication of ailments.

He was helped aboard the train, carried off on a stretcher on the team's arrival in New York, and spent weeks in a hospital. He did not appear again in a Yankee lineup until June 1.

Nor had all the lesson been yet fully learned. Later in the same campaign Huggins, exasperated beyond all measure at the Babe's wayward way of deporting himself, slapped a $5,000 fine on him for "misconduct off the ball field." It was the highest fine ever imposed on a ball player, and Ruth at first took it as a joke. But Huggins stuck by his guns, received the backing of Colonel Ruppert, who was now the sole owner of the club, and the fine came from the Babe's paycheck.

Now the lesson was learned and another startling change came over the Babe. He became, almost overnight, one of Miller Huggins's stanchest supporters. He trained faithfully in 1926, hammered forty-seven homers as against a meager twenty-five in 1925, and started the Yankees on another pennant-winning era. Sixty homers, a new record, sailed off his bat in 1927, and Ruth was a greater figure in baseball than ever.

Another pennant followed that year and still another in 1928, on top of which the Yankees swept through two World Series triumphs in those two years without the loss of a single game.

In the spring of 1929, several months after his first wife, from whom he had been estranged for a number of years, died in a fire in Boston, the Babe married Mrs. Claire Hodgson, formerly an actress, and to her also is given a great deal of credit for the complete reformation of the Babe, who in the closing years of his baseball activities trained as faithfully to fulfill what he considered his obligation to his public as it was humanly possible.

Simultaneously with this, Ruth suddenly became a shrewd businessman with an eye to the future. Giving heed to the advice of Colonel Ruppert and Ed Barrow, the Babe invested his earnings carefully. In 1927 he became the highest salaried player of his time with a three-year contract at $70,000 a year. In 1930 he signed a two-year contract at $80,000 per season, but in 1932, acceding to the economic pressure of the times, accepted a $75,000 stipend for one season.

That proved an excellent investment, for the Yankees won another pennant that year and defeated the Cubs in four straight games, Ruth causing a sensation by indicating to the spectators in Chicago where he meant to hit the ball when he made two home runs in the third game of the Series for the championship. The next year saw a further decline in the salary of the star to $52,000, and in 1934 he signed for $35,000.

At the close of his baseball career it was estimated that in his twenty-two years in the major leagues he had earned in salaries $896,000, plus $41,445 as his share of World Series receipts. In addition, he was reputed to have made $1 million from endorsements, barnstorming tours, movies, and radio appearances.

As a consequence, when he retired, the Babe was able to live in comfort, maintaining a large apartment on New York's West Side. For, despite his earlier extravagances, he later invested so well he was able to realize a monthly income of $2,500 by the time he had reached forty-five.

In addition to the great crowds he had drawn steadily to major league parks, he also brought vast sums into the Yankee coffers from spring exhibition tours. In 1929 and 1930 the Yanks booked two tours through Texas and the Midwest on their way north from the training camp in Florida and played to record-smashing crowds that stormed hotel lobbies and blocked traffic in all directions to get a glimpse of baseball's most famous character.

And through all this new homage showered upon him, he steadfastly remained the same Babe, more serious-minded, but as cordial and affable as ever. The youngsters he worshiped possibly as much as they worshiped him. In Waco, Texas, he broke up an exhibition game by inviting some of the kids to come out on the field and roll around on the grass. They poured out of the stands by the thousands, overran the field, swamped the local police, and ended the game.

Ruth came to the parting of the ways with the Yankees after the 1934 season. He had always aspired to be a manager, and that winter he asked Colonel Ruppert, with his accustomed bluntness, to make him leader of the New York team. Ruppert was satisfied with the results obtained by Joe McCarthy in winning the 1932 World Series after coming from the Cubs in 1931 and refused. However, he said that he would not stand in the way of Ruth if the latter could find a place as manager.

The opening came in the spring of 1935, when Judge Emil Fuchs, then president of the Boston Braves, offered Ruth a contract as a player at $25,000 a year, with a percentage from exhibition games and a percentage of the gain in the earnings of the club, together with a promise of becoming manager the following season. Ruppert gave Ruth his release and he joined the National League team at its training camp in St. Petersburg, Florida, that spring.

Ruth never was a success with the Braves. He was his old self as a batsman and player only in spots and the team sank into the National League cellar. On May 25, 1935, in Pittsburgh he showed the last flash of his former greatness when he batted three home runs in consecutive times at bat at Forbes Field, but a week later, on June 2, after a dispute with Fuchs, he asked for and received his release. He had several offers from minor league teams after that, but refused them all.

It was not until June 17, 1938, that his chance came to reenter the big leagues. Then he was named a coach of the Brooklyn Dodgers. Burleigh Grimes, the manager of the team, recommending the move, said, "you can't keep a man like that out of baseball." Although the team was a loser, Ruth entered into the work of upbuilding enthusiastically and was hailed with the usual acclaim around the circuit and in towns where he played in exhibition games.

Although Ruth's continued popularity helped the Dodgers to draw additional fans through their turnstiles, a service for which the club paid him a $15,000 salary, he was not reengaged as coach at the close of the 1938 season.

It was then that Leo Durocher was appointed manager to succeed Grimes.

Ruth, taking his dismissal in good spirit, explained that a new manager necessarily would want to make his own choice for the coaching jobs, and he wished the Dodgers good luck.

The Bambino once again became the retired businessman, and as he returned to the role of "baseball's forgotten man," he increased his activities on the links. His name soon became associated with some of golf's leading players, while his scores consistently ran in the low seventies.

However, he never overlooked lending a hand to his first love wherever baseball offered him some opportunity for showing himself. During 1939 he appeared at the World's Fair baseball school in the role of instructor, took part in the Old-timers Game in the baseball centennial celebration at Cooperstown, played a prominent role in the Lou Gehrig Appreciation Day ceremonies, and in the spring of 1940 appeared for a time with a baseball training school at Palatka, Florida.

During 1941, Ruth, principally through the medium of his golfing prowess, stayed in the public eye. During the summer he engaged in a series of matches with his old diamond rival, Cobb, the proceeds going to the British War Relief Fund and the United Service Organizations. Cobb, victor in the first match in Boston, 3 and 2, lost the second match at Fresh Meadow, New York, 1 up on the nineteenth hole, but came back to defeat the Babe in the deciding tilt in Detroit, 3 and 2.

Later in the year Ruth signed a contract to appear in the Samuel Goldwyn motion picture based on the life of his famous teammate, Lou Gehrig, with the Babe appearing as himself.

The Babe hit the headlines and frightened his friends before 1942 scarcely had begun. On the morning of January 3 he was removed to a hospital in an ambulance, the reason being "an upset nervous condition," partly brought on by an automobile accident in which he was involved.

But three weeks later Ruth was off on a hunting trip in upstate New York and by February was in Hollywood, teaching Gary Cooper (who was to portray Gehrig) how to bat left-handed and signing autographs for screen stars.

On April 9 Ruth went to the Hollywood Hospital suffering from pneumonia; he was described by his doctor as "a borderline case," but two days later the Babe's countless friends and well-wishers were cheered by the same physician's statement: "I believe he is over the hump." Ruth was out of the hospital by April 22 and back on the movie lot to complete his work in the Gehrig film.

During that and succeeding war years Ruth answered any and all demands for his appearance at war bond rallies and charity enterprises. He played in golf tournaments, went bowling, and sold bonds. On August 23, 1942, he paired with the late Walter Johnson, another of baseball's immortals, at Yankee Stadium to aid in a benefit show for two war services.

With Johnson pitching, the Babe came through, as he always had, by hitting a "home run" into the right-field seats and "rounding the bases" via a short cut from first to third base. That was his final homer.

Late in 1943 Ruth proved a bad prophet when he predicted that major league baseball would become a war casualty in 1944, "if not sooner." His prophesying was as wholehearted as his ball playing had been, for he said, "It's a cinch they won't open the ball parks next year."

Although never realizing an ambition to manage a major league club, Ruth became manager for a day in July of 1943, when he piloted a team of all-stars, including such players as Ted Williams and Dom DiMaggio, to a triumph over the Boston Braves as part of a charity field-day program in Boston. A dozen days later he filled the same role in a similar game at Yankee Stadium.

Ruth's activity in aiding war causes increased in 1944 and it was in March of that year that he was the subject of one of the oddest dispatches of the conflict. It came from Cape Gloucester, New Britain, where United States Marines were fighting the Japanese and recounted that when the Japanese charged the Marine lines their battle cry was: "To hell with Babe Ruth!"

The Babe didn't know, or care, that nine years before the Japanese sounded that battle cry a Japanese publisher had been assassinated by a Japanese fanatic and that Ruth was partly blamed for it. The assassin had said the publisher's crime was in sponsoring the Japanese tour of a group of American ball players, headed by Babe Ruth.

In June of 1944 Ruth went into the hospital once more, this time to have cartilage removed from his knee. Reports immediately followed that he might try to play ball again as a pinch hitter.

Early in 1946, Ruth took a trip to Mexico as a guest of the fabulous Pasquel brothers, "raiders" of American organized baseball. This resulted in a rumor that he would become commissioner of the Mexican National League, the Pasquel loop, but as usual nothing came of it.

On his return to New York Ruth disclosed that he had sought the manager's berth with the Newark club, owned by the Yankees, but that "all I got was a good pushing around" by Larry MacPhail. The Babe also praised the Pasquels and at the same time revealed that he had turned down an offer of $20,000 from the Federal League while getting $600 a season from Baltimore.

"I turned it down because we were told by organized baseball that if we jumped we would be barred for life. But nobody was barred for life and I just got jobbed out of $20,000 without a thank you from anybody."

There was scarcely room for real bitterness in the expansive and warm Ruthian temperament, but the big fellow undoubtedly did feel at times a resentment against the owners in major league baseball because no place in it ever was found for him. And whatever slight flame of resentment may have lighted in him was frequently fanned by many writers who openly chided the baseball moguls for sidestepping the great Bambino.

Through the unhappy medium of a protracted illness and a serious neck operation that kept him hospitalized from late November 1946 to mid-February 1947, Ruth came back into the public eye. Recurrent reports that his condition was critical resulted in a deluge of messages from sympathetic well-wishers.

There was general rejoicing among his legions of followers when he was sufficiently recovered to leave the hospital. That this feeling was shared in official baseball circles was promptly indicated when Baseball Commissioner A. B. "Happy" Chandler paid unprecedented tribute to the Sultan of Swat by designating April 27, 1947, as Babe Ruth Day.

All organized baseball joined on this date in honoring the man who contributed so much to the game. Ruth himself was present at Yankee Stadium, where a crowd of 58,339 turned out for ceremonies that were broadcast over the world and piped into the other major league ballparks.

Extremely conscious of his debt to the "kids of America," to whose loyal support he attributed his success, Ruth identified himself with welfare programs after his discharge from the hospital. He was engaged by the Ford Motor Company as a consultant in connection with its participation in the American Legion junior baseball program, and he was named by Mayor William O'Dwyer of New York a permanent honorary chairman of the Police Athletic League.

In May 1947, he established and made the first contribution to the Babe Ruth Foundation, Inc., an organization whose resources were to be devoted to the interests of underprivileged youth.

Although the ravages of his illness left little of his robust physique, the Babe, now gaunt and bent and his once resonant voice reduced to a rasping whisper, continued to astound his physicians by tackling his new job with all his old-time vigor. Throughout the summer he made innumerable public appearances all over the country.

On Sunday, September 28, the final day of the 1947 season, he returned to Yankee Stadium to receive another thunderous ovation. On this day, under the direction of MacPhail, a galaxy of more than forty stars of former Yankee and other American League world championship teams, assembled to engage in an Old-timers Day.

They included such immortals as Ty Cobb, Tris Speaker, Cy Young, George Sisler, Waite Hoyt, Bob Meusel, and Chief Bender, and with the Babe looking on from a box, the grizzled vets played a two-inning game. The entire day's receipts were turned over to the foundation.

Ruth continued his role as consultant, making appearances all over the country. He went to Hollywood to help with the filming of his life story. While there, the Babe was informed that the Yankees were planning to celebrate the twenty-fifth anniversary of Yankee Stadium. He readily agreed to participate in the ceremonies. He accepted the managership of the 1923 Yankees, who were to play an abbreviated exhibition game against later-year Yankees, to be piloted by Barrow.

June 13, 1948, was the date set for Silver Anniversary Day. It turned out to be a memorable day, one that Ruth, despite his physical condition, would not have missed for anything. Despite a wretched day—rain, fog, etc.—the Babe donned his old uniform with the number 3 on the back. When he was introduced and walked slowly to home plate, a thunderous ovation from 49,641 men, women, and children greeted him.

Many in the gathering wept as Ruth, in a raspy voice, told how happy he was to have hit the first homer ever achieved in the stadium; how proud he was to have been associated with such fine players, and how glad he was to be back with them, even if only for a day.

Bob Shawkey, Sad Sam Jones, Whitey Witt, Bob Meusel, Waite Hoyt, Carl Mays, Bullet Joe Bush, Wally Pipp, Mike McNally, Wally Schang, and others from the 1923 club that annexed the first world championship by a Yankee aggregation as well as Bill Dickey, Lefty Gomez, George Selkirk, Red Rolfe, and others who came later—all were on hand to pay homage to the Babe.

It was the last time that number 3 was worn by a Yankee player. For the Babe turned his uniform over to the Hall of Fame, retired for all time. It was sent to the baseball shrine at Cooperstown, New York, where it was placed among the Ruth collection there.

Ruth's team scored a 2–0, two-inning victory that day, and the man to whom a big league manager's job was never given managed a winner in the House That Ruth Built.

Finally, on August 16, 1948, Ruth succumbed to throat cancer.

The "Called" Home Run

By JOHN DREBINGER

Four home runs, two by the master hitter of them all, Babe Ruth, and the other pair by his almost equally proficient colleague, Columbia Lou Gehrig, advanced the New York Yankees to within one game of their third World Series sweep on October 1, 1932.

The American League champions once again overpowered the Chicago Cubs to win their third straight game of the fall classic after having taken the first two games at Yankee Stadium.

Those four blows made the final score 7–5. They crushed not only the National League standard bearers but a gathering of 51,000 that jammed Wrigley Field to the limits of its capacity and packed two wooden temporary bleachers outside the park. Included in the gathering was Governor Franklin D. Roosevelt of New York, then the Democratic presidential candidate.

It was by far the most turbulent and bitterly fought engagement of the Series. The Cubs, inspired by a show of civic enthusiasm, battled fiercely and courageously.

They even struck back with a couple of lusty homers on their own account, one by Kiki Cuyler, the other by Gabby Hartnett.

Both the game and all its trimmings provided a much livelier spectacle than either of the two previous encounters. In sharp contrast to the rather matter-of-fact manner in which New York had accepted the first two battles, the crowd in Chicago was as keyed up as the players, if not more so.

It was a warm day, clear and sunny, though rather windy. There was a gay, holiday spirit in the air that never forsook the gathering, for Chicago puts a great deal more fervor in its baseball than does New York. It seemed as though the fans of this midwestern metropolis simply would not believe how severely and decisively their champions had been manhandled by the mighty Yankees in the first two games in the East.

They roared their approval of every good play made by the Cubs. They playfully tossed bright yellow lemons at Babe Ruth and booed him thoroughly as the great man carried on a pantomime act while standing at the plate.

Then they sat back, awed and spellbound, as the Babe, casting aside his buffoonery, smashed one of the longest home runs ever seen at Wrigley Field.

It was an amazing demonstration by one of baseball's outstanding figures, who a few weeks ago was ill and confined to his bed. It confounded the crowd, which in paid attendance numbered 49,986 and had contributed $211,912 in receipts.

The Cubs took the field with their hopes resting upon the stout right arm of Charlie Root, but Charlie was unequal to the task. He failed to survive five rounds, retiring immediately after Ruth and Gehrig had blasted their second two homers. These came in succession in the fifth like a flash of lightning and a clap of thunder.

Both were held fairly well in restraint in the latter rounds by Pat Malone and the left-handed Jakie May. But aside from providing the crowd with a chance to give vent to boos, the earlier damage these two had inflicted proved far sufficient to carry the day.

Ruth and Gehrig simply dominated the scene from start to finish, and they began their performance early. When the two marched to the plate during the batting rehearsal they at once thrilled the crowd by uncorking a series of tremendous drives into the temporary wooden bleachers.

The Babe's very first practice shot almost cleared the top of the wooden structure, and he followed it with several more prodigious drives. Gehrig produced some more, and each time the ball soared into those densely packed stands the crowd gasped. The spectacle certainly could not have been very heartening to the Cubs.

And when the battle proper began, both kept right on firing. The Babe's two homers were his first of the Series, but they sent his all-time World Series record for home runs to fifteen. For Gehrig, his two gave him a total of three for the Series and an all-time record of seven.

Fittingly enough, the Babe was the first to touch off the explosion and his opening smash sent the Yanks away to a three-run lead in the very first inning. In fact, the crowd had scarcely recovered its composure after a tumultuous reception it had accorded the home team when it was forced to suffer its first annoyance.

There was a sharp wind blowing across the playing field toward the right-field bleachers that threatened to raise havoc with the players, and it did very shortly.

Eager and tense, the crowd watched Root pitch to Earle Combs, the first Yankee batter. It at once roared approbation as Combs sent a drive squarely into the hands of young Billy Jurges, who was playing shortstop for the Cubs in place of the injured Mark Koenig.

But the next moment the throng voiced its dismay as Jurges unfurled a throw that sailed high over Manager Charlie Grimm's head at first and into the Yankee dugout.

Root was plainly flustered as Combs, under the prevailing ground rule, was allowed to advance to second base. Root strove to steady himself, but he passed Joey Sewell and faced Ruth. Cheers and jeers mingled as the great Yankee batter made his first official appearance at the plate in Chicago's portion of the setting.

Root pitched cautiously, fearful of what would happen if he allowed the Babe to shoot one high in the air with that brisk breeze behind it. His first two offerings went wide of the plate. Then he put one over, and away the ball went. It was a lofty shot that soared on and on until it dropped deep in the temporary stands. Thus, the Cubs, who had planned to fight so desperately for this game, already were three runs to the bad.

But desperately they fought, nevertheless, and in the lower half of the same inning they gave their cohorts the chance to do some wholehearted cheering by getting one of these tallies back.

The wind, which had annoyed Root so much, also seemed to trouble Yankee pitcher George Pipgras. He passed Herman, whereupon the crowd set up a roar as though the Series already had been won. Woody English was retired on a fly to Ruth, who was performing in left field today in order to avoid the glare of the sun.

But Kiki Cuyler, who might have been the hero of this struggle had Ruth and Gehrig been playing elsewhere, lifted a two-bagger over Ben Chapman's head in right against the wire screening in front of the bleachers, and Herman scored amid tumultuous cheering.

But two innings later Gehrig, after an uneventful first inning, stepped into the picture. Leaning heavily into Root's pitch, he sent another mighty shot soaring into the right-field bleachers. That made the score 4 to 1.

At this point, however, the Cubs staged their most gallant fight of the day. With one out in the lower half of the third, Cuyler again produced a jubilant uproar by shooting a homer into the right-field stands, and this at once inspired his comrades to redouble their efforts against Pipgras. Riggs Stephenson slashed a single to right, and though he was forced by Johnny Moore, Manager Charlie Grimm lined a drive to right that Ben Chapman did not play any too well. The ball shot past the Alabama Arrow for a two-bagger, and Moore scored all the way from first.

That left the Cubs only one run in arrears, and in the fourth they drew even amid the most violent vocal demonstration of the afternoon. Jurges, eager to make amends for his earlier miscue, slapped a low liner to left, and the crowd howled with glee as Ruth failed in a heroic attempt to make a shoestring catch of the ball. Jurges gained two bases on the hit.

Good-naturedly, the Babe doffed his cap in acknowledgment to the adverse plaudits of the fans and the play went on. Tony Lazzeri made a spectacular catch of Herman's high, twisting pop fly back of second base. But the next moment Tony booted English's grounder and Jurges raced over the plate with the tally that tied the score at 4–all.

But it seems decidedly unhealthy for anyone to taunt the great man Ruth too much, and very soon the crowd was to learn its lesson. A single lemon rolled out to the plate as Ruth came up in the fifth and in no mistaken motions the Babe notified the crowd that the nature of his retaliation would be a wallop right out of the confines of the park.

Root pitched two balls and two strikes, while Ruth signaled with his fingers after each pitch to let the spectators know exactly how the situation stood. Then the mightiest blow of all fell.

It was a tremendous smash that bore straight down the center of the field in an enormous arc, came down alongside the flagpole and disappeared behind the corner formed by the scoreboard and the end of the right-field bleachers.

It was Ruth's fifteenth home run in World Series competition and easily one of his most gorgeous. The crowd, suddenly unmindful of everything save that it had just witnessed an epic feat, hailed the Babe with a salvo of applause.

Root, badly shaken, now faced Gehrig, and his feelings well can be imagined. The crowd was still too much excited over the Ruth incident to realize what was happening when Columbia Lou lifted an enormous fly high in the air. As it sailed on the wings of the lake breeze, the ball just cleared the high flagpole and dropped in the temporary stand.

Grimm, the player-manager of the Cubs, called time. Consolingly he invited Root to retire to the less turbulent confines of the clubhouse and ordered Pat Malone to the mound.

Pat filled the bases with three passes but he escaped the inning without further trouble. From then on the game, like its two predecessors, passed on to its very obvious conclusion with the exception of a final flurry in the ninth, including Hartnett's home run.

Another Piece of the Legend
By ROBERT McG. THOMAS, Jr.

There are those who will tell you that little Johnny Sylvester was never that sick and certainly not dying.

They will tell you that Babe Ruth never promised to hit a home run for him in Game Four of the 1926 World Series, and that the three home runs the Babe did hit in that game in no way saved the eleven-year-old youngster's life.

Any representations to the contrary, these people will tell you, were simply embellishments of a trivial incident by an oversentimental press in a hypersentimental age.

Such people are known as cynics. While their skepticism is understandable in view of the myriad of fulsome and contradictory contemporary accounts of the famous promise and its even more famous fulfillment, such doubt is mere chaff beneath the grindstone of a mighty legend, and as it turns out, against the hard kernel of fact.

As the record makes clear enough, Johnny Sylvester was severely ill in October 1926. And Babe Ruth did promise him a home run. And if the three homers Ruth hit against the Cardinals in St. Louis on October 6 did not bring about an instant cure, they most certainly did no harm.

For little Johnny Sylvester not only lived to tell the tale, he also spent the next six decades doing just that.

And when John Dale Sylvester died in 1989 at the age of seventy-four, it seemed occasion enough to tell it once more.

Sylvester was a 1937 graduate of Princeton University who served as a lieutenant in the navy in World War II and later as president of Amscomatic, Inc., a manufacturer of packing machinery in Long Island City, Queens.

There was nothing Sylvester could have done to match the pinnacle he reached in 1926 when he became the most famous little boy in America.

One reason the skeptics have had a field day debunking the incident is that a range of ailments were ascribed to Sylvester, among them blood poisoning, a sinus condition, a spinal fusion, a spinal infection, and a back problem.

According to his son, John D. Sylvester, Jr., and at least one contemporary account, the ailment was an infection of the forehead caused by a kick from a horse after the youngster fell while riding, in Essex Fells, New Jersey. His father, Horace C. Sylvester, Jr., a vice president of the National City Bank in New York, maintained an estate there.

Most accounts indicate the youngster was dying. One had his doctors giving him thirty minutes to live before he rallied after his father vowed to fulfill his last request for a baseball autographed by Ruth.

It is still unclear whether the youngster initiated the request for an autographed ball, or whether his father or an uncle decided such a present might cheer him up.

What seems clear enough, however, is that urgent telegrams went out from the family to the Yankees in St. Louis and back came an airmail package containing two balls, one autographed by the Cardinal team and the other with the signatures of several Yankees and a special message from Ruth: "I'll knock a homer for you on Wednesday."

(The version of the incident in the movie *The Babe Ruth Story*, showing Ruth delivering the promise at the youngster's hospital bed, seems to have been wrong on at least two counts. The promise was not made in person and the youngster was apparently never in a hospital.)

The Babe did better than that, of course, but even he was not invincible. A follow-up note from Ruth "to my sick little pal" dated October 9, the day of Game Six, said "I will try to knock you another homer, maybe two today."

Alas, Ruth went without a homer and the Yankees lost, as they did the next day when an unpromised Ruth home run was not enough to save the game or the Series for the Yankees.

Or as a consoling Johnny Sylvester told the Babe when Ruth made a well-publicized visit to the youngster after the Series, "I'm sorry the Yanks lost."

Babe Ruth Day
By LOUIS EFFRAT

Wherever organized baseball was played on April 27, 1947, Babe Ruth was honored. Ceremonies at Yankee Stadium, where the Babe was given the greatest ovation in the history of the national pastime, were broadcast throughout the world, and what Ruth and others had to say was piped to other ball parks.

However, for the real impact, for the fullest effect, and for the solemnity of the occasion, one had to be among the 58,339 followers of the game at the stadium, often referred to as the House That Ruth Built. This was Babe Ruth Day.

Older, grayer, no longer the robust Babe who wrote diamond history, George Herman Ruth stood before a microphone at home plate. He talked to the crowd, the biggest baseball turnout of the year. And what he had to say was extemporaneous. Babe said he did not need to write down things that came from the heart. Francis Cardinal Spellman delivered the invocation, Commissioner A. B. Chandler, American League President Will Harridge, National League President Ford Frick, and Larry Cutler, a thirteen-year-old lad who represented the American Legion players, were the other speakers.

A bit unsteady at the outset, the Babe, in a raspy voice that obviously had been weakened by recent serious operations, dwelt principally on the youth of the land. Ruth's main interest toward the end of his life was the American Legion baseball program, for which he served as a consultant, and it was to the boys that he directed his talk.

"Thank you very much, ladies and gentlemen," he began. "You know how bad my voice sounds. Well, it feels just as bad. You know this baseball game of ours comes up from the youth. That means the boys. And after you've been a boy, and grow up to know how to play ball, then you come to the boys you see representing themselves today in our national pastime."

Now the Babe's big smile was visible to everyone. Still a very sick man, he emphasized his remarks with a clenched fist and a wave of the hand.

"The only real game in the world, I think, is baseball," he continued. "As a rule, some people think if you give them a football or a baseball or something like that, naturally, they're athletes right away. But you can't do that in baseball. You've gotta start from way down at the bottom, when you're six or seven years old. You can't wait until you're fifteen or sixteen. You've gotta let it grow up with you, and if you're successful and you try hard enough, you're bound to come out on top, just like these boys have come to the top now.

"There's been so many lovely things said about me. I'm glad I had the opportunity to thank everybody. Thank you."

Then with a wave to the fans, the Babe walked down into the New York dugout. He had had his Day.

Several weeks of vacationing under a Florida sun brought the Babe to the stadium a tanned but still sick man. Just before he spoke, Ruth started to cough, and it appeared that he might break down because of the thunderous cheers that came his way. But once he started to talk, he was all right, still the champion. It was the many men who surrounded him on the field, players, newspaper and radio persons, who choked up.

Underneath the stands, Ruth again started to cough, and he had a few trying minutes before he was able to move to a box adjoining the Yankee dugout. There he joined Mrs. Ruth, his daughter, Mrs. Julian Flanders, and a friend, Emory C. Perry. Ruth remained until the start of the eighth inning of the Yankees-Senators game. He left with the score tied, 0–0, and did not see the Washington club score a run in the eighth and win, 1–0.

Cardinal Spellman was unable to remain for the ball game. Before he departed, though, there was a behind-the-scene get-together. "You've been a great inspiration to the boys and I want to tell you, you've been a great inspiration to me," said Cardinal Spellman, who then left with Monsignor Walter Kellenberg.

The crowd that had booed Commissioner Chandler cheered him when he paid tribute to Ruth. Presidents Harridge and Frick also paid their respects. The former gave Ruth a plaque, inscribed by American League club owners, while Frick handed the Babe a book containing autographs of every player, club owner, and official in the National League. Thirteen-year-old Cutler welcomed the Babe back to baseball.

The Yankees, for whom Ruth used to play, and the American League handed envelopes to the Babe. It was believed that these contained checks for sizable sums. However, the donors were reluctant to discuss this. President Larry MacPhail of the Yankees said, "Anything about what we gave Ruth will have to come from him."

The Babe's comment was, "I have not opened or looked at a single thing I received."

SECRETARIAT

1970–1989

By STEVEN CRIST

T HE FLAGS in the infield at Belmont Park were flying at full staff on the day he died because tradition says not to lower them for the death of a horse. One fan, who spoke for many, disagreed.

"He wasn't a horse," Bennett Liebman said sadly. "He was Secretariat."

Horse lovers were touched by the death of a champion who not only may have been the fastest who ever raced, but who also became a symbol of brilliance and beauty beyond his breed.

A son of Bold Ruler and the Princequillo mare Somethingroyal, Secretariat is survived by more than 300 sons and daughters, including Risen Star, 1988 Preakness and Belmont Stakes winner, and Lady's Secret, the filly who was named Horse of the Year for 1986. But it was Secretariat's sixteen-month racing career in 1972 and 1973, rather than his sixteen seasons at stud, for which he will be remembered.

"Horse racing was in a down period," said Penny Chenery, Secretariat's owner during his racing career. "The country was in a blue mood. It was the time of Watergate and the Nixon scandals, and people wanted something to make them feel good. This red horse with the blue-and-white blinkers and silks seemed to epitomize an American hero."

Secretariat is widely acknowledged as the greatest racehorse of the second half of the century, and only Man o' War and Citation are mentioned in the same breath when most racing fans talk of the great ones. Other horses compiled better records than his 16 victories in 21 career starts, and his earnings of $1,316,808 never approached record levels. But Secretariat's best days were the best performances that have ever been seen on a race track.

Born March 29, 1970, at the Meadow Stud in Doswell, Virginia, Secretariat was a colt of picture-book prettiness, with a glowing and coppery coat, three white stockings, and a white stripe that ran from his forehead to the tip of his nose. He would grow into a strapping colt with a barrel chest and a stride so enormous it defied belief.

Secretariat lost his debut at New York's Aqueduct Race Track on July 4, 1972, but then finished first in his next eight starts and was named Horse of the Year. He won that title again in 1973, when in five weeks during May and June he set new standards for the breed.

On May 5, he won the ninety-ninth Kentucky Derby by 2½ lengths and set a track record of 1:59⅖ for a mile and a quarter, which still stands. Two weeks later, he won the Preakness Stakes, and then on June 9 at Belmont Park

The Bettmann Archive

he turned in what remains the single most astonishing performance in American racing history. Despite setting a blazing early pace, he drew away to win by 31 lengths and ran the mile and a half in 2 minutes 24 seconds, still more than 2 full seconds faster than any other winning Belmont time.

Those three victories made Secretariat the first winner of racing's Triple Crown since Citation in 1948, and he became a national celebrity, knocking world news off magazine covers and requiring his owner's agent, William Morris, to handle demands for endorsements and personal appearances.

Secretariat, regularly trained by Lucien Laurin and ridden by Ron Turcotte, was retired after winning four of his next six starts, including the first Marlboro Cup. Mrs. Cheney had syndicated him for stallion duty for a record $6.08 million to save her father's farm.

For the next fifteen years he lived the lush life of a stallion at Claiborne Farm in Paris, Kentucky. At stud, Secretariat sired the first yearling to fetch more than $1 million at auction, and at least forty stakes winners. He regularly ranked among the world's top twenty stallions, but was unfairly regarded as a disappointment for failing to sire a flock of runners with talent equal to his own.

His popularity endured long after his racing career. He received dozens of letters and birthday cards each year from fans, and he was a shameless ham as well as a mischievous greeter to the thousands who visited him at Claiborne.

Secretariat enjoyed intimidating human visitors by charging them at full speed and then turning away at the last instant. He relished another game in which he would feign calmness, approach a visitor for a pat on the nose, then suddenly drench him with a mouthful of grass.

In the fall of 1989, Secretariat contracted laminitis, a painful and degenerative disease of the inner tissue of the hoofs that often affects older and heavier horses. His condition improved gradually and he was able to graze in his paddock each day, but then deteriorated suddenly.

The nineteen-year-old stallion was given a lethal injection on October 4, 1989, and buried near his sire, Bold Ruler, and grandsire, Nasrullah, at Claiborne.

The Triple Crown

By JOE NICHOLS

Secretariat won the 1973 Belmont Stakes with a finality that was incredible. The Meadow Stable star flashed to success in the 1½-mile event by the improbable margin of 31 lengths over Twice a Prince, his runner-up, and even with the big margin, he set a track record time of 2:24.

The performance was executed under a splendid ride by Ron Turcotte and was most noteworthy in that it enabled Secretariat to become the ninth winner of the Triple Crown for three-year-olds.

A quarter of a century earlier Citation turned the trick, and Secretariat was the first since then to do so. He won the Kentucky Derby at 1¼ miles on May 5, and the Preakness at 1³⁄₁₆ miles on May 19.

A crowd of 69,138 attended the 105th running of the race. It had five contestants, and the advance indications were that it would turn out to be a duel between Secretariat, whose payoff at the end was $2.20 for $2 to win and $2.40 to place, and Sham, who competed in the silks of Sigmund Sommer.

Sham was in there for a while, but he found the going too tough as the contest went on, and he wound up in the most unlikely spot—last place. The colt that finished back of Twice a Prince was Arthur Appleton's My Gallant, who was a half-length out of second place and 13 lengths ahead of C. V. Whitney's Pvt. Smiles. Sham trailed that one by three-quarters of a length.

The race had a gross value of $150,200, with the five starters, and the share to the winner, who is trained by Lucien Laurin, was $90,120.

In the day or two preceding the Belmont, Sham's trainer, Frank "Pancho" Martin, had said he would send a "rabbit," Knightly Dawn, into the race to test Secretariat with an early pace, but the morning of the race Martin changed his mind and withdrew Knightly Dawn.

The race, as regards tight competition, was hardly a tingler, considering the huge margin of victory. But it held continuous excitement because of the superequine achievement of Secretariat.

At the start he went to the front with Sham, who was ridden by Laffit Pincay, and for a spell the pair raced together, the others being "nowhere."

Approaching the three-quarter pole, Turcotte turned around to spot his pursuer, who was two lengths behind. Assured that his margin was a comfortable one, Turcotte just sped away to the score, which had to be the easiest one of Secretariat's career, while Sham cracked completely under the fast pace.

The fractional times, most of them set by Secretariat, were 0:23⅘, 0:46⅕, 1:09⅘ and 1:59. The mark that Secretariat shattered was 2:26⅗, set by Gallant Man in the Belmont Stakes in 1957. Each horse in the Belmont carried scale weight of 126 pounds.

It was obvious through the going that Turcotte was out for the record with Secretariat just as he had done in the Kentucky Derby of 1¼ miles. In that race Secretariat, in beating Sham by 2½ lengths, was timed in 1:59⅖, beating the standard of 2:00.

In the Preakness of 1³⁄₁₆ miles there was a misunderstanding about Secretariat's time, and the matter was finally resolved with a clocking of 1:54⅖, as against the standard of 1:54. Some clockers caught Secretariat in 1:53⅖. In that race Sham also was the runner-up, again by 2½ lengths.

When he returned to the winner's circle yesterday Turcotte corroborated the speculation that he was record-conscious. He said, "When we got to the stretch, and I saw those figures on the tote board, I knew that I was going to a record."

Incidentally, the world record for a mile and a half (on turf, and not on the dirt, like the Belmont), is 2:23, set by Fiddle Isle at Santa Anita in 1970. The American record on dirt, which was broken yesterday, was 2:26⅕, set by Going Abroad at Aqueduct in 1964.

To and from a Coronation

By DAVE ANDERSON

On a tiny portable TV set atop a midnight-green Cadillac parked outside the Meadow stable barn at Belmont Park just prior to the 105th running of the Belmont Stakes in 1973, a voice was saying, ". . . and that horse, named Secretariat. . . ." Minutes later, deep in the shadows of the green and white barn, the three-year-old chestnut emerged from his stall.

"Clear it out," somebody was yelling now outside the barn. "Clear it out. The horse is coming." About ten people, a few newsmen but mostly spectators, had been gathered at the barn for half an hour, the way people wait for a heavyweight champion to come out of his dressing room before a title fight. And now, with a blue bridle contrasting with his glistening chestnut coat, the horse followed a gray lead pony into the warm sun as a breeze fluttered the leaves of the small oak trees. Quickly, with his groom, Eddie Sweat, holding the blue reins, the horse turned down into the tunnel that leads to the paddock.

"Go get that money," somebody yelled.

"You see why everybody has fallen in love with this horse," somebody else said as dozens of people surged into the tunnel behind him. "He's beautiful, he's just beautiful."

"Stop crying," a man said to a child. "While you're crying, you can't see the horse."

Soon, the horse was moving under the tall trees of the paddock. As he circled the walking ring, applause followed him from the spectators who surrounded it. Above, on a balcony of the red brick-and-glass clubhouse, others peered through binoculars.

"Bravo," somebody called. "Bravo, Secretariat." Such was the crowd on the grass inside the walking ring that when Ron Turcotte was about to be helped into the saddle, the trainer, Lucien Laurin, was unable to get through to help him. The assistant trainer, Benny Hoeffner, had to do it. And then, as the horse moved through the darkness of the underpass toward the track, applause and cheers followed him again.

"Triple Crown, baby," a young man yelled. "Triple Crown in New York, baby."

When the horse appeared on the track, a roar from the 69,138 spectators thundered out from under the roof, as if a Sugar Bowl team had run onto the field.

"Look at those odds," a man said. "One to nine."

But that was only because the odds board doesn't have room for three digits, as the proper odds of 1 to 10 demanded. Soon, the bell clanged in the starting gate and the horses were hurrying toward the first turn, where a red helicopter hung in the air.

"You've got a hole, baby, go," a man yelled.

Moving along the rail, Secretariat accelerated through that hole into the lead. He was in command to stay. On the backstretch, he was lengthening his lead when the Teletimer on the toteboard flashed 1:09⅘ for six furlongs.

"He's got to come back," a man said.

But he didn't. At the mile, he had a seven-length lead. His time was flashed as 1:34⅘.

"If he doesn't come back," somebody said, "he's a super horse."

He didn't, and he was. He won by 31 lengths, the roar of the spectators rumbling to a crescendo in accompaniment as Secretariat pounded across the finish line, more alone than Greta Garbo ever was. Soon he was in the winner's circle, the first to sweep racing's Triple Crown in twenty-five years. But just as the names of thoroughbreds relate to their breeding, the names of Secretariat's owner and groom are symbolic, too.

His owner, being photographed with him now, is Mrs. Penny Tweedy, as in herringbone. His groom is Eddie Sweat, as in perspire.

RED SMITH

1905–1982

By IRA BERKOW

I N THE COLLEGE TEXTBOOK *A Quarto of Modern Literature*, between an essay by Winston Churchill and a short story by Dylan Thomas, there is an example of spot-news reporting by Red Smith. It is a column on a heavy-weight fight between Joe Louis and Rocky Marciano, written on deadline. It is the only piece of journalism in the anthology, and the only sports story.

To the legion of Red Smith fans, it was not surprising that one of his stories would be included among the works of the finest contemporary writers. For them, Red Smith was virtually without peer in his profession.

When he won the Pulitzer Prize for distinguished commentary, in 1976, Smith became only the second sports columnist ever to be honored with that award. Arthur Daley of the *Times* was the first, in 1956. The Pulitzer committee cited Smith's work for being "unique in the erudition, the literary quality, the vitality and the freshness of viewpoint."

He received innumerable awards and several honorary degrees, including one from his alma mater, Notre Dame, from which he graduated in 1927. He was pleased by the attention, but not necessarily impressed. He found trying to master his craft too challenging for that.

"Writing is easy," he once said. "I just open a vein and bleed." But he loved it, he admitted. And he had great respect for the "mother tongue." His knowledge of the language was so widely respected that he was on the board as a consultant for several dictionaries and encyclopedias.

He was as self-effacing as he was esteemed. In *Strawberries in the Winter-time*, the last of his five collections of columns, published in 1974, he wrote in the foreword, "Finding a title for such a mixed bag can be a problem. I consid-ered using a catchier title like *War and Peace, Wuthering Heights*, or *The Holy Bible* but they struck me as dated."

Instead, the title he used, he wrote, "happens to be the title of a piece about Willie Mays and it captures, I think, some of the flavor of the sportswriter's existence, which is what the late Bill Corum was talking about when he said, 'I don't want to be a millionaire, I just want to live like one.' "

Few newspapermen, even of the stature of Red Smith, live like million-aires. But some find their work fulfilling. Smith, apparently, was one. Sport is often considered less than important, but Smith believed that his job was signif-icant.

"Sports is not really a play world," he said. "I think it's the real world. The people we're writing about in professional sports, they're suffering and

living and dying and loving and trying to make their way through life just as the bricklayers and politicians are.

"This may sound defensive—I don't think it is—but I'm aware that games are a part of every culture we know anything about. And often taken seriously. It's no accident that of all the monuments left of the Greco-Roman culture, the biggest is the ball park, the Colosseum, the Yankee Stadium of ancient times. The man who reports on these games contributes his small bit to the record of his time."

But Smith wrote with a light touch and a wryness that put the games and the people involved into perspective. Covering a college football game, for example, he quoted, tongue in cheek, a program hawker: "Get your programs, folks—the names, numbers and salaries of all the players."

Praise for Smith through the years sometimes came from unlikely sources. The short-story writer Shirley Jackson, who knew almost nothing about sports, reviewed his book *Out of the Red*, and said that reading the book "has been, actually, an educational experience unlike almost anything I have known since first looking into Chapman's *Homer*."

And Ernest Hemingway, in his novel *Across the River and into the Trees*, described one of his characters starting to read the *New York Herald Tribune:* "He was reading Red Smith, and he liked him very much."

When the *Herald Tribune* advertised Smith's columns on subway posters, they used Beau Jack, the former boxing champion, for a testimonial. Mr. Smith was delighted by it. "Everyone knew," he said, "that Beau Jack was a functional illiterate."

A small man—he stood 5 feet 7 inches—with a florid face, Smith once described himself as "a seedy amateur with watery eyes behind glittering glasses, a receding chin, a hole in his frowzy haircut." In his later years, his once bright red hair had turned white. But he retained a youthfulness.

"I know I've grown more liberal as I've grown older," he said. "I seem to be finding this a much less pretty world than when I was younger, and I feel things should be done about it and that sports are a part of the world."

In a sense, Smith became the conscience of the sports world. In his later years he wrote bitterly of the owners of professional sports teams in their labor-management relations. He wrote the headlines for his columns, and he entitled one on employer-employee relationships in baseball, "Lively Times in the Slave Trade." He frequently criticized the International Olympic Committee, accusing it of trying to impress nineteenth-century ideas on a twentieth-century world.

He was the first columnist to propose publicly that the United States boycott the 1980 Olympic Games in Moscow because of Soviet intervention in Afghanistan. The idea appeared in his column of January 4, 1980, and President Carter formally proposed a boycott on January 20. Mostly because of the boycott, only 81 of the 147 eligible nations participated in the Moscow Olympics.

Walter Wellesley ("I hate the name") Smith was born September 25, 1905, in Green Bay, Wisconsin. He was the second of three children born to Walter Philip and Ida Richardson Smith. His father operated a wholesale produce and retail grocery business.

When he was growing up, he hiked through woods, fished, built lean-tos, and enjoyed the outdoors, as he would all his life. He was never very athletic, but he did become an avid fisherman and often enjoyed writing disparagingly about his efforts in that pastime. He said he had caught his casting line in trees all the way from the Andes to Finland.

At home in Green Bay, he also read the classics that were stored in a credenza in the family's living room. And influenced by an older friend who was studying journalism at Notre Dame, Smith decided to matriculate at the same school and major in the same subject.

He edited the school yearbook, *The Dome*, and briefly participated in track. He said his most notable achievement in college was not quite finishing in a mile race, the only one he ever ran.

He was, though, determined to be a newspaperman. And upon graduation in 1927, he recalled that "I wrote letters to about a hundred newspapers asking for a job. I got back one reply. That was from *The New York Times*. And it said no." Writing for the *Times* would come much later for Smith. Meanwhile, he caught on with the *Milwaukee Sentinel* after sending the city editor a letter of "arrant flattery." The pay was twenty-five dollars a week.

He covered stories ranging from murders to society news. One year later he took a job for forty dollars a week with the *St. Louis Star*, as a copy editor. "I hated the routine," he said, "but I've got to credit that job with teaching me about writing. The horrible examples that came over my desk daily shocked me into doing a little better."

A few months later the managing editor fired most of the *Star*'s sports staff. Smith was asked to shift to sports. "All I knew about sports was what the average fan knew," he said, "but I was the most dispensable copyreader."

His first assignment was a night football game, and he wrote his story from the viewpoint of a glowworm that envied the brightness of the stadium flood-lights. "It was cute," said Smith, "but people seemed to like it." From then on, his editors knew he was special.

In 1936, he joined the *Philadelphia Record* as a sportswriter and colum-nist, and in 1945 he began a column full-time for the *New York Herald Tribune*. His column was syndicated in ninety newspapers. In 1954, when Grantland Rice died, Smith became the most widely syndicated sports columnist.

When the *Herald Tribune* became part of the new *World Journal Tribune* in 1966, Smith became sports columnist for the new newspaper. When the publication ceased the next year, his syndicated column survived. His column in the New York area was picked up by the *Long Island Press* and, oddly, *Women's Wear Daily* in a column titled Sportif. In 1971, Smith was hired by *The New York Times* and joined Arthur Daley and Dave Anderson as sports columnists.

Smith recalled when he was hired. "There was a lot of electricity around our house," he said. "I felt like I was back playing the Palace." Without a large New York daily for an outlet, said his wife, Phyllis, "Red had been more unhappy than he either knew or admitted."

He was sixty-six years old when he joined the *Times*. "Within the *Times* family," said A. M. Rosenthal, then executive editor of the newspaper, "we always felt that bringing Red to our staff, even at an age when most men contemplate retirement, allowed us to fulfill a very special trust for sports. He embodied the spirit, vigor, and youth of sports. We remember him with affection and pride as a wonderful writer and a wonderful man."

Smith's three or four columns a week were syndicated by The New York Times News Service to 275 newspapers in the United States and 225 in about thirty foreign nations.

His work remained outstanding, and he continued to grow as a writer. For one thing, he worked to simplify his style, and he looked harder at his prose. "I have tried to become simpler, straighter, and purer in my language," he said. "I look at some of the stuff I wrote in past years, and I say, 'Gee, I should have cooled it a little more.' "

He continued to believe that his responsibility as a sportswriter was "to add to the joy of the reader interested in the games and to capture the grace and drama and beauty and humor."

He avoided the clichés and flowery approach that many sportswriters had adopted, and he tried to cover games and people with the accuracy and insights of a good reporter. He preferred covering sports like baseball, football, boxing, and horse playing ("not horse racing," he emphasized) and disdained what he called "back and forth" sports like basketball and hockey.

He combined his unusual style of a sports columnist with the style of a news-side analyst when he covered several political conventions. But in 1968, at the Chicago Democratic Convention, he was moved deeply.

"In the past," he wrote at one point, "it seemed to make sense for a sportswriter on sabbatical from the playpen to attend the quadrennial hawg killing where presidential candidates are chosen, to observe and report upon the politicians at play. After all, national conventions are games of a sort, and sports offer few spectacles richer in low comedy. . . . It is sadly different this week in the police state which Richard "The Lion-hearted" Daley has made of the city he rules. There is no room for laughter in this city of fear."

His serious view of subjects would increase. In earlier days, he was, by his estimation, guilty of "Godding up" the players. And some commentators on the sports world criticized him for giving the sports establishment's high-handed treatment of athletes a kind of sanction. He would begin to change.

Smith was a warm, generous man who was as witty and insightful in person as he was in print. To young writers, he was unfailingly helpful. He would answer letters seeking his advice. To one college student who sent Smith his school newspaper columns, he wrote back:

"When I was a cub in Milwaukee I had a city editor who'd stroll over and read across a guy's shoulder when he was writing a lead. Sometimes he would approve, sometimes he'd say gently, 'Try again,' and walk away.

"My best advice is, try again. And then again. If you're for this racket, and not many really are, then you've got an eternity of sweat and tears ahead. I don't mean just you; I mean anybody." And then he proceeded to make specific and pertinent suggestions.

He felt dearly about his friends and eulogized many in his columns. One of his closest friends was Grantland Rice. "He wrote of men he loved and deeds he admired," wrote Smith "and never knew how much bigger he was than his finest hero."

Smith's books included such collections of his columns as *Out of the Red*, *Views of Sports*, and *The Best of Red Smith*.

He died of cancer on January 15, 1982. His last column appeared four days before his death.

Write Less and Better?

By RED SMITH

Up to now, the pieces under my byline have run on Sunday, Monday, Wednesday, and Friday. Starting this week, it will be Sunday, Monday, and Thursday—three columns instead of four. We shall have to wait and see whether the quality improves.

Visiting our freshman daughter (freshwoman or freshperson would be preferred by feminists though heaven knows she was fresh), we sat chatting with perhaps a dozen of her classmates. Somehow my job got into the discussion. A lovely blonde was appalled.

"A theme a day!" she murmured. The figure was not altogether accurate. At the time it was six themes a week. It had been seven and when it dropped to six that looked like roller coaster's end. However, it finally went to five, to three, and back to four, where it has remained for years.

First time I ever encountered John S. Knight, the publisher, we were bellying up to Marje Everett's bar at Arlington Park. He did not acknowledge the introduction. Instead, he said, "Nobody can write six good columns a week. Why don't you write three? Want me to fix it up?"

"Look, Mr. Knight," I said. "Suppose I wrote three stinkers. I wouldn't have the rest of the week to recover." One of the beauties of this job is that there's always tomorrow. Tomorrow things will be better.

Now that the quota is back to three, will things be better day after tomorrow?

The comely college freshman wasn't told of the years when a daily column meant seven a week. Between those jousts with the mother tongue, there was always a fight or football match or ball game or horse race that had to be covered after the column was done. I loved it.

The seven-a-week routine was in Philadelphia, which reminds me of the late heavyweight champion, Sonny Liston. Before his second bout with Muhammad Ali was run out of Boston, Liston trained in a motel in Dedham.

I was chatting about old Philadelphia days with the trainer, Willie Reddish, remembered from his time as a heavyweight boxer in Philadelphia.

"Oh," Willie said apropos of some event in the past, "were you there then?" "Willie," I said, "I did ten years hard in Philadelphia." There had been no sign that Liston was listening, but at this he swung around. "Hard?" he said. "No good time?" From that moment on, Sonny and I were buddies, though it wasn't easy accepting him as a sterling citizen of lofty moral standards.

On this job two questions are inevitably asked: "Of all those you have met, who was the best athlete?" and "Which one did you like best?"

Both questions are unanswerable but on either count Bill Shoemaker, the jockey, would have to stand high. This little guy weighed 96 pounds as an apprentice rider thirty-two years ago. He still weighs 96 pounds and he will beat your pants off at golf, tennis, and any other game where you're foolish enough to challenge him.

There were, of course, many others, not necessarily great. Indeed, there was a longish period when my rapport with some who were less than great made me nervous. Maybe I was stuck on bad ball players. I told myself not to worry. Some day there would be another Joe DiMaggio.

AMOS ALONZO STAGG

1862–1965

I N THE SPRING OF 1888, as a slender Yale University undergraduate, Amos Alonzo Stagg pitched his baseball team to a 2–1 victory over the Boston Braves. Within a week the young pitcher was offered six professional contracts. He turned them down. He disliked the character of the professional game, he explained, and, besides, in several years he expected to enter the ministry.

In time, Stagg abandoned both of his early loves—pitching and preaching. But in seventy years as a college football coach, he was the most compelling single force for the tactical growth and ethical elevation of the game.

He pioneered the forward pass and the T formation. He molded thirteen charter students of the University of Chicago into the first of a long line of football powerhouses. He developed such great coaches as Fritz Crisler, who went on to Minnesota, Princeton, and Michigan, and Jesse Harper of Notre Dame. And before each game he gathered his players about him for a moment of silent prayer—not a prayer for victory, he often said, but a supplication that they might do their very best.

Stagg was older than college football. He was born on August 16, 1862, in West Orange, New Jersey, seven years before the first collegiate game. The fifth of eight children of an impoverished cobbler, Lon Stagg did odd jobs by the hour after classes at Orange High School and helped his father to mow and cradle hay in the summer.

Physical conditioning was a by-product of his life. He ran the mile between home and school each day because he was always either coming from a job or going to one. He once said that he was particularly fascinated by the tale of the Spartan lad who made no outcry while a fox, which he had hidden in his shirt, began to chew on his flesh.

In lieu of foxes, Stagg led a Spartan life of his own. He gave up coffee in high school, never drank, and never tasted nicotine. He chewed one-quarter of a stick of gum at a time—even when he could afford a whole piece. His only indulgence was sourballs and other hard candies.

At twenty-one, Lon Stagg entered Phillips Exeter Academy. He pitched its team to victory while living on soda crackers and waiting on tables. Offered a baseball scholarship at Dartmouth, Stagg turned it down so that he might enter Yale as a predivinity student.

A year leater, with thirty-two dollars and no overcoat, Stagg arrived in New Haven. He continued his soda-cracker diet until he was hospitalized with

malnutrition, then, more substantially nourished, pitched the Yale baseball team to five championships. He played end on the football team for five years and was named to Walter Camp's first all-America squad in 1889.

By the spring of 1890, after six years of athletic fame, Stagg was convinced that he lacked the ability to talk easily before a group. He quit the Yale Divinity School and became a faculty member at the Young Men's Christian Association training school at Springfield, Massachusetts. One of his colleagues there was James Naismith, the inventor of basketball.

While at Springfield, he coached the local college football team with such success that in 1892 he was invited to coach at the as yet uncompleted University of Chicago. The response to the football call at Chicago was not overwhelming. Thirteen boys showed up. Stagg suited up, placed himself on the roster as No. 14, and began the first of forty-one years of coaching there.

His teams won six Big Ten Conference titles and were unbeaten in five seasons. He became the first football coach to have a field named for him, the first athletic director to achieve faculty status, and, to thousands of students and fans, was as much a part of the university as its imposing Gothic buildings.

The university remembered him as a short, well-knit figure (he maintained his playing weight of 160 into his nineties) walking briskly about campus without an overcoat in winter, playing tennis with his son Paul or driving in a vintage electric runabout; a man who scorned the cold winds whipping in from Lake Michigan, the stiffening muscles of middle age, or the easy temptations of a materialistic era.

His influence and importance reached far beyond the Midway. He was selected to the Football Hall of Fame both as a player and as a coach. He was instrumental in the formation of the Western Conference. He was a member of five Olympic Games committees and one of the original members of the Intercollegiate Football Rules Committee, and he staged some of the first national collegiate track and baseball contests. Through trying moments on and off the field, the strongest word he ever used was *jackass.*

If a player made a series of mistakes, Stagg would call him a "double jackass" or even a "triple jackass." His players at the University of Chicago formed a "jackass club," and the coach's son Paul, the Maroon quarterback from 1929 to 1931, became a member. "He called me a double jackass once," Paul said.

Stagg was revered as the "grand old man," but in 1932, at the age of seventy, the university asked him to retire and accept an honorary position as supervisor of athletics. He refused.

"I could not and would not accept a job without work," he later said.

So, at a time when most men would be ready to call it a career, Alonzo Stagg went west.

"I went west when I was a young man," he said. "I'm going west again, and I'm still a young man."

For fourteen years, at the College of the Pacific, in Stockton, California, Stagg turned out big-time teams in a small school. At eighty-four, again asked to take an advisory role, Stagg moved on. He joined his son Amos Alonzo, Jr., at Susquehanna College in Pennsylvania. There he took charge of the offensive platoon and actively coached on the field for six years.

In 1953, when his wife become unable to travel between California and Pennsylvania, Stagg took an advisory job at Stockton Junior College.

His wife, Stella, not only had an avid interest in her husband's teams, but she also served as an aide on more than one occasion.

When Stagg was coaching at Susquehanna, Mrs. Stagg went off on a Saturday to scout Dickinson College, the next week's opponent. When she came back, she reported, "You can pass on their left halfback. He's slow."

Susquehanna beat Dickinson by the margin of one touchdown, achieved late in the game. It came on a pass, over the losers' left halfback.

On September 16, 1960, Stagg sent this note to Coach Larry Kentera of Stockton: "For the past seventy years I have been a coach. At ninety-eight years of age it seems like a good time to stop."

His record of 314 career victories stood until 1981, when Bear Bryant surpassed it.

According to his son Amos Alonzo Jr., he never singled out a favorite athlete.

"Father said, over and over, 'When you start picking favorites, it is unjust to the loyal men who have competed for you,' and he was proud of the loyalty of all his many outstanding Maroons.

"Father said he loved each and every one of his boys, as he called them.

"He had a real affection for them and considered each as a son. I never thought of myself as an oldest actual son, but one of the many men for whom he had deepest affection."

Who Is the Winningest?
By ROBERT McG. THOMAS, Jr.

"Who is college football's winningest coach?" That was the question posed by a public relations consultant for Susquehanna University in a series of letters sent to sports editors and writers in October 1988.

"If you answer Paul 'Bear' Bryant," the letters continued, "you're right. But if your choice is Amos Alonzo Stagg, Sr., you'd also be correct."

That, the letters asserted, was because while Bryant's total of 323 career victories exceeded Stagg's official record of 314, Stagg really had 21 victories that were never properly credited to him.

They were the games won by the Susquehanna Crusaders during the years 1947–52, when Stagg, having recently been retired by the College of the Pacific after fifty-seven years as a head coach, including forty-one at the University of Chicago and two at Springfield, joined his son, Amos Alonzo Stagg, Jr., as the Crusaders' co-coach.

Although players from those teams insist that the elder Stagg, who handled offense, really was the head coach, school records listed him only as an advisory coach, and the National Collegiate Athletic Association has consistently refused to credit him with those victories.

"I think it was a very grave error on the part of the NCAA," the younger Stagg said. "I'm still blistered about it."

The younger Stagg was ninety years old at the time (his father died in 1965 at the age of a hundred and two).

As for the question posed by the Susquehanna public relations consultant, his two "right" answers would seem to be a case of two rights making a wrong.

The "winningest" coach in college football is neither Bear Bryant nor Amos Alonzo Stagg. It is Eddie Robinson of Grambling, who had 346 victories at the time, and 366 at the end of the 1990 season.

CASEY STENGEL

1890–1975

C HARLES DILLON STENGEL of Kansas City, the man from KC, owned oil wells in Texas, was vice president of a bank in California, and controlled real estate that made him a millionaire. But for all his status, he was best known as a baseball man with a wrinkled, expressive face and a guttural voice.

He was transported to his early baseball games as a boy in Missouri in horse-drawn surreys and wound up flying coast to coast in jetliners. He reached the major leagues in 1912 when William Howard Taft was president and retired in 1965 during the administration of Lyndon B. Johnson.

He was a player, coach, or manager on seventeen professional teams. He was traded four times as a left-handed outfielder in the major leagues. He was dropped or relieved three times as a manager in the big leagues. He was even paid twice for not managing.

From 1910 to 1931, he played on four teams in the minors, then five in the majors, and finally two more in the minors. Then, as a manager, he lived through twenty-five years of frustration at both levels, finishing no higher than fifth in an eight-team league during one decade.

Then he suddenly graduated to the New York Yankees in 1949 as the fifteenth manager in their history of dominating the sport and won ten pennants and seven world championships in twelve years.

Finally, at the age of seventy-two, he wound up as the first manager of the New York Mets where he had started—at the bottom of the ladder.

Through it all, he was one of the busiest characters on the American scene—and one of the most theatrical. His pantomime, monologues, and story-telling defied description until he was accused (with some reason) of carrying on to distract the public from the less effectual performances of his teams.

He spoke in a nonstop style that came to be known as Stengelese—a kind of circuitous double-talk laced with ambiguous antecedents, dangling participles, a lack of proper names, and a liberal use of adjectives like "amazing" and "terrific."

He drew on baseball lore back to the days of John J. McGraw, his idol as a manager, and would clinch points in rhetoric by saying with finality, "You could look it up." When a listener's attention waned, he would recapture it by suddenly exclaiming, "Now, let me ask you," and would be off and running again.

The perpetrator of this commotion was born in Kansas City, Missouri, on

July 30, 1890. His father had emigrated from Germany in 1851 and had settled in the farm country across the Mississippi River from Davenport, Iowa. A first child, Louise, was born in 1886; a son, Grant, in 1887, and Charles three years later.

Charles became an all-around athlete at Kansas City Central High School and pitched and won the state championship in 1909. He turned professional the following year with the Kansas City Blues, who farmed him out to Kankakee, Illinois, in the Northern Association.

Baseball was a means to an end: Stengel was working his way through the Western Dental College in Kansas City. But two things swerved him from his course. He was left-handed, which raised some problems for his instructors. And left-handed dentists had a less riotous future than left-handed baseball players.

The dental college, Stengel recalled, also did not have the daring to turn him loose on society with a "weapon" in his hand.

For whatever reasons, he became a full-time ball player and was discovered by Larry Sutton, a scout for the Brooklyn Dodgers. In September of 1912, the Dodgers—then known as the Trolley Dodgers and Superbas—called him up from Birmingham, and he was in the big leagues.

For the next fourteen seasons, Stengel played the outfield in the National League—with Brooklyn until 1917, Pittsburgh until 1920, Philadelphia until the middle of 1921, New York until 1923, and Boston until 1925.

He batted .284 and hit 60 home runs in 1,277 games. His best year was 1922, when he hit .368 in 84 games with McGraw's Giants. His best moments came in the World Series of 1923, when he hit two home runs and won two games—only to be upstaged by the young Babe Ruth, who hit three home runs as the Yankees won the Series.

After the 1923 Series, Stengel was traded to the Boston Braves and two years later began his career as a manager with Boston's farm club at Worcester, Massachusetts.

He already had gained a sizable reputation as a brawler and clown and promptly increased it when the Boston club installed him as a one-man triumvirate at Worcester—president, manager, and right fielder.

Casey fretted until the final day of the season, then hatched a monumental triple play to escape. As manager, he released Stengel the player; as president, he dismissed Stengel the manager; and as Stengel, he resigned as president.

The owner of the Boston team, Judge Emil Fuchs, was outraged by this impertinence, but nobody was too surprised. After all, Stengel had long since become famous as "the king of the grumblers," a locker-room clique whose chief talent was trouble.

He had been the bane of umpires and of managers like Wilbert Robinson of Brooklyn, who became the butt of one Stengel prank at Daytona Beach, Florida, in the spring of 1915. On that occasion, Casey was inspired by the recent feat of Gabby Street, who had caught a baseball dropped from the Washington Monument. The question now became: could a man catch a baseball dropped from an airplane?

The airplane was supplied by Ruth Law, the pioneer woman flier, and the baseball was supplied by C. D. Stengel, except that somehow it became a grapefruit by the time it was dropped.

"Uncle Robbie," Stengel recalled, "was warming up this pitcher on the sidelines—we didn't have six coaches in those days. And this aviatrix—it was the first one they had—she flew over and dropped it. And Uncle Robbie saw it coming and waved everybody away like an outfielder and said, 'I've got it, I've got it.'

"Robbie got under this grapefruit, thinking it was a baseball, which hit him right on this pitcher's glove he put on and the insides of it flew all over, seeds on his face and uniform, and flipped him right over on his back. Everybody came running up and commenced laughing, all except Robbie."

In one of his most fabled escapades, Stengel returned to Ebbets Field in 1918 with the Pittsburgh Pirates, who had just acquired him from Brooklyn. He was greeted by a rousing round of catcalls from the fans. In reply, he marched to home plate, bowed with courtliness to the grandstand, doffed his cap—and out flew a sparrow. He had given them the bird.

On another occasion, he went to right field, found a drainage hole and simply disappeared from sight. A moment later he rose majestically, the manhole cover under his arm, just in time to catch a fly ball.

Later, when he became a manager, Stengel looked back on his wayward years and said, "Now that I am a manager, I see the error of my youthful ways. If any player ever pulled that stuff on me now, I would probably fine his ears off."

Stengel's success as a manager, meanwhile, was lean. In seven years in the minor leagues from 1925 to 1931, his teams won only one pennant. But he was developing skills that became his trademark in later years: he was thriving as a buffoon who could draw attention away from inept players to himself, and he was learning the business side of baseball—buying players low, selling them high, and converting farm clubs into pools of talent for the major leagues.

He also was branching out in his personal life. In 1924 he had married Edna Lawson, a tall, lively brunette from California who once had acted in silent films with Hoot Gibson, a western star, and who later was an accountant with a shrewd business sense.

They settled in a two-story house at the foothills of the Sierras in Glendale, California. And for the next forty years it was their base as both roamed the country on Casey's travels.

They had no children, but had hordes of relatives who lived nearby, plus young ball players who often stayed with them. They also had interests in real estate, established the Valley National Bank with Mrs. Stengel's family, and literally struck oil in Texas on a chance investment Casey had made with some baseball friends.

With all this going for him, Stengel was hardly considered the type of man who would flower late in life into a baseball manager of renown—not even when he was called to the Brooklyn Dodgers as a coach in 1932 and became manager two years later.

From 1934 until 1943, his teams at Brooklyn and Boston never finished higher than fifth in an eight-team league. Then in 1943, when he was struck by a taxi in Boston and suffered a broken leg, it appeared that his career was finally ended.

However, the following year he agreed to leave his swimming pool and patio in Glendale to take over the Milwaukee club in the American Association. He did it as a favor for a friend, but it proved to be a turning point. After one season as manager at Milwaukee and another at Kansas City, he spent three at Oakland in the Pacific Coast League, won 321 games, and suddenly at the age of fifty-eight was offered the job as manager of the lordly Yankees.

His selection as the replacement for Bucky Harris evoked surprise. It was widely thought that the Yankees had hired "Professor" Stengel to throw a screen of hilarity around the club for a season or two while rebuilding. But the "interim" manager, who had never spent a day in the American League, stayed twelve years, and the Yankees reached spectacular heights.

In 1949, his first season, the Yankees suffered seventy-two injuries. Joe DiMaggio even missed half the season. But Stengel kept juggling lineups, and the Yankees defeated the Boston Red Sox in the last two games, won the pennant, and defeated the Dodgers in the World Series.

A year later they won again, and they kept on winning until they had taken five straight pennants and world championships. It was a record streak for a team and a manager. In a rash moment Stengel remarked that if the Yankees didn't make it six in a row in 1954, the manager should be dismissed. They didn't, but he wasn't.

In 1955, they won the pennant again and also took it in 1956, 1957, 1958, and 1960. But they won only two World Series during that time, and in 1959 even slipped to third place.

Stengel was earning $85,000 a year by now and was the foremost manager in baseball. He was surrounded by stars like Yogi Berra, Whitey Ford, Phil Rizzuto, Mickey Mantle, and Roger Maris. But the second half of his administration was a somewhat troubled time, and he grew increasingly arbitrary with players and bitter to suggestions that he was "too old."

His bitterness reached a peak on October 18, 1960, five days after the Yankees had lost the Series to Pittsburgh.

In an acrimonious press conference at the Savoy Hilton Hotel, the Yankee brass—led by Dan Topping—announced that Stengel had "retired." A short time later George M. Weiss, Stengel's friend and sponsor, was released as general manager.

"I was fired," Casey commented.

After a year in the California sunshine, though, he was hired again—by Weiss, who now was organizing the Mets, the successors to the Giants and the Dodgers, who had left New York in 1957 for the West Coast.

So, at the age of seventy-two, Stengel began a new career, one that crystallized all his talents for teaching, acting, and enchanting the public. The Mets needed such talents, too, since they lost 452 games while winning 194 during the next four years, finishing dead last each time.

They were as downtrodden as the Yankees had been exalted. But they were cast in the image of the stumpy, waddling old man who directed them, a team whose sins were pardoned by an adoring public, whose life was surrounded by legend, whose bank account grew with the legend.

In 1965, Stengel's last year in a baseball suit, 1,768,389 persons paid up to $3.50 each to watch the Old Man and his celebrated Youth of America in their new Shea Stadium on Flushing Bay; and 1,075,431 paid to see them on the road.

The partnership began to fold on July 25, 1965, when Stengel fractured his left hip—somewhere between an old-timers' party at Toots Shor's restaurant, where he slipped and fell, and a house in Queens, where he slipped and fell again while getting out of an automobile.

In any event, he was in Roosevelt Hospital that afternoon while 39,288 persons celebrated his seventy-fifth birthday at Shea Stadium. Two days later he underwent an operation on his hip and one month later he retired to the side of his swimming pool as titular vice president of the Mets.

One year later, however, leaning on a crooked black cane, he limped into baseball's Hall of Fame at Cooperstown, New York, alongside Ted Williams. Stengel, the 104th person inducted into the shrine, told the crowd in valedictorian Stengelese, "I want to thank my parents for letting me play baseball, and I'm thankful I had baseball knuckles and couldn't become a dentist. . . . I got $2,100 a year when I started in the big league, and they get more money now. . . . I chased the balls that Babe Ruth hit."

He died at the age of eighty-five on September 29, 1975.

A World Series at Last

By JAMES P. DAWSON

Casey Stengel was so happy in the Yankee clubhouse after his team had routed the Brooklyn Dodgers by 10 to 6 to win the 1949 World Series in five games that he congratulated Commissioner A. B. Chandler for "doing a great job."

The Yankee skipper didn't mention whether the commissioner pitched air-tight ball, hit a couple of home runs, or plucked a homer out of the air before it fell into the seats. But the incident indicates the tremendous, delirious joy for the KC veteran, in the first flush of his paramount triumph, which had been so long denied him as a manager.

No adjectives can describe the scene in the clubhouse of the victors, though a number of them have been through these World Series triumphs before. They went in for extremes. Yells, whistles, shouts, shrieks, split the air in ear-shattering crescendo. Punches were like slaps—delivered good-naturedly, but resoundingly. Among the celebrants the miracle was that none was hurt.

The contrast? It was supplied by Charlie Keller. Off in a corner he sat, munching a sandwich while still and movie cameramen and writers flitted hither and yon, grabbing this one and that one, and well-wishers added to the general pandemonium by trampling players and working persons under foot to present their congratulations.

Off in a corner, like little Jack Horner, only he wasn't eating a pumpkin pie. The rugged veteran of five of these orgies now, survivor of the baseball campaigns as a Yankee from 'way back in 1939, he who used to be leading the parade to victory with his war club, just sat there, munching, unnoticed.

Oh, he was happy over the victory. He had contributed to the triumph up to his physical best. Although a lame back handicapped him, he had helped toward the American League pennant. But he took no actual part in this Series triumph, and he was letting the youth of the club have its day in the sun.

Just a few feet away from Keller photographers and writers were swarming around Joe DiMaggio, Cliff Mapes, Vic Raschi, Lefty Joe Page, Gene Woodling, Jerry Coleman, Tommy Henrich, as they quaffed beer or soft drinks or lunched on snacks. DiMaggio was smiling for the first time since the Series began. Everybody was smiling. The rushing tide of confusion swept along, but it brushed by Keller, never touched him. And he smiled when one who had seen him come up as a raw rookie and go out like the fighting man he is, clasped his hand and congratulated him on his contribution, however small.

Stengel was beside himself with joy. But he had no exclusive rights on this emotion. Everybody was the same. The Yankee skipper, whose pennant hopes had been dashed as a manager with Brooklyn and Boston, had taken an injury-riddled ball club and piloted it to baseball's heights in his first year back with the majors after going down to the minors, tagged a failure. His felicitations for his club knew no exceptions.

"The biggest thrill of my life? No. I wouldn't say it was," Stengel exclaimed, shouting hoarsely to make himself heard above the din. "I'd say the big thrill came when we got in there. If we hadn't won the pennant, we wouldn't be here. Winning the pennant took some doing, after all we'd been through.

"I'll say this. This is the greatest ball club a man could manage. Certainly the best I've ever known. We have been one happy family from the time spring training started. There has never been a sour note in the clubhouse, on the dugout bench, or on the field. A really great bunch of fellows and I am indebted to them for the way they came through for me. They won it. Not me.

"I won't say nothing happened through the season. But the only things that interrupted our happy family life came from out there on the field, injuries and accidents and sickness as the boys gave it all they had. A real good gang. Take my word for it. And, I'm thankful, too, to Mr. [Dan] Topping and Mr. [Del] Webb and Mr. Weiss for giving me this kind of a ball club. I don't know of another club that could come through like them

"If I said the Series went the way I expected I'd sound like I was popping off. It went the way I expected only in that we won. We won from a pretty good ball club, too. And, we won like real champions. I'm only sorry it had to be Brooklyn. I spent most of my playing days here. The fans here have always been wonderful to me, giving their support all the time. I hope they are glad we won.

"I had [Fred] Sanford warming up in the fourth, not because I was worried, but because I wanted to be ready. I was figuring on him as my pitcher for tomorrow if need be. Then I was coming in with [Tommy] Byrne and [Allie] Reynolds, again. You have to think of those things, you know. Our clubs were about on a par. They had a tough time winning their pennant. So did we. In the end, I guess it just amounts to the fact we lasted five days longer than they did."

The conquering skipper went across the room to shake the hand of the smiling DiMaggio and thank him for getting back into action when he should have been in a sickbed.

DiMaggio was happy over his home run into the left-field stands in the fourth inning. The master's stroke lifted some of the gloom that has hung over the Clipper because he never got to slugging through the Series. His eight-year-old son, Joe Jr., was at his right shoulder.

"Daddy, I lost one of your balls," said Joe Jr., explaining he had mislaid one of the autographed balls Wallopin' Joe was saving for friends.

"That's all right, son," smiled Daddy, "we can afford to lose one today. I lost one myself." DiMaggio is going to California without delay.

Joe Page was besieged on all sides. So were Raschi and Bobby Brown and Woodling, Jerry Coleman and the diminutive Phil Rizzuto and the unpredictable Yogi Berra and Mapes and Henrich. Page was almost speechless. Of his three relief jobs, this one was tops.

It wasn't generally known, but he entered the fray incapable of throwing a curveball. He had bruised the thumb of his left hand, his pitching paw, in the eighth inning of Friday's game, going out on a grounder to Jackie Robinson. He had to depend on his fastball.

"I tried one curve," said Page. "Fanned Robinson with it in the ninth." (He had previously fanned Duke Snider after Eddie Miksis doubled, swinging for Spider Jorgensen.) "I couldn't quite get it over for [Gene] Hermanski and he walked. But I fanned [Gil] Hodges on fastballs, and that was it. What a feeling. That ended it."

Page's last pitch was handed by Yogi Berra to Manager Stengel, a priceless souvenir. Somebody asked the Skipper for it. "Not this, no, no, no," yelled Stengel. "I'm keeping this myself."

Dodger Manager Burt Shotton presented his compliments to Stengel in the dugout runway under the stand. "He told me I did a good job, and I told him he did the same," said the Yankee pilot. " 'Winning the first one is always the best one,' says I."

Commissioner Chandler praised DiMaggio for his recklessness in leaving a sickbed to lift his club to the pennant. "Take good care of yourself; get a good rest. I hope you didn't overtax yourself coming back the way you did," said the commissioner.

Yogi Berra was disappointed. "I caught the best I ever did," said he. "But I couldn't swing that bat too good with my thumb."

Raschi was happy with the victory that ended the Series but disappointed at not being able to go the route. Three tough outings, against the Athletics and the Red Sox leading up to the pennant, and against Preacher Roe in the second Series game, had taken their toll. "They were must games," said Raschi. "I had to bear down all the way. I felt all right going into the seventh. I was thrilled when I fanned Billy Cox with the bases loaded to end the sixth, but when

Hodges hit that homer I knew it was the end. You can't take chances on a tired pitcher and I was tired, and weary. I'm glad we won it, although it would have been great for me to finish the first World Series game I've won."

A Stengel Sampler

By LEONARD KOPPETT

Charles Dillon "Casey" Stengel in his eighty-fourth year attended the 1973 World Series between the New York Mets and Oakland A's. He made some typical comments about the game and its participants.

A few excerpts (with translations and footnotes in parentheses):

On Yogi Berra:

"He was an awkward-lookin' player, like I was, and you could buy him three uniforms, and you'd only need one 'cause he'd look lousy in all." (It took listeners twenty-four hours to realize that this included Casey's definitive comment on Oakland's use of alternating combinations of green-and-gold uniforms.)

On how he thought the Series would come out:

"Now, I work for the New York Mets, who've been paying me for seven years and never said a word, so natcherly I'm for them, and I think it's been terrific."

On what he thinks of Yogi as a manager:

"Now wait a minute, let me ask you: who's played more big games as a player than him? He's played more than anybody in the world." (Yogi holds the record for World Series games played, and he played on fourteen pennant-winning Yankee teams.) "Why wouldn't you know the right plays after bein' in all them big games? You'd know it even if you was a dummy, which he ain't."

On experiences with Charles O. Finley, owner of the A's at that time:

"We're drivin' in his big limousine one day with this man here—go ahead, ask him, he'll tell ya—listenin' to the game on the radio." (The man indicated is Dave Condon, of the *Chicago Tribune*, nodding as Casey talks.) "Suddenly he [Finley] yells, 'Stop the car,' gets out, goes to a phone booth, calls the manager in the dugout, and yells: 'Get that donkey out of there,' into the phone." (That's right, Finley ordered a change of pitchers from a phone booth. Now he has a green telephone at his box seat behind the dugout.)

On life in the early days:

"There was this splendid man who knew all the rules, I'll give ya his name, and he became an umpire, Ernie Quigley, and in Fond-du-Lac, Wisconsin, they had this railroad right behind the right-field fence. So when it's time for the game, he comes out with that little thing, y'know, a megaphone, and tells the crowd behind home plate: 'Batterieeees for today's game . . . .' and he gives it to 'em. Then he trots out to right field, puts his arms up, gives a jump, and pulls himself up to the top of the fence, like chinning—and gives the batteries to the people sittin' on top of the railroad cars watchin' the game from out there. That was in 1910."

On a secret bit of baseball history:

"They used to say that in the American League they'd tell the pitchers not to throw over to first too much so there'd be more stealing and more excitement in the new league. I played in the National, and they'd throw over quick and scare you to death and the next nine times you wouldn't try to steal. But in the American, they had Ty Cobb, and that president—Ban Johnson, you know—sort of quietly let the word get around, and that was how they all played." (This was before Babe Ruth turned the American League, and eventually all baseball, into a home run oriented world.)

On the 14-inning game that Ruth pitched in the 1916 World Series for the Boston Red Sox against the Brooklyn Dodgers, still the longest World Series game by innings:

"That game was so famous they never used me." (Stengel was on the Dodgers then, but didn't get to play.)

On himself as a basketball player:

"I was taught in high school in Kansas City by a great man, Phog Allen, and I'd run around a lot and get knocked down, so I never made a basket, but I always got a lot of points on free throws."

On being platooned:

"When I was with the Dodgers, they had this very fast man, Jimmy Johnston, who stole ninety-nine bases in the Pacific Coast League, but they all said don't pay attention to that because they play twenty more games in that league, which they did, but now they play twenty more here and so what about that? So Robinson—Uncle Robby—the manager, would play him sometimes and me sometimes, but it wasn't lefty-righty. When I was with McGraw, he platooned me lefty-righty." (Casey was a left-handed batter and played for John McGraw's Giants in the early 1920s after playing for Wilbert Robinson's Dodgers before World War I.)

Three of the most prominent Mets—Cleon Jones, Tug McGraw, and Bud Harrelson—either played on Stengel's tenth-place Met teams or took part in spring training as minor leaguers in those years. And Ed Kranepool, of course, played regularly under him. Did he ever think, Casey was asked, that they would develop into a championship team?

"Well, it was tough while I taught some of those men, and who's been playing center field for eleven years for Baltimore, he was in the Met system, right? And you had to wait to get more men who could play." (Paul Blair, drafted out of the Mets' farm system, became an Oriole regular while the Mets still searched desperately for a center fielder.)

Casey seemed now to be getting around to his main point.

"They are very brave men," he said of Dick Williams and Yogi and various star players whom he has seen interviewed on television, "the way they talk right up. Now if it was me, I would double-talk."

Amen.

JIM THORPE

1888–1953

H ERO OF THE 1912 Olympic Games at Stockholm and a towering football figure, Jim Thorpe was probably the greatest natural athlete the world had seen in modern times.

King Gustaf V of Sweden said to the black-haired Sac and Fox Indian as he stood before the royal box, "Sir, you are the greatest athlete in the world." That was after Thorpe almost single-handedly gained the Olympic honors for the United States, setting a point-total record never before approached and dominating the games as no other figure.

Thorpe came back from Stockholm with $50,000 worth of trophies. They included a Viking ship presented to him by the czar of Russia and gifts from King Gustaf.

A month later the new American sports idol was toppled from his high pedestal when the Amateur Athletic Union filed charges of professionalism against him, accusing him of receiving pay for playing summer baseball with the Rocky Mount Club in the Eastern Carolina League. The amount of money was negligible, helping to tide him over at school, but the American Olympic Committee offered its apologies and sent back the gifts and medals lavished upon the young man to whom former President Theodore Roosevelt had cabled long messages of congratulation.

The medals were forwarded to the runners-up in the pentathlon and decathlon events at Stockholm. Thorpe had won four of the five events in the pentathlon and finished third in the other. In the decathlon he scored 8,412 out of a possible 10,000 points. His records were restored on October 13, 1982.

Thorpe's decathlon feats in the Olympics have been surpassed, but another Olympic great—Finland's Paavo Nurmi—declared that "Jim Thorpe could still beat them all."

In 1950 Thorpe's athletic prowess won for him selection as the greatest athlete of the twentieth century and the greatest football player in an Associated Press poll of sportswriters and broadcasters.

Before leaping into worldwide fame as the star of the Olympics, Thorpe had become a national sports figure through his deeds on the gridiron as a member of the famous Carlisle "Indians" football teams coached by Glenn S. "Pop" Warner. In 1911 and 1912 he was chosen as halfback on Walter Camp's all-America teams.

Thorpe played professional football for almost fifteen years, and in his prime at Carlisle and as a pro he never had to leave the field because of an injury,

such was his courage and stamina. In his last year at the Indian school he won letters in five major sports, and he was proficient in others. His activities included running, jumping, football, lacrosse, boxing, basketball, hockey, archery, rifle shooting, canoeing, handball, swimming, and skating.

He could run the 100-yard dash in 10 seconds flat, the 220 in 21.8, the 440 in 50.8, the 880 in 1:57, the mile in 4:35, the 120-yard high hurdles in 15 seconds, and the 220-yard low hurdles in 24 seconds. He broad-jumped 23 feet 6 inches and high-jumped 6 feet 5 inches. He pole-vaulted 11 feet, put the shot 47 feet 9 inches, threw the javelin 163 feet, the hammer 140 feet, and the discus 136 feet.

Thorpe was born on a farm at Prague, Oklahoma, the son of Hiram Thorpe, a ranchman. Dutch, Welsh, and Irish blood were understood to flow in his veins, but he was predominantly Indian. As might have been expected, he learned to ride, swim, and shoot almost as soon as he could walk, and he was punching cattle at the age of ten. His favorite diversion was following his hunting dogs in the forest, which helped to develop his magnificent body.

His mother gave him the Indian tribal name of Wa-Tho-Huck, or Bright Path. Official records, however, list him as James Francis Thorpe.

Young Jim was sent to the Haskell Indian School at Lawrence, Kansas, and then to the Carlisle School at Carlisle, Pennsylvania. He showed no particular interest in college athletics until Warner persuaded him to come out for football. That was in the fall of 1907 and he played as a substitute. The next year he became a regular and attracted attention as a ball carrier and kicker. He weighed around 178 pounds.

In the spring of 1908 Jim made the track team. Jumping and hurdling were his specialties. By the time he finished his five-year term at Carlisle in the spring of 1909, he had developed into a track star.

Thorpe returned to his home and played baseball in North Carolina. In the fall of 1911 he came back to Carlisle. Warner thought he would have a better chance of making the Olympic team if he returned and persuaded him to do so. That year he won all-America honors in football, as he did in 1912 also, performing sensationally against Harvard, Penn, Princeton, Army, Syracuse, and Penn State. Against Harvard in 1911 Thorpe ran 70 yards in nine plays for a touchdown and kicked three field goals from back of the 40-yard line.

President Dwight D. Eisenhower could attest to Thorpe's hitting power. When he was a cadet at the United States Military Academy, the Army team played Carlisle, the Indians winning, 27–6. Thorpe stopped Eisenhower time after time, and in the process the future general injured his knee and never played again.

In his track days Carlisle was booked to meet the Lafayette team at Easton. A welcoming committee was puzzled when only two men got off the train.

"Where's your team?" they asked.

"This is the team," replied Thorpe.

"Only two of you?"

"Only one," Jim said with a smile. "This fellow's the manager."

In the spring of 1912 he started training for the Olympics. He had confined his efforts to the jumps, the hurdles, and the shot put, but now he undertook the pole vault, the javelin, discus, and the hammer. In the Olympic trials held at Celtic Park in New York, his all-round ability stood out in all these events and so he riveted a claim to a place on the team that went to Sweden.

After his suspension as an amateur athlete, following his return from Stockholm, Thorpe left Carlisle in 1913 and signed with the New York Giants. He was optioned out to the Milwaukee club of the American Association and remained there until 1916, when he came back to the Giants for two seasons. After that he went to the Boston Braves and then it was back to the minors.

Although he never could be considered a star in the major leagues, having trouble hitting a curveball, Thorpe was good enough to last for seven seasons. In his last year, 1919, he batted a highly creditable .327 in sixty games, playing first base and the outfield for the Boston Braves.

Meanwhile, he went into the game he loved best—football—as a professional.

In 1915 he organized the famous Canton (Ohio) Bulldogs, which beat most of the good teams. Later he played with the Cleveland Tigers, the LaRue (Ohio) Indians, and the Rock Island Independents. Jim got heavier and found it more difficult to keep in shape, and he was appearing in New York at the Polo Grounds in a drop-kicking contest with Charley Brickley as an extra attraction to the game. He played with other teams in Hammond, Indiana, and Portsmouth, Ohio, and finally his competitive days ended.

After his retirement, Thorpe fell upon hard days. He went to California in 1930 as master of ceremonies for C. C. Pyle's cross-country marathon, known as the bunion derby. He settled down in Hawthorne, California, and got work as an extra in motion pictures, appearing in western serials and in short football features, but things got worse for him.

Thorpe was back in the news in 1943, when the Oklahoma legislature adopted a resolution that the AAU be petitioned to reinstate his Olympic records, but no action would be taken for nearly forty years.

In February 1952, a group in Congress made another unsuccessful attempt to have the medals restored. After an operation for cancer of the lip in the preceding November, he had been discovered to be nearly penniless and groups throughout the country raised thousands of dollars for him.

Although past the age for acceptance by the army or navy in World War II, he joined the merchant marine in 1945 and served on an ammunition ship before the conflict ended.

In the summer of 1949, Warner Brothers started work on a motion picture entitled *Jim Thorpe—All-American*, with Burt Lancaster in the athlete's role. The picture reached Broadway in the summer of 1951.

Thorpe married three times. His first wife was the former Iva Miller, whom he wed in 1913 and was the mother of his three daughters, Gale, Charlotte, and Frances, and his first son, the late James Francis Jr. He married Freeda Kirkpatrick in 1926 and they had four sons, Phillip, William, Richard, and John.

On June 2, 1945, Thorpe wed Patricia Gladys Askew of Louisville, Kentucky. She was with him when he died of a heart attack on March 28, 1953.

World's Greatest Athlete

He was the mightiest athlete at the 1912 Olympic Games in Stockholm through his winning of the pentathlon and decathlon—the five-event and ten-event contests. The world had never seen such a marvel of physical strength as was embodied in James Thorpe, the Carlisle Indian schoolboy. It has been stated by several writers that Goliath and some fabled strong men of history could hardly have competed successfully with Thorpe as an all-around athlete.

The figures he made in the various events in the Stockholm stadium attest that his like has never been seen and that probably no athlete who ever lived can boast of such all-around excellence in track and field work as well as in many other lines of physical endeavor.

He stood then preeminently as a refutation to the allegation on the part of critics all over the world that the American plan of developing athletic marvels is accomplished by specialization carried to unreasonable extremes. It was conceded by his close followers that he was a man of enormous strength, not so much because of his size—he weighed about 185—but because of his ability to concentrate his strength to the channels most needed.

Thorpe was found to be normal when he went to Carlisle as a lad. On entering the school he was 5 feet 5½ inches tall and weighed 115 pounds. As bearing on his physical development, figures at hand show that in 1908 he had jumped to 5 feet 11¼ inches, and his chest measurements at inspiration and expiration, respectively, were 41 and 35 inches. He then weighed 181 pounds.

Three years afterward, or on September 17, 1911, he was 6 feet 1½ inches tall, weighed 185, and inspiration and expiration measurements were 42½ and 35½ inches. Smooth, even development, without knots or bumps, marked the Sac and Fox Indian's progress all along.

To be sure, Thorpe had the training at school for the previous two years at the hands of Pop Warner, and he did nearly all his work in the Cumberland Valley, which was considered by some as giving the best athletic environment to be found in America. But in the building up of this marvelous youth, resort was not made to unusual methods.

Warner never stultified himself or his pupils by extreme treatment. Thorpe lived plainly, and while he conformed to Warner's general instructions as to his manner of living, he was not made an exception at the Carlisle School by special treatment or privileges.

Most remarkable of all possibly was the simple fact that he clearly demonstrated to the world by his marvelous performances at Stockholm that he was the greatest athlete in the world by only demonstrating a bare third of the possibilities that lay in his powerful, alert body.

It must be understood that in addition to the eleven representative sports included in his winning the pentathlon and decathlon, he was equally proficient in such sports as throwing the hammer, swimming, skating, walking, rowing, and possibly a dozen minor athletic activities.

In addition, he was a specialist, and probably the greatest in the world, at football. He ran, sidestepped, plunged, and dodged as well as the best football player that probably ever lived. He punted and kicked goals with strength and precision, interfered or followed interference with cunning, threw forward passes, and made inside kicks with the greatest veterans, and tackled and used the stiff ram with almost perfect technique. That he was elected captain of the 1912 Carlisle Indian football eleven was in itself a tribute to his complete knowledge of the intricate football rules.

Thorpe pitched at baseball, played any base, or occupied the field with equal distinction. At basketball he was little short of a marvel, playing any position. Included among the other sports that he mastered were lacrosse, tennis, hockey, handball, indoor baseball, indoor gymnastics, and medicine ball. Croquet, cricket, and golf were about the only sports Thorpe left alone. He was enthusiastic over horseback riding and hunting, being a dead shot with rifle and shotgun.

His easy method of approaching all of his athletic tasks was the subject of much comment at the time and for years to come.

Gold Medals Restored
By GERALD ESKENAZI

The two gold medals from the 1912 Olympic Games that Jim Thorpe was forced to return after he admitted he had once been paid to play baseball were restored posthumously on October 13, 1982.

The International Olympic Committee in Lausanne, Switzerland, which for many years had resisted returning the medals and restoring Thorpe's amateur status, agreed to do both after hearing a plea by William E. Simon, the president of the United States Olympic Committee.

The proceeding closed a chapter in one of the sports world's most intriguing and, for the Thorpe family, frustrating stories.

Since Thorpe's death on his sixty-fifth birthday in 1953, his widow, his seven children from two previous marriages, and President Ford in 1975, among others, had attempted to bring the medals back to the United States.

Thorpe's Olympic feats and his subsequent loss of the medals gave a poignant aspect to the larger-than-life heroics that surrounded the legendary American Indian athlete's career. Not only were the medals taken away, but his triumphs were expunged from the official Olympic record books as well.

But he is in the halls of fame of three sports—college football, pro football, and track and field—and was a major league baseball player. He lived to see the actor Burt Lancaster portray his life in a movie. And a town in Pennsylvania was renamed for Thorpe after his death.

When he entered the 1912 Olympic Games in Stockholm, he was probably this country's most famous college football player, enrolled at the Carlisle School, an Indian trade school in Pennsylvania. By the end of a week's Olympic activity, he had become the world's most acclaimed athlete as well.

For in that span he competed in two grueling competitions, the five-event pentathlon and the decathlon, with its ten events then spread over three days and climaxed by a 1,500-meter race.

Thorpe captured his first gold medal by winning four of the five pentathlon events and finishing third in the other. Then he went on to take four of the ten decathlon events and finish third in four others and fourth in two. He earned the gold medal in the decathlon—which is based on overall points in the events—after taking the 1,500-meter run by more than fifty yards.

A Massachusetts newsman saw Thorpe's picture in a newspaper and recalled that he had seen Thorpe play baseball professionally two years earlier. It turned out that Thorpe had earned about sixty dollars a month from teams in Fayetteville and Rocky Mount, in North Carolina. United States Olympic officials confronted Thorpe.

Then, the Olympics rules forbade any athlete from competing in the Games if he had been paid to play a sport—even if he did not compete in the Olympics in that sport.

Within six months of the presentation of the medals by King Gustaf V of Sweden, who called him "the world's greatest athlete," Thorpe had to return the medals.

"I was not very wise in the ways of the world and did not realize this was wrong," he said in a 1913 letter of apology to the Amateur Athletic Union.

Still, his fame never waned. In a 1950 poll by the Associated Press, Thorpe was voted the greatest athlete of the half century. His accomplishments included:

• Scoring 25 touchdowns and 198 points for Carlisle in 1912.

• A career in baseball as an outfielder that spanned seven seasons, including one in which he batted .327 for the Boston Braves.

• A pro football career of nine years that followed his baseball retirement.

"He never felt he did anything wrong," one of his four sons recalled after the medals were reinstated. The son, Richard Thorpe, the purchasing agent for the Oklahoma Senate, said, "It's a damn shame it took that long, but that's the way things work sometimes. I think it would have been restored long ago. But Avery Brundage was the chairman of the International Olympic Committee for many years. He competed in 1912 and got beat real bad by my dad. And of course, in 1912, there was a little bit of prejudice against Indians."

Brundage was a controversial figure in United States and international sports. He placed fourteenth in the 1912 decathlon and fifth in the pentathlon. He was among those opposed to restoring Thorpe's medals.

But in the late 1970s and early 1980s, the United States wielded more influence on the international committee, the governing body for the Games. The United States Congress passed resolutions, first in 1979 and again in 1982, requesting that the international committee return the medals. Also, the question of amateurism—the international committee has asked its members to redefine the concept—has become more complex than it was in 1912.

Finally, Mr. Simon, the former Secretary of the Treasury, went before the international committee to ask for the return of Thorpe's medals.

"The very first Olympic meeting I attended in 1965 was about Jim Thorpe and his medals," Mr. Simon recalled after returning from Switzerland. "I went home and told my wife after that meeting, 'Here's a guy took fifteen dollars a game in 1910 and we're still debating about him.' "

In the final meeting, Mr. Simon said, "Everyone just wiped off the Olympic record."

New medals—the originals were redistributed in 1913 to the second-place finishers—would later be presented by the president of the international committee, Juan Antonio Samaranch of Spain, to one of Thorpe's three daughters, Charlotte Thorpe of Phoenix, at a major Olympic meeting in Los Angeles in January 1983. Los Angeles was to be the site of the 1984 summer Olympic Games.

On hearing the news, Miss Thorpe said, "When my father died in 1953, it seemed to me his spirit invaded my body. It gave me such a heavy burden, and I've been pushing this ever since. I started saving newspaper clippings of him when I was a teenager, and I'm sixty-three now."

Miss Thorpe said that she would attempt to bring her father's body back to Oklahoma, where he was born. His third wife, Patricia, who is deceased, moved his remains twice after she was angered when the state of Oklahoma refused to allot $25,000 for a Jim Thorpe memorial.

Finally, in 1954, she was invited by the northeastern Pennsylvania towns of Mauch Chunk and East Mauch Chunk to bring his remains there. The towns had agreed to merge and change their names to Jim Thorpe, and build a mausoleum.

"Tourism is building up more and more," said Mayor Michael Hichok, who is a barber in Jim Thorpe, a town of 5,300. "We have his nice, clean mausoleum."

But Miss Thorpe said, "My next push is to get Dad's remains back to Oklahoma so his soul can rest." But as of this writing, she had not succeeded.

BILL TILDEN

1893–1953

A T THE HEIGHT of his remarkable tennis career, in sport's golden age of the twenties, Bill Tilden was a national and international hero, along with Jack Dempsey, Bobby Jones, Babe Ruth, and Tommy Hitchcock.

He won even more superlatives as a professional at an age when tennis players and athletes in other fields had long since closed their competitive careers. His victories, in his forties, over the world's foremost professionals established him as one of the real miracle men of sport, and he continued to be a headline attraction almost until he had reached the half-century mark.

His record shows:

• He won the national amateur championship seven times, from 1920 through 1925 and in 1930.

• He was the first American to win the men's championship of Great Britain at Wimbledon, in 1920, and he triumphed there twice again, in 1921 and 1930.

• He won thirty-one national crowns as an amateur indoors and outdoors in singles, doubles, and mixed doubles.

• He was ranked as the No. 1 player of his country as an amateur ten times from 1920 through 1929.

• He played on the Davis Cup team eleven years from 1920 through 1930, and that from 1920 through 1925 he was unbeaten in singles and lost only one match in doubles of a total of twenty-two cup matches.

It was as the ace of the American Davis Cup team that Tilden gained his greatest prestige, though from 1920 through 1925 he was so invincible that no player the world over stood a chance against him in any competition. A member of the team that went to Australia in 1920 to bring back the international team trophy to the United States, he stood as the bulwark of its defense until the Four Musketeers of France—René Lacoste, Henri Cochet, Jean Borotra, and Jacques Brugnon—broke America's long hold on the trophy in 1927, marking France's first victory in a Davis Cup challenge round.

In 1928, Tilden was the captain of the team that went to Europe seeking to win back the cup. Out of that trip arose the most celebrated of the many dramatic episodes in his career.

While in France he was removed as captain of the team and declared ineligible to play for his country because of his violation of the amateur rule. He was considered a professional by the United States Lawn Tennis Association

because he was writing for American publications about his playing experiences. Today there are no restrictions on a tennis player's ability to make money.

The United States defeated Italy without his services and qualified to meet France in the challenge round. When the French realized that he was not to be allowed to play against their team, their indignation knew no bounds.

This was the first time they were to have the honor of staging a Davis Cup challenge round. For the occasion, they had built a beautiful new stadium at Auteuil, indirectly a monument to the drawing power of Tilden. To put on the show without Big Bill was unthinkable to them. It was like putting on *Hamlet* without the Melancholy Dane.

The outcry was so great, feeling ran so high, that Ambassador Myron T. Herrick found it necessary to intercede for the sake of international amity. Upon his request, the United States Lawn Tennis Association restored Tilden to the team at the eleventh hour.

To add to the drama, Tilden threw a scare into the French by defeating the great Lacoste. Upon his return home with the team, which was beaten by the French, Tilden was brought up on charges of violating the amateur rule and was barred from competing in the national championships that year, 1928.

Except for that year and 1926, when he was beaten in the quarter finals by Cochet, Tilden was in every national championship final from 1918 through 1929. He was runner-up to R. Lindley Murray in 1918, to William Johnston in 1919, and to Lacoste in 1927. In 1930, his last year as an amateur, he was beaten in the semifinals by John Doeg, the first American to conquer him in the championship since 1919.

It was on the private court of the family country home that Bill Tilden had his introduction to tennis. There and at Germantown, Philadelphia, where he was born on February 10, 1893, he was playing the game when he was barely able to hold a racquet.

By 1910, young Tilden was widely known in competition around Philadelphia. He attended the University of Pennsylvania and played varsity tennis there.

In 1920, Tilden was named on the Davis Cup team that went to England for the qualifying rounds, and with his victory at Wimbledon began the most absolute sway tennis has known. From the age of twenty-seven to thirty-three he bestrode the court like a colossus. In the autumn of 1922, he suffered the amputation of the upper joint of his right middle finger as the result of an infection.

That might have ended the career of some, but Tilden overcame it, as he did physical frailties in his boyhood days and a knee injury later in his career. If anything, he was even more the master in 1923, 1924, and 1925. Then Lacoste and Cochet caught up with him in 1926 and 1927. He came back in 1929 to regain the championship, and in 1930, at the age of thirty-seven, he thrilled the tennis world by triumphing at Wimbledon on the same stretch of turf where he had been victorious ten years earlier.

In December 1930, Tilden said good-bye to amateur tennis. Like Bobby Jones, he made his exit by way of the motion pictures. He signed a contract to appear in a series of short films devoted to tennis, automatically disqualifying himself for amateur competition.

The next February, Tilden launched his career as a professional player at the age of thirty-eight at Madison Square Garden. He defeated Karel Kozeluh of Czechoslovakia. In May, he defeated Vincent Richards and again in 1932.

In 1939, Tilden settled in Los Angeles and remained there for the rest of his life. He was taken up by the movie colony, playing regularly on Charlie Chaplin's court. Even in his fifties many people regarded him as the best player in the world for one set.

In 1946, Tilden's luck ran out. He was arrested in a compromising situation with a boy of fourteen. He pleaded guilty and expressed contrition. But his palpable lie that he had never before committed any such act angered the judge. Instead of probation he was sentenced to a year in jail. He did seven and a half months. While still on parole he was arrested again, and did another ten months. Broke, abandoned, his portrait removed from the walls of the Germantown Cricket Club, his records destroyed by the University of Pennsylvania Alumni Association, he drifted like a ghost until his death on June 5, 1953.

On February 3, 1950, he was named the greatest tennis player of the first half of the twentieth century by an overwhelming vote in a poll taken by the Associated Press and is still regarded as one of the great practitioners of the game.

BILL VEECK

1914–1986

T O HIS FELLOW EXECUTIVES in the big leagues, Bill Veeck was a
rebel who owned the Cleveland Indians, the St. Louis Browns, and the
Chicago White Sox (twice), and who pulled outrageous stunts to promote them.
To the public, he was a creative genius and an original: a craggy dynamo of a
man who limped on an artificial leg, spoke in a hoarse voice, dressed casually,
without necktie or overcoat, and created excitement and controversy wherever
he staged events and drew crowds.

To himself, he was "Old Will," who expressed his sense of the entrepre-
neur's art in his books, *Veeck, as in Wreck*, and *The Hustler's Handbook*. He
was amused that his showmanship often alarmed his fellow club owners in
baseball or the racing establishment when he ran the Suffolk Downs track near
Boston. He was criticized and even ostracized, but to all his critics and doubters,
he offered one basic thought: "Tradition is the albatross around the neck of
progress."

In pursuit of that wisdom, he wooed the public with tricks, gifts, and
bargains. He gave orchids to the women, placed gift certificates beneath the
stadium or racetrack seats, sent circus clowns to the coaching lines, and even
held a Grandstand Manager's Day, during which the Browns' strategy for one
game was dictated by people in the grandstand, who were asked to signify by
applause when signs were hoisted asking INFIELD IN? or SHOULD WE WALK
HIM?

But his most memorable stunt came on August 19, 1951, when he was
running the Browns, a team of perennial losers that lost 102 games that season
and finished 46 games behind the Yankees, the pennant winners.

At a suitably dramatic moment in a game against the Detroit Tigers, he
sent in a suitably dramatic pinch hitter: Eddie Gaedel, a theatrical midget who
stood 3 feet 6½ inches tall. Gaedel promptly walked on four (high) pitches and
ended his career as suddenly as he had started it.

Bob Fishel, the late executive vice president of the American League, was
working as Veeck's deputy in those days in both Cleveland and St. Louis. He
remembered the short but spectacular career of Eddie Gaedel.

"It was Bill's idea," he said, "but I actually signed Eddie to a contract for
$100. After he went to bat, the president of the league, Will Harridge, ruled that
midgets were not eligible to play. But we had already released him. But Eddie
made all the big TV shows as a guest and made something like $17,000 in fees
for that one time at bat."

But Bill Veeck proved to be no mere stuntman. After he bought the Cleveland Indians in 1946, they won the American League pennant and the World Series in 1948 and played before 2,620,627 fans, a major league record at the time. After he bought the Chicago White Sox in 1959, they promptly won the pennant and set a club record by drawing 1,644,468 customers.

"Veeck was born into baseball and belongs there," Red Smith once wrote. "He is an independent thinker, imaginative, uninhabited, innovative. He is a promoter at heart but a baseball man at bottom."

Al Lopez, who was the manager of the White Sox in 1959, remembered Veeck at his dramatic best in that season: "He promised he'd eat crow at State and Lake if I would win the pennant with that team. The following year, he went out to State and Lake and ate crow—or pheasant, or something."

Bill Veeck was born into a baseball family on February 9, 1914. His father, Bill Veeck, Sr., was a Chicago baseball writer who became president of the Cubs, and young Bill would roam around Wrigley Field running errands and checking the turnstiles.

He studied law at Loyola University in Chicago and once wrote a letter to Kenesaw Mountain Landis, the commissioner of baseball, warning that the "reserve clause" in contracts was illegal and probably doomed. He suggested a solution: sign players to seven-year contracts, the way the Hollywood film studios were doing. Nothing happened, but forty years later the "reserve clause" was ruled illegal and the era of the free agent opened with revolutionary changes in sports.

In 1941, he took his first plunge into professional baseball as head of a syndicate that bought the Milwaukee Brewers, then a minor league team in the American Association. He hired the effervescent Charley Grimm as manager, and the two began to stage stunts and shows that turned the Brewers into a profitable team.

But two years later, he joined the Marines and was sent to the South Pacific, where his right leg was struck one day by the recoil of an antiaircraft gun. The leg was lost, and he later endured dozens of operations to mend the damage.

Back home, he returned to baseball in style in 1946: he was only thirty-two, but he headed a group that bought the Indians. The team finished sixth that season, but two years later won the pennant and the World Series before record crowds. That team included the outfielder Larry Doby, who had been signed the season before as the American League's first black player.

Three years later, Veeck turned his talents toward St. Louis and bought the struggling Browns, and struggled with them for three years in a city dominated by the Cardinals. His fellow owners refused to let him move the team, forced him to sell, and then quickly allowed the new owner to move the Browns to Baltimore.

It took Veeck until 1959 to wedge his way back into the big leagues, but he did it with a clatter. He headed a group of investors who bought the White Sox, and once more found instant success. The team couldn't hit, but it could pitch, and it won the pennant in his first season as the resident magician. But the next year, the White Sox dropped into third place. In 1961, seriously ill at the time, Veeck sold the club to his partners, Arthur and John Allyn, and more or less retired to a country estate in Easton on Maryland's Eastern Shore.

His immediate aim was to restore his health, but he said, "Old Will will be back." And he did come back—but this time as the operator of Suffolk Downs, where his creative mind was as sharp as ever. He staged Joe Fan Day, stashed a prize-winning certificate under one chair in the grandstand, and awarded the winner a three-year-old filly.

"Altruism is not one of my great gifts," he said. "The average racing fan is slightly over fifty years of age. If you don't create new fans, how do you insure future growth, or even future existence?"

But baseball remained his main interest. In 1970, he tried to buy the Baltimore Orioles but was blocked. In 1975, when the White Sox were packing to move to Seattle, he put together a financial group, bought them, and kept them in Chicago.

Veeck stayed with the club five years then tried to sell it to Edward J. DeBartolo, Sr. This time he was blocked by Bowie Kuhn, the commissioner of baseball, reportedly because DeBartolo owned race tracks and did not live in Chicago. Veeck argued and lost, then sold the team to Jerry Reinsdorf, a real estate executive, for twenty million dollars. This time, he left baseball for good.

"I didn't like the American League owners when I came into the league," he said, "and I don't like them going out of it. Of course, I'm sure the feeling is mutual."

Veeck died of a heart attack on January 2, 1986. He was seventy-one years old. In 1991 he was elected to the Hall of Fame.

The Pied Piper

By IRA BERKOW

Some will remember how Bill Veeck threw a post–leg-amputation party for himself—he was not about to wallow in self-pity—and danced the night away on his new wooden limb. That was in 1946, more than a year after he was injured. He had been a marine on Guadalcanal during World War II when an antiaircraft gun recoiled into his leg, and the leg became infected.

Others in recent years will remember—who can forget?—that wrinkled old face with that bright, boyish look in his eyes. And you had to remember his laugh, a deep, hoarse, genuinely delighted laugh, with head thrown back and stein of beer gripped solidly.

Others will remember him as the greatest hustler since Jack Falstaff. And perhaps it was no coincidence that when he was the owner of the Chicago White Sox he named the press quarters The Bard's Room. He understood that it couldn't hurt business to con the reporters some, too.

Bill Veeck will be remembered by many as the guy who brought midgets and orchids to baseball, or exploding scoreboards to the ball field, and signed the first black to play in the American League, Larry Doby, and put old Satchel Paige into a big-league uniform. And he'll be remembered by some as the guy who never wore a tie but who made starchy baseball owners so tight around the collar they got bug-eyed.

And some will remember how much he loved baseball. And some will remember how much he loved people. And some will remember both. "The most beautiful thing in the world," he once said, "is a ball park filled with people."

I have my own memories of William Louis Veeck, Jr. I remember him covering the Philadelphia-Baltimore World Series in 1983 for the *Chicago Tribune*. And in the outdoor press box in Philadelphia I noticed him at game's end set up his turquoise portable typewriter and begin to hit the keys. He had been forced for financial reasons to sell the White Sox three years before, but his heart was still in the game—it always would be—and now he would write about it. On deadline. He was no phony. This former big-league baseball owner wrote his own stuff. I remember reading one of his pieces afterward and enjoying it very much. He knew the game, had original insights, and stuck the adverbs and adjectives in all the right places.

I remember the first time I heard Veeck speak. It was in a hotel in Chicago in 1959—the first year that he ran the White Sox. He had placed billboards all around the city proclaiming "We will bring a pennant to Chicago." I remember that the hall in the hotel was filled. Veeck at the lectern fidgeted and he seemed to list because of his leg, but he spoke without notes and told stories—old stories, but fresh to my then-fresh ears—about how poorly the Browns in St. Louis drew: One day he asked someone to come to a Browns game. The person said, "What time does it start?" Veeck replied, "What time's convenient?" The crowd loved him. So did the rest of the city.

True to his word, he brought a pennant to Chicago that very first year and set another attendance record. He made Comiskey Park—often a dreary joint—a swell place for a few hours' entertainment. He not only cleaned up the old park and had it painted, he even installed washrooms and an outdoor shower for the people in the bleachers. For the nearly fifty years that Comiskey Park had been in existence, those who had been treated as the underclass in the bleachers had simply been inconvenienced.

Veeck cared enough about them—and his promotion—to do something about it. One of the people he brought with him to Chicago was Hank Greenberg, the Hall of Fame ball player who became Veeck's general manager there. Greenberg was also his assistant when Veeck owned the Cleveland Indians in the middle 1940s. Greenberg lived in Beverly Hills, and on the morning when it was learned that Veeck had died, I called him.

"I've lost a great friend and great partner—he was the most unusual man I ever met," Greenberg said. His voice was a little shaky. As we spoke, there were moments when Greenberg stopped to gather himself.

"Bill brought baseball into the twentieth century," he continued. "He sold baseball not just on the field, but off the field. Before Bill, baseball was just win or lose. But he made it fun to be at the ball park. Even if it was a lousy game that day, a lady could go home with an orchid he had handed out. Of course, he always wanted to win, and knew he'd draw more if he did.

"I remember the 1948 season in Cleveland when we set the attendance record of the major leagues with 2.6 million. I'd look out the window of the stadium and see these great crowds of people coming over the bridge and heading for the ball park. I told Bill, 'You're like the Pied Piper.'

"Bill wasn't just a guy trying to make a buck by running promotions. He really enjoyed people enjoying themselves. He was color-blind and race-blind and religion-blind. I first met him in 1947 and he talked to me about the Indians—I mean the ones in Oklahoma and Texas—and how unfairly they had been treated. I never knew from such things. This was so far advanced for me. I was a guy who was concerned with base hits and how to win a ball game. It opened up my eyes. When he brought Satchel Paige into baseball, a lot of people said he was making a mockery of the game, because Satchel was forty-eight or something. Remember, this was a day when a ball player was really old at thirty-two or thirty-three. Well, Satch was six and one for us down the stretch and we won the pennant."

Though Veeck was out of baseball for the last six years of his life, he couldn't stay away and was frequently seen in the bleachers in Wrigley Field. Greenberg recalled: "The last time we talked, Bill said, 'You know, I think I can get the Cleveland club.' I said, 'You're crazy. Why don't you go someplace where you have a chance to make some money? Why don't you go into the stock market, or some other business? With your talents you can make a lot of money at anything.' "

HONUS WAGNER

1874–1955

B ASEBALL CAN BE as controversial a topic as politics, especially when it comes to ranking the great players of the past and present. But, as with Babe Ruth, Ty Cobb, Christy Mathewson, and a select few other outstanding performers, there has been almost perfect unanimity among the experts that Honus Wagner belonged among the immortals of the game.

In fact, there are many who will argue that the Flying Dutchman should be placed at the top of the list. Be this as it may, there have been or are now no serious challengers to Wagner in his generally accepted designation as baseball's greatest shortstop.

It was at this position that Wagner performed for the greater part of his twenty-one consecutive years of major league service, from 1897 through 1917. In various emergencies, he filled in at other spots, in fact, playing every position except catcher. He still is regarded as the yardstick of excellence for shortstops.

Wagner also was one of the most noted batsmen of his day. He had a lifetime mark of .328, hitting more than .300 in seventeen successive seasons. He led the National League eight times, 1900, 1903, 1904, 1906, 1907, 1908, 1909, and 1911.

His lifetime fielding mark was .945, and he was first among the National League shortstops in 1912, 1914, and 1915. In addition, he led his league in stolen bases in 1902, 1904, 1907, and 1908.

Other records set by Wagner are the National League marks for playing the most games (2,785), leading the league the most times in batting (eight), hitting more than .300 the most times (seventeen), and making the most hits (3,430), the most runs (1,740), and most total bases (4,878). Of these, his records for leading the league the most times and hitting more than .300 still stand. His batting feats were all the more remarkable since he had to contend with such obstacles as trick pitches, long outfields, and a "dead" ball.

Wagner was modest and good-natured. He avoided disputes with the umpires and had no salary wrangles with his employers. He never was a holdout. In fact, it is said that he often signed blank contracts, leaving it to Barney Dreyfuss, president of the Pirates, to fill in a figure he considered fair.

His love for baseball went far deeper than the money he made in the game. He played for the love of playing and his interest in baseball survived his playing days, and he retained his active connections until the very end.

Wagner was born in Carnegie, Pennsylvania, on February 24, 1874. He was christened John Peter, but during his baseball career he was familiarly

known as Honus or Hans. The Flying Dutchman sobriquet, fastened on him by the fans, was indicative of the dash and speed he displayed in the field and on the baselines.

After gaining prominence on the sandlots while earning his livelihood as a barber, Wagner broke into professional baseball in 1895 with the Steubenville, Ohio, club. He received a trial at the insistence of his older brother, Albert, also a ball player, who refused to sign unless the club took Honus as well.

Wagner was an immediate success at Steubenville and the next year advanced to the Paterson, New Jersey, club of the old Atlantic League. His play at Paterson attracted the attention of the Louisville club, then a member of the National League and operated by Dreyfuss. Louisville purchased Mr. Wagner's release for $2,200, and he began his major league career with the Colonels in 1897, winning a regular position at the start.

In 1900 the National League circuit was reduced from twelve teams to eight, and Dreyfuss bought the Pittsburgh franchise, taking Wagner with him. The shortstop remained with the Pirates until he retired from active play in 1917 at the age of forty-three. In his final season he was made manager of the team, but the task was not to his liking and he gave it up after less than a week.

After leaving the Pirates, Wagner continued to play semiprofessional baseball in the Pittsburgh area until he was well past fifty. During this period he served as manager of a sporting goods store and in other ways kept in contact with baseball. He was appointed an assistant sergeant-at-arms in the Pennsylvania State Legislature in 1929 and once was nominated for the office of sheriff in Pittsburgh.

Wagner was brought back to his old team in an official capacity in 1933, when he was appointed a coach. He served continuously with the Pirates for the next eighteen years, and the sight of his rugged, bow-legged figure on the field awakened nostalgic feelings among the old-timers in the stands.

Throughout his career one of the outstanding features about Wagner was his vitality. One of the strongest players in the game in his active days—he weighed 190 pounds and was 5 feet 11 inches tall—he possessed an amazing vigor, even after he had passed sixty, and he often set the pace for his youthful charges in the pregame workouts of the Pirates.

During his term as coach of Pittsburgh, Wagner also served for several years as commissioner for the National Semi-Pro Baseball Congress, in which capacity he had jurisdiction over 25,000 sandlot teams.

In 1936, he was among the first group of stars named to baseball's Hall of Fame. He retired on a Pirate pension in 1951, and two years later the locker he had used as player and coach was shipped to the baseball shrine at Cooperstown, New York.

At the turn of the century the bat-manufacturing concern of Hillerich & Bradsby conceived the idea of having major league ball players endorse their product, with the players autographing their particular models. Wagner was the first to have his autograph appear on one of these bats. This was in 1905.

Although in his later years Wagner remained confined to his home in Carnegie, honors continued to be showered upon him. On the occasion of his eightieth birthday, in 1954, he was deluged with greetings, one of them from President Eisenhower.

With the opening of the 1954 season at Forbes Field in Pittsburgh, the Pirates, as part of the inaugural day ceremonies, presented a special plaque to Wagner as baseball's Mr. Shortstop.

A bronze statue of Wagner was unveiled in Schenley Park in Pittsburgh in 1955. A public campaign had provided the $30,000 needed for the statue. The great shortstop, weakened by age, saw the unveiling from an automobile parked near adjacent Forbes Field, where he had played for the Pirates half a century before.

He died on December 6, 1955, at eighty-one years of age.

There Weren't Any "Buts"

By ARTHUR DALEY

The way the story goes is that Ed Barrow made a trip down the Monongahela Valley to scout a ball player named Al Wagner. On the way he became fascinated by a big rawboned kid in dungarees who was picking up rocks along the railroad right of way and unconcernedly scaling them across the river. So Barrow forgot all about Al Wagner and signed Al's brother, Honus, the big kid in the dungarees.

When John McGraw insisted that Honus Wagner was the greatest of all ball players, the Little Napoleon might have been accused of being prejudiced in favor of a National Leaguer. But Barrow was the founder of the Yankee empire and an American Leaguer. He'd managed Babe Ruth and seen Ty Cobb. Yet Cousin Ed agreed with McGraw.

Much has been written about the fabled Flying Dutchman, but the story still is far from told. Now that Honus is dead at the age of eighty-one more acclaim is bound to pour down on this massive man with the granite features and the gentle heart.

Impossible to ignore is a tribute Casey Stengel paid him in one of his rambling dissertations. The general topic, when he stuck to it, was great ball players.

"They'd say that this feller was great but—" he said. "And then they'd tell you what his weakness was. With Wagner, though, there weren't any 'buts.' He was great, period." Casey could rattle along for hours on the subject of this unchallenged king of the shortstops until Honus soon sounded like Paul Bunyan, in a baseball suit. There was a Bunyanesque quality to him at that.

Poll Perritt, the pitcher, swore that he once served up a low fast ball to Wagner and . . . . But let him tell it.

"I was still in my follow-through," he said, "when the Dutchman swung. The ball shot under my arm and over the center-field fence."

Primarily, he was a line drive hitter with triples his specialty. But this eight-time National League batting champion had such tremendous power that he undoubtedly would have been a top home run hitter if he'd ever swung against the lively ball.

Honus was such a delightful storyteller that it generally was difficult to determine where fact and fiction parted company. There was a twinkle in his eyes when this reporter asked him to describe the greatest throw he ever made.

"The base runner was hung up between third and home," he said, "when I ran over to help in the rundown. But that feller was a cute one. He got between me and the catcher so that I couldn't throw home without hitting him. So I threw a curve that hooked right around him and into the catcher's glove."

Do you believe it? When Wagner was involved, you could believe almost anything.

Once when he was playing first base—he was so versatile that he was in the big leagues five years before he settled down at shortstop—he wanted a chaw of eating tobacco. He took off his glove and shoved his left paw into his back pocket just as the pitcher threw the ball. The batter grounded to short and the ball was fielded smartly.

Honus tried to yank his hand free. But his hamlike hands were so huge that his fist was imprisoned by the pocket. So the Dutchman made the catch with his bare right hand. They had to cut away the pocket afterward.

Considering the fact that he was a simple, guileless youth when he broke into the big leagues, Honus learned fast. He was prey for all tricks until he became a better trickster than any of the others.

One day he broke for second to take the catcher's throw on a steal. The throw was a mile over Wagner's head. Deadpan and serene, he went through the motions of making the catch, being careful to appear a fraction late in making the tag. Then he tumbled, all 200 pounds of him, atop the runner while outfielders frantically chased the ball to keep the runner from scoring.

"Don't move," said Honus to the runner in a hoarse stage whisper. "I've ripped the seat out of my pants and if you'll wait a minute, sonny, they'll bring out some pins to me."

The trusting runner waited while the ball was relayed back to the infield. That was one of the rare business lies that this wonderful man ever told.

The most he ever earned was $10,000 at the end of his career in an era when—to use his own words—"a glass of beer only cost a nickel."

When Barney Dreyfuss, the Pittsburgh owner, offered to double his salary to keep him from jumping to the American League, the loyal Honus refused.

"Cut the salary in half," he said, "or I won't sign. I'm just not worth it." Oh, no?

CY YOUNG

1867–1955

T RADED TO THE MAJORS from the minors for a suit of clothing, Cy Young thrilled the baseball world from 1890 to 1911 with a blazing fastball that set pitching records of towering proportions.

Six feet two inches tall and weighing 210 pounds, this Ohio farmer pitched and won more games than any major leaguer. When he retired at the age of forty-five because his legs had weakened, he had won 511 of 826 decisions in both leagues and for five teams. In all, he hurled in 906 games.

As the starting pitcher for the Boston Red Sox in 1903, Young threw the first pitch in a World Series game. Fifty years later, as a guest at the opening game of the World Series between the Brooklyn Dodgers and New York Yankees, he stood in the pitcher's box and threw a ceremonial strike to the Yankee catcher, Yogi Berra, to open the Series. He was eighty-six at the time.

During his career, he was a thirty-game winner five seasons; a twenty-game victor sixteen times. He pitched one perfect game, two other no-hit shut-outs, and performed the "iron man" feat of hurling and winning complete games of a doubleheader.

One of the early members of the Baseball Hall of Fame at Cooperstown, New York, Young pitched for the Cleveland Nationals, St. Louis Cardinals, Red Sox, Cleveland Indians, and Boston Braves. He won 291 National League games and 220 in the American.

For fourteen consecutive years, beginning in 1891, Young won twenty or more games. The 1892 season, when he posted a 36–10 record, was his best.

He pitched 23 consecutive hitless innings over a four-game span early in 1904 and amassed 2,836 strikeouts.

He was born on a farm in Gilmore, Ohio, on March 29, 1867. While pitching for the Canton, Ohio, club of the old Tri-State League in 1890, Denton True Young was nicknamed Cy. "I thought I had to show all my stuff," he recalled years later, "and I almost tore the boards off the grandstand with my fastball. One of the fellows called me 'Cyclone,' but finally shortened it to 'Cy,' and it's been that ever since."

The league disbanded during the 1890 season and the pitcher joined the Cleveland Nationals early in August of that year.

Still a gawky country boy, he made his major league debut against Cap Anson's Chicago White Stockings and won the game. Young won 10 and lost 7 for Cleveland during the late stages of the season. Two of those victories were

obtained on October 4, when he captured both ends of a doubleheader against Philadelphia.

In his first complete major league campaign the next year, Young won 27 and lost 22 games. For the next thirteen seasons he stayed above the .500 mark. He pitched his first major league no-hit, no-run contest on September 18, 1897, blanking Cincinnati, 6 to 0. His affiliation with Cleveland ended after the 1898 campaign, and he played with the St. Louis Cardinals in 1899 and 1900.

Young began eight years with the Red Sox in 1901. While blanking Philadelphia on May 5, 1904, he did not permit an opposing runner to reach first base. It was the third perfect game in major league history. On June 30, 1908, he won his third no-hit, no-run decision in the majors by shutting out New York, 8 to 0.

He was traded to the Cleveland Indians in 1909, and in the middle of the 1911 campaign was traded to the Braves. He retired to his farm near Peoli, Ohio, after that season.

He was eighty-eight years old when he died on November 4, 1955.

He'll Always Be First
By ARTHUR DALEY

When Cy Young had passed his eightieth birthday, his back was bowed ever so slightly by the weight of his years. But there was still the look of a former athlete about him. Perhaps it was the sweep of those wide shoulders that stirred visions of the gangling farmboy who shook the hayseed from his hair and then went on to baffle big-league batters for twenty-three seasons. Like Abou Ben Adhem, he is first on the list.

Yet there once was an occasion when a young man meeting old Cy for the first time professed his ignorance of history by asking a question of the white-haired gaffer.

"Pardon me, Mr. Young," said the boy, "did you ever pitch in the big leagues?"

"Sonny," said old Cy, his kindly eyes twinkling, "I'd like you to know that I *won* more big-league ball games than you are likely to see in your entire lifetime."

There was so much truth in that statement. The big right-hander won 511 games and not too many fans get to attend that many games in a lifetime. Some of the more youthful fans unaware of Young's existence are often so jarred to learn that someone had once reached the fantastic total of 511 that they ask for details.

For one thing this fireballing marvel had 14 straight seasons when he was a 20-game winner. Then he missed a pair and had two more. Five of those seasons were ultrafancy with 36, 34, 35, 31, and 32.

He came off an Ohio farm to try out for the Canton team. He wore no uniform. He had no equipment and no catcher as he pitched against the star Canton hitter, who didn't nick him for a loud foul as the ball crashed into the stands behind the plate.

"How's that kid pitcher?" asked the Canton owner of George Moreland, the manager.

"Just look at your grandstand," said Moreland.

" 'Pears as though a cyclone struck it," said the owner.

That's how Denton True Young got the nickname of Cyclone Young, later shortened to Cy.

He pitched for Cleveland in 1890 and finished with Boston in 1911, losing his final game, 1 to 0, to Grover Cleveland Alexander. He pitched in 886 games and never had a sore arm. He never even had a rubdown.

"Can't understand these modern fellows," he once remarked to this reporter. "I just pitched every third day. 'Twarn't nuthin' to it."

He was a big man, 6 feet 2 inches and 210 pounds. But there are even bigger pitchers around today and they can't stand the gaff. Perhaps farm life gave him the heritage of toughness. When he was seventy-five years old, he split 3,000 railposts just for the exercise.

He lived on the same Ohio ridge for most of his lifetime, which was a long one, because he didn't die until he was eighty-eight. His grandpappy got the deed to the land from Thomas Jefferson.

"All us Youngs could throw," he once remarked. "I usta kill squirrels with a stone when I was a kid. My granddad," he continued, his voice swelling with pride, "once killed a turkey buzzard on the fly with a rock."

Perhaps that explains the genesis of his ability to a certain extent. But it doesn't go all the way.

This remarkable pitcher had three no-hitters during a career that was split almost evenly in two centuries. The middle one was the best.

It had to be. It was a perfect game, one of only twelve in this century. He pitched it for the Red Sox against the Philadelphia Athletics and it was a real hair-raiser. Opposing him was the legendary Rube Waddell, and Young was the winner, 1 to 0.

"The odd part about that game," Young said speculatively, blue eyes gazing down memory lane, "is that there wasn't even a hard chance—until Waddell came to bat for the final out. He hit a sizzler but right at an infielder."

If a new generation of fans thinks that Nolan Ryan is extraordinary as he goes past the 300 victory mark, they are right. But this merely serves to put in truer perspective the feats of Cy Young, who won 511.

"It really should have been 512," said this dogged old gentleman, his faded blue eyes flashing fire even when he was more than eighty. "The scorer cheated me out of one more."

BABE DIDRIKSON ZAHARIAS

1914-1956

FROM THE TIME she made the headlines during the 1932 Olympic Games at Los Angeles, winning the javelin throw and eighty-meter hurdles, Babe Didrikson Zaharias reigned as the world's top all-around woman athlete. In 1949 she was voted the greatest female athlete of the half century by the Associated Press, a selection that surprised no one.

The athletic career of Mildred Didrikson was an unusual one. As a youngster—she was born June 26, 1914, in Port Arthur, Texas—she excelled at running, swimming, diving, high-jumping, baseball, and basketball in addition to being adept with the javelin and at going over hurdles.

She was a success at any sport she undertook and gave conclusive proof of this with her prowess in golf—a game she began to play in 1935.

At least part of Zaharias's success could be attributed to her powers of concentration and diligence. When she decided to center her attention on golf, she tightened up her game by driving as many as 1,000 golf balls a day and playing until her hands were so sore they had to be taped. She developed an aggressive, dramatic style, hitting down sharply and crisply on her iron shots like a man and averaging 240 yards off the tee with her woods.

She began winning golf titles in 1940. In that year she captured the Western and Texas Open championships. These victories were forerunners of many to come. By the end of 1950 she had the distinction of having won every available golf title. Asked whether she had any idea of retiring, Zaharias answered in characteristic style; "As long as I am improving, I will go on, and besides, there's too much money in the business to quit."

She turned professional in 1947, after her triumph in the British Amateur championship, a distinction that she was the first American to earn. In 1948 she won the world championship tournament and the National Open. She repeated her victory in the "world" event the next three years. She was the runner-up in the Nationals in 1949 and came back to win it in 1950.

Zaharias was an athlete almost from the time she was strong enough to lift a baseball bat. She beat the boys at mumblety-peg, outsped them in foot races, and outshone them in basketball and baseball. Her nickname of Babe, after Babe Ruth, was acquired after she had hit five home runs in a baseball game. She conditioned herself by using a backyard weight-lifting machine built of broomsticks and her mother's flatirons.

The athlete from Texas was a constant source of colorful stories. She once pitched for the St. Louis Cardinals in an exhibition baseball game. She toured

the United States, giving billiard exhibitions and showed her true versatility with a demonstration of needlework and typing. She could type eighty-six words a minute.

She met her future husband on a golf course in 1937. They were married a year later and eventually set up house in Tampa, Florida, just off a golf course they had purchased in 1951.

In April 1953, she underwent an operation for cancer in Beaumont, Texas. By July she had recovered—to play tournament golf again. Ten months after the surgery she won the $5,000 Serbin Women's Open Tournament at Miami Beach.

She regarded her comeback as complete when she won the 1954 United States Women's Open. Zaharias's margin was twelve strokes at Peabody, Massachusetts, as she recaptured the title she had held twice before.

"It will show a lot of people that they need not be afraid of an operation and can go on and live a normal life," she commented shortly after this triumph.

Early in 1955, however, a hip pain sidelined Zaharias. After an operation for a ruptured spinal disk, her physicians found that she was again suffering from cancer.

Zaharias accepted stoically the news that the disease had returned. "Well, that's the rub of the greens," she told her husband. Together they established the Babe Didrikson Zaharias Fund to support cancer clinics and treatment centers.

Her autobiography, *This Life I've Led*, as told to Harry Paxton, was published late in 1955. And shortly before her death, she established the Babe Didrikson Zaharias Trophy to be awarded annually to the American woman amateur athlete who had done the most during the year for women's sports.

Zaharias won many golfing prizes. One of these was the Ben Hogan Trophy, named for another famous golfing Texan. This was awarded to her in 1953 by the Golf Writers of America for overcoming a physical handicap to play golf. She was the first winner of this trophy.

During the latter stages of her career as a golfer it was estimated she was earning more than $100,000 a year for exhibitions, endorsements, and other activities connected with sports. She drew a considerable salary from a sporting goods company that manufactured equipment bearing her name. Zaharias also dipped into the journalistic field, writing instructional articles and a book entitled *Championship Golf*.

While she captivated many with her versatile stunts as a youngster, it was her achievements and deportment later in life that gained for her the most popularity. As a young girl she had disdained lipstick, plastered her hair back, and talked out of the side of her mouth.

But as a top player and drawing power in golf, her attitude and demeanor changed. The once lonely tomboy became a social success. She developed into a graceful ballroom dancer and became the life of many a social gathering. She was too skillful at gin rummy for most, and at times, to change the pace at a party, she would take out a harmonica and give a rendition of hillbilly tunes she had learned as a youngster.

This change was the cause of a more convivial feeling toward her by rivals.

In her younger days her desire to win had served to toughen her as far as any opponent was concerned. But in her later days, instead of greeting her rivals with, "Yep, I'm gonna beat you," she began encouraging the younger girls on the golf circuit.

Zaharias was the sixth of seven children born to Mr. and Mrs. Ole Didrikson. Her father was a Norwegian ship carpenter who had sailed nineteen times around Cape Horn before settling down at Port Arthur.

She died when she was forty-two years old on September 27, 1956.

Implausible Is Best

By ARTHUR DALEY

The team championship at the National Amateur Athletic Union track and field meet in 1932 was won by the Employers Casualty Company of Dallas. Its points were achieved through the winning of five individual championships and the tying for a sixth. The entire "team" consisted of one eighteen-year-old girl, Babe Didrikson.

Implausible is the adjective which best befits the Babe. As far as sport is concerned, she had the golden touch of a Midas. When she was only sixteen, she was named to the all-America women's basketball team. She once hit thirteen home runs in a softball doubleheader. Her top bowling score was 237. In the 1932 Olympics she won two events, setting world records in each, and placed second in the third test, although again breaking the world record.

But it was as a golfer in her later years that she gained most renown, dominating the the divot-digging pastime with awesome efficiency. Best remembered is the rueful flippancy Bob Hope tossed over his shoulder after pairing with her in a charity match.

"I hit the ball like a girl and she hits it like a man," he said. Hope was at least half-correct. The Babe hit the ball like a man.

But behind that steel-sinewed, square-jawed facade was feminine softness and gushy sentimentality. The first time the Babe ever had any extra money, she took her mother to a department store in her native Beaumont, Texas.

"Momma, pick you out a dress," drawled the Babe pridefully. Momma did.

"Pick you out another one," urged the Babe, glowing with satisfaction at the astonished look on her mother's face. The Babe kept urging until eight dresses were selected.

"Momma," said the Babe triumphantly, "now you got a dress for every day in the week and two for Sunday." Her devotion to her beloved Momma and Poppa was heartwarming.

There was a tender awkwardness to her romance with George Zaharias, the massive wrestler. They were mutually attracted the moment they met and their love story was a rich and rewarding one through courtship, matrimony, and beyond.

Babe Didrikson Zaharias made a strange confession in her autobiography

This Life I've Led. "Before I was even in my teens," she declared, "I knew exactly what I wanted to be when I grew up. My goal was to be the greatest athlete that ever lived."

And she did. The Babe became the greatest of her sex beyond question and her golf frequently attained unbelievable proficiency. It was no accident, no reliance on natural ability alone. She worked at it with the same indomitable ability with which she fought against the cancer that was to take her life.

Before she started out in the first golf tournament of her career, a reporter asked how well she expected to score.

"I think I'll shoot a 77," she said nonchalantly. This was a bit of bombast which she airily characterized as "Texas talk."

So the gal from Texas shot a 77. It was a freak, of course, and she did not linger long in the match play rounds that followed. But this experience impressed on her the need for giving polish to her game. She did it in typical fashion.

The Babe practiced sixteen hours a day each weekend. On weekdays she was on the course at 5:30 A.M. for a three-hour session. Then she went to her regular job. Most of her lunch hour was spent chipping balls onto a leather chair in her boss's office. After work she took lessons for an hour and practiced until dark.

"I'd hit golf balls until my hands were bloody and sore," she once grimly explained. "Then I'd have tape all over my hands and blood all over the tape."

The price for perfection was high, but she paid it willingly. The rewards were high, too. Yet there never were any shortcuts for the Babe in anything, either in getting to the top or staying there. Once she was leading a tournament when she discovered that she played the wrong ball out of the rough. She alone knew it.

"That's it," she said resignedly to the officials. "I've been playing the wrong ball and I have to disqualify myself."

"But no one would have known the difference," remarked some unthinking spectator.

"I'd have known the difference," said the Babe sharply, "and I wouldn't have felt right in my mind. You have to play by the rules of golf just as you have to live by the rules of life. There's no other way."

This was no mere muscle girl. The greatness of her athletic achievements permeated the entire character of Babe Didrikson Zaharias until the strength and splendor shone through. She was a remarkable personality.

INDEX